A

LONG RANGE PLANNING FOR MARKETING AND DIVERSIFICATION

Other books by the editors:

Pricing Strategy

Technological Forecasting & Corporate Strategy
  (with David Ashton)

Bradford Exercises in Management (with Thomas Kempner)

Handbook of Management Technology (with Ronald Yearsley)

Sources of U.K. Marketing Information

Marketing through Research

Marketing Research (with Joseph Siebert)

Management Thinkers (with Anthony Tillett
  and Thomas Kempner)

Organisational Design for Marketing Futures (with Roy Hayhurst)

New Ideas in Retailing Management

Marketing Logistics and Distribution Planning
  (with Martin Christopher)

Exploration in Marketing Thought

Contemporary Marketing

Technological Forecasting: the Art and its Managerial
  Implications

LONG RANGE PLANNING FOR MARKETING AND DIVERSIFICATION

collated and edited by
BERNARD TAYLOR
Director of Post-experience Programmes
and
GORDON WILLS
Professor of Marketing Studies,

both of the Management Centre, University of Bradford

BRADFORD UNIVERSITY PRESS
in association with
CROSBY LOCKWOOD & SON LTD
26 Old Brompton Road, London, S.W.7

© 1971 Bradford University Press and Crosby Lockwood

First Published in 1971 by Bradford University Press
in association with
Crosby Lockwood & Son Ltd, 26 Old Brompton Road,
London S.W.7

ISBN 0 258 96778 1

Printed in Great Britain by
Bristol Typesetting Co. Ltd, Bristol

Contents

Introduction   9
Gordon Wills

PART ONE: IN THEORY

1. Making Strategy Explicit   25
   Seymour Tilles

2. Corporate Strategy, Marketing and Diversification   51
   Harry Henry

3. Economic Analysis of Company Strengths and Weaknesses   71
   J. Roger Morrison

4. Identifying Market Opportunities   83
   Stephen King

5. Selecting New Products for Development   112
   Aubrey Wilson

6. Planning the Product Range   126
   Andrew Muir

7. Choosing the Best Product Ranges and Assortments   139
   James Rothman

8. Developing Strategies for Diversification   151
   Peter Baynes and Donald F. Burman

9. Planned Diversification of Industrial Concerns   160
   W. F. Rockwell, Jr.

10. Strategies for Diversification   172
    H. Igor Ansoff

11. Programme for Product Diversification   196
    Thomas A. Staudt

12. Planned Product Diversification   217
    W. E. Hill

13. Merger Objectives and Organization Structure   231
H. Igor Ansoff and J. Fred Weston

14. Organization Structure for Innovation   245
Rodney Leach

15. Conditions Favourable to Product Innovation   258
David Ashton, Russell Gotham and Gordon Wills

16. Technological Myopia   282
Gordon Wills

17. Long Range Planning and Creative Marketing   298
Ray Willsmer

PART TWO: IN PRACTICE

18. Some Management Lessons from Technological
Innovation Research   311
James Bright

19. Developing a Product Market Strategy as part of the
formal Corporate Planning Process—I.T.T.   325
Gerhard Simons

20. Increasing Penetration in Industrial Markets—
Rank Xerox   332
Michael Hughes

21. Increasing Penetration in Consumer Markets—
Cleveland and T.B.A.s   340
Wilfred Smolden

22. Planning a Future Product Market—Rolls Royce
R.B.211   352
Kenneth Bhore

23. Strategic Planning in a Dynamic Technology—
The Electronics Industry   363
Seymour Tilles and Ronald R. McFarlan

24. Expansion into an Allied Market—Massey-Ferguson   385
John Houston

25. Organizing for Profit and Growth—I.C.I. Plastics   397
Douglas Owen

26. Evaluating and Controlling Marketing Projects—
the Ford Capri   406
Roy Horrocks

27. Strategies for Diversification—Cadbury 422
    John Harvey

28. Growth Planning—Geigy 435
    Carl Eugster

Appendix List of participants at the National Conference
on Long Range Planning for Marketing and
Diversification, June 1969, at the University of
Bradford Management Centre 449

Index 459

Introduction

THIS book is intended for senior managers and directors, particularly those who are involved in developing plans for the future growth of their companies. It will be of particular interest to specialists in marketing and long range planning and to students and teachers in these fields.

Corporate development for profit and growth is becoming increasingly hazardous. Traditional markets quickly decline in the face of changes in patterns of consumption and distribution. Products are rendered obsolescent by new developments in technology. Large and threatening competitors emerge through take-overs and mergers, and through the invasion of home markets by foreign producers.

In response to these changes, top management is relying increasingly on corporate planning—the careful assembling of an integrated system of plans covering the whole range of company activities. The emergence of corporate planning as a management discipline has important implications for marketing.

This collection of viewpoints has grown from a conference held at the Management Centre in the University of Bradford, jointly with the British Institute of Management in June 1969, and a series of seminars held in the past three years.

Our objectives throughout were:

1. To consider systematically the various opportunities for increasing profitability and growth through improved strategic planning
2. To evaluate company policies and organization for the development of profitable new products and markets
3. To learn from the experience of companies which have profited from new organizational approaches and new techniques.

We are hence concerned with the whole process of developing corporate strategy—the setting of goals; the assessment of the company's competitive strengths; the analysis of market opportunities; and the development of an explicit strategy to guide corporate development. Contributors examine a wide range of strategic alternatives for corporate development as well as the problems of organizing and implementing, evaluating and controlling, long range planning for marketing and diversification.

A recent survey of America's fifty-three fastest growing companies suggests that firms succeed in their quest for rapid growth by adopting certain business strategies: conscious selection of fast growth industries and market segments, participation in industries which are in an early phase of growth, expansion into new markets, including foreign markets, adoption of new-product policies and acquisition of other firms. Against this background, we feel it will be especially valuable if, as this book is examined and read, three texts are borne in mind, which come not from Theodore Levitt but from a less well-known book of Peter Drucker's, *Managing for Results*:[1]

'Any leadership position is transitory.'
'Results are obtained by exploiting opportunities, not by solving problems.'
'Concentration is the key to real economic results.'

Transition

The first of our themes must focus our attention on the need to sustain and review product strategy on a continuous basis. Not only must a business believe that it should introduce new products from time to time to replace its declining lines. It must collect and collate the necessary control data from the customers in the market place, from the distribution channels, and from research, development, testing and engineering sectors to diagnose the life cycles of market offerings. (Life cycles incidentally to be viewed in the context of profit contribution and opportunity cost rather than in terms of sales volume; in terms of timing, of market entry, and its relationship to marketing investment cost rather than static longitudinal views of sales.)

Opportunity Results

The end product of all our business activities, these are normally generated almost solely from the sales revenue accruing as our products or services change hands. To achieve planned profitability, the product strategy must develop profit forecasts on the basis of the whole product range offered. Resources must be allocated to those activities which afford the required profitability rather than squandered on problems which even if solved hold out slender hope of making an adequate refund for the effort involved.

Concentration

Attention must be focused not solely on the job in hand but on the range of products and services which can effectively achieve the

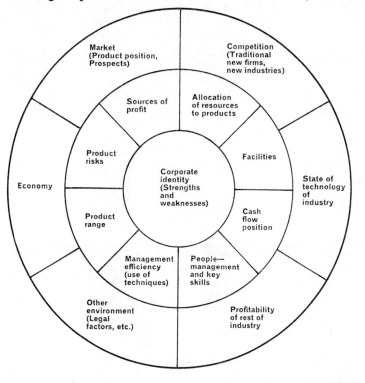

Fig. 1

Outer circle—external factors
Middle circle—internal factors
Inner circle—the corporate identity

results required. Concentration of vision on the target area, not myopia, is demanded. The glib recital of 'Leviticus' must be superseded by the multi-dimensional analysis of opportunities prior to corporate focus. To know what we are in the 'transportation' or 'food' business is hopelessly vague. It offers little guide to product strategy, although at a corporate level it may be somewhat more valid.

Developing Strategy—Although these three texts may cause you to nod and feel complacent, musing to yourself that you are well aware of them, we hope to explore in these pages ways in which our awareness can be translated into firm patterns of action and control. The gaps between awareness, planning and control are perhaps the most difficult issues to be faced.

No plan can be formulated, nor action taken and controlled, until we know our corporate selves. Far from proposing that a business should take its cue from its customers and their more vociferous needs, we propose we should turn the focus on the extent of business, its strengths and weaknesses. Fig. 1 (from David Hussey, 'The Corporate Appraisal', *Long Range Planning* 1, 2, December 1968, pp. 18-25) offers an effective framework for thinking.

Fig. 2   *Example: one method of summarising company strengths and weaknesses*

Part 1: Weaknesses/Limiting Factors

1. Management

	Immediate Strategic Implications
a. Chief executive aged 65, no obvious successor.	a. Recruitment, merger, or sale of business.
b. Weak middle management.	b. Recruitment training (Position can be improved but some weakness will remain for 5 years).
c. Marketing manager incapable of handling any expansion.	c. A serious block. Solve by organization change or replacement.

2. Marketing

a. 80 per cent of profits emanate from product A market declining at 5 per cent p.a. market share constant.	a. i. Reduce dependence.
	  ii. Changed market strategy to improve performance.
	  iii. Cost reduction to improve position—Introduce value analysis.

b. 25 products contribute no profit and have no potential.	b. Cease production re-deploy resources.

Part 2: Strengths

1. People
  a. A high level of technical expertise in production departments.

2. Marketing
  a. Strong image among consumers, particularly for quality, performance and after-sales service.
  b. Five established brand names.

3. Finance
  a. £500,000 available for expansion from own resources. Up to £2 m loan capital can be raised without difficulty.

Fig. 2, also taken from Hussey, gives specific instances of the sort of strengths and weaknesses to be considered. This is not the place to examine all aspects which Hussey itemizes; suffice it to point out that at a corporate strategy level we must. Our attention must be focused specifically on the review of our existing products and services, and both extrapolative and normative statements of future market offerings.

Analysis of current range—Two main approaches can be described. The first and most widely employed has been eloquently described by Drucker.[2]

1. Today's breadwinners
2. Tomorrow's breadwinners
3. Productive specials
4. Development products
5. Failures
6. Yesterday's breadwinners
7. Repair jobs
8. Unnecessary specialities
9. Unjustified specialities
10. Investments in managerial ego
11. Cinderellas.

Fig. 3 *Universal products company product analysis: a tentative diagnosis*

Product	Revenue	Diagnosis
A	£19 0	Today's breadwinner becoming yesterday's breadwinner. On way down. Considerably over-supported.
B	14 0	Investment in managerial ego. Withdraw all support?
C	14 0	Today's breadwinner. Inadequately supported to become 'tomorrow's breadwinner' and a leader.
D	11 0	Tomorrow's breadwinner. But will Prince Charming come before Cinderella gets old? Perhaps even a real 'sleeper'). NOT SUPPORTED.
E	7 0	Repair job needed on both product and management to cut out excessive service needs. Could then become a 'productive speciality', perhaps even a 'breadwinner'. Marginal today.
F G	4 0 } 4 0 }	Necessary? Have neither product, leadership nor prospects. Are either nuclei of new main product or 'unjustified specialities'.
H	3 5	Another investment in managerial ego.
I	4 0	The has-been. Breadwinner of the day before yesterday.
J	Under 1 0	Development. Not a product yet. Potential leader as new high-speed equipment comes into customers' plants. Do we know the market yet?

Once completed, the very act of classification implies the appropriate course of action required. Fig. 3 shows a possible product range for Universal Products Co. Ltd.

All our organizations have strengths and weaknesses in product terms; we are always out of balance. Our product strategy must be designed to move us continually towards a more balanced range to meet our corporate goals and our profit plans.

The second additive approach to the analysis of our extant product range has been described by Simmonds.[3] He proposes as insightful, the analysis of the customer, distributive, product and productive characteristics of our market offering. He lists 17 common dimensions for such analysis and implicitly extends the concept of market sequentation to a strategic segmentation of 'offering'.

Fig. 4 Some Common Dimensions

Customer characteristics
Age
Sex
Loyalty (No. of previous purchases)
Income bracket
Social class

Order characteristics
Size of order
Time of year
Credit arrangements

Outlet characteristics
Type
Size
Location

Product characteristics
Size of item
Material
Design

Production characteristics
Technology required
Skills employed
Machines used

Meaningless uni-dimensional proposals for revamped product strategies, e.g. vertical or horizontal, can be replaced through such analysis by meaningful multi-dimensional specification for new product search. It is a search, however, which must continually check back to the total corporate situation and objectives. This constraint can be well illustrated by the influence of size of company on its operating results with a semi-fabricated product. Fig. 5, cases A and B make the comparison clear.[4]

Search framework—We have already identified the need to formulate corporative objectives and to match our current market offerings to those objectives.

Fig. 5 *Break-even charts for manufacture of speciality semi-fabricated product in large and small companies*

CASE A   Actual Results in Large Corporation

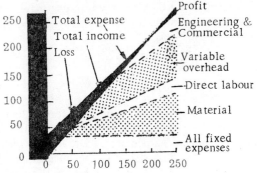

Annual sales in thousands of pounds

CASE B   Estimated Results in Small Independent Operation

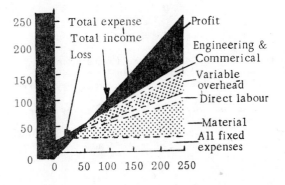

Annual sales in thousands of pounds

Gaps will be apparent, preferably in the form of small cracks rather than yawning chasms, but there will normally be gaps.

In the context of company strengths and weaknesses we can develop a *normative statement* of our product strategy. We can then develop a statement of the policy we must pursue to attempt to meet the strategic requirements. This is not the full range of possibilities however. Two detailed checklist approaches have been formulated. The first by Johnson & Jones[5] is given on page 17; the second by Karger and Murdick[6] is given on pages 18-19 and 20-21. This form of matrix analysis appears frequently in the chapters which follow.

*   *   *

We gratefully acknowledge the support accorded to the University in organizing the Conference, particularly by the British Institute of Management in the persons of Dr. John Marsh and Tom Cauter. We also thank most sincerely the businessmen who gave so much of their time and their thoughts to the preparation of papers and/or discussions thereon. Permission to reprint a number of articles published elsewhere is gratefully acknowledged. Miss Helga Werwie and Mrs. Margaret Firth met our secretarial needs.

Management Centre   Gordon Wills
University of Bradford   *Professor of Marketing Studies*
October 1st, 1969.

REFERENCES

1 Drucker, P. (1964) *Managing for Results,* Heinemann.
2 Ibid
3 Simmons, K. (1968) 'Removing the Chains from Product Strategy', *Journal of Management Studies,* 5, 1, 1968, pp. 29-40.
4 Kline, C. H. (1965) 'The Strategy of Product Policy', *Harvard Business Review,* July/August.
5 Johnson, A. & Jones, C. (1957) 'How to Organise for New Products', *Harvard Business Review,* May/June.
6 Karger, F. & Murdick, K. (1966), 'Product Design, Marketing and Manufacturing Innovation', *California Management Review,* Winter.

←——— Increasing Technological Newness ———→

Product Objectives	No Technological Change	Improved Technology	New Technology
		To utilize more fully the company's present scientific knowledge and production skills.	To acquire scientific knowledge and production skills new to the company.
No Market Change		*Reformulation* To maintain an optimum balance of cost, quality, and availability in the formulas of present company products. Example: use of oxidized microcrystaline waxes in Glo-Coat (1946).	*Replacement* To seek new and better ingredients or formulation for present company products in technology not now employed by the company. Example: development of synethic resin as a replacement for shellac in Glo-Coat (1950).
Strengthened Market To exploit more fully the existing markets for the present company products.	*Remerchandizing* To increase sales to consumers of types now served by the company. Example: Use of dripless spout can for emulsion waxes (1955).	*Improved Product* To improve present products for greater utility and merchandizability to consumers. Example: combination of auto paste wax and cleaner into one-step 'J-Wax' (1956).	*Product Line Extension* To broaden the line of products offered to present consumers through new technology. Example: development of a general purpose floor cleaner 'Emerel' in maintenance product line (1953).
New Market To increase the number of types of consumers served by the company.	*New Use* To find new classes of consumers that can utilize present company products. Example: sale of paste wax to furniture manufacturers for Caul Board wax (1946).	*Market Extension* To reach new classes of consumers by modifying present products. Example: wax-based coolants and drawing compounds for industrial machining operations (1951).	*Diversification* To add to the classes of consumers served by developing new technical knowledge. Example: development of 'Raid'—dual purpose insecticide (1955).

←——— Increasing Market Newness ———→

Classification of new products by product objective (after Johnson and Jones)

Expand sales into new classes of customers.	No change in product, but new classes of customers reached, probably involves finding some new uses for product. Can occur without expansion of sales to old classes of customers; can even occur when sales to customers are decreasing. Finding new uses for product may involve technical or new product assistance.	No change in product, but new classes of customers reached. Probably involves finding some new uses for product. Can occur without expansion of sales to old classes of customers; can even occur when sales to customers are decreasing. Finding new uses for product may involve technical or new product assistance.	Expanded sales new classes of tomers will not a matically occur. such expanded occur it will be cipally for same sons as those for unchanged produc
Strengthened market in existing classes of customers.	Remerchandizing and/or other sales effort to expand sales. Sell more customers of the same type previously served.	Remerchandizing and/or other sales effort to expand sales. Sell more customers of the same type previously served.	Market coverage present classes customers likely increase due to provements in duct characteris and merchandiza ity. The general is always to re cost, increase p margin, and only crease price when solutely necessary.
No market change.	No change in product characteristics and no change in market penetration.	No change in product characteristics and no change in market penetration.	Positive ma change likely to result, however, s adverse market p meters could sales constant, or e let them slip.
	No product change.	Product characteristics remain same but changes in components formulation, production techniques, etc., made to keep costs in line and quality at same relative level.	Minor design mo cation. Improveme in product charac istics to yield gre utility to custom and / or incre merchandizability. ample: side - b trimmer on Sunbe electric trimmer.

INCREASING MARKET NEWNESS

INCREASING PRODU

Product/Market Matrix (a

effect, the :eting func- is here erned with . is essenti- a new pro- , complete all the lems associ- with a new uct.	Opening of new markets because of introduction of a replacement does not automatically follow. Unless changes in characteristics and/or resultant price obviously opens new markets, new applications must be actively sought and aggressively exploited when found in order to reach new classes of customers.	Addition of new product lines makes it possible to attract new classes of customers, especially where previously incomplete line made it necessary for certain classes of customers to buy from several manufacturers. New marketing programmes involving promotion channels of distribution, and emphasis required.	Addition of new product lines makes it possible to attract new classes of customers, especially where previously incomplete line made it necessary for certain classes of customers to buy from several manufacturers. New marketing programmes involving promotion, channels of distribution and emphasis required. If first to use the new technology, may mean entirely new markets.
a major de- modifica- of a pro- , is usually :trengthened :et because sales de- nent has ideas to note.	Replacement product usually lends itself to a remerchandizing campaign resulting in greater penetration of existing markets.	If new product will be used by existing customers, the hold on them will be strengthened, especially if new product relates in some manner to existing product line.	If new product will be used by existing customers, the hold on them will be strengthened, especially if new product relates in some manner to existing product line. If company is the first to use the new technology, significant market gain may result.
tive market ge likely to t, however, e adverse :et para- :ers could sales con- :.	Product changes drastic enough to change market penetration. Example (possible little effect on market): synthetic resin instead of shellac in Johnson's Glo-Coat in 1950.	Not applicable.	Not applicable.
or design, ification. nple: IBM :tric Type- ar.	Replacement of an existing product by new but related technology. Example: replacing tube-type portable radio with transistorized model.	Diversification: addition of new product line (could be a new company introducing the product) involving existing technology, but new to the company. Examples: Bulova Accruton. Tensor lamp, G. E. computers.	Diversification or product line expansion using new technology. Involves development and/or expansion of the new technology.

WNESS ————————————→

rger and Murdick)

| | Expand sales into new classes of customers. | No change in product, but new classes of customers reached. Probably involves finding some new uses for product or developing new pricing policies or service arrangements. Can occur without expansion of sales to old classes of customers; even when sales to old customers decreasing. May involve technical or new product assistance. | No change in pro[duct,] but new classes of [cus]tomers reached. [Prob]ably involves fin[ding] some new uses for [pro]duct. Can occur [] when sales to [] classes of custome[rs de]creasing. Finding [new] uses for product [may] involve technical or [new] product assistance. |
| ↑ | Strengthened market in existing classes of customers. | Remerchandizing and/or other sales effort to expand sales. Sell more customers of same types previously served. | Remerchandizing o[r ex]ploiting improvem[ents] in quality or red[uced] cost of production. |
| INCREASING MARKET NEWNESS | No market change. | No change in processing or in market penetration.

No processing change. | Hold market pos[ition] by means of kee[ping] cost and/or qualit[y in] line with competiti[on.]

Minor modificatio[n of] existing plant pro[cess]ing (materials an[d] methods). |

INCREASING PROC[ESS]

Process/Market Matrix (a

duct line extension
s t i n c t possibility.
inged product char-
:ristics may meet
ds of new classes
customers. Lowered
ts may permit serv-
new classes of cus-
ier.

New products usually
involved which usually
means news classes of
customers. A major co-
operative, concurrent
effort by marketing,
manufacturing, and en-
gineering a v i t a l
necessity.

New products usually
involved which usually
means news classes of
customers. A major co-
operative, concurrent
effort by marketing,
manufacturing, and en-
gineering a v i t a l
necessity.

p r o v e d and/or
nged product char-
:ristics must be ex-
ited. Costs associated
h this usually are
iced and permit
:e reduction; how-
r, they may be raised
t balanced by im-
ved product char-
:ristics). Major pro-
ing change may also
olve product line ex-
s i o n, permitting
ngthened market.

Possible where techno-
logy involved provides
better product char-
acteristics or reduces
cost. Can also involve
expansion of product
line which aids market-
ing. Such changes often
make possible major
remerchandizing effort.

Could be involved, but
new processing would
affect costs and product
characteristics, assuming
no major change in pro-
duct line involved.
Lends itself to major
remerchandizing effort.

t normally applic-
.

Not normally applic-
able.

Not applicable.

jor modification of
i s t i n g processing
hods and/or materi-
Example batch vs
tinuous production
at degree of auto-
ion).

Introduction of new
type of processing. Ex-
amples: Replacing elec-
tro-mechanical w i t h
electronic s w i t c h i n g
(help from engineering
required). New products
(designed by engineer-
ing) for existing line or
to begin new line.

New-to-the-world manu-
facturing methods or
processes. Examples:
'Float' plate glass. High
energy rate of forming
of metals. Use of laser
to perform machining
operations.

WNESS ————————————————→

rger and Murdick)

Part 1
IN THEORY

1 | Making Strategy Explicit

by SEYMOUR TILLES

MANAGERS of successful companies have frequently pursued a strategy of one kind or another without a conscious analysis of their own actions. More and more, however, corporate experience indicates that there are substantial advantages in making strategy explicit.

As companies get larger, and as they encompass many points of strategic initiative, it becomes more and more difficult to reconcile co-ordinated action and entrepreneurial effort without an explicit statement of strategy. This need becomes particularly pressing as policy-making is delegated to divisional managers who act on the basis of their own assumptions concerning the availability of corporate resources and the degree of corporate support.

As companies find themselves encompassing a broader and broader range of businesses, an explicit statement of strategy on the part of the divisions becomes an essential aspect of corporate review. At the corporate level, it becomes a necessary basis for making trade-off decisions.

As companies find themselves facing a broader range of specific options in each of their businesses, an explicit strategy becomes important as a basis for using overall strength in pursuing particular opportunities.

For these reasons, an increasing number of companies are attempting to say what strategy they and their divisions are follow-

DR SEYMOUR TILLES is a consultant with the Boston Consulting Company. The paper was first printed as one of their 'commentaries' and was presented to a *Seminar on Strategic Planning* held at the University of Bradford Management Centre, April 1968.

He has served as Special Assistant to the Assistant Secretary of the Navy, and was a Lecturer at Harvard Business School. Dr Tilles was also Visiting Professor of production management at Technische Hogelschol, Delft, Holland. From 1953-1958 he acted as consultant within the Technical Assistance Programme of the United Nations, advising on questions of industrial productivity in Israel and Brazil. He has also taught at Purdue University, and has been associated with Timken-Detroit Axle Company.

ing. As they try to do this, they discover the need for a framework to help make the abstract concept of strategy more concrete and specific. This Special Commentary discusses the challenge of strategy development.

Why have an explicit strategy?

The need for an explicit strategy stems from two key attributes of the business organization: first, that success depends on people working together so that their efforts are mutually reinforcing; and second, that this must be accomplished in the context of rapidly changing conditions.

In the absence of an explicit concept of strategy, members of the same organization can easily find themselves working at cross purposes. Functional perspectives can blur strategic priorities—as when the financial group vetoes new plant investment this year because interest rates are so high, leaving the door open to competitors to achieve real scale advantages. Similarly, the intentions of the corporate leadership can remain a mystery to people several levels down who are being depended upon for implementation. For example, one company trying very hard to penetrate an export market on the basis of reliable delivery discovered that export shipments were consistently given lowest priority in the packing room.

In the absence of an explicit statement of strategy, obsolete patterns of corporate behaviour are extraordinarily difficult to modify. Where there is no clear concept of what current strategy is, the determination of what might be changed, and why, must rest on either subjective or intuitive assessment. This becomes increasingly unreliable as the pace of change accelerates.

A conventional way of addressing the future in an organized fashion is to develop a 'long range plan'. But while long range planning may be a useful contribution to thinking about the future, its utility is limited in many companies by its being exclusively focused on factors which are completely controllable and internal to the organization. Most companies concentrate on a detailing of what the company itself proposes to do. Rarely does it consider explicitly how competitors are likely to act, what major trends exist in the environment, and what the dynamics of the industry are. As a result, it is quite possible to have a long range plan which represents a reasoned sequence of actions consistent with available resources, but which proves to be an expression of an unsuccessful strategy. For example, Monsanto's entry into the detergent field with a branded product was well timed, but nevertheless had to be terminated as vigorous opposition was encountered from consumer products companies who were major customers for detergent materials.

Unfortunately, many companies have tried to tackle the problem of managing their evolution by going directly to the development of long range plans without first constructing meaningful competitive strategies. As a result, many executives view planning as merely an extension of the budgetary process, rather than as a careful delineation of basic strategic decisions.

This approach misplaces the emphasis among factors influencing future performance. The primary consideration in budgeting is how much money can be obtained from the corporate pot against the competition of other divisions and projects. The primary consideration in strategy is how much money can be obtained from customers against the claims of competing companies and products. The customer is by far the most significant source of future funds, and the key to the customer is strategy.

At its worst, a long range plan is an extrapolation of past performance for several years into the future, developed by a staff group established for the purpose, and expressed in purely numerical terms. This approach suffers from several major shortcomings:

It assumes that the conditions which led to past performance will continue to be true in the future.

It makes numbers explicit, but leaves the underlying concepts and assumptions implicit.

It does not provide an adequate framework for dialogue among senior executives with respect to corporate direction.

It unnecessarily separates the responsibility for describing the corporate future from the responsibility of making it happen.

At its best, a long range plan is a statement of strategy, sequenced over time, expressed in terms of resource requirements and funds flows, and representing a consensus of the top management team.

Developing such a statement requires an effort that is creative both in terms of concept and process. Not only does it require ideas which are novel in the business context; it also requires methods of behaviour which many executives will at first find unconventional. If strategic planning is to work, in the sense of making strategy explicit, agreed upon and periodically reappraised, it often requires fundamental changes in the way executives interact with each other. This is frequently the major stumbling block to companies which are at the threshold of a formal strategic planning effort.

(Some of these behavioural issues have been discussed by my colleague, Dr. Robert Mainer, in his Commentary, 'The Impact of Strategic Planning on Executive Behaviour.')

Concept and process are closely related in developing a strategy. Just as the existing organization structure dictates how the question of strategy determination must be approached, the emerging strategic concepts frequently justify the process changes which may be required. The desire to put new strategies into practice may make organizational changes acceptable which might otherwise appear arbitrary and capricious.

In this Commentary, our essential concern is to examine what it is exactly that has to be agreed upon before a company can feel that it indeed has an explicit strategy. This will include a close look at such ideas as corporate objectives, the business mix, competitive tactics, and industry dynamics. Making these explicit is still an untried idea in many companies.

Strategy in the context of a 'business'

Most companies are engaged in a variety of businesses. Either they have a diversified product line, sell to widely different customer groups, or use a number of very different distribution channels (such as to both original equipment and replacement markets). Consequently, it is important to look at the range of businesses that the company is engaged in and to consider the strategic issues inherent in each. Only then can strategy, as it applies to the company itself, be discussed.

Within an individual business, a statement of strategy should include:

The business definition.

The tactics which will be used as a basis for competitive success.

The rate of additional commitment of resources to the business.

The contribution of the business to the overall company.

Why define the business?

The problem of carefully defining an individual business has been discussed at great length in the business literature, especially by Peter Drucker and Theodore Levitt. Both have stressed the significance of starting with a definition of the major businesses of the company as a point of departure in strategic planning. The most important reason for doing so is that defining a business permits the following strategic issues to be explicitly dealt with:

1. What is the critical competitive arena within which tactics must be formulated?
2. What are the dimensions and implications of the potential size of the business?
3. What are the specific requirements for competitive success in the business?
4. What is our relative strength in the specific business compared to current or potential competitors?
5. What are the major opportunities for innovation through redefinition of the business?
6. What are the major trends influencing competitive performance in this particular business?

How do we define the business?

The basic concept of a business is that of a match between a given product or product group and a given market. In this context defining a business involves three elements: a definition of the product, a definition of the market, and an explicit determination of the connection between the two.

Each business consists of a specific product group sold to a particular market segment. The question of strategy requires an analysis of both product groups *and* market segments. For example, typewriters may be considered a product group; but typewriters sold as office machinery are a completely different business with different strategic problems from portable typewriters sold to individuals through retail channels. In this sense the office typewriter business is different from the portable typewriter business.

One can also make the mistake of defining a business *only* in product terms. One often hears talk about the softwood lumber business or the pulp business. Actually, selling lumber in the auction market is a very different business from selling lumber to home builders, and selling pulp to large chemical producers is quite a different business from selling pulp to small speciality paper-makers.

While the definition of the product is important, the definition of the match between the product and some specific market is even more important. Business strength comes from the ability to serve a market, and this requires more than just a good product.

Defining markets from a strategic point of view

A market may be considered as a group of customers having some common characteristic that is strategically important. For example, the *location* of customers might be of prime importance.

A customer for shipping containers in Chicago is a different kind of business problem from a customer for shipping containers in Pierre, South Dakota.

Size of customer is another important characteristic in thinking about market definition. Customers who are very large users of particular products are very different business problems from those who are small users. Similar distinctions may be drawn in terms of distribution channels and service requirements.

Within each of his businesses, the manager has to decide which particular groups of customers are going to represent the focus of his strategy. He cannot really expect to have an equal chance in appealing to *all* kinds of customers. He has to select that customer group for which he offers some specific appeal, and then design a combination of tactics which will give him a competitive edge in that well-defined market. The selection of that customer group, and the design of that combination of tactics, are important strategic choices. They will influence his company's performance at least as much as anything else his subordinates can do.

Defining the product from a strategic point of view

The decision as to what the product *really* is is another significant strategic choice within each business. As we have already implied the product is rarely just the physical material itself. The automobile industry long ago discovered that what people bought was not just a car—they were equally concerned with more abstract concepts such as status appeal, reliability, and service. The same is true of all other products.

A good example of this is the difference in competitive themes that have been adopted by companies in the forest products industries who sell what might almost be considered commodities: pulp, paperboard, and paper. Some companies have been very successful in differentiating themselves from others selling similar materials. Rayonier has had great success through the emphasis of chemical services to speciality pulp users, and Container Corporation has been able to make itself look different to potential customers by making packaging design services the basis of its market appeal.

Business definitions and levels of generalization

A critical issue in defining a business is to do so at the most meaningful level of generalization. Unfortunately, there is a prevalent notion that if one merely defines one's business in increasingly general terms—such as transportation rather than railroading—the path to successful competitive strategy will be clear. Actually, this is hardly ever the case, and more often the opposite is true. In the case of the railroads, passengers and freight represent very different problems, and short-haul vs. longer haul are completely different strategic issues. Indeed, as the unit train demonstrates, coal handling alone can be isolated as a meaningful strategic issue.

Competitive tactics

The area of competitive tactics is a very broad one, since a company has a very wide range of choice in selecting what mix of things it will emphasize in its attempt to react its market objectives. It may choose advertising impact (Alberto-Culver), service reliability and field training (IBM), prestige appeal (as with Franklin National's new branch bank in New York), or door-to-door selling (Fuller Brush).

In general, competitive stance refers not so much to a single tactic, but to a whole broad range of policies. These may range from research policy through labour relations to facilities planning and marketing mix. While the market is the payoff point, a division's marketing effort is merely the iceberg's tip. Without all the rest, the tip could not support itself.

It should be emphasized that there are two very different kinds of tactical objectives. One is superior performance with respect to those companies already in a particular market segment. The other is dissuading companies not yet in a particular market segment from entering. Early in Xerox's development, the company was equally concerned with successfully competing against other copying processes and keeping the major office equipment and technology companies from entering its field. Similarly, the high margin of some of the chemical companies in the petrochemical fields was for a time considered evidence of competitive success. However, it provided an added inducement to the petroleum companies to integrate forward. As this illustrates, the most dangerous competitors may be those who have not yet entered a market.

Competitive tactics: Innovation

Innovation is frequently the most successful competitive tactic because it offers the potential of radically changing competitive relationships. It can do this either by creating new product concepts which set the company apart, or by creating a new market or marketing concept which has the same effect. For example, the Wilkinson razor blade, *Playboy* magazine, and Kearney & Trecker's

Mult-au-Matic machine tool—all illustrate the dramatic impact that a new product concept may have on the fortunes of a company.

The opportunities for innovation with respect to markets are no less than with respect to products. The great successess of Avon Products in cosmetics, and Servomation in food vending are examples of the impact that innovation in distribution can have. And Bobbie Brooks is an exciting case of business success built on a creative concept of a distinctive market for women's wear.

Competitive tactics: Concentration

Many successful growth companies illustrate the principle that growth is obtained by concentrating one's strength in markets where a competitive advantage can be obtained by doing so. A good example of this is Control Data.

Control Data successfully entered the computer business against IBM and other larger competitors by concentrating on the market for large computers for scientific use. It had the technical capability to develop such computers, and the market was one where it could achieve a competitive advantage. The great strength of its major competitor, IBM, was a large and skilful sales forces and broad range of customer services. The cost of supporting these, however, was built into the computer's price.

Control Data perceived that the users of large computers are generally capable of evaluating a machine on its own merits, developing their own software, and providing their own services. A good machine at a competitive price was therefore possible as a commercial success for a small company. Further, once Control Data launched its attack on this market segment, IBM could not counter its price requirements because of its own requirements for consistency across a broad product range. Control Data was therefore able to grow rapidly, so rapidly that it has now expanded beyond its original market segment and must revise its strategy.

Competitive tactics: Timing

Markets are dynamic. As they are always changing, there is a big payoff to the company that can understand the markets dynamics well enough to identify the time of occurrence and prepare effectively for probable future trends. For example, one company that has benefited greatly—and also been hurt—by market shifts is the Jim Walter Corporation. It made the crest of the wave of demand for shell homes but has been hurt by the move away from shell homes to more expensive housing.

Mr. Robert A. Weinberg, of IBM, makes the point that the

biggest mistakes in corporate affairs are frequently those of timing. He cites as an illustration the case of General Dynamics, which lost a great deal of money, in large measure because it had the right product (the Convair 880) at the wrong time.

Competitive strengths and weaknesses

A frequent component of strategic planning is an assessment of the strengths and weaknesses of a company. However, for this to be a meaningful exercise, it must be related to each specific business in which the company is engaged: one company prided itself on the effectiveness of its expensive order-handling system. This was a real competitive advantage in dealing with customers who ordered many items in small quantities, but it imposed a heavy overhead charge on customers who bought relatively few items but in very large quantities. Consequently, while it was a strength for one customer group, it was a weakness for the second.

The careful identification of the particular business says a great deal about the essential strengths required for successful operation. For example, assume a business producing specialized machine tools which are sold primarily to the automative manufacturers. To operate successfully in this business context requires (1) a high degree of sophistication in terms of design, since parts are produced in such heavy volume that a new machine may be ordered as a result of a design change in a single part of an automobile; (2) careful quality control, since any delivered machine must without fail operate in accordance with established specification; (3) a strong service organization, since a breakdown is a major crisis to the customer; and (4) the financial skills to deal with a highly cyclical pattern of orders. Customer credit is not a problem, nor is competition from abroad.

By way of contrast, consider the requisite capabilities of a company in a related but different business: producing general-purpose machine tools which are sold primarily to repair shops. This business is far less cyclical than the one described above, and while designs and quality control are important, they are not critical. The crucial functions are marketing and credit, and competition from foreign manufacturers is likely to be severe.

Within each specific business, the real significance of a strengths and weaknesses analysis is what it says about the company's competitive posture. For example, having an unparalleled manufacturing capability may not be worth very much in an industry where competition is primarily on the basis of styling and distribution. Simi-

B

larly, having a first-class marketing group scores no competitive points if many other people in the industry have a marketing group that is equally first class.

Another important reason for analysing strengths and weaknesses is the insight it gives into the company's ability to adapt to unforeseen developments. Since no one can predict the future, every company must be reasonably sure that it has the required ability to exploit unforeseen opportunities or respond to unanticipated threats. In some companies, reliance is placed on the R & D function, which is counted on to come through in the clutch with the new products required to either stave off a competitive development or exploit a suddenly expanding market. In other companies, the marketing group is the foundation on which adaptive capability is built. And in still others, it may be the ability of the production people to move rapidly with the high quality and low cost.

The relative skills that a company has in such areas may be evaluated in a number of ways:

The number and calibre of people engaged in a particular activity.
The organizational status of their function.
The budget of the activity.

However, a company may have as its basic superior capability a skill that has not been formally designated—for example, its willingness to move rapidly into new areas of opportunity or to experiment objectively with important parts of its business. Whatever the skill that is relied on as a competitive base, the continuing assessment of its current validity is a constant management challenge.

Strategy in the context of an industry

An industry may be thought of as a system of related businesses and competitors. From this point of view corporate performance is influenced not only by what the company itself does in its present and potential businesses, but also by the major trends in the industries of which it is a part. The determination of strategy for the company must rest on an analysis of the dynamics of the industries in which it has a major interest. Indeed, one way in which the essential problem of corporate strategy can be defined is in terms of the relationship between the unique attributes of the company and the particular dynamics of the industry or industries in which it competes. The problem is to relate one to the other so as to achieve a high probability of accomplishing corporate objectives.

Industry dynamics is a neglected aspect of strategic planning, yet it is frequently the key to the development of successful strategies. The dynamics of an industry can be described in terms of:

The effect of cyclical swings in the relationship between supply and demand.
The effect of dynamic technology.
The effect of broadening geographic systems.
The effect of economies of scale and learning.
The effect of integration, both forward and backward.

Each of these is a way of describing what the companies in the industry are doing, and what effect it has on their relative competitive position.

Effect of cyclical swings in the relationship between supply and demand

A major determinant of corporate profitability is the supply-demand relationship in its industry. A period of excess demand provides opportunities for high profit, while a period of excess supply puts great pressure on profit margins; both cases are due largely to factors beyond the scope of the enterprise itself. Consequently, to estimate its future profitability, a company must pay careful attention to its own investment plans, its competitors' investment plans, and projected variations in demand.

In some industries, demand is relatively stable, but there are major fluctuations in supply. This is especially true where additional capacity tends to come on stream in very large increments, but it may also come about when individual companies in an industry act without reference to competitors' actions.

In the forest products industry, for example, a rough analysis of published data suggests that companies in the industry have characteristically tended to a policy of reinvesting their cash flows. The effect of such a policy is to cause a situation in which increases in demand produce more sales, which produces more cash flow—leading to additional investment in capacity, and the result is that not much money is made in the industry by the average producer.

The significance of this effect can be particularly great where estimates of supply and demand lead to heavy investment in equipment. Large machines and mills have such drastically different economic performance with just a few percentage points difference in proportion of output to capacity that timing can greatly influence earnings. In addition, where the market size is limited relative to companies who may enter, being first with additional on-stream capacity may be a prime strategic advantage.

Supply-demand relationships are so important a factor in performance that they should be made explicit. This can be done by identifying the factors which influence demand and supply in a given business, and then estimating how much they are likely to change over a given time period. Making these assumptions explicit is an important responsibilty of management.

Effect of dynamic technology

Where the technology in an industry is dynamic, the characteristic pattern of product evolution is an important backdrop to strategy determination.

A characteristic cycle for many products can be discussed in terms of an introduction phase, a take-off phase, and a maturity phase. In the introduction phase, the major requirement for competitive success is R & D capability. At this point in the cycle, the total demand is low, the price and margins high, and the rate of new technological development very rapid. As the product moves into the take-off stage, volume increases very sharply, and the rate of technological development slows somewhat. Frequently, demand far outruns supply, and the essential competitive skill is the production know-how which permits reliability to be achieved and new capacity to be brought on-stream quickly. Colour television is currently in this phase.

As the product reaches maturity, the rate of technological development slows even further, and the basis for competitive success becomes marketing. At this point the essential factors are: having broad distribution capability, identifying significant market segments and matching design to them, and engineering to carefully determined price ranges.

This pattern of evolution poses major issues of strategic choice to any company wishing to participate in such an industry. A company must determine whether or not to play the game at all with respect to a particular product. For example, Westinghouse has stayed out of computers, but tried jet engines and is into atomic power. Also, it must decide at what stage it wishes to enter, and how long to stay in. General Electric likes to come into the market heavily as a product is approaching maturity, in contrast to Varian, which likes to be in the market-place very early in the introduction phase.

Effect of widening geographic horizons

Earlier, an industry was described as a system of competitors, in the sense of a group of companies which have an impact on each other's performance. From this point of view the nature of the competitive problem changes substantially as the geographic boundaries of the system are changed. One important strategic issue is how a company brings its combined strength to bear in a particular geographic area. Another is how a company identifies and compares major new opportunities for investment around the world. For many industries today, the world has become the only valid perspective for considering competitive stance. As logistic and political barriers to international commerce have rapidly dwindled, sourcing abroad overseas investment, foreign competitors, and third country markets have become increasingly significant aspects of strategy.

Effect of economies of scale and learning curves

Economy of scale is so basic an economic concept as to hardly need emphasis. It is well known that in a wide variety of industries costs come down as volume goes up. However, for the strategic implications of this observation to be clear, some additional factors must be examined. One of these is the distribution of scale position among companies in the industry. A second is the economical size for incremental capacity.

In the automotive industry there is a substantial spread in scale position. GM has so high a volume as to be a very low cost producer, Ford and Chrysler have an intermediate position, and American Motors has so low a volume as to be a marginal producer despite the fact that it makes many thousands of cars. On the other hand, in the garment industry, the economics of the process are such that low cost production is reached at relatively modest volume, leaving plenty of room for the small producer. One important question for a company is whether its industry is more like automobiles or garments. Another is where it stands in this range and what this implies in terms of competitive tactics.

In a number of industries, the economic size of incremental capacity is increasing. This has significant implications for concentration in the industry. Larger units generally mean concentration in the production of commodity grades, because only the bigger companies can afford the big units. The smaller companies must either sell out or retreat to the lower volume specialities. The scale effect also influences financial performance. Large new units generally make existing capacity uneconomic with subsequent write-offs of undepreciated assets.

The impact of the learning curve is similar to that of economies of scale; costs tend to decrease as volume increases because of the greater skill of the more experienced organization. Consequently, the learning curve gives a competitive advantage to the company that first increases its volume, even against other companies with installed capacity of equal magnitude. This effect can be used by leading producers in some industries to maintain a significant and continued discrepancy between their own profit margins and those of their competitors. By lowering prices as it benefits from the effects of the learning curve, the leading producer can squeeze those having smaller volume.

Effects of integration

One of the significant shifts taking place in a number of industries is the extent to which companies have broadened the degree of their deployment so as to encompass a greater number of processing stages. Examples of this are the move of some producers of plastic items backward into the production of polymers, the move forward of the petroleum companies into petro-chemicals, and the emergence through merger and acquisition of large integrated producers in the textile and forest products industries.

Integration, or potential integration, presents every company in an industry with the same basic strategic problems. The most important is the problem of deployment. Second is the extent to which internal capacity will be balanced, in the sense of having external sales or purchase requirements. Third is the question of the arrangements which should be made for either securing sources of supply or markets on a long-term basis.

The single-stage company in an industry where integration is increasing faces a continuing strategic problem. Competition comes not only from others offering the same service, but also from the possibility that its own success may induce down stream companies to move back a notch, or up stream companies to move forward. This company is especially vulnerable to price swings in its materials and product markets, while its integrated competitors can absorb these in their overall operations.

Combined effects

In many industries all of the effects mentioned here occur simultaneously. As a result, the determination of competitive posture for a company requires that these effects be considered, both individually and in relation to each other, before stating the company's competitive position.

Strategy and industry dynamics

In the context of an industry, the basic strategic issues are those of definition, deployment, and timing.

Industry definition

As with individual businesses, definition of the industry is the essential point of departure in a consideration of strategy. While the issue may at first appear to be merely one of semantics, it has very direct and significant strategic implications: for example, the manufacturers of cans thought of themselves for many years as being in the 'can' industry. As the tin can encountered increasing competition from other packaging materials, some companies changed the concept of their industry from 'cans' to 'packaging'. As soon as they did, they found themselves up against a completely different set of competitors and opportunities than was previously the case. Their industry strategy in the can business did not change, but they found that they could improve their overall corporate performance by using their capabilities to market glass, plastics, and paper containers to the same customers and through the same channels that they had developed with their traditional product.

Many factors in the environment contribute to the constant change in industry boundaries. Perhaps the most significant is the rapid rate of technological development. For example, advances in electronic technology have put RCA, IBM, and AT & T in the same industry. Similarly, the development of synthetic sweeteners has put many chemical companies and food companies up against each other as competitors. If attempts to synthesize protein from organic chemicals economically are successful, the petroleum companies and the food companies could become arch-rivals.

Because industry boundaries shift so rapidly, industry definition cannot be a one-time decision. As with most other strategic variables, its continued redefinition is a significant element in maintaining competitive position.

Deployment

Deployment is the degree and extent to which the company participates in the various businesses which comprise an industry. In a sense, strategy may be thought of as the change in deployment over time. A company's mix of businesses, described in terms of a corporate 'profile', expresses what the company's current deployment is. An analysis of the corporate profile can be a basic device in defining what the company's present strategy is. It is also a way of being able to say in a more detailed fashion than is otherwise possible how the company compares with its competition. Since strategy in an industry requires the exploitation of the unique attributes of the individual company, its deployment, compared with that of its major competitors, is critical.

Some of the major purposes for making deployment explicit are: to review the relative mix of earning opportunities currently being exploited by the company; to relate the currently projected investment flows with the currently projected earnings flows; and to assess whether the projected future mix of earning opportunities is consistent with what management wants the company to do.

Timing

Timing includes several subordinate issues:

When to enter (or withdraw from) a given industry sector.
What the rate of commitment should be in the various industry sectors.
What the lead time is between action and result.
What the appropriate time horizon should be.

These issues are, of course, very close interrelated. Entry cannot be considered without relating that decision to magnitude of entry and rate of penetration; and both must be carefully related to the assessment of how long it will be between decision and result.

To make investment timing decisions on an informed basis, a knowledge of the dynamics of an industry is required. For example, many companies have only a crude feel for supply-demand relationships in their industry, and are therefore unable to assess the impact of competitors' moves on their own investment returns. The result is that investments which seem to promise high payouts under the conditions that prevailed at the time they were made prove to have unsatisfactory returns when they are brought on stream.

Timing is the most difficult aspect of strategic planning because dealing with it effectively requires not only an intimate knowledge of the dynamics of the industry but also a knowledge of the dynamics of the company. At one time this could be handled by senior executives relying on their experience, but the increased rate of change and breadth of corporate deployment make this problem increasingly difficult to deal with intuitively.

Where the concern of senior executives is only for this year's performance, or indeed only through next year's performance, many significant strategic variables cannot be meaningfully addressed. One of the strongest arguments for a more extended time horizon in management thinking is that, in the larger organization, the lead time for any basic strategic re-orientation is likely to be far longer than just a year or two.

Contingency planning and industry dynamics

An essential reason for being concerned with industry dynamics is the help which it provides in dealing with what might otherwise be totally unforeseen contingencies.

Dealing with contingencies does not mean merely trying to dream up things which might conceivably happen, so the company may be prepared for them. To develop realistic contingencies requires careful analysis of events outside the company that may have a substantial impact upon it. This involves a careful study of characteristic behaviour of competitors and industry dynamics.

Some common kinds of contingencies that companies have had to deal with are the following:

Capacity constraints or excesses due to swings in gross economic activity.

Price attrition caused by competitors' initiative.

Research breakthroughs on the part of competitors.

Shift in the basis for competition through change in industry maturity or structure.

Entry into the market of major new competitors.

Dealing with each of these contingencies has several points in common. They can only be dealt with if there is (1) a forecasting capability, (2) a model which relates the impact of forecasted changes on corporate performance, and (3) a basis for selecting a particular adaptive response.

The development of a forecasting capability, whether economic or technological, and the development of models which relate environmental changes to corporate performance are significant aspects of strategic planning. While the general level of practice concerning these issues is still quite primitive, the state of the art is rapidly advancing. As more and more sophisticated models of industry economics are developed, the identification of most probable contingencies becomes more and more reliable.

Corporate strategy: Designing the business portfolio

A company may be thought of as pursuing a set of objectives by means of engaging in a given mix of businesses. From that perspective, the major strategic issues become: (1) what is an appropriate set of objectives for a particular company given its deployment, and (2) what is an appropriate mix of businesses, given the corporate objectives. The problem is to achieve consistency between objectives and mix within the constraints imposed by established policies.

Setting objectives

The basic part of any statement of strategy is the determination of corporate objectives, for these determine the ends which will be used to justify a broad variety of means. The choice of objectives is a basic part of the process of choosing a future course of action and an essential foundation on which specific competitive moves and tactics should be based. For example, we often hear of companies which have chosen to pursue a 'growth strategy', or others which have chosen a 'defensive strategy'. These terms imply *both* choice of objectives and how they are to be accomplished.

The choice of objectives is so critical a part of selecting a strategy that it deserves to be thought of as the most important variable subject to management control rather than as something which is static or fixed. For lower levels in the company they can be treated as 'given' from above; for the top level in the company objectives must be treated as a variable which it is their responsibility to determine.

Whichever objectives are chosen, they should be expressed dynamically. That is, one should talk about X per cent growth per year, rather than Y dollars by year Z. While this may seem like a pedantic distinction, the problems involved in sustaining a given growth rate are fundamentally different from those involved in reaching a given level of volume without any thought as to what subsequent levels should be. The most meaningful objectives are those which describe capabilities as well as results.

Moreover, objectives should be determined in qualitative as well as quantitative terms. The company which is dedicated to being 'Number One in the hospital care field', or 'the world leader in maritime propulsion', is being guided by as real a set of objectives as the company which wishes to achieve 10 per cent after tax earnings growth compounded annually.

An essential issue, often raised when objectives are made explicit, is the perception of a fundamental discrepancy between numerical and qualitative objectives that have been set. For example, one company which established for itself a rather ambitious growth rate also decided that it wished to remain within its traditional industry. The growing appreciation of the inherent conflict between these two objectives produced useful analysis and clarification of the corporate future on the part of the senior management group.

Where more than one quantitative objective has been established, discrepancies may also occur between the quantitative objectives themselves. For example, a unit may be asked to achieve a very high return on investment and a very high growth rate over the next few years. These conflict in most cases, in the sense that going after one usually means that the other has to be foregone to some extent.

In most companies, objectives are expressed both in terms of aspirations and constraints, with both do's and don'ts in their corporate objectives. Some companies would like to achieve rapid growth while remaining entirely within related businesses, or without diluting equity, or without exceeding a certain debt limit (which in some cases is zero). Getting these do's and don'ts identified and agreed upon is an early step in making corporate strategy explicit.

The primary criteria for evaluating a set of objectives is the degree of risk that it represents. The determination of the company's objectives should represent a careful weighing of the balance between the performance desired and the probability of its being accomplished. This balance is critical. Strategic objectives which are too ambitious result in the dissipation of assets, the destruction of morale, and create the risk of losing past gains as well as future opportunities. Strategic objectives which are not ambitious enough represent lost opportunity and open the door to complacency.

Consequently, objectives cannot be set in a vacuum. They must be related to the available resources, the characteristics of competitors, industry dynamics, and the market opportunity.

Developing an appropriate mix of businesses

Once objectives for a company have been established, the portfolio of businesses engaged in can be evaluated by applying the following criteria:

1. Criteria related to individual performance
    Probable contribution
    Minimum standards
    Trade-offs.

2. Criteria related to the total mix
    Risk level
    Synergism
    Extrapolation
    Resource requirements.

Criteria related to individual performance

Probable Contribution. An important point of departure in thinking about corporate strategy is an estimate of what the existing businesses will contribute to corporate performance if no major changes are made in competitive practice. If a reasoned and valid estimate can be obtained and compared with the corporate objectives, the quantitative extent of the strategy problem may be determined.

This comparison is frequently a major motivating factor in launching a serious examination of strategy. In most cases, it is a result of the estimates falling short of what the company would like to accomplish. However, the difference is not always a gap. One company found itself faced with such glowing estimates of performance—and requirements for resources—that it felt compelled to take a closer look at the assumptions underlying the numbers.

Minimum Standards. This is really the question of disinvestment. If a company has standards of performance which cannot be achieved, given the existing mix of businesses, performance can frequently be improved by getting out of some businesses or parts of them.

The mark of a well-managed company is that it has a procedure for disengaging from unsatisfactory situations, as well as one for identifying attractive new opportunities.

Trade-offs. Establishing standards for unit performance in the context of a portfolio requires that the trade-off decisions underlying such standards be made explicit. For example, one of the essential trade-offs which must be made with respect to every individual business is that of growth vs. profitability. A second is that of short-term profitability vs. long-term profitability. These decisions will frequently be made with three considerations in mind: the overall corporate objectives, the expected contribution from other businesses, and the appraisal of specific opportunity inherent in the particular businesses under consideration.

Criteria related to the overall mix

Risk Level. An essential consideration in looking at the mix of businesses is the degree of risk which the portfolio represents. For this reason it is quite common to find within a single company conglomerate groups of businesses whose major reason for association is that the risk inherent in the package is less than would occur if the pieces were separate. An example of this would be the Martin-Marietta combination, in which the high risk Martin business enjoys some of the benefits of the relatively stable cash flows of the Marietta group of companies. Similarly, the wave of mergers and acquisitions that has swept through the machine-tool industry during the past few years is further evidence of the risk reduction to be achieved in a highly cyclical industry through grouping into broader units.

One very common kind of portfolio risk is that which arises in international companies. Frequently in such situations careful attention is paid to the geographic deployment of assets, since this has direct implications for expropriation risks and for risk of devaluation.

Synergism. Synergism refers to the nature and extent of mutual reinforcement which the individual businesses provide for each other. It may be either operational or financial.

Operational reinforcement arises where the two businesses operating jointly enhance the company's strategic advantage. This may occur because of a broader product line to the same market, because of economies in marketing (as in the American Safety Razor-Philip Morris merger), or because of manufacturing economies (as in the case of General Motors' automotive divisions).

Financial reinforcement may occur either because of the relative pattern of funds generation and demand, or because cyclical swings in earnings of one division are counterbalanced by swings in another, or because the combination is more attractive to the financial community than the pieces would be separately.

Determining the kind of synergism which should exist, and the extent to which it should exist, are strategic issues reserved to the corporate management.

Extrapolation. A key attribute of the mix of businesses is the range of additional opportunities for which it may provide a platform. Indeed, major differences in the valuation of a company may arise from different interpretations of where the company may go from its present position, and what would be required to do so.

From an internal point of view, this frequently arises as a problem of the 'n + 1' division, the critical strategic issue of what should be the next division added to the existing range of businesses. The basis for such a decision should be the considerations of business strategy, industrial dynamics, and synergism that have already been discussed.

Funds Requirements. A universal constraint in any corporate strategy is the balance between the funds requirements it imposes and the resources available for successfully meeting them. Consequently, any strategy must be translated into funds flows projections if the strategy is to be rationally assessed. This is invariably an extremely difficult thing to do: magnitudes of investment are difficult to predict—even when the money is spent for physical plant. Where the money is allocated for research activities, the amount required is notoriously uncertain. Nevertheless, the determination of a schedule of funds flows is an important element of a corporate strategy.

A key reason for constructing such a schedule is that it permits the longer-term implication of a given move to be examined. Most investment projects, whether they be research, new plant, or acquisition, are not self-contained. They are moves in a continuing game, and a game in which a continuing stream of bets will have to be made. As a result it is the overall schedule, rather than the individual project, which should be assessed when considering investment alternatives. The ability to visualize such a schedule is what distinguishes a strategic move from a blind gamble.

Policies

One way of summarizing the thinking of the executive team is to develop a set of basic principles which they can agree should govern the evolution of the company. These should be stated in terms of what the company *will* do, rather than in terms of what the company will *not* do, and should be in terms of general principle rather than specific instances. For example, the statement that 'we will actively pursue international opportunities by encouraging geographic specialization of plants, local promotional efforts, and minimization of exposure to depreciation losses' is general enough to serve as a guideline for a broad set of specific instances.

In a sense, a policy is a decision rule, and the basic corporate policies are those which state the fundamental value trade-offs of the company. If these are to be consistent, there must be some unifying strategic concept.

The attempt to develop such a statement of policies will inevitably produce a considerable amount of soul searching with respect to terminology, and a great deal of discussion concerning interpretation, but this is perhaps its greatest value. Such an effort provides a context within which any lack of consensus concerning future direction can legitimately be discussed.

A statement of objectives addresses itself to *what* should be accomplished. A set of policies addresses itself to *how* that should be accomplished, both in terms of identifying specific directions of evolution and a consideration of specific constraints.

For example, one of the common kinds of questions which any strategy raises are those related to the mobilization of resources. In the financial area debt policy and equity dilution are two issues about which some statement of policy may be useful.

In general, a set of policies will be helpful if they are a comprehensive statement of what the company wishes to emphasize as a basis for its future growth. These may include such issues as: those things which will distinguish the particular company from other companies in its industry; what this company sees as the particular opportunities open to it because of its size and deployment; the skills which are most critical to the achievement of its corporate objectives; and qualitative criteria which new opportunities would have to meet if they were to be seriously considered.

Few companies have ever made such a statement of policy explicit. However, it is clear that many companies have acted as if they had such a set of policies. In one company a senior executive presented the chief executive officer with a statement of principles which he had developed from a consideration of prior decisions made and the policies they implied. When these statements were presented, the chief executive officer took exception to virtually all of them. His disagreement was the clearest indication of the potential value of attempting to make a statement of policy explicit.

The process of developing a statement

Having written up to now of the concepts involved in a statement of corporate strategy, I would like to discuss the process by which such a statement may be arrived at. This is particularly significant because the important end product of developing an explicit corporate strategy is not only the statement itself, but also the benefit that derives to the company from the process. In this context it is particularly valid to say 'you may not learn much from reading a statement of corporate strategy—but you learn a great deal from trying to write one'.

A consideration of the characteristics of the process is, therefore,

as important as a consideration of the contents of the statement—
perhaps more important. To provide its potential benefit, the process of developing a statement of corporate strategy should be (1)
reiterative, (2) political, (3) experimental, and (4) conceptual.

The process of developing a statement of corporate strategy is
reiterative because the full implications making the initial decisions
early in the process are usually not apparent until later decisions
are considered. Consequently, it is important to be able to cycle
through the whole process several times before settling on an interim
solution. For example, objectives may be completely changed once
their resource requirements are explored.

Second, the process is political because it is necessary that the
major source of political power in the executive group be represented in the planning process. One of the commonest explanations
for the existence of elaborate plans which nobody pays any attention to is a sharp separation between the centre of the planning
activity and the centre of political power.

Third, it should be emphasized that the process of developing a
statement of corporate strategy is purely experimental. It ought to
be seen primarily as a way in which the company learns from its
experiences rather than as a straitjacket imposed on divisional management. If it is to be experimental, then there should be a substantial amount of time devoted to a consideration of why certain
things are expected to happen, and a careful review after the fact
of whether they did. This review should be essentially for the purpose of improving the company's understanding of its own decision
processes. In this regard it is interesting to note how many companies make investments year after year without ever reviewing
whether the justification of those investments at the time they were
made proved to be valid.

Finally, it should be emphasized that the process of developing a
statement of corporate strategy should also be conceptual in the
sense of contributing to the formation of new concepts about the
company and its environment. Many companies do not realize their
full potential because they remain confined within concepts of themselves and their environment that are no longer useful guides to behaviour. A company that thinks of itself as American when the
market has become international, or that thinks of itself as stable
when its industry is changing rapidly, is likely to be continually surprised and to have performance results significantly below those
of competitiors who are more sophisticated.

The ultimate reason for going through the demanding process of
developing a statement of corporate strategy is not to produce a

document but to attain superior competitive performance. Whether or not this indeed happens will be influenced by many variables— among them the contents of the statement, the process of developing it, and the way it is implemented. A statement of strategy in itself provides only the usual prelude to action.

Getting started

One of the major difficulties in developing a statement of corporate strategy is that in most companies the attempt to do so coincides with the beginning of a formal planning effort. As a result, all of the complex conceptual and procedural issues related to the corporate future tend to get bound up with the first groping efforts to work out a viable mission and programme for the corporate planning activity.

The most common causes of difficulty are the premature establishment of a formal planning department and the separation of the responsibility for the future of the company from the responsibility for managing current operations. Many companies feel that the way to start developing a statement of corporate strategy is to designate someone as planning officer and then turn the whole job over to him. They invariably discover that they have to pass beyond that point of view in order to make any progress.

Strategic planning is not what the planner does but rather what the management does. If the management finds that it is so deeply involved in the process that it requires some additional assistance, a planning officer may provide this. But to view the planner as synonymous with planning is to assume that a statement of corporate strategy remains a document rather than a creed.

Some companies which avoid this pitfall fall into another: the separation of responsibility for the future from current operation. It is increasingly common to find the chairman of the board, whether or not he is also chief executive officer, or a vice chairman, or some other senior executive, viewing his position as essentially responsibility for the future welfare of the organization. Such a division of responsibility between current operations and future direction invariably produces acute stress, unless both points of view can be incorporated in the same decision-making body. This can be achieved in the context of a formal committee or an informal group. But unless it is accomplished the interaction of present and future, and the trade-offs which must frequently be made between them, will not be adequately achieved.

The way to get started, then, is to have those who are responsible for the present welfare of the company as well as those who are responsible for its future prosperity involved in trying to develop a statement of strategy. In so doing, they may wish to have a member of the executive group act as a co-ordinator or recorder of their own efforts; but whichever procedural decision they take, they ought to recognize that developing a statement of corporate strategy takes a lot of time and trouble. Those few companies who have one feel it was worth it. In every one of those cases, however, it was the chief executive who was the moving force behind it. The idea seems to sell easier from the top down.

2 | Corporate Strategy, Marketing and Diversification

by HARRY HENRY

I PROPOSE to consider the relationship between the corporate strategy concept and the marketing concept. You will remember how St Paul found that the Athenians spent their time in nothing else but either to tell or to hear some new thing, and I think it possible that he would have discovered the same phenomenon in the higher levels of management debate in the Western world today. The corporate strategy concept, being only about five years old, is currently extremely fashionable: the marketing concept, now almost twenty years old, has lost a good deal of its glamour. Since it is characteristic of most of us to seek for new management techniques which will give us better results without actually requiring us to modify in any substantial degree the way in which we conduct our businesses, we are naturally inclined to turn our enthusiasm to concepts which have not yet come to the crunch, in the hope that this will enable us to sweep under the carpet earlier concepts, the later stages of implementation of which are beginning to cause us some embarrassment. In fact, of course, the introduction of the corporate strategy concept in no way supersedes or vitiates the marketing concept. Indeed, it is largely meaningless without it, while a good deal of the difficulty involved in the implementation of the marketing concept arises from the fact that this latter needs to to be viewed against the background provided by the corporate strategy concept itself.

Before we examine the interaction between corporate strategy and marketing, however, we might begin by setting down what we

HARRY HENRY is Visiting Professor of Marketing in the University of Bradford Management Centre and until recently a Deputy Managing Director of the Thomson Organization Limited. This paper was first presented to *The National Conference on Long Range Planning for Marketing and Diversification*, sponsored by The British Institute of Management at the University of Bradford, in June 1969.

understand by the corporate strategy concept as a whole. Despite
its relative novelty, the subject has already accumulated a pretty
massive literature, though it is difficult to avoid the impression that
many of the contributions are saying the same thing in slightly
different words. This is not because of any lack of insight or integrity on the part of their authors: it arises from the fact that
there are relatively few main components of the concept, and that
once they have been listed out it is virtually impossible to think
of any others. What might be regarded as the standard work on the
subject, for example, Professor H. Igor Ansoff's *Corporate
Strategy*, has so far defied all attempts on my part to discover in it
any major lacunae, and I have yet to read an article or paper re-
vealing any significant factor which he has not already mentioned.
But the complexity of the subject, and hence the opportunity it
offers for re-exposition, arises from the fact that most of its components can be seen as interacting with each other in almost any
sequence or combination you care to select, and that one particular sequence and combination will attach different significance than
another to a specific component.

What is meant by this will perhaps become rather clearer if we
look at a very simplified hierarchical diagram of the corporate
planning process, consisting merely of four questions:

1. What are our corporate objectives?
2. What business are we in?
3. What are our relevant strengths and weaknesses (internal and
    external)?
4. So where do we go from here?

The fourth question, of course, will automatically break down
further into sets of options and plans, and the first three questions
will prove on examination to be nothing like as simple as they
might seem at first sight. They will be discussed at a later stage:
what we are concerned with at the moment is to indicate that we
cannot answer the first three questions (and hence put ourselves in
a position to tackle question 4) simply in the order 1, 2, 3: other
orders could be just as relevant, or even more so.

Suppose, for example, one of the corporate objectives is set as
a materially increased Return on Capital Employed—there is some
doubt about the wisdom of such an objective, but it is often used—
and the company is engaged in an industry where (a) capital employed consists largely of fixed plant, and (b) the market in which
the industry operates provides only a low return. Unless the company can find some much more efficient method of operating, un-

known to its competitors (which may be possible, but is improbable), such an objective might be unattainable until Question 2 has been answered by saying 'some other business than our present one'. But before you can say this, you have to answer Question 3, which covers not only the skills inherent in the business but also such things as the nature of the assets. Even if you decide to get out of the business, how do you do so? If you sell the assets on their earnings performance, you are no better off, and you can probably sell them on their capital value only if you are lucky enough to find some megalomaniac competitor obsessed with growth.

This is only one example: it is not too difficult to think of others which will equally well serve to illustrate that these three questions cannot meaningfully be answered in any fixed hierarchical sequence. And, obviously, if we run into this sort of difficulty in so simplified a model, the complications that arise when we start treating the concept more realistically, and therefore in greater detail, will increase exponentially.

Objectives for corporate strategy

I have mentioned corporate objectives without so far attempting to indicate what these may be. For reasons which will later become obvious I do not propose to suggest what they should be: let us at this stage simply look at some of the areas which have been suggested as appropriate objectives for corporate strategy, starting off with what may be called the 'economic' ones. In most cases the word 'growth' may be assumed as being attached: what that means we can come to later.

AREAS OF POSSIBLE ECONOMIC OBJECTIVES

> Return on equity
> Return on assets (variously defined)
> Price/earnings ratio
> Volume of business
> Size of operation
> Liquidity
> Flexibility
> Risk reduction
> Share of market.

Not all of these, I hasten to add, necessarily belong in this list, but before we deal with them we might consider other objectives which, though non-economic and frequently not made explicit, can

be just as significant to the management or the shareholders of a
company. In practice they loom largest when the management *are*
the shareholders, or at least the controlling shareholders, but that is
another matter. These include:

AREAS OF POSSIBLE NON-ECONOMIC OBJECTIVES

Survival of the business
Security for management
Security for personnel
Size of operation
Company prestige
Social responsibility.

It may seem a little surprising that 'survival of the business'
should be listed among the non-economic objectives, and that 'size
of operation' should appear on both lists. But before these para-
doxes are explained it would be as well for us to consider what we
mean by 'growth' and also to make reference to the question of
time.

Economic objectives

The investor who puts his money into equities, as against fixed-
interests stocks, does so today for two reasons. One reason is as old
as investment itself; he is putting his money at risk in the expectation that his foresight and judgement will be suitably rewarded, by
a higher rate of return than he could hope for if he sought greater
security—say in government bonds. The second reason, resulting
from the general acceptance of the fact that we shall live forever in
conditions of regular inflation, is his desire to maintain his return
at least constant in real terms.

Under present conditions in the money market the average investor does not attempt to separate in his mind these two components of his expectation: it is not at all certain that even the
institutional investors do. But it is probably important that corporate managements should, in order that they may determine what
degree of 'growth' they feel obliged to provide. Clearly they are
required to furnish sufficient growth in return on equity to counter
inflation: equally clearly they are required to provide some special
return on equity to remunerate the shareholder for his risk. But
whether that special return should itself be subject to growth—inflation apart—is by no means so obvious, particularly if such growth
involves any increase in the size of risk.

The need to counter the effects of inflation underlines the time element involved in corporate objectives. But, even without this, corporate objectives must necessarily be long-range, taking into account not only likely changes in market needs and the probability of developments in production technology, both within the firm itself and outside, but also other external circumstances subject to change, and the consequences of the company's long-range strategy itself.

Indeed, at any particular moment of time corporate objectives must be determined by the nature, structure and situation of the company in question, and the relevant criteria may differ not only quantitively but also qualitatively. What may be appropriate for a giant corporation with equity widely distributed in public hands may not be acceptable to the middle-sized company still basically in family hands: in the latter case particularly, non-economic objectives may be of major significance. Further, such operating objectives as increased return on investment, growth in scale of operations and reduction of risk, may often be incompatible one with another: how, therefore, the company will choose among these must depend upon its current position and the requirements of its owners.

At this point we may return to a more detailed consideration of the areas of possible objectives, beginning with the economic objectives. Growth in return on equity has already been discussed: an alternative objective might be growth in return on assets. There is vigorous controversy about which criterion is the better, and, indeed, about how 'assets' are going to be defined. I do not want to get involved in this, but I would draw attention to one especial difficulty which manifests itself in my own industry and presumably in others which operate in a like manner. This stems out of the problem of goodwill.

The principal asset of a viable newspaper or a magazine is its goodwill—indeed, in the case of a magazine printed externally by contract, goodwill is its only asset apart from a few typewriters and salesmen's cars. When we buy a successful magazine as a going concern we buy the goodwill, which naturally goes into the balance sheet as an asset, but when we start one of our own we make no such payment. Yet if it becomes successful it develops an inherent goodwill of its own which we could sell at any moment of time for good hard cash. The manager of that magazine thus has charge of a very real asset, on which we expect him to make an adequate profit. But the value we should put on that asset, the price we might get in the open market, is simply a multiple of the net maintainable profit, the multiple being determined by external market conditions. If the manager increases the profit of the magazine, then its market value goes up proportionately, so that the rate of return he is producing on assets employed—assets being taken at their market value—remains constant whatever he does, and equally does so whether the profit increases or decreases. Of course, we have other and more pragmatic methods of determining how such a manager is performing, but this situation creates at the corporate level a very real dilemma which I imagine may well be shared by other industries where goodwill overshadows net tangible assets.

It is unusual to list growth in price/earnings ratio as a possible corporate objective, but I think it legitimate at least to consider it in this context. Since a high P/E ratio reflects the judgement of the money market that a particular company has considerable growth potential still to be developed, it cannot be expected to be maintained for ever, but in the short term—which may well be four or five years, the current conventional period for long-range planning —it may be of major importance to a company planning growth by acquisition and intending to use shares rather than cash for that purpose, or indeed, to a company planning to go to the market for more equity. Whether what is thus essentially a tool of growth may legitimately be regarded as an objective in its own right is an interesting philosophical point, but in practice it is difficult to separate the two, certainly over the sort of time-span we are considering. At the same time, a high P/E ratio is some defence against being taken over, and if the avoidance of take-over is a legitimate objective of the business—something we shall examine among the non-economic objectives—then the same considerations apply.

I have listed growth in the volume of business, along with growth in the size of the operation, as among the possible corporate objectives, because a number of people regard them in this light. I do not: growth for its own sake seems fairly pointless. It may, of course, provide the necessary mechanism for growth in profitability (as measured by return on equity or return on assets) but in this case it becomes a tactical manoeuvre, not a strategic objective. It may inhibit the growth of a competitor to a position of market dominance, but before such inhibition is accepted as a necessary corporate objective it is as well to be sure that the threat of competitive market dominance is real and not merely emotional or superstitious. Unless there is some reason to suppose the threat actually to exist, then growth in the size of the operation unrelated to growth in profitability ought really to be included among the non-economic objectives. And the same considerations apply to growth in market share, which is simply another aspect of the same subject.

It may be added that growth in volume of business, even if it does not result directly in any increase in the return of equity, could be conceived as likely to have beneficial side-effects, resulting from an increase in the overall scale of operations. But this is probably looking at the matter through the wrong end of the telescope: if the overall corporate objectives of the company entail a higher level of activity, then that higher level might perhaps be considered a means rather than an end in itself, as indeed might the effect of being in an expanding business on the morale of the executive staff and on the company's success in staff recruitment. At this point, however, we are running up against the problem to which I referred at the beginning of this paper—the difficulty of considering the corporate objectives of the company separately from the assessments of the company's strengths and weaknesses.

Liquidity and flexibility should perhaps be considered together. Whether or not a change in either or both of them is an appropriate corporate objective—and, if so, in which direction—must depend entirely upon the nature of the business, the industries in which it is operating, its existing capital structure, and the requirements of its owners in terms of both economic and non-economic objectives. Again, whether such changes should be regarded as objectives in their own right, or merely as tactical operations in the interests of higher objectives, is something about which it is not easy to be dogmatic: yet again, it might be argued that a tactical objective which is going to take a long time to fulfil could well be considered a strategic objective.

Non-economic objectives

Let us now consider the examples listed of non-economic objectives, of which the first is survival of the business. Here we must define our terms: clearly it is no part of anybody's corporate objectives to run a company into bankruptcy. The economic objectives concerned with return on equity or assets look after this, however, and when we talk about the survival of the business in this context we mean its survival as a separate entity, which is quite another thing.

It may well be to the economic advantage of the owners of a company—that is, the shareholders—that the company should be taken over at a good price and submerged in some other company. Indeed, the equity markets and the tax laws being what they are, a very considerable number of shareholders live in hopes that this will happen to some of their investments. In these circumstances the fight which managements put up to fend off take-over bids may sometimes be viewed with a jaundiced eye by at least a substantial minority of shareholders. On the other hand, the ultimate decision rests in the hands of the shareholders as a whole, and the question of the right of a Board of Directors to run a company in such a way that it is not particularly attractive to a potential take-over bidder, so that the shareholders are not led into temptation, raises questions about the duties and responsibilities of Directors which it would certainly be out of place to discuss here. And while it is true that non-economic objectives of the type listed may sometimes be held by a mass of outside shareholders—there have been some quite surprising instances of this—it is equally true that they are more usually found to exist in companies where the management holds equity control, and more particularly in family businesses.

In this context, the objective of security for management may simply mean that the family would rather have a given level of profit, and jobs, than a higher level of profit and no jobs. This is their right, as is their right to choose the other objectives listed. Size of operations and company prestige, insofar as they are not implicit in the company's economic objectives, fall into this same general category of decisions which it is the right of managements to take as a matter of personal preference when they are also the owners of the business and thus wasting their own money but which are possibly beyond their proper powers when they are not. On the other hand, the questions of security for personnel and social responsibility are nothing like so easy to deal with in these terms, and open up major issues well beyond the orbit of corporate planning. All that can really be said here is that if these are regarded by the management of the company as legitimate objectives then the corporate planning procedure has no option but to accept them as constraints on the economic objectives.

One other consideration might be mentioned here. It could happen that long-term strategies are entered into, designed to lead eventually to a material increase in the profitability of the company and its return on equity, which entail a considerable sacrifice of profitability in the short term. Situations of this sort have a magnetic attraction for the take-over bidder, who may be able to see into the future better than can the stock market as a whole, or even the company's shareholders. In such a circumstance the survival of the company as an entity could conceivably be regarded as an economic objective rather than a non-economic one.

What business are we in?

The second question we asked in our simplified model of the corporate planning process was 'what business are we in'. This is the question on which the most popular attention has been focused in the recent literature of management, and it has produced some very odd answers, the basic philosophy underlying many of them being enshrined in Theodore Levitt's now classic article on 'Marketing Myopia',[1] and encapsulated in his observation on the buggy whip industry, which read:

> 'No amount of product improvement could stave off its death sentence. But had the industry defined itself as being in the transportation business rather than the buggy whip business it might have survived. It would have done what survival always entails, that is, changing.'

This particular example has so tickled the fancy of management enthusiasts that it is almost heresy to ask just what it means. But it is by no means clear what it *does* mean, or what is supposed to be understood by 'the transportation business', or who defined buggy whips as being part of it, or what the buggy whip makers were in a position to change to. Another example from the same article unconsciously underlines the difficulty even more strongly:

> 'The railroads did not stop growing because the need for passenger and freight transportation declined. That grew. The railroads are in trouble today not because the need was filled by others (cars, trucks, aeroplanes, even telephones), but because it was *not* filled by the railroads themselves. They let others take customers away from them because they assumed themselves to be in the railroad business rather than in the transportation business. The reason they defined their industry wrong was because they were railroad-oriented instead of transportation-oriented; they were product-oriented instead of customer-oriented.'

Now I yield to no man in my contempt for excessive product-orientation, and I have been fulminating against it for the best part of twenty years. But a market cannot really be defined except in relation to the products serving it, as we shall see a little later, and the hard fact remains that railways are in the business of providing rail transportation, not transportation in general. If the market for their category of product is declining, so that they wish to invest elsewhere, then obviously it makes sense for them to look at the possibility of, say, running an airline, and to see whether their existing railway operations and experience would give them a competitive edge in the airline business. If this is not the case, then there is no particular reason for them to choose airlines as a diversification rather than, say, the manufacture of jelly-babies. Equally, if railways were regarded as being in the same business as airlines, then locomotive-builders would be in the same business as aeroplane constructors. It is rather a pity they are not: it would be pleasing to see Concorde driven by steam, and with a cow-catcher in place of a droop-nose.

Theodore Levitt's approach in general is, of course, an extremely stimulating one, and has led to a good deal of valuable mind-stretching. But the warning I am sounding here is one against being misled by words. When the Thomson Organization bought a major section of the packaged holiday business—some tour companies and an airline—and we were asked why, we answered that we were in any case in the communications business. I was responsible for that piece of logodaedaly, and naturally feel rather proud of it, but it is really somewhat difficult to see any sort of logical connection between publishing the *Sunday Times* and carrying holidaymakers on packaged tours to the Costa Brava. We bought into that business because we saw the opportuntiy of acquiring, on reasonably advantageous terms, an operation which we reckoned we had the skills to manage and which admirably suited our profitability and cash-flow requirements at that moment of time in the company's development.

Indeed, there is some case for suggesting that the business a company is in can only be defined as the business of meeting its corporate objectives. How it ought to go about this is something which derives, not from Cartesian definition-mongering, but from a meticulous appraisal of what means it has to that end: in current Corporate Planning terminology, what are its strengths and weaknesses?

Strengths and weaknessses in corporate planning

These means fall into three main categories:

1. Production resources and skills.
2. Marketing structures and skills.
3. Financial resources and availabilities.

Production resources and skills include, of course, R & D facilities, and the financial resources and availabilities will naturally condition the two other categories. (It may be noticed that I have not included in this list anything that can be identified as 'general management skills'. This is because I personally do not believe that such generalized skills exist independently of the specialized skills already listed. General management has skills, of course, but these represent a mix (in various proportions) of the major business skills in production, marketing and finance. The thinking that sometimes leads companies into enterprises they do not know how to operate, that 'we understand the art of management' is perhaps on a par with that of those of us who came out of the services after the last war having as our only qualification 'I know how to control men'.)

The means and resources existing within the company, or available to it, must then be measured against the markets to which these are appropriate, and against likely developments in those markets. In fact, the appraisal of the company's strengths and weaknesses, though it is likely to be time-consuming and to entail a lot of work, is conceptually the simplest part of the task. Where the real difficulty is encountered is in delimiting the relevant markets.

Here, as in so much else in management theory, we run straight into problems of definition, and (unless we are careful) into various semantic pitfalls. In the first place, we have to decide whether the word 'market' is defined by use or by geography: the question of geography is not unimportant, and we shall return to it later, but at this stage it is desirable to confine our definition to that of use.

But even at that we can find ourselves in some confusion, since whatever definitions are selected are likely to be either too narrow or too wide. What, for example, is the market for breakfast cereals? If we define it in terms of the present volume of consumption of the product category we have something which at least is clear-cut, but which is liable to have a very restrictive effect on our thinking: if, on the other hand, we try to define it in terms of the potential market, then there is no breakfast cereal market at all—merely a breakfast market, in which each brand of cereal battles for market share not only against all other brands but also against grapefruit, porridge, eggs, bacon, sausages and kippers—and, indeed, against nothing at all, an option always open to the commuter in a hurry. Similarly, should not the market for frozen vegetables be defined in terms of the total market for vegetables—frozen, canned and fresh alike? We are back here, in effect, with the problem of whether the railways are in the transportation business or in the rail transportation business, and it is probably true to say that most manufacturers are inclined to take the narrower definition. On the other hand, some service industries adopt the much wider definition, and declare, for example, 'we are in the entertainment business' or even more widely, 'we are in the leisure business'.

The conceptual framework which has been put forward as providing a basis for decision in the light of corporate objectives and the company's resources, the product/market matrix, does not help a great deal with this problem. This, like so much else in Corporate Planning theory, is Professor Ansoff's, and takes the following form, under his title of 'Growth Vector Components':

Product Market	Present	New
Present	Market penetration	Product development
New	Market development	Diversification

Fig. 1

though he uses the word 'mission' instead of 'market' for classification purposes, in order to make a distinction between the need being served and the actual customer.

I would suggest, however, that this is possibly not the most useful breakdown. It seems to me that a market can only be defined as the market for a product, and that in this case the product itself defines the market. Thus a present product cannot be said to have the potential of a new market—that is, if we are ignoring the geographical sense of the term. A new market otherwise is only open to a new product. At the same time, however, there could sometimes be a case for considering a market as being defined by a certain type of distribution structure: we shall see an example of this later.

We might consider here an alternative matrix, based on the classification of present markets as 'saturated' or 'extensible'. Saturated markets are those where the total volume of sales is unlikely now to increase very rapidly whatever the industry does about it, such as toilet soap, or cigarettes, or toothpaste, so that a new product can only gain a foothold at the expense of existing products: extensible markets are those which can be regarded as capable of being expanded either through an increase in the number of consumers or an increase in the average per capita volume of consumption. It is possible that this is rather more in line with the realities of modern markets, and it produces the following schedule of growth vectors:

Market \ Product	Existing	New
Saturated	Market penetration	Product development
Extensible	Market development	Product/market development
New	--	Diversification

Fig. 2

At this point it is necessary to consider what difference is made if we take into our thinking the definition of markets in geographical terms. This approach is, of course, far more common in the United States than here, because of the much more regionalized nature of the US economy, and when we ourselves adopt it we normally do so in terms of export markets.

Conceptually, however, it makes remarkably little difference: though the product may be an existing one so far as our production processes are concerned, it is a new product in marketing terms for the market in question, and though the particular vector thus involved might perhaps be better described as 'market extension' rather than 'diversification' yet the fact that we are probably going outside our established marketing structures and skills could well justify our continuing to regard the operation as a diversification.

The precise point at which a particular market ceases to be 'extensible' and becomes 'saturated' is, of course, likely to be very much a matter of degree and of judgement. Nor is the distinction always clear between 'existing' and 'new' products: indeed, the difficulties here are likely to be not only conceptual but also practical. Continuous product improvement is the rule rather than the exception for most industries today, and the point at which such improvement turns an existing product into a new one is not easy to identify. Yet this can be of considerable importance in leading a company to decide which growth vector offers the greatest potential for the effort and resources likely to be involved. For an existing product in a saturated market, for example, market penetration can only come from more skilful marketing (broadly defined): a clear product improvement, however, could shift the operation over towards the product development vector, where the return might be materially greater.

This problem becomes even more intractable when we turn to those industries which are in the habit of producing new models at reasonably frequent intervals, and possibly most intractable of all in connection with cars. The Capri and Maxi are certainly new products, but to what extent can the Hillman Minx Convertible Coupé Series IIIC introduced in July 1961 be regarded as a different product from the Series IIIB which had been introduced in October 1960? And in the newspaper and magazine business we produce a new model with every issue. However, if we follow this line of thought too persistently we shall eventually find ourselves speculating how many angels can dance on the point of a needle: it is probably sufficient at this point to note that the problem exists, and needs to be taken into account where appropriate.

Selecting the operational vectors

We have now been most of the way through the simplified model of the corporate planning process outlined at the beginning of this paper. We have examined the problems of formulating corporate objectives, have come to the conclusion that the question 'What business are we in?' is rather a meaningless one, and have considered briefly what we mean by our relevant strengths and weaknesses. We have also gone part of the way towards deciding how to determine where we should go from here, by systematizing the various growth vectors in which our options lie. It now remains for us to review briefly how we go about selecting which are the vectors in which we are going to operate, in the light of our corporate objectives and the production, marketing and financial resources and skills of which we dispose.

The growth vectors are, as we have seen, identified by the interrelation between alternative product conditions along one dimension and alternative market conditions along the other. To a major extent the product conditions may be regarded as being under our control, insofar as we can lay down specifications and, according to our skill, have those specifications met at one price or another. But market conditions are largely outside the control of the firm, and have therefore to be taken as externally determined. It therefore follows that in any market/product interaction it is, with rare exceptions, the market which calls the tune, and it is to this fact that I was referring when, at the beginning of this paper, I pointed out that the corporate strategy concept in no way vitiates the marketing concept, but needs to take it in.

Marketing concept

The marketing concept can be described in various ways. One fairly all-embracing definition is as 'a managerial philosophy concerned with the mobilization, utilization, and control of total corporate effort for the purpose of helping consumers solve selected problems in ways compatible with planned enhancement of the profit position of the firm'.[2] This refers to corporate effort, but puts as its goal simply the enhancement of the profit position of the firm, which, as we have already seen, goes only part of the way towards fulfilment of overall corporate objectives. A simpler description of the marketing approach refers to it as acceptance of the fact that the ultimate commercial success of any manufacturing or service enterprise is the satisfaction of a user need, and suggests that the channels into which production activities are directed should be drawn backwards from the consumer, not onwards from the factory. This again is too narrow in its outlook for our present purposes: it works well enough from a purely marketing viewpoint, but it ignores the corporate strategy requirements. If, to hark back to an earlier example, you own a large capital-intensive plant engaged in the manufacture of railway locomotives, for which the demand is declining, it does not really make much sense to decide to start making aeroplanes there instead.

But in making it clear that the marketing concept should be subordinate to the corporate strategy concept we must not overlook the fact, already pointed out, that marketing considerations must always be important, and may well be dominant in any implementation of corporate strategy. For product development requires that the product thus developed shall be acceptable to the consumer, by meeting a consumer need; market development assumes that the market for an existing product is extensible, because latent needs exist which can be exploited; diversification presupposes that a market/product organism can be found in an area of which the firm has no direct knowledge.

Market penetration

We have described the market/product vectors as growth vectors, but one at least of them need not be so unless we wish so to identify it. Market penetration, the vector made up of an existing product in a saturated market, does not necessarily imply growth. If the corporate strategy is simply to jog along as before, relying on price inflation to keep step with cost inflation, in line with corporate objectives which are probably mainly non-economic, then no growth is called for. A considerable number of small and middle-sized firms remain quite happy with this situation—at least until death-duties strike—and abstention from growth is equally possible in extensible markets, where market development potential exists but is regarded as of no particular interest. By the same token, product development in either saturated or extensible markets may not necessarily subsume growth for the firm as a whole: it may simply involve the updating or replacement of models which are becoming obsolescent.

If, however, the corporate strategy calls for growth, then growth potential can be found in any of the vectors we have considered, the size of this growth being a function of the external market conditions and, as has already been said, of the production, marketing and financial resources and skills available.

Growth in market penetration, for example, will require in particular the application of marketing skills and of financial resources: the volume of these required may well need to be considerable, since within a saturated market increased market share can only be obtained at the expense of competitors, who will probably fight back. Market development, though it may involve less need to counter competition from other producers, may equally involve a heavy investment of marketing skills and financial resources to create the increased demand from consumers. In both these vectors, however, the enterprise will normally understand something about the dominant variable, the nature of the market, and it may sometimes be felt that companies are too prone to wander off into the more uncharted forms of expansion, and even into outright diversification, before there has been adequate exploration of the growth potential immediately to hand—including the possibilities in such dull preoccupations as better housekeeping. Product development will call most heavily upon production skills—particularly upon R & D facilities, the long-term operations of which may entail a very major drain upon financial resources—while product/market development calls upon all three of production, marketing and financial resources, and though the payoff may be correspondingly greater so may the risks.

Growth vectors and resources

In considering which growth vector to go for, therefore, the firm has to examine what resources it has available which may be appropriate and how far their allocation is likely to be justified by the likely outcome, having regard to the long-term corporate objectives of the company. Leaving aside the question of financial resources, which casts its shadow over every option which is likely to exist, the decision frequently boils down to a choice between expansion along the production channel and expansion along the marketing channel.

A company which is making cars, for example, may decide to start making fire-engines (historically, we have examples the other way round, but we need not let that worry us). So far as production techniques are concerned, this is a logical development. But difficulties might arise because cars are sold to private individuals through car-dealers, whereas fire-engines are for the most part sold to public authorities direct, and the two sets of marketing skills required may have little connection. This does not make the adventure an impossible one, but it does mean that the problem must be recognized. John Houston explains how Massey-Ferguson tackled a similar problem (p. 385).

On the other hand, a firm which manufactures certain types of foods and sells them to grocers may decide that its most relevant skills lie not in its existing food-production technology but in its marketing structures, so that its expansion strategy lies in selling to those same grocers other foods of which it previously had no direct knowledge. John Harvey tells us about the Cadbury experiences with this policy (p. 422), but it is of some interest to note that one of the products in question is dried milk. A superficial judgement would suggest that the people who could best sell dried milk would be the same people who sell fresh milk—that is, dairymen—but a little consideration given to the nature of the consumer market, and the circumstances in which the housewife is likely to want to buy this product, would detect the fallacy in this judgement. And I hark back here to the buggy-whip over-simplification: had the milk combines decided that they were in the business of selling milk at large they might have tried to make a major entry into the dried milk business which would probably have proved unprofitable: in fact they are in the business of distributing fresh milk, to which it is feasible for them to attach other products which, like milk, are highly perishable and need to be delivered at daily intervals— cream, yoghourt and (by extension) eggs: dried milk is not covered by the relevant criteria.

Integration

I ought not to leave the subject of expansion vectors without mentioning another sort of approach to the problem—that of integration, either horizontal or vertical. Both of these can be fitted into the corporate strategy model, but they complicate it considerably and really form a subject of their own. I would only say about vertical integration that the judgement that it will serve the company's corporate objectives is frequently based upon an assessment of its appropriateness to the company's resources, which is emotional rather than realistic. There are not a few examples in my own industry of publishers who enter forlorn-hope publishing ventures in order to feed hungry printing presses, and most of them get what they deserve. On the other hand, it is true that D. C. Thomson and Company who, in order to print over a million copies weekly of the *Sunday Mail,* have to maintain large printing presses which during the week are under-employed in printing a relatively smaller circulation morning paper and evening paper, are able to use their surplus capacity to produce at marginal cost a whole raft of children's comics so cheaply that no other publisher can make any headway in this market at all.

Diversification
We have so far not dealt with the last of the growth vectors—diversification. The word itself is often used in a rather slipshod fashion and is frequently applied to activies which, in strict Ansoff terminology, are more accurately defined as expansion: I fear some carelessness in this connection has found its way into the programme for this book, and even into the title of this chapter, But in the conceptual structure we are considering how 'diversification' is limited to the combination of new products with new markets, which in its purest form represents the entry of the firm into a market unrelated to its existing markets with a product unrelated to its existing products. It will be obvious that here in particular the appraisal of the company's strengths and weaknesses, and consideration of the appropriateness of its skills and resources, are of supreme importance. I have indicated earlier my doubts as to the meaningfulness of the concept of generalized management skills, independent of the special skills—production, marketing and financial—which go to form the management mix, and if this disbelief is accepted it follows that the resources which a company can put into such a new venture must be viewed in specific rather than in general terms. Though the corporate objectives of the company may seem to call for diversification, very little purpose will be served by a diversification exercise which falls flat on its face because the company is unable to make a success of it.

Of course, the possibility always exists that the special skills required may be bought in. This assumes in the first place that the company understands enough about its new business to know what to buy, which is by no means always the case, but even if it is reasonably successful in this the difficulty still remains that corporate management, with whom lies the ultimate responsibility, may not possess the skills necessary to manage the operation, and may not be able to acquire them in the necessary time-span.

The conglomerate

This leads on, in fact, to that special form of multiple diversification which is the conglomerate. The problems of conglomerates are far too large a subject to be entered into here, but they do bring into focus a major distinction, advanced in a recent editorial in *Management Today,* between 'control' and 'management'. Conglomerates control, rather than manage, and they do so by the application of their financial skills and resources. Their control mechanisms are normally financial rather than through the application of production and marketing skills, and the question which is beginning to nag is whether, in these circumstances, the warning financial signals arrive too late after the non-managed production and marketing errors have been committed for the damage to be easily repairable. In considering diversification of this order as a growth vector, therefore, the company whose corporate objectives call for growth will need to give very detailed attention to the question of whether it is not likely to run less risk by a policy of expansion in those areas with which its existing production and marketing skills have some sort of relationship. In contradistinction to this hypothesis, however, we have the case of the Rank Organization, which over the years has expanded from the base of its original film business into other activities having some sort of logical connection with it and where the mystic word 'synergy' might be expected to apply: at the same time it has diversified into xerography, with which it had really no logical connection at all. It is really no secret to anybody which of these two types of growth strategy has been the more successful.

Two points may be made in conclusion. The first is that we have been dealing here with corporate planning, which is *ad hoc,* of indefinite time-span, and involving top corporate management: this must be distinguished from long-range planning at the operating unit-level, which is routine, of limited time-span, and decentralized to operating managements. The second point is that I have been concerned essentially to discuss the conceptual framework, which is helpful and, indeed, probably indispensable as a background to any corporate planning operation. But the way in which any particular company chooses to go about the job in practice is likely to be unique, because that company's situation is unique: there is no system or routine which can be adopted as a general standard. I think it more than possible that some consequent variations in style may well be distinguishable in the chapters that follow.

REFERENCES

1 *Harvard Business Review*, July/Aug. 1960.
2 King, Robert L. (1965) *Science in marketing.* ed. George Schwartz (John Wiley).

3 | Economic Analysis of Company Strengths and Weaknesses

by J. ROGER MORRISON

SOUND economic analysis is the foundation of all management planning. Properly carried out, it enables management to grasp the major problems and opportunities facing a company. The emphasis in this chapter is more on delineating the logic to be followed in making an economic analysis than on specific case examples. Before examining the individual steps it is important to understand what economic analysis is and the steps in economic analysis.

Economic analysis is the examination of (1) a company's industry and (2) the company's competitive position within that industry in order to *identify significant improvement opportunities*. Thus economic analysis is a diagnostic process that is essential in carrying out strategic planning, determining a company's organization, identifying management information requirements and evaluating marketing strategy.

The five steps in economic analysis

There are typically two broad areas of examination in economic analysis. First, a review of the total industry; and second, an examination of a company's competitive position within that industry. However, these two areas are so broad that it is worth while, for the purpose of this paper, to divide the process of economic analysis into five main steps:

J. ROGER MORRISON is a consultant with McKinsey Company Inc. This paper was first presented at the *National Conference on Long Range Planning*, sponsored by the *Financial Times* at the University of Bradford Management Centre, November 1967.

1. Analysis of the basic forces affecting industry supply and demand in order to determine *the key factors for success* in the industry.
2. Identification of significant industry trends in these forces of supply and demand, to highlight *the need for changes in the key factors for success* in the industry, or to identify *new problems or opportunities* that may arise in the industry.
3. General appraisal of the company's competitive position within the industry in order to highlight major problems and opportunities.
4. *Specific* appraisal of the company's competitive performance against the key factors for success in its industries in order to identify the *critical problems and opportunities* facing the company.
5. Development of *specific action programmes* to capitalize on these opportunities or to solve these problems.

The five basic steps are individually discussed in this chapter. However, it is important to recognize that each step is not a separate analysis that can be completed before moving on, but that the process of economic analysis is continuous and simultaneous.

Step 1. Analysis of the basic forces affecting industry supply and demand

The purpose of this first step is *to identify the key factors for success* by examining the forces or factors that typically control industry supply and demand. These factors fall into four broad categories, each of which is discussed below: market characteristics; price-cost-investment characteristics; technology; and industry structure and profitability. Having analysed these four characteristics, the last section discusses how they can be used to identify the key factors for success.

Marketing characteristics

The investigation of six main market characteristics determines the outlook for growth and the forces affecting demand for the products in any business. These characteristics are:

1. Product Line. One basic question is involved in the examination of the product line:

What are the industry's products? The product line should be broken down by price, quality, performance and/or end use categories.

2. *Customers.* The complex nature of this characteristic requires several questions to be answered :

Who buys the products? Each specific customer or user of every product category must be identified.
In what quantity are the products purchased?
How frequently are the products purchased?
When are products purchased?

3. *Channels of Distribution.* These queries occur in defining distribution channels :

Where can consumers buy the products?
How do products reach the point of sale?
What functions are performed by each of the units in the channel of distribution?
What compensation—e.g. trade margins—is given by manufacturers to each of the units in the channel of distribution?
How do the trade margins given to these units on this industry's products compare with the margins typically given for other products handled by the units?

4. *Use of Product.* To understand how the product is actually used, four points should be considered.

What are the specific applications of the products?
What products could be substituted for the same application?
Is a product a necessity or a luxury?
How long will a product last?

5. *Basis of the Buying Decision.* This critical marketing characteristic can be understood best by asking :

How do customers choose between the products offered by different manufacturers and what is the relative importance of price, service, brand name, quality etc. to the consumer when selecting the product of an individual manufacturer?
Who influences the customer in making his buying decision?

It is important to understand the basis of the buying decision precisely instead of making generalized comments. For example, when considering impulse ice-cream products sold through a confectioner, it is extremely important to know if the consumer typically decides to buy ice-cream before entering the shop, or whether the decision to buy largely arises from seeing ice-cream, i.e. is ice-cream a planned purchase? Will the consumer go to another shop in search of a particular brand of ice-cream, or will he take what the shop offers?

These two questions would obviously be crucial to an analysis and understanding of retail distribution strategies in the ice-cream business.

6. Pricing. In theory, product prices should be the balancing factor between supply and demand. For example, the price of a product should reflect the consumer's rationale for its purchase. Since this theory is not always valid in practice, we will also want to discover:

The logic for setting prices used by management in the industry.

Cost versus 'value to the consumer' versus market price—e.g. commodities.

The extent to which individual producers are able to achieve price differentials for essentially similar products—and why.

The price leader in the industry.

The trend of produce prices compared with industry cost trends and the general level of other industrial or consumer products.

The end result of these investigations should be a clear understanding of the factors affecting the demand for the products and their outlook for growth.

Price-cost-investment characteristics

These characteristics will significantly affect industry supply. The specific questions to be answered in looking at these characteristics are:

1. Relative Significance of Cost and Investment. It is important to get an overall appreciation of the relative costs and investment for the whole business and to understand how these costs and investment vary between each of its major functions. For example:

In simple business like food products, the major functions may merely be manufacturing, wholesale distribution and retail distribution. The fixed and variable costs *and* investment associated with these three functions can easily be identified.

In more complex businesses such as metals, chemicals and petroleum, the analysis by function of cost and investment becomes more complex for two reasons: (1) the company may not be involved in each of the major functions of that industry—e.g. a producer of plastic polymers may not participate in the fabricating phase of the plastics industry—and obtaining information may therefore be more difficult; (2) an intermediate profit is frequently earned at each stage in the process between receipt of the major raw materials and the sale of the final product to the consumer— e.g. in the copper industry a separate profit is typically earned at the mining, smelting, refining and final fabrication stages.

In analysing the costs and investment of each function, it is also important to understand how these costs and investment would vary with the scale or size of the unit.

Thus, in effect, we must gauge the impact of the scale of enter- prise on the economics of the business. While the concept of 'mini- mum economic size' and 'economies of sale' is generally considered in terms of the manufacturing units in an industry, it may also be applied to physical distribution, advertising or size of retail outlet —e.g. how much business must a manufacturer do with a retailer before it is economic for the retailer to devote any effort to the product?

2.   *The Source of Industry (Company) Profits.* It is vital to know the major sources of company profits and how they vary between end use markets, product groups, customers, geographic areas or manufacturing units. We must look at profitability in terms of the *total* contribution to profits and the per unit—or percentage of sales —contribution.

3.   *The Effect on ROI of Price, Volume, Cost and Investment Changes.* The dynamic analysis of the industry's price-volume-cost- investment characteristics is usually presented in a break-even or 'profit/volume sensitivity' chart.

This type of analysis gives a quantitative basis for appraising the relative significance of improvements or trade-offs between any of these variables. This can be illustrated by contrasting the important variables in food, drugs and footwear. For example:

A 10 per cent increase in drug volume would result in a 60 per cent increase in ROI

A similar increase in the volume of footwear would result in only a 10 per cent increase in ROI because

Variable costs are only 30 per cent of the sales price in the drug industry, but

Variable costs are 75 per cent of the sales price in the foot- wear industry

A 10 per cent decrease in distribution costs in the food business would result in a 14 per cent increase in ROI

A similar decrease in footwear would result in only a 2 per cent
improvement in ROI because
    Physical distribution costs amount to 33 per cent of total costs
    in food.
    Similar costs are only 8 per cent of the total costs in footwear.

In summarizing the importance of these variables, it is important
to select meaningful variations in cost, price and volume. We should
not, for example, use a 10 per cent increase in volume automatically, but should select a range of volume increases that appear to be
reasonable in the light of the company's current market position
and industry growth trends.

*4. Profit Implications of Strategic Alternatives or Economic
Trade-Offs.* In any industry there are certain 'trade-offs' or decisions
which management can make that have a significant impact on the
present and future profitability of the business. Since these strategic
alternatives usually require a change in the company's policy or
strategies, they are important to top management.

The strategic alternatives will obviously vary from industry to industry. Typically they arise from actions to alter the relative balance
between:

Functions in the industry. Increasing the proportion of crude oil
    requirements supplied from petrol company wells.
Products. Shifting from gas to middle distillates.
Markets. Increasing sales in New England States as proportion of
    total US sales.

Technology

The technology inherent in producing an industry's product
affects the degree to which supply is flexible and the extent to which
other products can be made with the same resources. The questions
warranting examination are :

1. How interrelated are product and process? Is it necessary to
develop a new process before a new or revised product line can be
introduced—e.g. a new synthetic fibre—or can a new product be
produced using existing processes—e.g. aero-engine parts? The
interrelationship of produce and process obviously determines the
speed with which manufacturing capacity will respond to increases
in demand as well as the speed with which new or improved products can be launched on the market.

2. What is the typical lead time for a new product's design and development? For example, it takes three years to design and develop an aero-engine or a car, but six–eight weeks to develop a new line of cosmetics—excluding market testing. The length of lead time not only affects the speed of launching new products but also the decision-making cycle and the risk factors in the business.

3. How could changes in the production/distribution technology affect the economic characteristics of the industry? For example, the bolt maker that replaced five separate machine tools previously required for the five steps in the cycle for manufacuting bolts substantially reduced the investment required and allowed the entrance of a large number of small bolt manufacturers into the industry. This in turn resulted in substantial price competition on high volume lines, the prices of which had previously been maintained by the four or five major manufacturers.

4. How does the nature of the production process affect industry's ability to increase and decrease the supply of products? In most process industries, such as cement and oil, there is a maximum capacity that manufacturers cannot exceed without investing in further major expansion. Similarly, until this capacity is reached it is relatively easy for manufacturers to step up production as they have only to run the facilities perhaps six days a week instead of five. This typically means that incremental pricing is a feature of the industry when demand falls significantly below capacity. In contrast, production of food and footwear products—which require a high labour content but relatively simple machines—can be modified almost in line with demand by merely adding or subtracting men and machines.

5. What is the rate of product and process innovation in the industry? Changes in the rate of product and process innovation could have a substantial impact on the economics of the industry.

6. How have new products or technological innovations affected the growth of the industry? For example, the emergence of a large number of new synthetic fibres substantially increased the total textile market. However, the large number of new breakfast cereal products developed yearly in the US has not increased the market for cereals (in terms of *per capita* consumption) but has altered individual manufacturers' share of that market.

Industry structure and profitability
The structure of an industry typically determines the extent and nature of competition in that industry. It is a reflection of:

1. The number and make-up of companies in the industry. This might specifically include:

The degree of concentration in the industry:
  Four aluminium manufacturers account for 90 per cent of the aluminium industry
  One hundred footwear manufacturers are required to represent an equivalent proportion of the footwear industry.

The extent of integration in the industry:
  Aluminium companies have integrated from the raw material (bauxite) to the fabrication of final consumer products
  Major copper mining companies do not typically manufacture the final user products.

2. Financial and non-financial barriers to entry:
The high capital investment required for participation in some industries acts as a barrier to entry by small enterprises—e.g. the steel or cement industries.

3. Extent of excess capacity:
Both short-term and long-term excess capacity affects the price and profitability structure in the industry.

4. Nature of competition:
Competition may be essentially local in nature—e.g. cement companies. It may be confined by national boundaries—e.g. food products, or may be international in scope—e.g. aircraft.

5. Competitive arrangements:
The industry may have a history of 'friendly' competitors, industry associations or informal meetings, or may be characterized by 'arms length' competition.

6. Extent of diversification into other businesses by major companies in the industry:
Some companies' diversification may affect the economics of the business.

7. Industry profitability and the relative performance of individual Companies:
The main focus of this analysis should be on the trends in profitability and ROI in the industry as a whole.

Analysis of characteristics
Having analysed these four forces affecting supply and demand,

we can now identify the key factors for success in the industry or industries in which the company is operating. These key factors for success can be identified by two steps:

1. Select the forces affecting industry supply and demand that are UNIQUE to the industry:

> In almost every industry there are certain characteristics high-lighted by the preceding analyses that will be generally unique to that industry. For example:
>
> Good plant location in the cement industry
> The high transportation cost of both raw materials and finished products places a premium on locating production facilities to minimize the transportation costs
> Sophisticated financial controls in the car industry
> The three-year lead time between product design and manufacture means that excessive costs can be 'designed into' the car that will not be highlighted until production is imminent.

2. Specify the unique skills—or advantages—of each company in the industry:

> This step can lead to the identification of other key factors for success and verify the soundness of the factors derived from the analysis of the industry characteristics. For example:
>
> General Motors' financial control system was considered to be one of the major reasons for its success and the Ford 'whiz kids' initial task in reorganizing Ford was to install a similar system.

Step 2. Identification of significant industry trends

The second major step in economic analysis is to identify the significant industry *trends* in market characteristics, price-cost-investment characteristics, technology and industry structure and profitability, as well as the general political and economic climate. For example:

> *Market trends:* Increased home storage capacity that results from the growth in home refrigeration in the United Kingdom should create a substantial opportunity for expansion of the take-home ice-cream market.
>
> *Technological trends:* The development of micro-wave transmission means that the use of underground cables for the transmission of telephone messages could decrease. Since these cables

account for twenty per cent of the total cable market, this represents a major problem for producers.

Industry structure: If a steel company acquires manufacturers representing sixty per cent of the drop forging market for steel, competitors will lose this market when excess steel-producing capacity arises.

General economic and political trends: The abolition of the fifteen per cent EEC tariffs on paper products means that Norwegian producers could sell commercial grade papers at about seven per cent below the UK producers' price, thus threatening thirty per cent of the total industry production and creating a major problem.

Changes in other industries: Changing trends in other industries have also altered the key factors for success.

Step 3.   General appraisal of the company's competitive position

The third step in economic analysis identifies major problems and opportunities by assessing a company's general competitive position. A more specific targeting and evaluation of its competitive position *vis-à-vis* the key factors for success is covered in Step 4. The major areas for assessment are:

1. Product Strengths and Weaknesses.

A qualitative and quantitative assessment of a company's current product line must be made:

Performance characteristics for each end use application of the product must be studied. Generally, these performance characteristics must be considered in the light of the price level of the products. The quality of the product is typically considered as part of performance.

By comparing individual items in the company's product line with the competitor's product line we may discover what gaps occur and why.

2. Comparative Market Position.

This is an analysis of the company's share of market position by:

Product
End user market
Channels of distribution
Geographic area.

3. Technology.

It is often difficult to make any precise quantifiable distinction between the technology and manufacturing skills of a company and those of its competitors. The simplest way of making this evaluation is to list—for each major process—the significantly different types of equipment or processes used by competitors, their advantages in terms of output etc., and the manufacturing technology on which they or their competitors have a patent (or unique) position. In certain instances it may be possible to measure technical performances.

4. Financial and Cost Results.

This involves a comparative financial analysis of the company with its major competitors. Generally, such analyses are based on published financial statements from competitors and, although they may not give precise data on the detailed cost performance of a company, they can show and have shown where overall costs are out of line.

This evaluation of a company's general competitive position can and should highlight the major problems and opportunities facing the company.

Step 4. Appraisal of the company's competitive position to identify specific problems and opportunities

The fourth step in economic analysis identifies specific problems and opportunities by analysing company performance on the key factors for success. This, in effect, is merely a refinement and pinpointing of the general competitive analyses made in the previous steps but with the focus on performance *vis-à-vis* key factors for success. The analyses required are relatively simple and fall into two categories:

1. A statement of the key factors for success developed in Steps 1 and 2
2. The development of a quantitative or qualitative basis for assessing the company's performances on each of these key factors for success.

For example, statistics could be developed to show the proportion of missed promises in an industry where delivery performance was essential for success.

In an industry like cement, where plant location is essential to success, maps and comparative transport costs showing company and competitors' position could be developed to evaluate the company's performance on the key factors for success.

Step 5. Development of specific action programmes to solve problems and to capitalize on opportunities

At this stage in the process economic analysis will have identified the major problems and opportunities facing the company. Some will be defined in very broad terms, e.g. improving the utilization of fixed investment. Others may be quite specific, e.g. improving the company's position in the take-home food products market. However, the critical fifth step in the total process of economic analysis will not yet have been completed—developing specific actions to capitalize on the opportunity or to solve the problem. This in turn requires:

The listing of possible specific alternative courses of action that may be appropriate

The evaluation of the pros and cons of each alternative and of the relative benefits that would accrue from implementing individual action programmes.

The end result of this step can be a simple summary outlining key problems and opportunities, and the major action steps that management must carry out to capitalize on them.

In summary, the following five steps lead to specific action programmes to capitalize on the major opportunities for a company:

1. Analyse the basic forces affecting industry supply and demand to identify the key factors for success
2. Examine major industry trends to identify the need for changes in the key factors for success and to identify major problems and opportunities
3. Assess the company's general competitive position to investigate the major problems and opportunities that may be involved
4. Evaluate the company's performance on the key factors for success to identify the specific problems and opportunities facing the company
5. Develop specific action steps to allow the company to capitalize on opportunities and to overcome the problems highlighted in the previous steps.

4 | Identifying Market Opportunities

by STEPHEN KING

THE gap between theory and practice is probably wider in new product development and diversification than in any other aspect of marketing. What is written in most of the books does not look very like what happens in most companies. Success has often come through breaking the rules: indeed in happy ignorance that there might be rules to break. Equally a determined effort to be rational about the whole thing has often ended in failure. After all, all products were new at one time, most markets were 'growth markets'; many of today's most successful businesses started from a hunch. We have to steer some sort of middle course between accepted theory and current practice. The conventional theory can be idealistically unattainable, and is often unreasonably based in any case. It tends to leave out the aspirations and fears of the people expected to achieve it; it tends to forget that we have a great capacity for self-deception and a great desire for ready-packaged magic solutions. And what many companies actually do most of the time is probably wrong anyhow. Certainly there are impressive statistics to support the high failure rate of new products and attempts at diversification.

What I have tried to do in this chapter is, first, examine a little more critically than usual some of the accepted theories (whether culled from books or the conventional wisdom) of the new product development/diversification business. Then I have tried to build up a suggested approach based on the practice and experience of some successful companies. First, then, to some of the accepted theories.

STEPHEN KING is Head of Account Planning at J. Walter Thompson Limited. This paper was first presented to the *National Conference on Long Range Planning for Marketing and Diversification,* sponsored at the University of Bradford Management Centre by The British Institute of Management, June 1969.

Identifying marketing opportunities

It must surely be clear that there is no such thing as a market opportunity in a vacuum. It must be able to be exploited by someone before one can call it an opportunity, rather than a gap in a market or a product that would be nice to have. It would be very nice to have a car that ran on water instead of petrol, and it would not be too hard to market it (until water became heavily taxed, that is). But, for the moment, this is not in any real sense a market opportunity, since as far as I know no company can see a remote chance of exploiting it. As Harry Henry has convincingly pointed out in Chapter 2, no company can possibly say what is a market opportunity for itself unless it has begun to answer such questions as 'What do we want to do as a company? Where do we want to be in five years' time—twenty years? What are we good at now? What makes us different from our competitors? How long will this difference last? Where could it lead to?'

There *might* be marketing opportunities practically anywhere. Provided that a product type is related to some fundamental and continuing human need or desire (like the need to eat and drink, desires for shelter, movement, warmth, appeal to the opposite sex, and so on), there is no reason why there should not be a marketing opportunity within it. It all depends whether the company can make something that appeals sufficiently to this need at a price related to the importance of the need and to what other companies might do. It depends a lot whether the company *wants* to make and exploit a market opportunity. It hardly seems worth belabouring such an obvious point. And yet, in my experience, practice is very different. Many companies do not seem to have clearly formulated objectives; many do not have clear-cut assessments of their production skills, marketing skills and financial skills. It is as if, in the transition from the one-man business (or company dictatorship) to the collection of specialist management skills, they have left out either long-term planning skills or the desire to meet some sort of specific objectives.

All too frequently new product development people, either in the manufacturing company or in outside agencies, are in effect asked to 'come up with some ideas and we'll let you know if you're on the right lines'. And since it can take a lot of time to work out ideas in detail (forecasts of market sizes, of profitability and so on) a great deal of time and energy is spent on projects which are not in line with the unspoken company policy. One reason for this is perhaps that the theory is not quite as easy to put into practice as it sounds.

It is a fact that many people running companies have reached their positions after a near-lifetime of specialization in research or production or accounting or some other part of the total business. Practically all their time will have been spent in dealing with short-term situations, the year's targets, sudden crises, hiring and firing. Many will have had little experience in long-range planning, even in their own specialist spheres. It may be unreasonable to expect them, on reaching positions of power, to be able straight off to look at the business dispassionately as a total entity, predict the very complex inter-relationships needed for change and take long-term views.

It seems to me that here is an area where we must accept some sort of compromise between theory and current practice. By all means we must constantly urge top managements to be clear about company long-term objectives and about assessment of strengths; and, of course, to pass on such decisions to middle management. But I think we must also accept that the correct model for this process is one of feedback rather than single flow. Management may not be able to make final decisions concerning the right direction for the company without a flow of ideas about where there might be opportunities. However, it is surely true that the ideas will quickly dry up unless the management gives some sort of boundaries to the area of search. And of course it is up to the management to make the first move and to get this feedback system of communication going.

Then the difficulty arises of the terms in which to set the company objectives.

Company objectives

One of the most common company objectives that is passed down the line is the purely financial one—to make so much profit this year, to achieve so much return on equity or assets, to reach a certain price earnings ratio. These are no doubt excellent short-term objectives, but they are not the only objectives. All too often the other corporate objectives remain unspoken and maybe are taken for granted by the employees, since they share a lot of them. This may work all right for a going concern, but there are problems when it comes to new product development.

The fact is that it is of no help at all to development people to be told that the corporate objectives are new products that will return 20 per cent on investment. This is just as bad as being given no objectives at all. All it says is that the market opportunities to be identified must be good ones. I have known this to happen with companies wanting to diversify, and as a new product consultant, all one can do is start out on a questionnaire: 'Would you go into property on the south coast? Banking? Dairy farming? Electricity generation? Transistors? Cheese?' Until finally the manufacturer is goaded into thinking and saying what would be acceptable.

There is perhaps a more subtle danger in over-concentration on financial objectives, and that is the gap between theory and practice. Many managements will talk publicly about their objectives in profit terms and imply that the sole purpose of the company is to make profits, that the sole obligation is to the shareholders. Much of the literature of management theory supports this view. But from middle management down, employees (through whom the policy is carried out) do not act as if this were so. On the whole employees act as if the corporate objectives were to preserve and strengthen the continuity of the company and its products. Loyalty tends to be given to the company as a collection of people, to the products and to customers. There is not very much sense of obligation to shareholders; after all, the shareholders will be the first to desert if the company runs into trouble. As a result companies tend to develop very specific personalities, which are formed mostly by the nature of the product and tend to be reinforced as managers recruit in their own image and teach by example. These personalities usually change very slowly and greatly affect new product development/ diversification. They are a very important factor in deciding what is a market opportunity for any company and what is not.

What companies are for is a very complex issue, with many social and ethical overtones. Different companies act in different ways, and maybe we are moving more towards the sort of large company with widely experienced professional managers who can take a wholly dispassionate view of the company personality and the nature of their brands. But on the whole I would say that the main motivations of middle managers in most companies are a desire for continuity of company and brand, a desire for success for both and a striving for some sort of personal attainment. Profits are a *measure* of all these, just as sales, market share and company growth are. They are not really ends in themselves.

If this is so, then it clearly does not make too much sense to set objectives for development in purely economic terms. They simply will not work very well, unless the commitment of employees can be obtained. In other words, the objectives must be set in terms of the sort of business the company should go into, in order to strengthen the personality or nature of the company and tie in with the motives of the people working in it. Profit objectives fall naturally into place as criteria of the success of the development: in a sense they are most useful as a description of the company personality—its patience or impatience, its adventurousness, its attitude to risk.

New products and top management

Here, following directly on from setting the wrong sort of company objectives, is another gap between theory and reality. Or, the cynic might say, an extract from the Chairman's Speech (as drafted by the Advertising Manager). New products involve the long-term growth of a company and its long-term profits. They relate to the nature and diversity of the company in the long term. Frequently they have a direct bearing on investment in new plant and skills. Always they involve risk.

One thing is common to all these areas: they are the province of top management. There are plenty of other people who will deal with short-term problems and keep the company on its course. It is only top management who can decide what the company is to be and do in the future. New product development is the top management function *par excellence*. And yet it is all too common for management's interest in product development to be fairly superficial—making speeches about it and examining with interest the ideas that are put up. Actually bringing the new products to the starting line is delegated far below. There are many arguments for and against any particular departmental placing of the responsibility for new product development. In consumer goods companies there have been both successes and failures when responsibility is lodged with the R & D Department; or with the Production Department; or with the Marketing Department; or with a special New Product Development Department. I personally think that the weight of argument strongly favours the specialist department, but it all depends on the Company structure and personality and on who does the job.

The key principle in organization for development seems to me to be that of closeness to management decision-taking. However organized, the actual practice of development/diversification should be regarded as part of management. It is not enough for top management to be interested in the results of development work. It should thoroughly understand development processes and the time periods involved; and it should take the initiative in stimulating and guiding the work. I would judge that the biggest single difference between success and failure in *making* new market opportunities lies in the degree of this management involvement. This is an area in which I think we should not accept any compromise between theory and practice. The theory say that development of the company and its products is the province of top management; practice must catch up with theory.

The marketing concept

The marketing concept is a very complex idea with a wide variety of meanings in common use, but no self-respecting company will nowadays omit it from the creed. Yet here too there are fairly wide gaps between theory and practice with which we must come to grips.

There have been many theoretical definitions of marketing in the literature (some of which I do not pretend to understand). In most of them there are three central ideas:

1. Marketing is a philosophy embracing the long-term planning and management of the whole company.
2. Its objectives are those of the company as a whole (including profits and growth).
3. It assumes that success will be based on the idea that consumers will buy more of, and pay more for, what they want than what they do not.

This is certainly not the precise meaning implied by common use in most companies. For instance, most Marketing Departments do not cover all three of the ideas in the theoretical definition. In some companies the Marketing Department is very little more than a new fancy name for the Sales Department; objectives are seen as annual sales targets, in cases or tonnage. As a development from this, some companies have separate departments for marketing and sales; but then one finds that the Marketing Department is staffed exclusively by ex-salesmen. These ex-salesmen may be admirable people, full of drive and initiative, but really the work done by salesmen is not very good training for the analysis, creativity and management of abstract ideas needs in the Marketing Department —let alone the general management implied by the formal definition of marketing.

In the larger consumer goods companies, the Marketing Department is much nearer the definition. Brand or Product Managers are in theory acting as general managers for their brand. But all too often they are bright young men with little experience, who are equally given little freedom or responsibility. They are still listened to more intently by salesmen than by production or finance men.

They are still apt to define markets in a rigid and blinkered way. There is still a gap between theory and practice, which maybe time will reduce—but I suspect not entirely. (It will depend partly on the supply and demand situation for bright young men, and thereby the length of experience or depth of training to be expected in people filling certain roles. American experience suggests that the average age and special training of marketing professionals will increase, but slowly.)

There has been an attendant danger to this tendency to view marketing in practice as one part only of the total management of a company. For the last ten or twenty years marketing has been seen as the glamorous part of manufacturing and trading companies, and it has attracted the most public attention and the most University graduates. It has developed its own language, mysteries and magic solutions—from demand curves to media optimization models.

Imbalance

The trouble is that this has unbalanced the relationship between finance, marketing and production. The production men have often sunk in estimation as the marketing men have risen. Their salaries have not risen as fast of those of marketing men: and production tends to find it harder to recruit the best brains, on a long-term basis. The pendulum may have swung too far. In the bad old days it was a question of 'Here's the product. Let's find some slick salesmen to sell it'. But are we any better off if we are saying 'Here's what we could sell (or here's a market opportunity). Let's find some horny-handed production man to make it'?

In my experience (and I suspect most people's), what goes wrong or proves most difficult in new product development is almost always on the production side. And this is not very surprising, because it is very much the hardest job. There is the problem of inventing the new formula or new design in the first place; then a huge leap from the laboratory to pilot plant then a lesser, but still difficult, leap from pilot plant to production run.

Here we have the people responsible for the hardest job in product development generally held in the lowest estimation of all those involved. It is not surprising that the success rate is low. The Research and Development people tend to suffer, too, from an overclose association with production. The result can be that they either end up as a glorified quality control department or retreat into an esoteric boffinery.

The greatest prophets of the marketing concept have maybe

added to the imbalance. I share this ambivalence towards Levitt and
'Marketing Myopia'. On the one hand, his theories have been one
of those very rare blinding revelations: afterwards one looks at
markets and development in a totally new way, and one cannot go
back to the old ways. On the other hand, I think he has dazzled
us into believing that one part of the development operation is the
whole thing. I am quite sure it would have been easier for the
American railroads to go into, say, catering or food manufacture
(not in the 'transportation business' but not too difficult on the production side) than into car manufacture or running an airline. This
is for two reasons. First, learning about new consumers and new
motivations or about new channels of distribution is a great deal
easier than learning new production methods and processes. It
seems to me that Levitt may be seeing production too much as a
science that can be bought and sold, too little as an art. Secondly, I
think that Levitt is leaving out the whole idea of commitment to a
product and to its continuation, which is one of the major motivations of the individuals in the company. Would the railroad companies have made a success of railroads, if they had not been
product-oriented, committed to railroads as products?

I have a feeling that Levitt is entirely right as far as product improvement is concerned; and wrong when it comes to complete
diversification, because the theory ignores the people in a company
—what they can do and what drives them on. Fairly obviously,
there is no clear dividing line between product improvement and
diversification. But if there is in practice—whatever the theory—a
boundary beyond which it is difficult to get committed company
people, and production men in particular, to go on developing
new products, then clearly this must be taken into account in real
life.

This is where corporate planning comes in. If what Marketing
Departments do were exactly the same as the theoretical definition
of marketing, there would be no need for it. The marketing men
would be initiating and controlling the total corporate effort (including production) to achieve total company objectives by satisfying
consumers. But most marketing men are in no position to do that;
it is only the corporate management which is.

It becomes essentially an organizational problem. In the pure
theory, one might agree that product development/diversification is
a marketing activity. In practice, it means a combination of the
skills exercised in the Marketing, Production, R & D and Finance
Departments. And it usually means also strengthening production
skills and status if there is to be any chance of going beyond the

boundaries of the current product commitment. This last is extremely difficult and it often comes in the end to acquiring a new company. But unless it can be achieved market opportunities will remain gaps in markets.

Generation of new product ideas

The marketing literature often seems to imply that the first task of development people is to invent the wheel three times a week. Reality is duller but probably more profitable in the long run. It is true that there have been, dotted over history, a few dramatic instances of 'new product ideas' in the wheel-invention sense, gunpowder, the jet engine, canning, carbon fibres, hover-propulsion, frozen food—even stainless steel razor blades. But most new products (and I suspect practically all the wheel-invention types too) emerge gradually from modification of existing ideas and technology, from putting together familiar things in a slightly new way. They do not spring fully-formed, ready-packaged from some special market research process.

One of the results of the combination of a high status for marketing and the tendency of many people in marketing departments to be either rather inexperienced or drawn from rather non-intellectual sources, has been a voracious quest for magic solutions. Each new technique for the measurement of advertising or the statistical manipulation of data has its brief vogue. The same is true for the generation of new product ideas. There seems often to be a feeling that there ought to be a single best method, if only we were 'sophisticated' enough to work it out. Modest aids to the process of thinking are blown up out of all proportion—particularly if they are linked in any way to computers—well beyond the claims of their protagonists; gap analysis, for instance.

In fact, there are several useful ways of stimulating a creative approach to new products. But they are just that, no more. And this is what in practice is most valuable. We do not need a magic method of invention; what we need is an inventive approach by everyone involved.

Growth market prediction

A good deal of long range planning theory is very properly concerned with prediction of the future. This has always been and will remain an extremely difficult business, with luck playing a very large part. There will always be unpredictable events, like wars.

Government reactions cannot be predicted very far ahead (even by the Government). The forecasts of basic statistics can go astray very easily—the Registrar General, for instance, is constantly having to revise population forecasts. Nevertheless, forecasting has to be done and, with all due reservations, becomes the basis for corporate planning. But corporate planners have only too often asked the forecasters to concentrate on predicting 'growth markets'. Once these 'growth markets' have been identified, the company will decide which ones to investigate. But the underlying theory that market opportunities lie only (or mainly) in growth markets seems both dubious and unrelated to past practice.

First of all, it goes back to the error of looking for market opportunities in a vacuum. There may well be an opportunity for Company A in some growth market, but not for Company B. The market for cars has been a rapidly growing one and will for many years continue to be. It was quite clear from the early 1950s that it would be. It has provided an excellent marketing opportunity for Ford and quite a good one for the companies now making up BMLH. It was not much of a marketing opportunity for Heinz or Procter and Gamble. But of course they have succeeded in exploiting many marketing opportunities within the food and cleaning material markets—hardly to be described as growth markets.

Secondly, there is a strong element of self-fulfilling prophecy in all this. Just as a company can 'prove' the life-cycle theory by removing support from a brand in temporary trouble, so the speed of growth of a market will be determined largely by what companies think and do about it. If they think it will give them a marketing opportunity, they may act skilfully enough to ensure that it does, growing rapidly into the bargain. The potato market has not really been a growth market (expenditure on potatoes has grown on average by about 5 per cent a year—barely enough to keep up with inflation). But within it there have been market opportunities, partly as a result of improved products, but mainly through companies' decisions to make opportunities. Would the instant mash potato market have been a growth market without the determination of Mars and later Cadbury to make it one? Was the potato crisp market a growth market before Imperial Tobacco decided there was an opportunity within it? Would it have become a growth market without 'Golden Wonder'? Who knows? What seems clear is that the rate of growth was related to company actions, with heavy investment both in marketing activity and in product improvement. It was not something that was in some way intrinsic to the market *per se*.

There is something very compulsive about the idea of natural growth markets, and since people wondering about the 1980s often come to much the same conclusions, there come to be fashions in predicting them. And of course if a lot of companies follow the fashion and enter a market, it may grow but may be very unprofitable. One of the fashions once was the aerosol, and some very extravagant predictions were made of its rate of growth. In fact, growth was fairly fast, but very few companies selling ranges of products in aerosol packs made much profit out of them. The price of the container was too great in relation to the value of the contents; manufacturers had little elbow room for building profits through product differentiation, and quickly competiton forced down prices. Not a great marketing opportunity, after all. Many of the currently fashionable predictions for growth markets look equally unlikely to provide automatically good marketing opportunities—for instance, dish-washers, boats, men's toiletries, slimming products, electronics, and so on.

Theory v. practice

This analysis of theory and practice does suggest that the gap is dangerously wide. The theory all too often seems to ignore people and the irrational way in which they act; and could thus be called bad theory. The practice could in many cases be greatly improved, by working towards a theory and not being merely haphazard. Certain conclusions emerge fairly clearly:

(1) Top management must take the responsibilty for forward planning in new product development and diversification. It must not fail to grasp the clear distinction between the idealistic 'marketing concept' and what most marketing departments do in practice. Development/diversification is not just one of the marketing department's tricks, for which they provide magic methods.

(2) The organization of product development within the company is of crucial importance. It must suit the style and circumstances of the company, but it will usually involve people from the production, R & D accounting/finance and marketing departments. They will have to be co-ordinated by someone who has a fair understanding of all four and is a member of, or has the ear of, the top management. There must be a balance of these skills, and it is perhaps most likely that the production side will be the weakest; it may need strengthening from the outside, particularly if the company wants to go beyond the boundaries of current product commitment.

(3) Perhaps the most important task, and one of the hardest for top management, is specifying company objectives. Nothing very valuable is likely to emerge if they are not set. Indeed not much will emerge unless they are set in terms that take into account the motivations and practice of the people of the company. That is, they should be related to the company personality and/or its current products, and recognize that the continuance of them is a powerful, if at times unconscious motivator. To set objectives purely in terms of financial criteria is more likely to lead to mental paralysis.

(4) Even when the management has made a start towards setting objectives, the model of development will normally be one of feedback rather than single flow, and of experiment followed by modification rather than simple invention. It is not so much a matter of setting up an invention machine; it is more that all the people involved should think and act inventively. These patterns of communication and action are often very unlike those used by companies in their day-to-day work, in which communication tends to be hierarchical and single-flow, routine is frequent and experiment is rare. These new working methods are obviously related to organization and staffing.

What it comes down to is that 'identify market opportunities' is not a very useful concept. It is hardly meaningful at all in the abstract—it must be an opportunity *for someone*. A market opportunity only exists when it is exploitable. In a sense it comes into existence only when it is being or has been exploited—in which situation it is not too difficult to identify it. In any case, there is often an implication that this identification of marketing opportunities is the right starting point. But it obviously cannot be if it is the exploiting that makes a gap into an opportunity, if the exploiting depends on what the company can do, and if what the company can do depends on what it wants to do. (A possible exception to this is the situation where a company intends to diversify by 'pure acquisition', by simply supplying capital to the company taken over —not management or operational skills or plant. Here a search for opportunities is the logical starting point. But I would regard this as investment rather than company development, and the methods used would be like those for identifying long-term opportunities on the Stock Exchange.)

What we should really be talking about is not identifying but *making market opportunities*. All the techniques of prediction and market research come in, but as part of this process of exploitation, of feedback and experiment.

In the second part of this chapter, I suggest how a company might approach the task of making market opportunities—looking at it from the point of view of packaged consumer goods. The approach is basically one of analysing successful practice and evolving theory from it.

AN APPROACH TO DEVELOPMENT

What is the basis of a successful brand?

The best starting point for evolving a realistic theory seems to me to be an analysis of the brands that have reached a successful position in the chosen area of activity. (I am assuming that the company has already chosen this broad area as a result of a careful analysis of its strengths and weaknesses in production, finance and marketing, and by working out the current and desired company personality.)

In most packaged consumer goods the really profitable brands—successful both in their performance and in the satisfaction they give to people working in their companies—are the leaders: brands like Persil, Kelloggs Corn Flakes, Guinness, Birds Eye, Oxo, Kit-E-Kat, Andrex, Heinz Baked Beans. The food business is much less prone to technical obsolescence than most, and the greater number of these brands have held this position of profitable leadership for some time, with many product improvements but relatively little radical development. An analysis by Nielsen of twenty-seven grocery product fields between 1958 and 1962 demonstrated their resilience. It showed that, on average, brand leaders gained share of the market, from 51.4 per cent to 53.1 per cent; and this was at a time of growing competition. And on the whole since then, in markets which face strong attacks from private label brands, it has tended to be the market leaders who have held out best.

What then do these dominating brand leaders have that other brands do not? Clearly they have sustained a continuous high standard of efficiency in production, quality control and day-to-day marketing. But that is true of many brands that are not market leaders. What is that they have extra?

One vital advantage seems to come from starting first. Another Nielsen analysis of twenty-seven grocery product fields shows that (after a minimum of three years on the market for any brand) the pioneer brand on average sells rather more than twice as much as the first 'me too' brand and nearly four times as much as the second 'me too' brand.

However efficient the marketing mix, innovation seems a vital element in sustained success in consumer goods in terms of sales and profits. And this is why I harp on the need for corporate management to strengthen the production side of the business and the 'applied' R & D side; to get more high-powered and inventive people and see that they have time to invent. There are two particular reasons for this. First, the rate of change in technology is undoubtedly accelerating. Secondly, in packaged goods markets private label brands, with built-in advantages in distribution/display and pricing, are increasingly quick to copy success. This is not to say that all successful brands have been, and all successful new brands will have to be, radically different in physical form and performance from everything that has gone before. There is obviously a continuum between the straight copy and the utterly revolutionary; what the new brand has to do is be seen as nearer the innovative end of the continuum.

In fact, this is not solely a matter of the physical form. What is needed is an innovative and unique *product mix*. The clearest idea of the difference between the two comes from analysis of blind versus named product tests. Here is an example of one (the results are typical of this sort of test):

Two brands, A and B, both well established, were given to two matched panels of housewives to try in their own homes. One panel received both brands in blank packs, the other in their normal market-place packs. The housewives were asked for an overall preference. The results were:

	Blank Packs per cent	Normal Packs per cent
Preferred Brand A	47%	41%
Preferred Brand B	28%	39%
No preference	25%	20%
	100%	100%

It is quite clear that there is something about the *totality* of Brand B (or the result of its product mix) that brings it level with A, even though the physical elements of Brand A appear to perform better. It is equally clear that Brand B may be endangering its brand leadership by weaknesses on the production side.

In this example, Brand B is certainly an older brand than

Brand A, but it was not the first on the market. Clearly over long periods of time the pioneering effect wears off. We can see that being first is a specific example of a general rule—that of *uniqueness relevant to consumer wants*. If a brand has a fair run as a pioneer, it obviously has a good chance of making all subsequent brands in its market seem copies.

Why unique? What is the relationship between uniqueness and sustained profitability, via brand leadership? It seems to me that there are two basic elements in profitability in any competitive situation—efficiency and monopoly. Clearly a company can sustain high profits if it produces and markets exactly the same as competitors, but more efficiently. The effective selling price ends up at the level just sufficient to keep the competitors in business, and at that price the efficient company makes a good profit. This efficiency is related both to size (economies of scale) and experience, and is clearly part of the reason for the resilience of brand leaders. But it seems clear that it is becoming a less important factor: the general standard of production and marketing efficiency has risen, and private label brands are beginning to set new lower price levels. And when we are dealing with development, with going into new markets, efficiency seems an even less important factor. Although there are many exceptions, as a general rule it is hard to imagine going into a new market and getting a market advantage in efficiency over the incumbent companies.

Monopoly therefore becomes the more important element in sustained profitability; to be more accurate, a tendency towards monopoly, or semi-monopoly. Clearly there is a continuum between the pure monopoly, a product or service for whose function there is effectively no substitute, and the commodity product which is virtually the same wherever one buys it. The owner of a monopoly product can exert tremendous leverage on the price, the owner of the commodity product very little. The whole history of branding is one of turning commodities into semi-monopolies. If a brand is unique, there is no direct substitute for it. The further away the brand is from its competitors, the more monopolistic it becomes and the higher price it can command within the boundaries of supply and demand in the mini-market it monopolizes. In other words, to achieve sustained profits in packaged consumer goods, what a brand has to do is establish a unique product mix and thus make a unique appeal to consumers. The appeal must be broad enough to attract a reasonable number of people; it must be formed in such a way that it can maintain the distinction and avoid being caught up by copyists (other manufacturers' or private label brands).

D

So to make marketing opportunities we have to invent brands with this sort of unique appeal. Before we can say what market research techniques will best help in developing such brands, it is necessary to analyse rather further the ways in which brands do appeal to consumers.

How does a new brand appeal?

There are four main elements to the total satisfactions given to consumers by a new brand which are relevant to the way in which a development programme and a consumer research programme is planned:

(a) First, a new brand is essentially a new means of satisfying people's wants, desires or needs. The wants, desires or needs themselves are likely to be very well established.

This is where, whatever the reservations, Levitt's gospel is a basic text. We must look through research at the needs met by products, not become caught up in the current means of meeting them. There are plenty of recent British examples of marketing myopia. For instance, it was not the lino manufacturers who developed vinyl floor coverings; it was not the pen manufacturers who led the boom in ballpoints; it was not the makers of hard toilet paper who made a market opportunity for soft toilet paper. The traditional lace curtain industry is nearly dead, yet people still put up net curtains; the old-established lace curtain manufacturers failed to invest in the warp knitting machines which now make them.

What this implies is that development people must ask (and use research to help answer): in our chosen area of operations, what do people *really* want? What are their most important motivations? How far do existing brands satisfy these wants and motivations? Can we imagine a better/quicker/easier/cheaper way of satisfying them? If we do not go deeply enough into the real needs we will always be striving to produce a new improved horse, instead of a car.

(b) The second element concerns *the way* in which a new brand meets a need. In other words, how exactly does it appeal to people? For practically all brands there are three sorts of appeal. They are interrelated and each brand has a different blend of the three:

(i) *Appeal to the senses*
   e.g. Soup: taste; texture; smell; colour, etc.
   Toilet soap: perfume; shape; lather; colour, etc.
   Floor polish: consistency; colour; perfume, etc.

(ii) *Appeal to the reason* (functional appeal)

Soup: convenience; type or amount of ingredients; contains protein, etc.

Toilet soap: contains germicide, deodorant, cold cream, purer ingredients; lasts longer; costs less, etc.

Floor polish: easy to dispense, use or apply; deeper shine; longer lasting finish; cleans/disinfects as well as polishes, etc.

(iii) *Appeal to the emotion*

Soup: plain English; farm house; continental; sophisticated, etc.

Toilet soap: medical or cosmetic; down to earth or luxurious; masculine or feminine, etc.

Floor polish: tough or delicate; synthetic or natural; quick and superficial or hard work and satisfying, etc.

A new brand can succeed through improvement in appeal to the senses, the reason or the emotions; or a new combination of all three. It can come through meeting directly the specific balance of requirements of an identified sub-group of people—and this is usually the pattern of markets that fragment (e.g. the soap market). So research needs to analyse the appeal of existing products and the basic needs in terms of appeals to the senses, the reason, and to the emotions.

(c) The third element of what a new brand is follows on from this. To a consumer it is a combination of a *physical thing* and *communication*. On the whole, sensual appeals are conveyed mainly by the physical thing; appeals to the reason partly by the physical thing, partly by communication—name, styling, pack, advertising, merchandizing, word-of-mouth and other associations; appeal to the emotions mainly by communication.

The balance between the physical thing and the communication varies according to the product field. For instance, a new physical product may be especially important for a successful new soup, perhaps a little less for a floor polish, still less for a toilet soap, and hardly at all for a cosmetic. Important as it may be to try to develop a brand with a physical improvement over competitors, it must be remembered that today it may not be long before competitors catch up. They are far more likely to copy the physical thing than they are to copy the communication. It may well be that the greater part of the uniqueness, the basis of sustained profitability, lies in the communication—while physical product improvement becomes a constant and continuous process. This is certainly true of most of the brand leaders in highly competitive markets.

(d) The fourth element of a new brand is quite simply that it is a totality. It may be made up of a blend of different effects and appeals, but to a housewife a brand is one thing, not an aggregate of bits. Housewives buy things, not concepts or naked physical products or propositions or attributes. Blind versus named product tests make it quite clear that it is the totality that matters.

To enshrine a cliché, a brand is very much like a person. It has certain physical aspects and can do certain things. What unifies it and makes it unique is a total personality, which is formed from many individual physical attributes and actions, elaborated by clothing, company and associations. This means that all the elements of a new brand must be developed co-operatively and tested as a totality. The advertising and the pack are not mere useful additions —they are part of the essence of the brand and its uniqueness.

Approach to developing a new consumer brand

This sort of analysis can go a long way towards working out an approach to making market opportunities in packaged consumer goods. The same sort of thinking could be applied to industrial goods or services, and in the same way an approach to development will emerge. This is not to say that such an approach will automatically work—that will clearly depend on the skills of the individuals involved. But at least it will help management to decide what sort of individuals are needed and to make the conditions that will allow them to succeed.

The conclusions I would reach on packaged consumer goods, from the analysis above, are:

(a) The aim must be to start the stage of actual development (that is, people producing physical products, packs, names, styles, etc.) from a brief which outlines the total brand appeal aimed at. This total appeal would be expressed in terms of desired appeals to the senses, to the reason and to the emotions.

(b) Thus the groundwork for making the marketing opportunity must be an analysis of the fundamental consumer needs and desires which are (to some extent) being catered for by current brands. This is followed by analysis of the ways in which current brands are appealing at the sensual, rational and emotional levels; and of the different blends of appeal required by different groups of people.

(c) There must then be a creative leap from the way in which brands are currenty satisfying people to the way that a new brand *might* satisfy people. In which of the areas of appeal could we realistically look for an improvement? In which areas is there dissatisfaction? Where are there gaps?

There are certainly ways of stimulating the inventive process, but I do not think there are or ever will be substitutes for it. Setting the brief for a new brand is in many ways as creative an act as producing from the brief. (Just as setting corporate objectives from an analysis of strengths and weaknesses is creative.)

(d) The process, as throughout development work, is one of feedback not single flow. It is impossible to set the brief at all without some prediction of whether it would be possible to meet it. As such predictions are frequently inaccurate, it is necessary to be constantly modifying the brief as one goes along.

(e) Since the brand must end up as an internally consistent totality, and since physical product and communication interact to make appeals to the senses, the reason and the emotions, it is vital that production and communication people work together from the start. The new brand brief will be a poor one if they have not worked it out together.

This poses very real organizational problems for most companies, since production skills are internal and deeply involved in the company and its current products; communication skills are usually hired externally—often on a short-term basis and from a variety of sources, some of which have very little involvement. But unless these problems are solved, the company is going into new brand development with one hand tied behind its back.

Running through these conclusions is one strong theme: there are no magic methods. The right approach is more like the true scientific approach: that is, someone has a theory and tries it out. The theory comes intuitively: it is based on a background of knowledge, but does not derive directly from it. (James Watson's 'The Double Helix' shows how this worked for the discovery of the structure of DNA.) What is needed is the right organization, methods based on feedback and experiment, and above all an inventive approach by all concerned—to achieve the uniqueness that will bring sustained profitability.

In the last section, I have summarized some methods of consumer research to provide the background of knowledge and some useful ways of stimulating this inventive approach.

SOME AIDS TO THINKING FOR DEVELOPMENT

Background knowledge

(a) Current market sizes, etc.

Company objectives, we hope, have defined a total area in which the company is interested—partly in terms of type of interest (e.g. anything sold through chemists shops; anything made by an AFD process), partly in terms of human activities (e.g. anything related to playing games; anything to do with cleaning; main meals) and partly in terms of specific markets (e.g. boats; electrical goods; prepared puddings). A basic part of background knowledge will be market sizes, which manufacturers are in them, what sort of share they have and what sort of profits they make.

Some of the main sources of information for this are:

(i) Government statistics—Census of Distribution, National Income and Expenditure Blue Book, Trade and Navigation Reports, etc.

(ii) Government surveys—Family Expenditure Survey, National Food Survey, etc.

(iii) Media owners' and other published surveys—IPC surveys of branded goods, EIU, Neilsen, etc.

(iv) Manufacturers' associations—BEAMA, etc.

(v) Trade magazines, and their editors.

(vi) Company reports.

(vii) Traders, wholesale price lists, etc.

It really should not be necessary to go beyond desk research and asking the trade to establish market sizes and market shares, in the early stages of making market opportunities. For background information one needs only the broadest of figures.

(b) Predicting changes in market size

There are many different methods used for forecasting changes in market size, and most of them can be appallingly inaccurate at times. In fact, it is more sensible to think of different stages of forecasting (or give them separate names, such as projection, prediction and forecast). Many of our difficulties arise from not making clear which stage we are thinking of.

(i)   In the first stage—normally projection or extrapolation—it is a matter of saying what will happen, if things go on as they have been doing. Methods include putting rulers across pages or continuing curves by eye; working out trend lines or by the least squares method; exponential smoothing or trend analyses. The validity of the answer will not depend so much on the precise method as the accuracy of the original data and the validity of the assumption that things will go on as they have been doing.

(ii)   The second stage—prediction—is more complex, but uses the same methods. It says, in effect, that the size of market A is affected by several variables (say, GNP, number of marriages, age of marriage, average birth-rate, interest rates, advertising expenditure, rate of technical innovation and disposable income). These variables are then extrapolated and the future size of Market A worked out from the extrapolations.

This can be more accurate, but it needn't be. It depends on the accuracy of original data (higher probably than for market data—e.g. GNP); the accuracy of the judgement of the relative importance of each variable; the validity of the extrapolations for each variable; and the assumption that in the future the relationship between the variables and the market size will remain constant.

(iii)   The third stage—or forecast—is far more qualitative. It is essentially applying to a prediction the presumed effects of presumed or known future events. What will be the effect on the market size of decimalization, metrication, a change of government, a value added tax, joining the Common Market, etc.? The forecast is thus open to the same limitations as predictions, with a bit of crystal ball thrown in.

Two examples put this into perspective. The National Plan, which is something of a classic, was inaccurate before the ink was dry. Many of the extrapolations and predictions were no doubt as well worked out as expensive economists with high-powered methods could do them. But a number of simple ideas were fed into the forecast (like that the rate of exports would increase, but not how this would happen) and very quickly turned out to be wrong.

In 1960 it was vitally important for frozen food companies to forecast the future size of the market, in view of the heavy investment required in plant and storage. Market statistics were fairly full (from retail audits and published by Birds Eye) and a great deal of American data was published. A straight-line projection, based on the average growth from 1956 to 1960, put the market size (at retail prices) for 1965 at £92 million. A projection based on the growth curve of 1956 to 1960 put it at £104 million. A prediction based on the rate of growth of the US market (taking US 1940=UK 1958) made it £146 million. One actual forecast, based on the idea of an increasing rate of progress and the Birds Eye forecast of £93 million in 1963, but modified by ideas of conservatism in the UK, lower incomes relative to the US, slower development of self-service, lack of space for car parks, lower ownership of and space for refrigerators, etc., estimated £105 million retail sales for 1965. The actual figure was £74 million, substantially lower than any of the estimates that was looking only five years ahead.

In 1966 JWT did two experiments to help us judge the value of projection. In the first experiment, the trends in actual expenditure over past years were projected forward. We took each item of expenditure from the Family Expenditure Surveys, and projected 1963 figures on the basis that the change between 1959 and 1963 would be exactly the same as that from 1954 to 1959 (which is true of total family expenditure).

The second experiment was more complex, and was based on a theoretical calculation of income elasticity of demand. That is, it was based on the idea that the proportion of income spent on any product is related to the total amount of income (which is true— it is well-known, for instance, that as income increases the proportion spent on food decreases). Thus theoretically by predicting future total income in real terms one ought to be able to predict actual expenditures.

Here are results of the two experiments:

Number of items in 1963 forecast:	Experiment 1	Experiment 2
Underestimated by 30% plus	7	11
Underestimated by 10-30%	18	13
Accurate within 10%	36	25
Overestimated by 10-30%	15	10
Overestimated by 30% plus	15	21
	91	80

Neither method seems particularly good, but if anything the simpler method gave better results. In most of the cases of gross inaccuracy it was easy to think of qualifications to the projection that most alert marketing men would have made in 1959; that is, these projections could in real life have been turned into reasonably accurate forecasts.

As far as product development and diversification are concerned, we must get market forecasting into perspective. At best it is a very chancy business, but in any case there is no clear correlation between market growth and market opportunity. It may make very little difference to our development decisions if we are a bit out anyhow.

(c) Consumers' attitudes and behaviour

The market research techniques that are used for getting background data on consumers' attitudes and behaviour are all well established. The value of consumer research will lie not so much in the ingenuity of technique (though this can make some difference), but in the way in which the scope and structure of the research is planned.

For instance, ordinary structured survey techniques can easily cover all that it is useful to know at this stage about behaviour in a certain area. But if this background information is going to be useful for development work, then the scope must be defined widely and from the consumer's point of view. We must plan research on the basis of 'what do people do about cleaning things in the home?' not 'how do people use washing powders?' In this way we can ultimately break up cleaning behaviour into a series of systems, each of which offers scope for improved products. For instance, there are many elements in the clothes-cleaning system. There are sorting; conveying to laundry or dry-cleaners or washing machine or hand-basin or mending-basket; pre-soaking; soaping or other forms of dirt-removal; rinsing; drying; airing; starching; ironing; storage. There may be ways of combining stages; improving the effectiveness of stages; substitution of stages; inventing new stages; eliminating stages; inventing materials to improve stages. For instance, a machine to wash and dry the hand wash; special pre-soaking powders (e.g. enzyme products); grease-proof materials; ultrasonic cleaning; dirt inhibition; clothes-softening products; throwaway clothes. The basis for seeing and making opportunities must be a *complete* picture of current behaviour.

Our analysis of the way a brand appeals makes it clear what sort of research is needed to produce a full picture of consumer attitudes. First, qualitative research in depth to get an idea of the real motives that lie behind any particular market. Why do people want to clean clothes? We cannot easily invent new brands unless we have some idea of the balance between desire for a crisp feel, desire to avoid disease, desire for prestige, desire to express personality, and so on. Why are some clothes washed more than others? Again, only a fairly complete picture will be an adequate background for seeing openings.

Then we can use research to discover the specific appeals to senses, reason and emotions of the existing brands; product tests for sensual responses; structured attitude research for rational responses; unstructured attitude and motivation research for emotional responses.

Some aids to constructive thinking

There are in fact many devices for helping the process of invention, and I think they have to be looked on as just that. I hope this chapter has made it clear that in the matter of 'identifying market opportunities' we have to follow a fairly subtle middle course. We must not expect these devices to produce the right answer straight out of the hat. We must not work so utterly rigidly and logically that nothing new emerges at all. We must not try to invent with such freedom that we are overwhelmed by a flood of impracticable ideas and are later disillusioned by their rejection. I think that some of the following approaches can help us to keep to the middle course:

(a) Methods of analysis

There are several methods of analysis that can be applied to the background data (collected as above on some area of human activity) which are specifically designed to show gaps or opportunities. They are based on what is sometimes called spectrum analysis and very simply entails placing brands along a bi-polar scale and seeing where there are gaps. For instance,

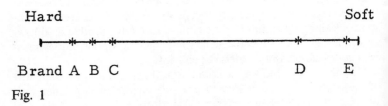

Fig. 1

In this case, there might be an opportunity for a brand that is half-way between hardness and softness.

Other methods are elaborations of this. The next stage is two bi-polar scales:

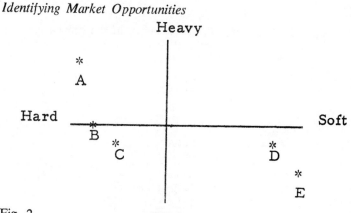

Fig. 2

The gap here is for a brand in the heavy and soft segment. This approach can clearly be extended to a large number of dimensions, provided that one can handle the data. The amount of data grows very rapidly as new dimensions are added, and computer programmes have been devised to carry out such Gap Analysis (with various refinements thrown in). There is certainly plenty of room for adding dimensions—they can be product attributes, users, types of use, styles, associations; in fact anything that can serve to discriminate between brands. The difficulty is to prevent it getting out of hand.

Other types of elaborate analysis are possible. Factor analysis, for instance, can show the relationships between beliefs about a brand or product type, grouping beliefs into main factors and ending with a matrix of correlations between all pairs of beliefs. Again, one can spot gaps by looking at low correlations.

These techniques can be useful, but must be treated with extreme care. First, the results can never be any better than the quality of the original data, and it is impossible to be sure of the real meanings implied by simple scales. Secondly, the whole structure is based on current views in current circumstances, and such views might be radically altered in new circumstances (as might be brought about by a new brand). On the whole it seems best to use such methods as a stimulus to thought, a sort of intellectual doodling. There is of course no absolute need to use research for spectrum analysis; it is still a useful way of ordering one's judgements.

(b) Check lists
The check list can be particularly valuable in forcing people to think when they could easily find excuses for not doing so (includ-

ing oneself). They are useful, for instance, in the crucial area of specifying company objectives and analysing company strengths. It is not too hard to make a list of points under the headings of production, finance and marketing to act as a check list of areas of strength and weakness. For instance:

Production
Current plant
Rate of obsolescence/depreciation
Production techniques
Manual skills
Knowledge of processes outside own business
Seasonality of production
Factory space, etc., etc.

The same list can be used to follow through from current position to future intentions and policy. And then it can stimulate screening systems as criteria for ideas.

One might end up, for instance, with a screening system that worked by scores. Out of a total of 100 points, say, ease of production might be given a weighting factor of six and raw material availability a weighting factor of three, etc., etc. Each might then be judged a scale running from 0 (bad) to 7 (good). Then one would have a way of evaluating two projects—e.g.

	Weighting	Project A Rating Score	Project B Rating Score
Ease of production	6	× 3 = 18	× 4 = 24
Raw materials	3	× 4 = 12	× 6 = 18
Market growth	5	× 6 = 30	× 1 = 5
Use of current sales force	2	× 0 = 0	× 4 = 8
		60	55

Project A would be judged the more promising. Once again, very strong warnings about being taken in by one's own guesses. This sort of screening is very very crude. The judgements about weightings and ratings are very rough, and in a sense one can hardly say how important market growth is in relation to ease of production without considering specific projects. But it can be a way of pinning down managements to statements of policy and it is a good agenda for one of the 'feedback' discussions central to the whole process of development.

I have found one of the main values of screening systems is that of public relations. If representatives of production, marketing, etc., are doing the screening (as they must, their technical skills being required), they can far more easily see themselves as part of the development process. It does not become a matter of Them landing us with a *fait accompli*.

(c) Non-technical forecasting

One can help oneself think constructively by using the techniques of research and forecasting in a judgmental way. For instance, one can make a list of likely social trends, and then ask what effect each will have on the chosen area. For instance:

Trend	*Effect on sitting room furniture*
1. Younger marriages	Working wives? More convenience needed? Vinyls? Replaceables? Zips? Throwaway covers?
2. More home ownership	Central heating? No focal point? Use of walls? Storage under sitting furniture? Use of walls to support furniture, so no wood needed? Moulded foam? Blow-up furniture?

and so on.

This is using the disciplines used in research and forecasting to break up consumer behaviour into pieces, and using the pieces to stimulate new thought.

(d) Aids to thinking

There are several well-tried methods used to stimulate creative thinking *per se*. Brain-storming—getting together people with an inventive turn of mind with the express purpose of inventing, working to a few simple rules. Synectics—a more elaborate version of brain-storming, with its own methods, including 'living out' problems, free associations, analogies. Lateral thinking—a term coined to describe the sort of thinking that deliberately sets out to avoid the logical progression from the *status quo* that is our normal mode.

These techniques are much used in advertising agencies, and not nearly enough in manufacturing companies. The point is that they should become an accepted way of operating for everyone involved in development—not a once-off method of generating a hundred new product ideas. They would be particularly valuable on the production side, where rigidity of thought is often deeply ingrained. In the United States a great deal of effort today is going into technological forecasting. The literature has become fairly elaborate, but the techniques are basically the same as those listed above for market forecasting, non-technical forecasting and thinking.

(e) Research techniques to stimulate thinking

There are several research techniques which can be used to stimulate thought—either by getting consumers to do the thinking or by groups of development people trying them on themselves. Group discussions, run by a psychologist, in which people talk within a loose framework about a topic can suggest new ideas to the listener; the interaction in a group often produces thoughts that would not arise from single interviews. Repertory Grid is a technique which is based on presenting people with brands in threes, selected randomly, and asking in what way two are similar and the third different; ultimately an exhaustive list of ways of looking at brands can emerge. Pseudo-product tests, in which people are asked to evaluate an existing product placed in a pack labelled 'New formula' or 'New improved' can be valuable; the way in which people think the brand is improved can be a guide to the way they would like it improved.

(f) Look abroad

Finally, there is nothing wrong with looking at what has happened in the US or Japan or Sweden. International plagiarism in new product development can often be very profitable.

REFERENCES

Adler, L. (1966) Time lag in new product development. *J. of Marketing*, Jan.

Booz, Allen & Hamilton. (1964) Management of new products.

de Bono, E. (1967) *The use of lateral thinking* (Jonathan Cape).

Gordon, W. J. J. (1956) Operational approach to creativity. *Harvard Business Rev.* Nov/Dec.

Jantsch, E. (1967) Forecasting the future. *Science Journal*. Oct. (1967) Technological forecasting in perspective. OECD, Paris.

Kelly, G. A. (1964) *Psychology of personal constructs* (Norton, New York).

King, S. (1968) Advertising research for new brands. *J. of Market Research Society*. July.

Levitt, T. (1960) Marketing myopia. *Harvard Business Rev.* July/Aug.

AC Nielsen Co (1966) How to strengthen your product plan. *The Researcher.*

Quinn, J. B. (1968) Technological strategies for industrial companies. *Management Decision.* Autumn.

Technological forecasting. *Harvard Business Rev.* March/April.
Robinson, C. (1968) Forecasting system and techniques. *Management Decision.* Winter.

Wills, G. (1968) Technological forecasting. *J. of Market Research Society.* April.

Zinkin, M. (1969) A child's guide to planning. *Applied Economics.* May.

5 | Selecting New Products for Development

by AUBREY WILSON

PRODUCT planning has been defined as the determination of a company's basic product policies, of what products the company will make and sell and what the specifications of these products will be. Whether new product ideas abound or whether they are as precious as diamonds, the problem always remains for a company to decide how extensive its technical and marketing research should be before committing itself to production. The doubts which surround new product developments stem as much from the competing advocacy of its supporters and detractors, each with a bias towards or against some aspects of the proposed development, as from the unknown factors of the market size, competition and the product's place in the total product line.

In deciding whether to develop and market a new product, there are perhaps seven or eight hundred questions to which it would be desirable to have answers. These deal with such diverse factors as the ability of the company to meet price competition and its facilities for disposing of the waste products of the production processes.

Clearly, in attempting to evaluate all the factors in one broad sweep, management's knowledge and ignorance, recent information and familiarity, affect any assessment. Only in the most exceptional cases is it possible to examine objectively, weigh and apply every factor which requires consideration before deciding whether to make a product or provide a service or to divert resources elsewhere.

The qualitative screening process

A new management tool, the 'qualitative screening process', has

AUBREY WILSON is Managing Director of Industrial Market Research Limited. This chapter first appeared in *Scientific Business*, 1, 4, Winter 1963.

Qualitative screening process

Product

A Section	B Coding	C Factor	D Weighting	E Rating	F Score
Stability	a	Durability of the market	3	1	3
	b	Breadth of the market	2	1	2
	c	Possibility of captive market	1	2	2
	d	Difficulty in copying	1	2	2
	e	Stability in depressions	2	1	2
	f	Stability in wartime	1	1	1
Growth	a	Unique character of product or process	2	2	4
	b	Demand-supply ratio	3	0	0
	c	Rate of technological change	1	2	2
	d	Export possibilities	1	2	2
	e	Utilization of management personnel	2	2	4
Marketability	a	Relationship in existing markets	2	1	2
	b	Company's image in allied fields	1	2	2
	c	Ease of market penetration	1	2	2
	d	Company's ability to give technical service requirements	2	1	2
	e	Competition with customer's products	2	2	4
	f	User stratification	1	1	1
	g	Few variations required	1	1	1
	h	Freedom from seasonal fluctuations	2	1	2
Position	a	Ease of development of manufacturing process	2	2	4
	b	Value added by in company processing	1	0	0
	c	Exclusive of favoured purchasing position	1	2	2
	d	Effect of purchasing position	1	0	0
	e	Availability of raw materials within company	2	2	4
	f	Effect on negotiating position	1	1	1
R & D	a	Utilization of existing knowledge	1	0	0
	b	Relationship to future development planning	2	2	4
	c	Utilization of existing laboratory or pilot plant equipment	1	1	1
	d	Availability of R & D personnel	1	2	2

Product

A Section	B Coding	C Factor	D Weighting	E Rating	F Score
Engineering	a	Reliability of process or know-how	2	1	2
	b	Utilization of standardized equipment	1	2	2
	c	Availability of engineering personnel	2	2	4
Production	a	Utilization of idle equipment	1	2	2
	b	Utilization of surplus stores, electricity and water capacities	1	2	2
	c	Utilization and upgrading of by-products	1	2	2
	d	Utilization of process familiar to company personnel	1	0	0
	e	Availability of production and maintenance workers	2	2	4
	f	Plant maintenance requirements	1	0	0
	g	Ability to cope with waste disposal problems	1	2	2
	h	Ability to cope with hazardous operating conditions	1	2	2

Overall Weighted Rating (Score) + 15
Maximum Weighted Rating (Score) + 116
Minimum Weighted Rating (Score) − 116

been devised to assist the objective assessment of most of the major factors and not only to rate them in accordance with their suitability to the firm's plans and resources, but also to weigh the factors importance relative to each other.

First phase
The first stage of this qualitative screening process is the preparation of an inventory of the company's resources. Some of the headings which have been found to be meaningful are as follows:

Financial strength. Money available or obtainable for financing research and development, plant construction, stocks, receivables, working capital, and losses in the early stages of commercial operation.

Raw material reserves. Ownership of, or preferential access to, natural resources such as minerals and ores, brine deposits, natural gas, timber.

Physical plant. Manufacturing plant, research and testing facilities, warehouses, branch offices, lorries, tankers, etc.

Location. Situation of plant or other physical facilities related to markets, raw materials, or utilities.

Patents. Ownership or control of a technical monopoly through patents.

Public or user acceptance. Brand preference, market contacts, and other public or user support built up by successful performance in the past.

Specialized experience. Unique or uncommon knowledge of manufacturing, distribution, scientific fields, or managerial techniques.

Personnel. Skilled labour, salesmen, engineers, or other workers with definite specialized abilities.

Management. Professional, administrative and technical skill.

Every company is unique. As a result of its history, experience and personnel, it has certain strengths and certain weaknesses that distinguish it from other business organizations. The ideal product policy exploits the company's strong points and avoids placing additional strain where it can least be borne. The inventory ensures the objective identification of these areas.

Second phase
From here, the next stage is to prepare the first coarse screen to identify factors which, if negative, would be sufficient on their own to warrant discontinuation of not only the screening process, but any further activities within the firm relative to the product's development.

For example, assuming a product had strong indications of suitability for the firm but it was apparent that supplies of a vital constituent material were unavailable through monopolistic and competitive supply, then it is clearly not one which warrants further attention. Alternatively, if it were to be sold into cotton textile manufacturing industry, because of the declining demand for British inexpensive cotton fabrics, the outlook would be poor and certainly would not warrant any development other than in the very short term.

Depending upon the product (or service), the industry and the markets into which it would be sold, the coarse screen might consist of such factors as consideration of the firm's ability to meet price competition, ability to finance investment in necessary plant or research, or the existence of strong patents. Products or services not eliminated in the first screenings are then ready for detailed consideration and fine screening.

Third phase

The next step of the qualitative screening process is to select those questions to which answers would be desirable in decision making. The choice is wide and if the process is not to be unwieldy, it is necessary to synthesize many of the questions. The selected questions are then grouped generically into a series of factors relative to such aspects as: stability of the market, market growth, research, development and production facilities. The generic groupings are then integrated into a table of perhaps thirty or forty vital questions (Column 'C').

A practical grouping, devised by the W. R. Grace Company, the American chemical manufacturers, was found to be easily adaptable to the needs of other industries.

Stability factors

First to be considered in the qualitative screening process is a group of six stability factors.

1. Durability of market. A basic commodity such as sulphuric acid, for which there will always be uses, will be rated very good on this factor. On the other hand, a product going into a textile end-use which is starting to become obsolete will rate very poor.

2. Breadth of market. A product used both nationally and abroad by a wide range of industries and customers will be rated very good, while another used in just one step of a process peculiar to a small number of manufacturers located in one geographical area or industrial sector will be given a very poor rating, unless this might be improved by favourable long-term contracts with reliable purchasers.

3. Possibility of captive market. An average rating will be given to a product for which there is a potential use within the company but which can be bought from outside suppliers at such favourable prices that the return on investment from the firm's own facilities would be borderline.

4. Difficulty of copying. A product covered by a strong patent and manufactured by a unique process from intermediate materials produced only by the company will rate very good.

5. Stability in depressions. A product distinctly in the luxury class, where purchases can easily be postponed, will be rated very poor, while one that is an essential constituent in staple low priced consumers' perishables will get a rating of very good.

6. Stability in wartime. A product which would almost immediately be denied allocations of critical raw materials in wartime will draw a rating of very poor, whereas a product which would be in heavy demand as a replacement for other more critical items will be rated very good.

Growth factors
Among the growth factors which can be taken into account are:

1. Unique character of product or process. A product that can fill an important unsatisfied need or that can rapidly—and without interference—replace a higher-priced material will rate very good on this factor.

2. Demand-supply ratio. Although the product may not be unique, if there is room for a new supplier because the demand is expected to out-grow the supply, it will rate very good so far as this factor is concerned.

3. Rate of technological change. If there is a wave of change developing on which the new product can ride, it draws a rating of very good. On the other hand, a product which is merely expected to grow commensurately with the economy on a whole will get a rating of average on this factor. A product that is fast losing ground technologically will rate very poor.

4. Export possibilities. If the sales growth of the new product can be markedly accelerated by adding export sales to domestic sales, it deserves a rating of very good.

5. Utilization of management personnel. A new project will rate very good on this factor if it offers an opportunity to promote potential management talent into enlarged responsibilities, yet does not unduly deprive existing products of their essential management and does not unduly tax top management's time and effort.

Marketability factors
Marketability factors may be summarized as follows:

1. Relationship to existing markets. A product which can be sold to existing customers through the present sales organization rates very good. A product that requires an understanding of an entirely different field from any in which the firm is now selling, requires an entirely different sales organization, or must be marketed through entirely different distribution channels, rates very poor.

2. *Company's reputation in allied fields.* Although prospective customers in a new field may not be the ones to whom the firm is now selling, if they are highly regarded in an allied field they may nevertheless have an advantage and the product should be rated very good on this factor.

3. *Ease of market penetration.* If other suppliers have neglected their markets and handled their trade relations badly, the firm can give the new product a rating of very good on this factor. But if the other suppliers have not only served their customers extremely well but buy from these customers as much as they sell to them, the ratings will be very poor.

4. *Company's ability to meet customer service requirements.* If the firm has a modern, well-equipped and well-staffed laboratory, a new product will rate very good, particularly if the product and its applications can be studied and demonstrated with the same equipment. If it is closely related, it will rate good; but, if it has no relationship whatsoever to any of the techniques the firm is currently using, it will have to be assigned a rating of very poor.

5. *Competition with customers' products.* A product is rated poor or very poor if it is the same type of product the firm's customers make, or if it is a different type but would tend to take business away from them or detract from their business profitability.

6. *User stratification.* When customers buy in large volume, selling and servicing expenses ordinarily will be relatively low. Larger customers may have adequate evaluation facilities which may be of importance during the development stage. All these conditions will give the new product a rating of very good, which to some extent offsets a very poor rating on the breadth-of-market factor listed under the 'Stability Factors' heading.

7. *Few variations or styles required.* If it is evident that a new product requires a wide assortment of grades, styles, and packages that will result in poor manufacturing economies and cumbersome inventories, the product will have to be rated very poor on this factor—especially if style changes could leave the company with obsolete stocks.

8. Freedom from seasonal fluctuations. The product that rates very good on this factor is one that can be made, stocked and sold at a steady rate all year round. The rating must be lowered as seasonal factors apply, particularly if the off-seasons coincide with the off-seasons of other products made in the same plant or sold through the same channels.

Position factors
Another group of factors concerns position:

1. Time required to become established. The position is more secure if development work can be completed, facilities built and the product established before there is any serious change in economic, technological or competitive conditions. The new product which can be commercialized most rapidly therefore rates very good on this factor, whereas the one which has a long, difficult development period must be rated very poor.

2. Value added by in-company processing. The position is more secure, and the new product's rating on this factor will be higher, if the firm can handle the entire processing, rather than act merely as a converter at one step.

3. Exclusive or favoured purchasing position. If the firm can absorb the entire output of a scarce and particularly advantageous raw or intermediate material that is produced by a highly reliable contract source, the position is more secure than if a competitor has access to the same material.

4. Improved purchasing position. If the new product's commercialization steps up purchases of materials into the bulk quantity class or enables the firm to contract more favourably for raw materials, a very good or good rating is assigned to this factor.

5. Availability of raw materials within the company. This factor rates very good or good if a raw material for the proposed product is already manufactured or can be made elsewhere within the company.

Research and development factors
In the screen used, as the table shows, there are four research and development factors:

1. Utilization of existing knowledge. The less the uncharted territory to be explored in the laboratory, the more the chances of success and the better the rating on this factor.

2. Relationship to future development activities. A project which is closely related to the main lines of the company's future activities and will broaden the know-how fundamental to those activities will receive a far better rating than one which diverts from their main activities.

3. Utilization of existing laboratory or pilot-plant equipment. This saves time and money and, if favourable, commands high rating. The necessity for constructing new research facilities or acquiring and learning to operate large amounts of new equipment swings the rating towards the unfavourable side.

4. Availability of research and development personnel. The lack of availability of the right talent within the company and the difficulty of locating it outside (unless it can be obtained by contracting out research to university or consultant laboratories) is a factor to be weighed carefully and rated accordingly.

Production factors
Finally, among the production factors for concentration are:

1. Utilization of idle equipment. The advantages of this possibility are obvious.

2. Utilization of surplus utilities. Surplus steam, electricity, and water capacities should be reviewed as to other possible future demands on them, and if truly surplus, should be considered a strong plus value in rating the new product on this factor. If, on the other hand, the new product will only fit into a plant where, for instance, expansion of water supply would be very expensive, it will receive a very poor rating on this factor.

3. Utilization and up-grading of by-products. In either case, the rating will be affected accordingly.

4. Utilization of processes familiar to company personnel. The high cost of training employees in new processes, where necessary, warrants a poor or very poor rating.

5. Availability of production and maintenance workers. If the new product is being considered for manufacture at an existing plant, both the quantity of labour available and the new categories of jobs required should be weighed and rated.

6, 7 and 8. Freedom from hazardous operating conditions, difficult maintenance requirements and waste disposal problems. All three of these factors, will, of course, be estimated quantitatively when the operating costs are projected, but they also deserve a qualitative appraisal during the screening process.

Fourth phase

Having formulated and selected the questions—and it is emphasized that those quoted are only examples—the next stage of the process is the *weighting* of the questions relative to each other. It is not feasible to design a constant numerical weighting for each of them. It is feasible to apply judgement and to discount any ratings where the question is of relatively minor importance. For example, while it may be of importance to be able to cope with toxic materials, this in most instances would not be of equal importance to the durability of the market. Thus, using a simple numerical or any other suitable *weighting* factor, each of the thirty or forty questions can be considered against the background of the firm's particular resources, experience, facilities and requirements assessed in the first phase audit, and they can be *weighted* relative to each other (Column 'D').

The fine screening process consists of asking each of the selected questions relative to each product and awarding a *rating* (Column 'E') based on a simple semantic scale: 'very good; good; average (or fair); poor; very poor'. The rating is then quantified. 'Very good' might rate +2 and 'very poor' −2.

When all the questions have been answered the values for the *weighting* are multiplied by the value for the semantic *ratings* to give the sums which are then added together to produce the overall *score* (Column 'F').

Take as an example, bituminous materials for spreading compositions. Spreading compositions are used in increasing quantities in roofing, flooring, damp course materials, tanking operations and tank linings, ships' deckings, tarpaulin coatings and road surfacings. Bituminous materials are not, however, favoured in many of these industries because of their characteristic 'gas works' smell. Thus, the wide market for spreading compositions is very much narrowed down to poor rating (−1). 'Breadth of market' factor is, however, of considerable importance (3) and the poor showing of the product on this factor is reflected in the score (−2). This situation is somewhat offset by a good rating for 'durability of the market' (+1), which is also an important factor and is weighted accordingly (3), giving a fairly high score (+3).

The total score of +15 is only slightly better than 'average', and therefore the product would not be regarded as a particularly favourable one for further consideration.

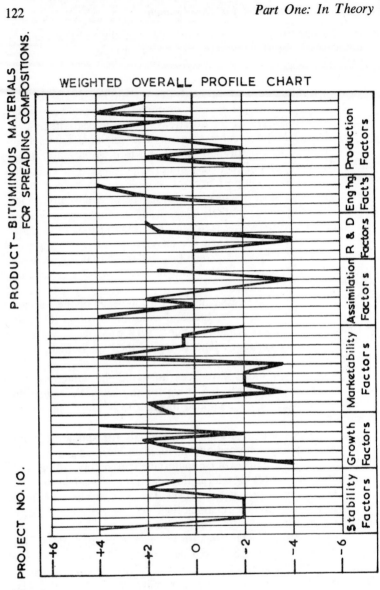

Fig. 1

It is important to note that if a positive series of *ratings* is used, scores do not accurately reflect the position. A bad score, say on a 1 to 5 scale, grossed up by a high, and therefore important, factor *weighting*, gives a higher *score* when, because of the importance of the factor, it warrants a low score. A 1 *rating*, which is very poor (or equivalent to − 2) with an important factor *weighted* 3 becomes 'average' (centre point of the scale) when in positive and negative terms it would be − 6, 'very poor'.

The table shows the working of the system. In Column D the *weightings*, which have been applied in the knowledge of the firm's facilities and resources, are given. Column C is the integrated questions in a shortened form. Column E shows the *ratings* to the answers to the questions relative to the product and Column F the *scores* (the product of D and E).

The grand total at the bottom can then be compared with:

(a) the maximum and minimum scores possible;
(b) the average score;
(c) alternative products under consideration;
(d) competitors' products.

Further, the individual score values can be charted to produce a profile (Fig. 1). This chart shows clearly how the product or service compares with the maximum and minimum and average scores and can be superimposed on alternative product profiles or competitors' product profiles. It serves a further purpose by graphically illustrating where the weaknesses of the project lie. If the factors for Research and Development have a low score this is something which can be remedied if the company so chooses. If, however, the end-product market is declining, this generally lies outside the scope of the company to adjust.

The table and the chart thus form the basis for assessing whether:

(a) the product or service should be subject to further detailed investigation;
(b) the profile can be improved by the action of the firm; and
(c) the product's priority as compared with that of alternatives considered for technical and marketing development.

When a product 'passes' a screening procedure, it must still be compared with other products which together form the pool from which the developments are drawn for further work to be carried out on them.

These early screenings are essentially qualitative (although some answers based on quantification are often incorporated) and their purpose is to winnow out the 'non-starters' and to prevent the allocation of resources to products which are not commercially viable or where profit possibilities do not conform with the corporate planning of the firm.

The value to the company is that once a product has passed through a preliminary screening test, a costing exercise has been carried out and the product has been deemed worthy of further investigation, there is every likelihood that these further investigations in greater depth will subsequently reveal a suitable situation for the firm's entry and indicate the quickest and most economic method of market penetration. The qualitative screening process is not marketing research and is no substitute for it. Its purpose is to limit marketing research and other expenditure to those projects on which there is a high probability of finding a profitable market.

There is nothing magical in the qualitative screening process and any company can carry it out. It requires time, technical expertise of a high order, objectivity and some marketing research experience within the appropriate industry.

Experience has shown that qualitative screening, whether carried out by the company or by specialist firms equipped for the task, is an economic exercise since it prevents expenditure on projects which have little prospect of commercial success.

The combination of company skills and assets, products and customers which makes the basis of successful business today, may not do so tomorrow. Product objectives need to be constantly reviewed and re-defined in the light of changes that may take place in the market, in product technology and in the nature of competition. These changes are generally more evolutionary than revolutionary. For this reason, they often escape observation. The qualitative screening process fulfils a secondary but nevertheless important function in that it enables infant trends to be espied and indeed ensures that all aspects of the firm's activities are reviewed. However, like the conditions which it seeks to evaluate, the screen itself is subject to change, both in the questions to be incorporated and in the weightings. Thus, it is important that if it is to be used, it must be constantly scrutinized to be certain that it has not moved out of line with corporate and ambient events.

REFERENCES

Corey, E. Raymond (1956) The development of markets for new materials. *Harvard Business Rev.* (1962) *Industrial marketing—cases and concepts* (Prentice Hall).

Levitt (1963) Creativity is not enough. *Harvard Business Rev.*, May/June.

Miller, T. T. (1959) A major shift in emphasis. Developing product strategy. *American Management Ass'n.*

Stacey & Wilson (1963) *Industrial marketing research* (Hutchinson).

6 | Planning the Product Range

by ANDREW MUIR

EVEN in the best run business there is a tendency for the range of products offered for sale to grow; in fact it is often a sure sign that a company is progressive if it is constantly extending its product range. An active research department will be seeking to improve quality and performance and to reduce costs by introducing new materials, new designs, and new methods of manufacture. Similarly, an enterprising marketing unit will seek sales expansion by developing new territories and markets, and by extending the possible applications of the company's products. All of these factors provide a stimulus to increase the product range.

And yet there is a limit to the number of lines that a company can afford to carry. A wide range of goods entails larger investment in stocks, less economic production runs, an increased burden for the production controller and a greater risk of inefficiency and muddle. Unfortunately, the energies that prompt the introduction of new products are rarely directed to cutting out the unprofitable ones. Indeed, as long as a product appears to be making a positive contribution to the general overheads, there is a reluctance to remove it from the sales list—and even if it is not, the sales force may well press for its continued inclusion as a loss-leader to support the turnover of other more profitable lines.

Thus the product range may be allowed to grow until it becomes obvious to all that it is sapping the strength of the company, at which stage drastic pruning is prescribed. This horticultural analogy is perhaps an apt one because there is almost certainly a right time to prune the product range and, furthermore, to do so regularly and with discrimination is more likely to promote vigorous growth than to engage in savage and sporadic attacks.

Nevertheless, the question remains on how to carry out such an

ANDREW MUIR is now a consultant with John Hoskyns. This paper was first presented to a Seminar at The University of Bradford Management Centre, March 1967.

operation, which products should be cut and when it should be done. In this chapter some ways of tackling this problem are examined.

Product groupings

The very first difficulty that may have to be resolved is that of dividing the range into a manageable set of homogeneous product groups. Where a company is offering a small range of perhaps fifty or a hundred well-defined products, each readily distinguished from the others, the problem does not exist. But more often than not the number of theoretical combinations of alternative specifications can run into the hundreds of thousands. Thus, although the car manufacturers may only produce five or six basic model types, if different arrangements of engine size, body colour and options are considered, the number of specifications can take on astronomical proportions. Similarly, although the manufacturer of rivets may market only a dozen basic types, if different diameters, lengths and finishes are taken into account, the total number catalogued by a single company can exceed half a million. And, in the extreme, the company that manufactures to customers' specifications in theory offers an infinite range.

In many cases common sense will determine the appropriate groupings, but it is as well, before fixing on a particular method of grouping, to consider the criteria that will be used to decide whether or not to discontinue a product group. These criteria will be covered in more detail later on, but in general they come under the three headings of revenue, costs, and productive capacity.

The factors that determine revenue are principally those of pricing and discount structures; however, the uses of a product and the interdependence of one on another cannot be ignored. The principal costs that affect the profitability of an item are the direct costs of production, such as materials and labour charges; it may, however, be necessary to consider other variable costs such as those incurred by frequent or lengthy set-up times, significant stockholdings or even installation expenses. Finally, where bottlenecks occur as a result of limited machine capacity or lack of sufficient skilled labour, it may be necessary to divide products into groups with homogeneous demands for each of these scarce resources.

When a large range of products is made it is advisable to break them down into a manageable number of product groups whose relative profitabilities can then more easily be measured. Since the main factors that determine profitability are price, direct costs and utilization of manufacturing capacity, it is essential that each group contains only those products with similar values of each.

In a study carried out for a manufacturer of electric motors the product range was broken down by:

  (i)   motor type: AC, DC, enclosure, final use
  (ii) pole classification: 2 pole, 4 pole, multi-pole
  (iii) frame size:
  (iv) specially built-up motors, stock motors.

Motor types were separated because they determined the method of manufacture and hence the demands on the different machine centres. The classification by pole numbers was necessary particularly because the 4-pole motors had especially high sales and a different price structure from the others. Lastly, built-up motors were differentiated from stock motors since the markets for the two were quite distinct and their costs differed. Ignoring all products with a sale of less than 50 units a year, 98 per cent of the turnover was covered by 317 groups, each of which was acceptably homogeneous. As a general rule, product groups should be so defined that if any one of them should be discontinued it will not be necessary to add to or modify the other groups.

Ranking by profit contribution

An exercise that is sometimes carried out is to calculate the annual revenue for each product group and then to rank the groups by the amount of revenue they produce. While such an analysis has the merit of computational simplicity, as a tool for judging which products to exclude from the range it is not very discriminating. A better approach is to calculate for each group, the direct or gross profit, defined by the net selling price (i.e. less discounts and commissions) minus the total variable costs (principally material and direct labour charges). If these are ranked, an indication is given as to which groups might profitably be discontinued.

The table below shows the monthly sales volume, revenue and direct profit of a range of twenty-four separate product groups. They have been ranked in descending order of direct profit, and the cumulative gross contributions to the overheads are plotted in the adjoining graph.

Product Group Units	Sales Vol. £	Sales Revenue £	Direct Profit £	% Cumulative gross contribution
A	108	9 900	4 844	13.5
B	454	10 229	3 734	23.9
C	308	7 937	2 887	32.0
D	144	6 614	2 757	39.7
E	420	6 934	2 621	47.0
F	51	4 952	2 455	53.9
G	28	4 088	2 356	60.4
H	351	5 520	2 204	66.6
I	325	4 262	1 751	71.5
J	59	4 226	1 731	76.3
K	182	3 825	1 360	80.1
L	78	3 117	1 236	83.5
M	132	2 617	1 053	86.5
N	29	2 083	946	89.1
O	140	2 354	940	91.8
P	76	1 895	657	93.6
Q	11	1 174	570	95.2
R	19	1 354	537	96.7
S	60	1 068	427	97.9
T	38	984	281	98.6
U	2	278	146	99.0
V	23	530	143	99.4
W	2	278	135	99.8
X	9	177	63	100.0
TOTAL	3 409	£86 426	£35 834	

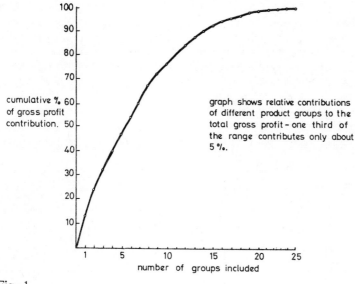

cumulative % of gross profit contribution.

graph shows relative contributions of different product groups to the total gross profit – one third of the range contributes only about 5 %.

number of groups included

Fig. 1

F

The graph illustrates a typical situation where a significant proportion of the product range makes little apparent contribution to the total overheads. Were any product group to show a negative contribution there would be a *prima facie* case for dropping that line. In such a situation the onus would be on the sales department to show good reason for continuing to offer it for sale. When each product group makes a positive contribution, however small, to the company's profit, a decision to drop a group can only be justified if it will result in increased sales of a more profitable group. This would be the case if its withdrawal led to a switch in orders to more profitable lines, or because it released manufacturing capacity for sales expansion in those other lines.

Capacity as a critical factor

In certain instances, where capacity is known to be a critical factor in determining real profitability and where the manufacturing process is mainly concentrated on a single production line, there is a better measure than simply gross contribution. This is to calculate for each group the direct profit per manufacturing hour. The direct profit is calculated as before, by subtracting the variable cost from the net selling price for a single unit. This result is then divided by the total number of direct manufacturing hours required to produce that unit. Sometimes these manufacturing hours will be machine-hours and sometimes man-hours—the choice depending on whether the machine or the man is the dominating restriction. It is also useful to calculate the fixed costs incurred per manufacturing hour by taking the total annual fixed costs and dividing by the total number of manfacturing runs available. In general, those products whose direct profit rates do not cover the fixed cost per manufacturing hour should be discontinued (or repriced if this is possible) unless the sales department can justify their continuation.

In the accompanying table are shown the calculated profits per

Product group	Profit per direct hour £/hr.	Product group	Profit per direct hour £/hr.
a	3.0	j	1.8
b	3.0	k	1.5
c	2.9	l	1.5
d	2.5	m	1.5
e	2.3	n	1.4
f	2.2	o	1.4
g	2.2	p	1.0
h	2.0	q	0.9
i	1.8	r	0.6

direct manufacturing hour for a company making specialized
machinery ranging in price from several thousand to several hundred thousand pounds. The estimated fixed costs per hour were 16s
per hour. Thus one group was not profitably using the production
capacity available.

Optimal product mix

The foregoing analysis is not applicable in those cases where the
different product groups use different machines or other production facilities in different amounts. In such situations the relative
profitability of different product groups will depend not just on the
calculated gross contribution but also on the use they make of the
more scarce resources. In such cases there is no simple way of
measuring the cost of limited capacity. Since we are concerned
with the product range, the solution lies in finding what combination of the existing product range is best made under the existing
capacity limitations. In effect, this requires a systematic examination of the possible product mixes until the one returning the
greatest profit is isolated. This can be done by using the method
of linear programming.

A company makes two product groups, A and B, which yield
direct profits of £140 and £100 per unit respectively. Demand for
both products exceeds supply and at present the company produces seventeen of A and six of B each week. Is this the most profitable product mix?

Product A requires the use of two types of machine (X and Y),
and product B also uses two machines (Y and Z). The hours required on each of the three machine centres to make a unit of
either A or B are given in the table together with the total machine
hours available each week.

Type of machine	Number in use	Hours avail- able	M/c hrs req'd per product	
			A	B
X	1	40	1.5	—
Y	2	80	4.0	2.0
Z	2	80	—	8.0

The existing solution (seventeen of A, six of B) produces a gross
profit of £2 980 per week, with spare capacity on machines X and
Z. The output is restricted by lack of capacity of machine Y. But
is this the best mix?

A	17 at £140	=	2 380
B	6 at £100	=	600
			£2 980

One obvious solution would be to make as many as possible of the more profitable product. This policy yields a lower gross contribution, with machine Y still providing the bottleneck.

A	20 at £140	=	£2 800
B	nil at £100	=	nil
			£2 800

It is less profitable than the previous solution because it does not make such good use of existing production facilities, a factor not reflected in the gross profit contribution.

A little experiment will show that the most profitable mix is fifteen of A and ten of B, giving a yield of £3 100 per week, and with no spare capacity on either Y or Z.

A	15 at 140	=	£2 100
B	10 at 100	=	£1 000
			£3 100

The technique of linear programming can compute the optimal product mix, given any number of product groups and any number of capacity restrictions.

In any real situation there may be several hundred different product groups to be considered and manufactured on a wide range of different machines. In such cases it would hardly be surprising if the company were not operating at the best mix with the right number of products. However, the optimal mix for any number of product groups can readily be calculated on a computer using linear programming. The information that is needed to execute such a programme is:

1. Net selling price of each product group
2. Total variable costs of each group
3. Capacity restrictions for each production centre
4. The manufacturing requirements at each centre for each group.

In addition to the optimal mix the solution of the linear programme will provide estimates of the reduction in direct profit that would be needed for a product group not to be included in the solution. Since these 'shadow prices', as they are called, represent the real profitability of a group, ranking by them provides a crude assessment of the best lines.

Increasing profitability by linear programming

In an earlier example the gross profits of twenty-four product groups were listed in order and their cumulative contribution to overheads plotted on a graph. In this table are shown the original data (based on an actual case study) together with the optimal mix of products calculated, using the method of linear programming.

Product Group	SALES Volume	Selling price	Monthly Revenue	Direct Profit	Gross Profit	OPTIMAL Product mix	Resultant revenue	Resultant gross profit
	units	£/unit	£	£/unit	£	units	£	£
A	108	91.7	9 900	44.9	4 844	136	12 471	6 106
B	454	22.5	10 229	8.2	3 734	508	11 430	4 166
C	308	25.8	7 937	9.4	2 887	257	6 631	2 416
D	144	45.9	6 614	19.1	2 757	181	8 308	3 457
E	420	16.5	6 934	6.2	2 621	431	7 112	2 672
F	51	97.1	4 952	48.1	2 455	64	6 214	3 078
G	28	146.0	4 088	84.1	2 356	36	5 256	3 028
H	351	15.7	5 520	6.3	2 204	326	5 118	2 054
I	325	13.1	4 262	5.4	1 751	252	3 301	1 361
J	59	71.6	4 226	29.3	1 731	42	3 007	1 231
K	182	21.0	3 825	7.5	1 360	229	4 809	1 718
L	78	40.0	3 117	15.8	1 236	97	3 880	1 533
M	132	20.1	2 647	8.0	1 053	166	3 337	1 328
N	29	71.8	2 083	32.6	946	37	2 657	1 206
O	140	16.8	2 354	6.7	940	176	2 957	1 179
P	76	24.9	1 895	8.6	657	—	—	—
Q	11	106.7	1 174	51.8	570	14	1 494	725
R	19	71.3	1 354	28.3	537	—	—	—
S	60	17.8	1 068	7.1	427	75 ·	1 335	533
T	38	25.9	984	7.4	281	—	—	—
U	2	139.0	278	73.0	146	4	556	292
V	23	23.0	530	6.2	143	—	—	—
W	2	139.0	278	67.5	135	4	556	270
X	9	19.7	177	7.0	63	11	217	77
Totals	3 409		86 426		35 834	3 046	90 646	38 430

It can be seen that the optimal solution using the same production facilities requires fewer product lines to be sold. Virtually the same volume is produced with an increase in turnover of 5 per cent and profit yield up by over 7 per cent—or over £30,000 p.a. It is of interest to notice that none of the four lines excluded was the least profitable by any conventional analysis.

Summary of Expected Annual Result

	present mix	optimal mix	% change
Units sold	36 600	36 600	nil
Net turnover	£1 037 000	£1 088 000	+4.9%
Gross profit	£430 000	£461 000	+7.2%

Implementing the optimal mix

Almost always the optimal mix of products (as determined by existing production capacities) will show considerable differences from the current market mix, both in the number of lines and the volumes sold of each line. This will be the case especially when a large variety of products is marketed and it has not previously been possible to carry out such a detailed analysis as is possible with an LP. Although it would be naïve to suppose that the market will conveniently acquiesce to the manufacturers' optimal pattern, it is nevertheless possible to progress to an optimum by a series of positive steps.

Before doing so it is advisable to include certain market restrictions in the formulation of the LP in just the same way as the production limitations are imposed. These restrictions can be of two kinds: either minimum or maximum requirements for any (or every) product group. The former are included when it is mandatory that certain items must be made available for sale, either as loss-leaders or because it has been shown that customers would switch their purchases of the profitable groups to a competitor if the unprofitable groups were not marketed.

Maximum restrictions are usually necessary to insure that the optimal product mix is within the realms of achievement and does not include impossibly high sales of any product group. In practice these upper and lower limits can only be set after a thorough analysis of sales by type, industry and customer, and only after close consultation with the sales management.

Once an acceptable solution has been derived, the product groups can be arranged in order of profitability. This order is now determined not by the direct profit per unit of each group but by their shadow prices in the LP. In practice these take into account not only direct profit but also manufacturing capacities and marketing requirements. Those products not in the optimal solution should be reviewed with a view to their being discontinued. However, the problem remains to encourage the sale of the more profitable lines at the expense of an inevitable reduction in volume of the less profitable ones. To some extent a solution to this problem can be promoted at the production planning stage by giving the favoured lines priority when forward loading over the less profitable lines. If selective delivery dates are quoted the sales can be steered towards the desired pattern.

Should it not be possible to achieve the optimum pattern in this way, it may be necessary to review the prices and discounts. A lot may be achieved simply by tightening up the discounts actually allowed (often quite different from the official policy). Any price changes that are contemplated should be examined in conjunction with the shadow prices. Theoretically, it is possible to calculate what the prices of each product group should be so that the current mix would also be optimal. In practice, since a price change itself would change the present mix, such a solution would be of little value. Instead a limited number of price changes might be considered, particularly to discourage the unprofitable lines (and at the same time make them more profitable) and encourage the most profitable lines.

Capital programmes

One effect of calculating the optimal product mix is that manufacturing bottlenecks are highlighted. They become apparent when, for example, a product with a high profit content is relegated to a low position by the LP because it makes extravagant use of scarce resources. A routine by-product of the LP solution is a list of those production centres that are acting as a barrier to greater profitability. It is natural, therefore, to want to use the LP as a basis for evaluating the real return of investment in additional production capacity. Too often investment in a machine tool is considered on a replacement basis—'we need to replace the existing braiding machines; which of the new ones available is the best buy?' Thus the comparison is made in isolation from other production factors. With the LP model it is possible to make a direct comparison on the profit yield of the total production set up by investment in any or all of the overworked production centres. And, of course, what applies to machines can equally well apply to other resources such as labour.

In one situation recently studied by OR workers it was shown that an investment of £8 400 in a single machine would increase the annual net profits (before tax) by over £13 000, giving a net return of 140 per cent. In another study it was possible to demonstrate that the addition of one skilled worker in an understaffed department would increase pre-tax profits by £74 000. In both of these cases the results came as a surprise to the management who had never before been able to take into their calculations the complex interactions of many products, seeking different amounts of production capacity in a variety of machine centres.

Rationalization

The use of the LP model that has been formulated need not stop at this point, that is as a means for deciding on the range of products to be marketed and as a tool for evaluating alternative investment programmes. Consider, for example, the situation facing a large company with two or more factories manufacturing an overlapping range of products. Sensibly, a study might start by constructing LP models for each of the factories to obtain the optimal product mix for each. However, larger benefits are likely to come from constructing a *single* LP model for all the factories, the results of which could lead to far-reaching rationalization of them. In particular, the solution would indicate which factories should make which products—a solution based not on the accidents of history, but on the realities of the economics of the existing situation. Such a study is particularly relevant prior to a take-over to evaluate the optimal profitability of the proposed group and compare it with the optimal profitabilities of the separate concerns. By having such a study carried out by an independent company, it is possible for both parties to have before them figures comparing their own best possible performance with that of the merged companies.

Following a successful take-over, the rationalization of the separate manufacturing units will almost always be most efficiently and effectively carried out by instigating the sort of studies that have been indicated.

A central system

Before considering the development of a systematic product review system, let us briefly summarize what has already been said.

The simplest method of assessing the relative profitabilities of the different product groups is by calculating the gross profit contribution for each of them; where this is negative there is a *prima facie* case for removing that group from the list. However, such a measure will not indicate how the total profit contribution could

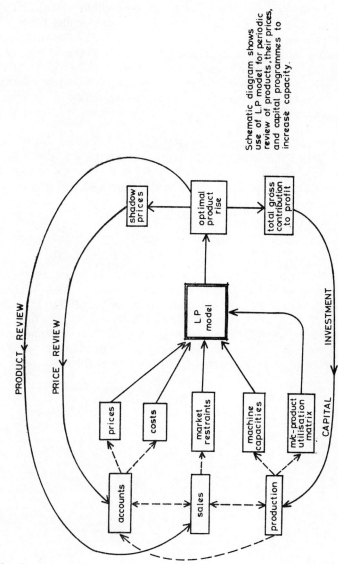

Schematic diagram shows use of L.P model for periodic review of products, their prices, and capital programmes to increase capacity.

Fig. 2

be increased if product groups which appear to be profitable were discontinued to release capacity for more profitable lines.

In certain situations this problem can be solved by calculating the gross profit per hour and where this is less than the fixed cost per hour, again there are grounds for discontinuing these lines. In the more common manufacturing situation a range of products makes different demands on the factory, and a more sophisticated approach, using LP, is necessary. Basically, this technique makes it possible to calculate the optimal product mix, taking into account not only direct profit but also the manufacturing and marketing restrictions.

Since the LP model is essentially a static representation of the economics of the company, it cannot seriously be considered as a means for making a one-off decision. Its real value is as a tool to help in the continual review of three main problem areas:

1. The product range
2. The price structure
3. Investment in productive capacity.

The diagram shows a simple breakdown of the inputs required and how the output is used. The precise way in which the model would be used would depend on the particular aspects of the company's problems and the systems that already exist for handling data and taking decisions. What is shown and is important to recognize is that the LP model integrates the three major aspects of the profitability of the product range and *ipso facto* ensures that no one of these is considered in isolation from the other two.

7 | Choosing the Best Product Ranges and Assortments

by JAMES ROTHMAN

How can a low price brand be promoted in such a way that it gains sales from its competitors and not from another, more expensive brand made by the same manufacturer?

A firm has taken over a company operating in the same field as its own. The managing director wishes to know if he should include the new company under his own corporate umbrella, or continue to sell its products as if they came from a separate manufacturer.

A brand is sold in a range of flavours. Should each one be advertised separately, or should the range be advertised as a whole, or should one flavour be used to spearhead the advertising for the whole range?

A bank wishes to know if the addition of another service will gain it sufficient additional customers to warrant the cost of the service.

Should a range* of products in related fields be sold under the same name or under different brand names?

A fashion product is sold in a range of different designs. Each additional design costs a certain amount to produce and market. The manufacturer wishes to select the optimum number and combination of designs for his range.

These are all questions on which my own company's advice has been sought in recent years. Their common feature is that when researching them we have to consider a number of different items

---

JAMES ROTHMAN is Chairman of Sales Research Services Limited. This paper was first given to the 1966 ESOMAR Conference at Copenhagen and has appeared in the Journal of the Market Research Society, *Commentary*, January 1967, and in *Management Decision*, Summer 1967.

* For definition of the terms 'ranges' and 'assortments' and 'multiple brands' see end of chapter.

—for example, all the different brands produced by a manufacturer, the different items in a range of consumer durables, and so on.

This type of situation occurs more frequently in marketing than one might gather from reading research reports. Few manufacturers these days produce nothing but a single version of a single brand. Moreover, the firm selling a range of versions of a brand or a range of brands in a product group can be very successful. Research, therefore, which points to the conclusion that there is a best brand or a best flavour must be based on false assumptions. For example, when compiling a range of designs, a procedure which is frequently used is to test possible versions separately and then to make up the range from, say, the ten designs having the best test scores. But if we do this we are left with questions like this:

It would be possible to take the design with the highest test score and produce ten versions of it which differed from each other only in minor details. If these ten versions were sufficiently similar to each other, each of these would score higher in our tests than the nine other designs which we had originally planned to include in our range. But would a range containing ten very similar designs sell better than one containing ten which differed quite considerably from each other? If not, how different should the designs in the range be?

Preliminary research

Before actually carrying out research to improve the formulation or promotion of ranges or multiple brands, some preliminary research may be required to determine the nature of the market they are in. In the case of both ranges and multiple brands, research may be required to establish the extent to which they are mutually supporting. In addition, research may also be required to establish the true nature and extent of the way in which the market is segmented.

Research techniques which are suitable for non-mutually supporting ranges and multiple brands would not be appropriate for mutually supporting ones. In many cases, the likelihood of the occurrence of mutual support can be anticipated directly from a knowledge of the market. For example, it would not appear to be likely that the range of grades of a brand of petrol were mutually supporting. In other cases, however, the situation will not be so clear, and the first research that will be required will be to establish the extent of mutual support that exists within the range of versions of a brand or brands.

This research might consist only of straightforward interviewing on behavioural patterns and on the degree of knowledge that already exists concerning the product fields. The area, however, is also one which is convenient for research by means of direct experimentation. For example, attitudes towards different brands can be measured, the sample can then be split, half the sample can be informed of which brands are made by which manufacturers, and then further attitude scales can be administered. The direction and extent of the change in attitude that takes place amongst the test group who have received information about the manufacturer of the brands, as compared with the control group, will then indicate the extent to which the range is mutually supporting.

Again, when testing designs or colours in a range, respondents can be given one item to evaluate and then be shown a range of items and asked to pick a pre-determined number. In this latter half of the test, half the sample would be informed as to which items belonged to the same brands and, in particular, which set of items were of the same brand as the item which they were originally asked to evaluate. The other half of the sample would not receive this information. We then study the choice patterns of the two halves of the sample to see whether the test group tends to pick items from the same brand group to a greater or lesser extent than the control group.

Research on market segmentation

Two methods are available for establishing the nature and extent of the way in which a market is segmented. In a product field, such as that for either cleaning and polishing materials or confectionery, the market is normally segmented by the manufacturer into a number of different product fields according to their characteristics—such as sugar and chocolate confectionery, liquid and powder detergents. The consumer, however, may mentally divide the products into a different set of categories. Thus, as far as the market is concerned, a brand which, in the eyes of the manufacturer, is in a different segment and is therefore not competing with another brand, may in fact appear to consumers to be a closely related substitute for it, so that the two brands are, in fact, in competition.

The first method that can be used is to ask a sample of women to rate a number of brands in the product area which are of interest on a series of semantic differential scales, as, for example:

Fattening — Not fattening

These ratings can then be studied by the statistical technique known as factor analysis, to determine the relative subjective distances between the different brands in order to see whether brands which were thought to be in the same market segment as each other were, in fact, separated by smaller subjective distances than brands which were thought to be in different market segments. This method is, however, rather laborious, particularly since the number of different brands to be rated and scales to be used would normally be so large that respondents would either have to be paid to complete the ratings or else the samples would have to be split so that only a proportion of the brands were rated by each respondent.

A new method is now available for overcoming this difficulty. This method depends on the principle that, if the distances between pairs of points drawn from a set are known, it is possible to determine whether the points all lie on a straight line or are spread over a two-dimensional plane, and so on. Moreover, if the distances between the pairs are known, it is possible to plot the relative positions of the points in this space. For example, if A, B, C and D represent four locations on a map and the following distances in miles apply

A	−	B	10		
B	−	C	20		
C	−	D	30		

A	−	C	30
A	−	D	60
B	−	D	50

then it will be seen that the points lie along a straight line like this:

A	B	C		D

| 10 | 20 | | 30 | |

MILES

and similar arguments can be used for points covering any number of dimensions.

Consequently, if we ask respondents to estimate directly the subjective distance between pairs of brands, it is possible to establish in how many different ways they are seen to differ from each other, and also to determine their relative locations. Here again, we can then examine the results of these tests to assess whether the true segmentation of the market corresponds to the categories normally used by manufacturers.

In both the above cases, if no *a priori* segmentation is known, or if the *a priori* segmentation is found to be incorrect, the methods of taxonomic analysis described by Joyce and Channon[1] can be used to establish the true system of segmentation.

Research for ranges in a non-mutually supporting field

In this case, the objective is to build a range in such a way that each item added to the range makes the greatest possible appeal to people to whom the items already in the range do not already appeal. For example, the following procedure is appropriate for building a range of designs in a home furnishing product, where each customer would only be likely to buy one of the designs. This means that we need to ensure that each item added to the range makes its greatest possible appeal to people who would not have purchased one of the items already in the range.

For this purpose, the potential designs are tested alongside those of the competition. Respondents are not informed that any of the designs are of common manufacture. They are then asked to indicate which of the designs they like best, which they like second best, and so on.

A gift choice technique is often a suitable means of establishing these preferences. In the case of furnishing products, however, it may also be necessary to obtain preferences separately for each room in the house. The results then require weighting by the importance of the different rooms before analysis. A maximum of five rankings is normally sufficient, and in most cases three will serve.

In analysing the results, all the designs are assessed according to the number of first choices they receive. Next, the design of the client which has received the smallest number of first choices is eliminated and the second votes of those who preferred this design are then allocated to the other designs. The procedure is then repeated with the client's design which now has the lowest score, and so on until the number of client's designs left is the same as the number which he wishes to have in his range. The similarity between this procedure and that of the single transferable vote used in elections will, of course, be appreciated. In this case, the purpose of using the procedure outlined above is that it is likely to ensure that the range is reduced in such a way that the smallest possible number of first choices is allocated to a competitive design, rather than to another one of the client's own designs.

More complex analysis procedures could be used to achieve the same end with marginally greater efficiency; however, this procedure has the advantage of being simple to understand and economical to programme.

Methods for assortments and mutually supporting ranges

These cases are, perhaps, the most difficult to research in a manner likely to yield useful decisions, since the interaction between the items in the assortment or range makes it essential that the group be tested as a whole. The following case history, which refers to research carried out some time ago, illustrates the complexity of this subject.

A firm was marketing a confectionery assortment containing a number of different sweets. The proportions of the different varieties contained in the assortment had been selected on the basis of the manufacturer's own judgement. The manufacturer then consulted us to obtain our advice on how to adjust the proportion of the different varieties in the assortment to achieve the maximum possible sales.

We proposed the hypothesis that people may buy more of an assortment that contained a smaller proportion of their favourite sweets than they would of one that contained a larger proportion. There are three basic arguments for this point of view:

(a) People may become sated with their favourite sweet if it occurs too frequently in an assortment

(b) Within reasonable limits, people may buy a sufficient quantity of an assortment to provide them with, over a period, a certain quantity which they feel to be adequate of their favourite sweet. Consequently, if these sweets are rare they will buy more of the assortment to achieve this supply

(c) Some people may enjoy the act of searching through an assortment for the sweets they like, or the gamble of finding them by chance.

In order to test this idea, the following research procedure was evolved. Each variety in the assortment was rated by a sample of consumers. The varieties were then ranked in order of the ratings they obtained. A new assortment was then made up in such a way that the proportion of the different types of sweet which it contained was roughly *inversely* proportional to their popularity—in other words, there were fewest of the most popular sweets in the assortment and larger proportions of the less popular ones. This assortment was then product tested against the assortment which the manufacturer was currently marketing in the following fashion.

Two matched samples of respondents were recruited, each sample was kept supplied with the assortment of the sweets for a period and their ratings of them obtained at periodic intervals. Initially, it was found that the standard assortment achieved a higher rating than the new assortment. However, as the respondents consumed more of the sweets, the ratings given by the panel trying the new assortment overtook those given by the panel trying the old assortment, so that at the end of the test the new assortment was rated significantly higher than the old one.

After this encouraging product test result, the new assortment was test marketed against the old one, and here again a sales improvement was found.

Finally, the new assortment was marketed nationally, and its subsequent sales confirmed that an assortment made up in this rather unusual fashion had a better sales potential than an assortment chosen by other methods.

It should be noted, however, that although our original hypothesis that an assortment should not contain large proportions of the most popular varieties was justified in this particular case, it does not follow that it would prove to be correct for other types of confectionery assortments, let alone for assortments in other product fields. Moreover, it should also be noted that only two assortments—the standard one and the inverse proportion one—were tested; it might well be that some other assortment of similar type but with slightly different proportions might have been even more successful—for example, we do not know whether an assortment with even fewer of the more popular sweets might not have been even more successful; or, again, it might have been better to have slightly increased the proportion of the more popular sweets while still maintaining the rule that the more popular sweets should be rarer than the less popular ones.

We see, then, that the only effective means of testing assortments is to treat them as a whole. On the other hand, the number of possible assortments that could be produced from any reasonable number of different varieties is too large for all the possible combinations to be tested. Preliminary research is therefore required to help us pre-select the combinations most likely to be successful. We can, for example, obtain ratings of the individual items and examine their preference patterns in the same way as was done in the case of non-mutually supporting ranges. Varieties having different overall preference patterns can then be made up and these can be tested in order to find what is the optimum preference pattern for the assortment. Again, the individual members of the assortment can be categorized according to the extent to which they are similar or dissimilar from each other and, as a first stage in the test, items which are seen on the whole as being similar to each other can be treated as being equivalent.

The methods outlined earlier for establishing segmentation patterns can also be used with advantage.

Methods such as these, then, can be used to reduce the number of potential assortments for test to more manageable levels which can then be evaluated by testing them against each other.

The case of mutually supporting ranges of products is to some extent simpler because firms seldom wish to produce a whole range *ab initio*. The question, therefore, is confined to which of a number of alternatives either might be the most successful addition to the range or, alternatively, which of the members of a range should be used as a spearhead for advertising the whole group. Here again, as we have already indicated, the items cannot be considered in isolation but each one must be evaluated in terms of what its effect will be on the range as a whole. However, the number of possible permutations is only the same as the number of items in the range, and consequently is more manageable than in the case of assortments.

Research for multiple brands

Finally, we come to the research needed by a manufacturer producing more than one brand in the same product group—the multiple brand situation.

This is essentially a question of how the manufacturer should attempt to change the image of each of the brands which he produces in order to maximize his total profits. In order to do this, we have to remember that different individuals have different images of any given brand, and that, again, they may have different physical or psychological requirements which they seek to fulfil when they buy the product.

Successful research in this field therefore means that we must consider each individual in our sample separately and establish how changing his image of any one brand is likely to affect his purchasing behaviour.

I have described the method for doing this in another paper,[2] but briefly what we do is measure brand images and individuals' product requirements—that is, their ideal brands—on a series of semantic differential or other attitudinal scales, which we then subject to principal component analysis to yield a limited number of orthogonal dimensions.

This is just a shorthand way of saying that we measure attitudes towards the brands on scales representing items such as 'glamor-ousness', 'fattening ability', 'warmth', and so on. When we analyse the results from these scales, we will find that if, say a person rates a brand as being 'feminine', they may also tend to rate it as being 'glamorous'—in other words, the scores on this pair of scales are correlated. We therefore analyse the pattern of correlations between all the different pairs of scales and find different ways of combin-ing the scale scores together to produce a smaller number of scores which will fulfil the following conditions:

(i) The new scores are not correlated with each other
(ii) If we know the scores that respondent has given to a brand, it should be possible to predict with reasonable accuracy from these the rating she gave to the brand on all the different scales.

By this means, we simplify the problem of examining a large number of different scale scores and allowing for all the correla-tions between them, to one of dealing with a smaller number of factor scores which we know to be uncorrelated.

Generally speaking, one finds that four or more factors are critical, but to simplify the argument we assume here that in a given product field brands are only found to differ in two respects —their glamour and their potency. We are now in a position to study the way in which one individual in our sample sees the pro-duct group. This is shown in the diagram below.

Here we see that this particular individual requires a product which is, on the whole, rather glamorous and not too potent. Again,

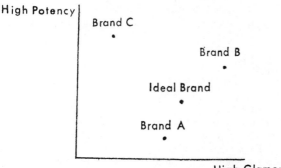

Fig. 1

we see that he thinks of Brand A as coming closest to his requirements. This individual is therefore likely to buy Brand A.

Suppose, now, that Brands A and C are made by the same manufacturer, who wishes to improve Brand C's image. As far as this individual is concerned, if an effort were made to make Brand C appear to be rather more glamorous and rather less potent, the individual might be persuaded to buy it. On the other hand, since he already buys Brand A, which is made by the same manufacturer, our client's total sales to this individual would not have increased.

This argument may seem rather lengthy to apply to each of the members of a sample of a thousand or more individuals in turn; but, in fact, by using a computer, once the basic data has been established it is fairly easy to simulate the effect that changing the image of any one brand in a given fashion will have on the sales of each of the others, so that a series of alternative changes in brand image can be tested to yield a recommendation for use when the manufacturer is planning future advertising.

These, then, are some of the research techinques which are appropriate when dealing with ranges, assortments and multiple brands.

What I have tried to do in this chapter, however, is not so much to describe research techniques, but to demonstrate the importance of this field of marketing, and to show that it is one where the techniques we use in researching single items are likely to be inadequate.

To place the argument at its most general level, when designing research in this area consideration must be paid to the way in which each item produced by the manufacturer interacts with the others. This can usually be done by considering the behaviour of each individual separately, and by considering the product field as a whole.

Definitions

Ranges

A range is defined as being a number of different versions of the same brand. While this definition covers the situation where a product is sold in a number of different sizes, the types of range which are of greater interest to us are those where the items in the range differ along some other dimension than that of size—such as price, colour, design, flavour, or even product.

Ranges themselves can be categorized according to the extent to which the items in the range support each other. By this, we mean the extent to which adding a new item to a range or making any change to an existing item, including its removal, will affect the sales of other items in the range, in comparison with the effect on the sales of the altered item.

To take an extreme case, we might have a dinner service whose items were sold separately; here, a woman who has bought one item will clearly be likely to buy other items as well. The same is true, but possibly to a lesser extent, in the soup market, where a housewife, having liked a brand in one of its flavour forms, may on other occasions try different flavours of the same brand. It should be noted, however, that there is a distinction between these two cases, since, in the case of the dinner service, the woman may reject the whole set if it does not include in an acceptable form all the items which she wishes to own; whereas, in the case of soups, a housewife might be more prepared to buy two different brands in order to achieve the full range of flavours which she wished.

At the opposite extreme, we have cases such as are found in the petrol market, where few motorists vary their grade of petrol. Consequently, although each manufacturer produces a range of grades in order to cover the requirements of the whole market, the addition of a new grade is unlikely to have a beneficial effect on the sales of other grades of that brand. However, even here it is just possible that the promotion of a special high quality grade might improve the image, and therefore the sales, of the whole brand.

If this were the case, it would represent a special case of the theory which has been advanced[3] that the quality image of a price range is largely determined by that of its highest priced member, while purchase is often initiated by the lowest priced member, even though the customer may end by buying a more expensive item.

On the other hand, one cannot stretch a price range too far. If this is correct, then one might employ something similar to a price confrontation technique to find out the maximum acceptable difference between the cheapest and the most expensive item in a range, and the maximum and minimum acceptable intervals between adjacent prices.

Assortments

An assortment is defined as a number of different versions of a product designed to be sold simultaneously to the same purchaser. The most common assortments are, of course, found in the field of confectionery. However, variety packs of cereal or assortments of biscuits are also known, and one might even assign a newspaper or magazine with regular features to this category.

Multiple Brands

Multiple brands are brands made by the same manufacturer which fall into the same or related product fields. For the purpose of assessing whether a manufacturer does produce multiple brands, we should use the broadest possible definition of a product field, such as cleaning products, foods, and so on. Examples of multiple brands are numerous—e.g. cigarettes, detergents or confectionery—and the same situation arises in many other product fields as well.

In some cases, there may be argument as to whether multiple branding truly exists, since one might claim that the product field is segmented into a number of different markets and that the manufacurer only has one brand in each of these fields. In some cases the market is only segmented by price; but in other cases, such as the polishing market, the market may be segmented more severely according to the purposes for which the product is designed. However, the segmentation of this nature is often found to exist in the mind of the manufacturer rather than in the mind of the consumer, and research is required to establish its true extent.

Again, in some cases, where both the manufacturer's name and a separate brand name are employed, research may even be needed to establish whether the items represent examples of a product range or of multiple branding.

REFERENCES

1 Joyce, T. & Channon, C. (1966) Taxonomic approaches to survey analysis. Market Research Society Conference paper. March.

2 Tate, B. & Totham, L. J. (1964) Research techniques for minority or maniple marketing. *Research in Marketing,* Market Research Society, March.

3 Oxenfeldt, Alfred R. (1966) Product line pricing. *Harvard Business Review,* July/Aug.

8 | Developing Strategies for Diversification

by PETER BAYNES & DONALD F. BURMAN

DIVERSIFICATION is today a fashionable word—so fashionable that it is in danger of becoming, like many other expressions in business and in politics, a mere cliché. The establishment of objectives, the assessment of the environment, the evaluation of strengths and weaknesses are all part of a new terminology akin to the so-called new morality. These supposedly new concepts are, it seems to me, the result of an analysis of practices which have developed over the past century and the attempts to formalize them by experts, like myself, who under the impact of University 'learning' and 'environment' of a brave new world felt that this was our life.

I take the subject to have two main aspects: the idea of diversification, and its strategic application.

There is of course a third and most important part—its implementation.

I had originally to consider the idea of diversification when I joined the Board of Trade location of industry team, and so far as I know the idea was first publicly promulgated by the Scott and Uthwatt Committees in the late 1930s as a solution to the problems of the depressed areas. The idea was to recast the industrial structure of an area so that if one industry declined, then the others were in sufficient balance to absorb those thrown out of work.

There were, and are, certain assumptions in this of which the most basic was that work must be taken to the worker and not vice versa. There were, and are, all sorts of ways of doing this, of which the most successful—and it is successful—is that of industrial

PETER BAYNES is Manager of the Strategic & Commercial Planning Division, P.E. Consulting Group Ltd. DONALD F. BURMAN is a consultant in the same group. This paper was first presented to the *National Conference on Long Range Planning,* sponsored by the *Financial Times,* at the University of Bradford Management Centre, November 1967.

estates. In essence, I think the problem of diversification facing an industrial or commercial organization is the same as that facing a locality. A simple question arises—has it, the locality or firm, too many eggs in one basket? Or better perhaps—has it run out of road? A firm does not *have* to diversify; it *can* merely fold up, which indeed is what used to happen to depressed areas before we became more democratic—before the balance of political power shifted a little.

My first assumption is that for the maintenance of present living standards in our country, let alone the attainment of better ones, many firms ought to fold up rather than diversify. Unless they do we shall be stuck with industries and processes which have no place in a modern market or technology. The thought of having everybody stay in business, even diversified into new fields, if it were remotely practical, seems to me either a Utopia or a 1984 nightmare.

My second assumption is my first rule: Diversify from strength. Briefly this means before you run out of resources—financial and markets. We must not wait for something to turn up—we do need a strategy which can be described, well I think, as 'calling one's hand.' This chapter outlines an approach to formulating a strategy. It describes what we mean by diversification, suggests some basic components of strategy, and then puts forward a systematic procedure for constructing a diversification plan using these components.

Meaning of 'diversification'

Diversification is a concept which cannot be defined precisely; it has different means for different people. The important thing is to recognize and to interpret this concept in relation to one's own particular circumstances. A broad definition is therefore given, followed by some qualification, to provide a basis for analysis.

Broad definition: Diversification is the term applied to the action of re-deploying resources available to a business enterprise into activities substantially different from those followed in the past.
Qualification: This action generally involves engaging in industries, technologies and markets which are new to the enterprise, with products (or services) which are also new to it. Almost invariably, new financial investment is necessary.

Reason for diversifying—the performance gap
The basic reason for diversification is the belief (or reasonable

supposition) that the prospects for the existing line of business are such that the required future performance of the Company will not be achieved. In a competitive society, the ultimate criteria of performance are expressed in terms of volume or growth of sales, profits and returns on investment. Ideally, early warning of failure to meet performance requirements is given by the forecasts of these quantities in a company's forward plan. The need for diversification is shown by a 'gap' between what is required and what is achievable by development of the existing line of business. With less fortunate companies, which do not (or perhaps cannot) plan ahead, the first indications of this gap are often a reducing current order book, or idle production capacity.

Forms of diversification

Diversification has a broad spectrum, ranging from limited ventures into closely related activities at one extreme ('narrow' diversification), across to engagement in completely foreign activities at the other extreme ('wide' diversification). As a first step in tackling the problem, it is desirable to carry out a simple analysis of this spectrum.

Two major divisions are evident:

Unrelated diversification: In which the common factors are generally limited to finance and business management. This situation is typical of investment houses and industrial holding groups.

Related diversification: In which additional common factors are present, such as technological 'know-how', marketing facilities or expertise, or production facilities.

Within this division we have what has become known as 'vertical integration', in which a company deploys its resources to set up or to acquire organizations which supply materials used by the company and/or organizations which provide market outlets for its products.

Against this background, three distinct diversification motives may be distinguished:

Replacements: For existing product-market combinations which have declining life characteristics, in consequence of obsolescence or excessive competition.

Complements: For existing product-market combinations which have reached maturity or saturation, where growth potential does not justify the employment of all the funds and resources available.

Insurance: Against recession or future saturation conditions, by spreading investment and risk over a number of activity fields.

These motives may exist singly or in combination, according to the particular circumstances of each company. The diversification path followed should be planned carefully in relation to these circumstances.

Approach to diversification

The need for planning

Whatever the reason and objectives involved in diversification, the company must be prepared for unfamiliar products, technologies and markets. New expertise must be provided to support the new operations. Significant investment and risks are involved. Acceptance of risk is fundamental to the business operation but costs and risks should be minimized as far as possible by careful planning. All organizations plan to some extent, but unless it is recognized as a formal activity, planning tends to be of a piecemeal nature. Under these conditions, the requirement of obtaining an optimum return from the available resources is often unfulfilled.

Significant components in planning—objectives, strategy, tactics

Successful diversification involves the recognition and subsequent profitable exploitation of new business opportunities, making optimum use of available resources. Essential procedures in planning are therefore concerned with evaluation of available resources, identification of business opportunities, and the construction of specific project plans as the basis for selection, decision and exploitation.

In practice, these search and evaluation procedures can be time-consuming and expensive. It is highly desirable to establish some boundary conditions for the field of search—that is, to establish company objectives and to outline the strategy by which these might be best achieved with the available resources.

The great advantage of limiting the field of search is that available manpower and experience can be focused upon those sectors which are compatible with the resources available to the company. A possible disadvantage is that good opportunities outside the boundaries might be lost, but in practice there is little point in evaluating projects that are beyond the capabilities or inclinations of the company. The extent to which the field is limited will de-

pend upon the form of the available resources and, in some instances, upon the urgency factor.

Final decisions concerning the new activities are strongly influenced by considerations of how to enter and to exploit the
markets concerned—that is, by the operational tactics necessary for
successful participation.

Diversification objectives

These describe the type of business in which the company wishes
to engage, and the overall performance it wishes to achieve. Since
companies essentially comprise groups of people, objectives will be
influenced by the personal views and aspirations of individuals—
owners and directors.

Product-market strategy

This element is concerned with the specification of the characteristics of the products and markets in which the company might
engage and the manner in which it seeks to exploit them. For
planning purposes, product and market must be considered in conjunction, since specification of the characteristics of the one implicitly specifies characteristics of the other. In practice, it is convenient to describe product-market strategy in the following terms:

Operational scope

Describes the sectors of the environment in which the company
might engage—

Type of industry: for example, engineering, agriculture, food-
stuffs, chemicals, etc.

Type of products: for example, mechanical handling equipment,
animal foods, ethical pharmaceuticals, etc.

Location of markets: regional, national, international.

For the majority of companies it is convenient to express these
descriptions in terms of the Orders and List Headings of the Standard Industrial Classification or the equivalent overseas. This defines the product characteristics explicitly and the market characteristics implicitly.

Operational scale

A stratification across the nominated sectors of the environment—

Type of application: professional, industrial, or consumer.

Type of end product: finished or part-finished goods, main contractor or sub-contractor.

Level of technology: in the products, in production and in supporting services.

Levels of quality: performance, appearance, costs and prices.

Levels of quantity: individual, batch or flow-line production.

Commercial approach

Describes the commercial philosophy of the company, which is generally dictated by the resources available and the financial strategy, but which in practice is often strongly influenced by the personal inclinations of management. Three main themes may be identified, which may be pursued singly or in combination—

Pioneering: developing new markets with new products incorporating new ideas or technology, with the intention of establishing and maintaining a dominating position. This is the 'catch-us-if-you-can' approach. The rewards can be high, but relatively substantial investment may be necessary before returns can be expected. There are corresponding risks—of the market not developing as expected, of being overtaken by later entrants, the 'followers'.

Following: into markets which are established but still in the stage of rapid growth, with straight-forward developments of existing products, capitalizing upon the investments (and possibly the mistakes) of the pioneers. This is the 'me-too' or 'bandwaggon' approach. Good marketing and efficient production are of prime importance.

Attacking: in markets which are well established but not yet in the decline stage, on the basis of improved products and/or better marketing tehniques. This is the 'better mousetrap' approach. Excellence of design is the key factor.

Synergy

The components of strategy described are interdependent to some extent—definition of any one imposes some conditions upon the others.

This final component links the others directly with existing skills and resources. Synergy means 'working together', and it expresses the extent to which the existing operation and any proposed new operation would be mutually supporting. It provides useful criteria for comparing the relative merits of different propositions—industries to enter, products to take on, companies for acquisition.

In making this assessment, it is important to look not only for supplementation of skills and resources, but also for complementation. A classic instance of synergy in diversification is the acquisition of the small design firm which has good products but no facilities, by the large manufacturing firm which is running out of products. The large firm supplies management and administration, finance and plant—the small firm provides product designs, specialist personnel, and possibly a name which is accepted in the market. Taken separately, the potential of each firm is low, but the potential of the combination is high.

Diversification procedure

The purpose of defining overall strategy is to enable attention to be focused on the appropriate sectors of the commercial environment. When suitable areas of opportunity have been found, major problems are those of how to enter and to exploit the markets.

Possible tactical approaches are:

internal research and development based on ideas generated within the company or obtained from the environment through market intelligence;
acquisition of specialists, individuals possessing ideas and 'know-how';
acquisition of licences for products already developed and/or 'know-how', etc.;
acquisition of other firms already possessing suitable products, markets, 'know-how', etc.

The choice of tactics will often be indicated by initial consideration of resources and objectives, and by the urgency of the company's requirements, but the final choice will depend heavily upon the circumstances of the environment and the specific opportunities available at the time.

Stage 1. Analysis of company

The first stage is concerned with defining the present business situation of the company and with establishing a set of boundary conditions to guide the planning work.

The Company Diversification Profile

This is a first, provisional diversification plan which uses the planning components of Section 2 in outline form to describe *existing resources*: financial, technological, marketing and personnel, available for diversification.

Stage II. Analysis of environment

This stage is concerned with detailed assessments of the fields of activity to be considered. These studies involve research and analysis of the selected user markets, producing industries, patterns of production and trade. Economic, technological and marketing studies are made.

The economic studies are concerned primarily with analysis of factors which influence growth of industries, markets and trade, and with forecasting future developments. The results provide the general background to the study of the environment, but, in practical terms, indicate only broadly the relative potentials of the nominated fields of activity. The technological and commercial studies are concerned with identifying commercial opportunities and the requirements for exploiting these opportunities in terms of specific products, investment, organization and facilities. Generally, we may say that the economic studies define the strategic possibilities and the technological and commercial studies indicate the operational forces and tactics necessary for success.

Stage III. Identification and evaluation of specific opportunities

The final decisions concerning which fields of activity should be entered and the tactics to be used, depend not only upon the relative theoretical merits (compatability with resources, market growth prospects etc.) but also upon the practical opportunities available for entering and exploiting the markets.

Stage III is the logical continuation of Stage II. It is concerned with identifying specific opportunities and with constructing forward-looking project plans as the basis for the final decision. It is presented as a separate stage in this planning procedure, since in practice these processes require more time than the analytical processes of the previous stages, and management decisions are desirable before substantial expenditure is incurred. In instances in which the need for new products is urgent, Stages II and III are carried out concurrently.

Search processes

For each field of activity nominated the search for specific opportunities is focused, according to circumstances, upon:

Ideas and/or designs for specific products
Individuals with specialized knowledge
Licences for products and/or 'know-how'
Companies for acquisition.

A variety of sources of information is used, depending upon circumstances and requirements—including members of the company, consultants, merchant banks, patent agents, business brokers, universities and Government-sponsored organizations, trade associations, contacts in other companies etc.

Screening and evaluation processes

Systematic search usually will produce numerous propositions, of which only a small proportion will be accepted ultimately. The ideas generated, or the opportunities identified, are first briefly screened for feasibility against the diversification criteria. Feasibility is taken here to mean that the proposition has merit sufficient to warrant more detailed investigation. The survivors are screened in greater detail for viability and those accepted are developed into provisional forward plans, in terms of investment required and probable returns. Additional analytical work might be necessary in these evaluations—specific market research, or appraisal of companies for acquisition. Various techniques are available for this screening process but space does not allow me to describe them.

More often than not diversification means working against time. To diversify in less than a year requires far more luck than we should expect and much more risk than we should take, which brings me back to my opening remarks—diversify from strength before you are out of road—in time—or in the interests of the UK economy, fold up!

9 | Planned Diversification of Industrial Concerns

by W. F. ROCKWELL, Jr

IN the business sense of the word, *diversification* usually is taken to mean growth that is generated in an enterprise by adding new products for new markets and seeking a stronger position in the market. This definition is accurate enough as far as it goes. However, it fails to suggest some other aspects of diversification that go deeply to the heart of a modern business concern. Among them is the capacity of the enterprise to marshal capital and brains when major changes become mandatory for, say, competitive reasons. Or, to respond to customer needs decisively and effectively with high calibre research, development and technical services. Or, *not* to be outgrown by its management executives for lack of opportunities to advance.

Over the course of about thirty years, diversification has been a predominant force in the growth of the Rockwell Manufacturing Company. Our experience may offer some useful commentaries on the subject which has come in for a considerable amount of discussion among businessmen.

Rockwell has not had direct experience with all of the methods by which diversification could be accomplished, but has followed

WILLARD F. ROCKWELL JR. is vice-chairman of the board and chief executive officer of Rockwell Manufacturing Company, and chairman of the board and chief executive officer of North American Rockwell Corporation, unrelated organizations.

He is also chairman of the Board of Rockwell Parsons Corporation, a company jointly owned by North American Rockwell and Reyrolle Parsons Ltd of Newcastle-upon-Tyne, England.

Mr Rockwell serves as a director for nine major companies in the United States, England and Australia. His interest and concern for conservation led to his recent appointment by President Nixon to serve as vice-chairman of the National Industrial Pollution Council.

This chapter is reprinted with permission from: *Advanced Management*, May 1956.

several of them consistently and has taken a searching look at most of the others.

The result of our diversification: Starting in 1925 as a specialist manufacturer of residential gas meters and regulators, with 200 employees, Rockwell's 5 400 employees now produce water meters and commercial and industrial metering devices as well, plus valves, power tools, gas and liquid regulating and control equipment, taxi meters, parking meters, and allied products which are used in most of the basic industrial and engineering fields. Today Rockwell has twenty plants in twenty communities.

By all odds the most valuable result of our diversification is our management and supervisory organization, of which naturally we are very proud. In the main it was this movement that brought together what we consider to be an able and versatile team of men and women.

This record may have in it the essence for another useful definition. Rockwell has diversified by widening and extending product lines through research and development efforts as well as by joining forces with other companies by acquisition. Either way, however, it has been the resulting enlargement of management coverage that furnished the key to success.

Our own definition, then, comes closer to these terms:

Diversification means the entry of a company into a new field of productive operations for which it can give effective management or add new management talent as part of the transaction.

The purpose of diversification, of course, is to gain a better future performance with the *total* resources involved. And, obviously, the specific goals that add up to a better performance should be fixed at the outset.

It is a process that calls for a concerted approach, analysis, consummation and follow-through which means, simply, *planning*.

The foregoing statements rest on the assumption that no enterprise can afford to 'stand pat'—can not safely rely on what prevailed yesterday or exists today. If a manager subscribes to the philosophy that his job is to conduct his business *ahead of itself*, making preparation simultaneously for the day after tomorrow, next month, next year, and even beyond, then he should not fail to appraise anew the potentials of diversification.

Corporate security goal

The pattern of diversification followed by our company was established by our founder and chairman, Colonel W. F. Rockwell. He

E

coined the term *corporate security,* as we use it. It means taking good care of what *you* have and, at the same time, taking a firm hold on opportunities that promise to bring more and better results from the human resources and physical property at hand.

Regardless of the diversification methods open to a manager, corporate security is subject to the standard tests for business performance, notably the 'dollar sign' measurements of costs, sales, earnings and all the rest. There are, however, other gauges. Technical leadership surely is one, and this force may be in evidence long before the figures begin to bear it out. To my mind, a number one result of our diversification programme has been the technical-management leadership we have generated in the process. Two men who exemplify the point are L. A. Dixon, Sr., our executive vice-president, and W. F. Crawford, one of our vice-presidents. Mr. Dixon began his Rockwell career with our predecessor company and in a succession of jobs mastered all aspects of plant operations. He headed an independent company, presided over a major division of Rockwell, and now is in charge of administration for all company operations. Mr. Crawford was president of Edward Valves, Inc., when it was bought by Rockwell. He still heads the Edward subsidiary, now a more broadly-based enterprise, and has important central corporate responsibilities in addition.

Obviously a plus from diversification, such as the contributions of unusually talented managers, must measure out ultimately in terms of corporate security. Clearly, an unprofitable business cannot long furnish security of jobs and investment, nor can it be relied upon, by customers or suppliers to fulfil the ordinary commitments stipulated in the industrial market place.

Diversification is not a cure-all for a sick company suffering from management anaemia, because the dose is likely to kill the patient. But for the small and large business alike, soundly conceived and well-managed diversification affords opportunities for long-term growth along with a significant reinforcement of the elements constituting corporate security.

As has been suggested, Rockwell has sought diversification in part by acquiring concerns found to be compatible with the corporate picture, but this is only part of the story. A majority of its new products and much of its versatility have been 'home-made', growing out of our own research and development efforts.

Whatever the method, going into something new calls for a higher calibre of analytical planning than perhaps any other field of management. Our course of planning for diversification starts with a simple set of criteria we apply to any proposal at the very outset merely to determine whether the matter bears detailed investigation:

1. Does the venture promise long-range, continuous operations? Rockwell is not interested in 'spot' opportunities or temporary advantages.

2. Are the added product lines or operations adaptable to the fields where Rockwell's experience and management talents can be applied? We subscribe to the axiom that there is enough of our own kind of business to attend to.

3. Is the venture otherwise compatible with the main lines of Rockwell's corporate procedures and policies? For one thing, we do not propose to compete with our customers.

Thus, at Rockwell we have found that opportunities for diversification can be tested initially by small and informal meetings of executives. At this stage, an affirmative finding is merely the decision to look into the matter further, investing the time and effort needed to make a thorough analysis.

Diversification criteria

The establishment of a similar set of criteria is strongly recommended to the enterprise newly interested in diversifying itself. Like a safety programme or good controllership, this essential first 'screening' is invaluable for the prevention of mis-steps.

The process of working up a diversification appraisal and plan merits time, effort and study. Overnight judgement cannot be relied on as a substitute for market studies, technical investigations of operations and products, financial analyses, conference time and, perhaps, the services of outside experts to perform a part of the fact finding. Indeed, such background may be necessary just for the initial decision of whether or not to go ahead with the idea in earnest. The appraisal may disclose that the proposition is a good one—but for somebody else.

Careful planning

To prescribe planning as the keystone of a diversification decision is not to say that modern management has discovered a new principle. The point is to re-emphasize the necessity of *complete* planning. In view of the complex character and the accountability of industry nowadays, all decisions seem to carry a broad range of implications: the public interest is to be reckoned with—the stakes usually are very high in terms of prospects and pitfalls in marketing —our responsibilities to the owners and to employees are so acutely realized—the human factors in business rank higher than ever before.

All of the many reasons cited for diversification bear out the principle of corporate security while achieving maximum benefits for the business through initiative and the best use of the people and resources concerned. So many good answers have been written to the question 'Why diversification?' that it hardly seems useful to compile yet another statement of them. It is sufficient to mention only the main headings of the 'checklist' classifications of reasons for diversification under the headings of:

Survival (such as moves to counteract adverse market, production or materials influences);

Stability (such as bringing productive balance to a cyclical business);

Productive utilization of resources;

Adaptation to changing customer needs;

Growth;

and the inevitable *Miscellaneous* category encompassing tax advantages, reputation-building, personal ambition of the owner or manager, acquiring new management talent, and so on.

In any single instance, a number of reasons for diversification might figure importantly, but the lesser influences of others may sum up to tip the decision one way or the other. Planning assures management that all potential advantages or disadvantages have been explored and appraised. Further, accountability—preparing owners, employees, customers, suppliers, and others for the move, and explaining its meaning to each—is a vital part of the performance and follow-through stage. Of itself, planning generates the background and mastery needed by management representatives for communications and interpretation.

The methods of diversification also have been dealt with extensively in the business and management press. It seems to us that diversification calls for such flexibility of approach that none of these methods should be ruled out at the outset. Each diversification opportunity calls for analysis on its own merits and all methods available should be considered.

We observe that diversification programmes generally work out to be predominantly one or another of the following types:

Adaptation. Existing personnel and facilities are employed to achieve a further diversity of products or services. This method is a 'natural' in a company whose personnel is imbued with the spirit of research and development. Rockwell relies on adaptation to a considerable extent, often coupled with expansion as defined immediately below.

Expansion. New capacity is gained by adding to the facilities and organization, often enabling the company to go into a new product line.

Acquisition. A going concern already engaged in a chosen field is acquired by purchase for either cash or stock, or a combination of the two. This method has been a principal diversification method on the part of Rockwell. Because the owners and managers usually acquire an equity or career interest in Rockwell, management coverage shifts both ways. That is, central corporate functions are extended to the new division, and management skills of the acquired concern begin to figure in the over-all picture.

Merger. A union of companies of approximately the same size and engaged in businesses considered compatible by the owners is arranged.

Affiliation. A participating or controlling interest in a company is acquired by another concern, but the affiliate continues to operate as an independent entity.

Investments. Arrangements involving cash, management talents, technical skills, patents, or other resources are made so that a company may secure some direct benefits, such as an assured raw material supply or investment returns, or the benefits of collaboration. In some cases a new corporation may be formed, as was the case in the 'partnerships' formed by companies going into the titanium business together.

Missionary. Encouraging a supplier or customer to change, diversify or expand his operations. In a large sense, customer requirements on the industrial scene may be characterized as a great missionary force for diversification.

Diversification approaches

The variations on such a list undoubtedly could be given at length, because each diversification situation has its own unique aspects. Of the types open to us—and we would rule none of them out of consideration—Rockwell has relied primarily on two for its diversification up to now: Adaptation and Acquisition.

Adaptation covers diversification measures which are generated within the existing resources of the concern, although an enlargement of the work force, expansion of plant facilities and other developments may result. Usually, we find, this type of diversification move centres around marketing realities or prospects. For example, our Delta division has designed, developed and introduced a metal lathe for industrial purposes and a radial arm saw primarily for home workshops, both new products complementing existing lines. The Deltashop was developed as a home workshop 'package' of basic tools, ideal for individuals who wished to establish themselves in a do-it-yourself hobby, perhaps in limited space. However, the full line of more versatile individual Delta power tools now frequently replaces the combination set in home workshops as the amateur craftsman masters his hobby and tools up for more complex projects. A central body of experience in a special field enabled Edward Valves to develop the 'Mud-wonder' valve for oil field use, whereas its main line of activity had been in the power plant field. Similarly, Rockwell meters were developed to measure and regulate the flow of hard-to-handle liquids such as concrete and sugar syrup, one of the departures from metering devices for such household 'staples' as water and gas.

Adaptation decisions

In our experience, diversification by adaptation grows out of intensive and continuous attention to developments along the main channels of our business. Thus, the 'Products Committee' of headquarters executives, including the president, consults representatives of sales, manufacturing, engineering, research, and all others whose judgements and responsibilities bear on a proposed new product idea.

The decision on a new product is based on a complete appraisal that provides affirmative answers to a sequence of questions which, in essence, are:

1. What do we know about the need? and about the product to fulfil the need?
2. Can we make it efficiently?
3. Can we sell it at a profit?

Rockwell's pattern of diversification by acquisition centres around the principle of corporate security on both sides. Rockwell has never considered allying itself with any but going concerns that would give us additional strength and talents. Because they have been successful, the inclination to seek a union with a larger company grows out of business reasons of their own. As noted by one diversification-minded corporation president, 'The businesses purchased often are family-owned or closely held concerns, simply because they are not popular investments with larger individual and institutional investors. Such companies often are willing to sell out because they have limited opportunty to raise permanent or long-term capital for expansion or modernization, because owners of closely held concerns face difficult tax problems, and because it is hard for them to diversify their investments.'

In other words, the advantages of an acquisition extend to both sides. The head of one company which decided to join Rockwell stated it bluntly: 'We're buying you,' he said, referring to the shifting of investments and of careers that occur when the owners and employees accept Rockwell stock and Rockwell jobs.

Our approach to the subject of diversification always has been on a 'situation' basis. Each case is studied on its own merits and all ideas of any substance are first given consideration in informal consultations at headquarters.

We have discovered that information of record and our own sources and representatives in the market furnish us with sufficient background for an initial checking of a proposed acquisition along lines of the criteria given earlier.

If the proposition is promising, we are prepared to devote considerable time and effort on the part of top management executives and staff specialists for a thoroughgoing analysis, based on a detailed check list which has evolved into its present form over a period of years (see Check List on page 168).

When Rockwell is prepared to consider an acquisition in earnest, representatives of the other concern are of course given every assistance in their own analysis of our company. At this point a mutual resolution has been formed to size up one another in terms of what each offers to the other. A complete exchange of information is essential for the negotiations that follow an affirmative agreement in principle. And equally important, it constitutes the groundwork for integrating the new unit into the Rockwell picture.

We can attest to the values of an aggressive diversification programme because it guarantees an open mind whereby all opportunities and good ideas are, at least, given some consideration. Because our diversification has been planned around the objective of corporate security, the decisions we reach are tempered by a reliable process of planned analysis. We believe there are other values as well. Not the least of these is the awareness generated within the company of its own character and qualities as others assess them. We have been enabled to see ourselves as others see us—and, in these days when the effectiveness of an enterprise depends in large measure on its standing with constituent groups such as owners, employees, customers and suppliers, the ground rules for sound diversification apply with equal force to the general conduct of the business.

Diversification check list

This check list has served usefully as a guide or reminder of points to be covered, when applicable, in preparing detailed background for judging a specific diversification situation.

A. General
1. Statement of proposed transaction and objectives.
2. History of business and general description.
3. List of officers and directors; affiliation.
4. Stock distribution—number, principal holders, etc.
5. Organization chart.
6. Policy manual.

B. Financial
1. Latest financial statements.
2. Last available statements.
3. Ten year summary of statements.
4. Projected operating and financial statements.
5. Full description of securities, indebtedness, investments, and other assets and liabilities other than normal day-to-day accounts.
6. Chart of accounts and/or description of accounting practices with inventories, fixed assets, etc.
7. List of bank accounts, average balances.
8. Credit reports from banks and Dun & Bradstreet.
9. Federal income tax status; i.e., excess profits tax credit, any loss or unused EPT credit carry-forwards, latest year audited, any deficiency claims, etc.
10. Summary of state and local tax situation; i.e., applicable taxes, unemployment tax rate, any deficiency claims, etc.
11. Tax status of proposed transaction; recommendation for best method of acquisition.
12. Complete list of insurance policies, including description of coverage and cost; workmen's compensation rate.

13. Statement of responsible officer of business as to unrecorded or contingent liabilities.
14. Nature of inventory.

C. *Sales*

1. A brief description and history (if any) of the product line.
2. A ten year record of product sales.
3. A long range forecast of growth or contraction trends for the industry related to the product line.
4. A three to five year forecast of demand for the product.
5. An estimate of the industry's ability to supply present and anticipated demand.
6. A three to five year forecast of sales expectations for this company (share of the market).
7. An analysis of the effect of anticipated increased volume and/or cost reduction on:
   (a) Product demand and share of the market.
   (b) Market saturation and over-capacity.
8. An analysis of the effect of the geographic location of the new facility on:
   (a) Product demand and share of the market.
   (b) Distribution costs (freight savings, warehousing, etc.).
   (c) Competitive position.
9. A review of present sales management, selling force, advertising and sales promotion policies for adaptability and adequacy in relation to new facility.
10. A review of present competitors and their practices including:
    (a) Description of *competitive* products.
    (b) Location.
    (c) Estimated share of market.
    (d) Pricing policies.
    (e) Methods of distribution.
11. An analysis of present and/or probable pricing policies for the product line considering:
    (a) Competitive position.
    (b) Cost pricing.
12. An analysis of present and potential domestic and export clients.
    (a) Major types of customers and their per cent of sales.
    (b) Geographical location.
    (c) Buying habits.

D. Manufacturing
1. Description and layout of plant and property.
2. List of principal machine tools—age and condition.
3. Opinion *re* maintenance and 'housekeeping.'
4. Utilities—availability, usage, rates.
5. Estimated total annual fixed cost.
6. Organization, departments.
7. Transportation facilities.
8. Description of area, including climate, hazards from flood, etc.
9. Opinion *re* adequacy of auxiliary equipment—tools, patterns, material handling equipment, etc.
10. Detailed expense schedule.
11. Building codes, zoning laws, etc.

E. Purchasing
1. Principal materials used.
2. Relation of material costs to sales.
3. Purchasing methods.
4. List of principal suppliers, items, location.
5. Inbound freight costs.
6. Work load—last twelve months.
   (a) Number of purchase orders issued.
   (b) Value of purchase orders.
   (c) Value of outstanding commitments.

F. Research and Engineering
1. Description and condition of facilities.
   (a) Drafting room and office.
   (b) Experimental room.
   (c) Laboratory.
   (d) Special test equipment.
2. Engineering personnel—quality and quantity of technical talents—employed—unemployed.
3. Product designs—evaluation; condition of drawings.
4. Patents and trade-marks—coverage, applications, litigation.

G. Labour
1. Analysis of present employee force—number, sex, age, etc.
2. Direct, indirect, administrative; number and cost.
3. Number of potential job applicants from surveys or census.
4. Determination of types of skills available in the area from state employment service and other sources.
5. Location and availability of students from high schools and technical schools.

6. Union—copy of contract.
7. Labour relations history.
8. Appraisal of working conditions.
9. Statistics on turnover; reasons.
10. Description of incentive system: average rates, incentive and hourly.
11. Employment and personnel policies.
12. Accident frequency.
13. Ratio of total labour cost to sales.
14. Pension and welfare plans.
15. Appraisal of transportation, recreation facilities, housing.
16. Evaluation of labour situation.

10 | Strategies for Diversification

by H. IGOR ANSOFF

THE Red Queen said, 'Now, *here,* it takes all the running *you* can do to keep in the same place. If you want to get somewhere else, you must run at least twice as fast as that!'[1] So it is in the American economy. Just to retain its relative position, a business firm must go through continuous growth and change. To improve its position, it must grow and change at least 'twice as fast as that.'

According to a recent survey of the hundred largest United States corporations from 1909 to 1948, few companies that have stuck to their traditional products and methods have grown in stature. The report concludes: 'There is no reason to believe that those now at the top will stay there except as they keep abreast in the race of innovation and competition.'[2]

There are four basic growth alternatives open to a business. It can grow through increased market penetration, through market development, through product development, or through diversification.

A company which accepts diversification as a part of its planned approach to growth undertakes the task of continually weighing and comparing the advantages of these four alternatives, selecting first one combination and then another, depending on the particular circumstances in long-range development planning.

DR ANSOFF is Professor of Management and Dean of the Graduate School of Management, Vanderbilt University, Nashville, Tennessee.

Dean Ansoff began his career as a student and teacher at Stevens Institute of Technology. He received his Ph.D. in applied mathematics from Brown University, and spent nine years with the Rand Corporation. He was Vice-President and General Manager, Industrial Technology Division, Lockheed Electronics Company, a division of Lockheed Aircraft Corporation in 1963, when he was appointed Professor of Industrial Administration at Carnegie Mellon University.

Dean Ansoff is active internationally as a lecturer and management consultant, and his book *Corporate Strategy*, has been translated into four languages.

This chapter is reprinted with permission from: *Harvard Business Review*, Vol. 35, No. 5, pp. 113–12., September/October 1957.

While they are an integral part of the overall growth pattern, diversification decisions present certain unique problems. Much more than other growth alternatives, they require a break with past patterns and traditions of a company and an entry onto new and uncharted paths.

Accordingly, one of the aims of this chapter is to relate diversification to the overall growth perspectives of management, establish reasons which may lead a company to prefer diversification to other growth objectives. This will provide us with a partly qualitative, partly quantitative method for selecting diversification strategies which are best suited to long-term growth of a company. We can use qualitative criteria to reduce the total number of possible strategies to the most promising few, and then apply a return on investment measure to narrow the choice of plans still further.

Product-market alternatives

The term 'diversification' is usually associated with a change in the characteristics of the company's product line and/or market, in contrast to market penetration, market development, and product development, which represent other types of change in product-market structure. Since these terms are frequently used interchangeably, we can avoid later confusion by defining each as a special kind of product-market strategy. To begin with the basic concepts:

1.   The *product line* of a manufacturing company refers both to (a) the physical characteristics of the individual products (for example, size, weight, materials, tolerances) and to (b) the performance, characteristics of the products (for example, an airplane's speed, range, altitude, payload).

2.   In thinking of the market for a product we can borrow a concept commonly used by the military—the concept of a mission. A *product mission* is a description of the job which the product is intended to perform. For instance, one of the missions of the Lockheed Aircraft Corporation is commercial air transportation of passengers; another is provision of airborne early warning for the Air Defence Command; a third is performance of air-to-air combat.

For our purposes, the concept of a mission is more useful in describing market alternatives than would be the concept of a 'customer', since a customer usually has many different missions, each requiring a different product. The Air Defence Command, for example, needs different kinds of warning systems. Also, the product mission concept helps management to set up the problems in such a way that it can better evaluate the performance of competing products.

3. *A product-market strategy,* accordingly, is a joint statement of a product line and the corresponding set of missions which the products are designed to fulfill. In shorthand form (see Fig. 1), if we let π represent the product line and μ the corresponding set of missions, then the pair of π and μ is a product-market strategy.

With these concepts in mind let us turn now to the four different types of product-market strategy shown in Fig. 1:

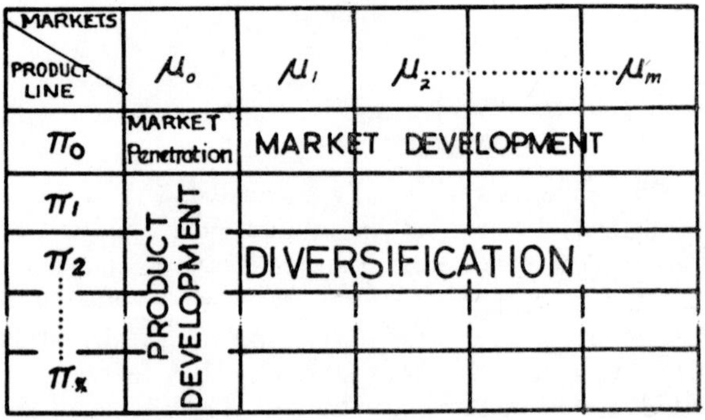

Fig. 1   *Product-market strategies for business growth alternatives*

1. *Market penetration* is an effort to increase company sales without departing from an original product-market strategy. The company seeks to improve business performance either by increasing the volume of sales to its present customers or by finding new customers for present products.

2. *Market development* is a strategy in which the company attempts to adapt its present product line (generally with some modification in the product characteristics) to new missions. An airplane company which adapts and sells its passenger transport for the mission of cargo transportation is an example of this strategy.

3. *A product development* strategy, on the other hand, retains the present mission and develops products that have new and different characteristics such as will improve the performance of the mission.

4. *Diversification* is the final alternative. It calls for a simultaneous departure from the present product line and the present market structure.

Each of the above strategies describes a distinct path which a business can take towards future growth. However, it must be emphasized that in most actual situations a business would follow several of these paths at the same time. As a matter of fact, a simultaneous pursuit of market penetration, market development, and product development is usually a sign of a progressive, well-run business and may be essential to survival in the face of economic competition.

The diversification strategy stands apart from the other three. While the latter are usually followed with the same technical, financial, and merchandizing resources which are used for the original product line, diversification generally requires new skills, new techniques, and new facilities. As a result, it almost invariably leads to physical and organizational changes in the structure of the business which represent a distinct break with past business experience.

Forecasting growth

A study of business literature and of company histories reveals many different reasons for diversification. Companies diversify to compensate for technological obsolescence, to distribute risk, to utilize excess productive capacity, to re-invest earnings, to obtain top management, and so forth. In deciding whether to diversify, management should carefully analyse its future growth prospects. It should think of market penetration, market development, and product development as parts of its over-all product strategy and ask whether this strategy should be broadened to include diversification.

Long-term trends

A standard method of analysing future company growth prospects is to use long-range sales forecasts. Preparation of such forecasts involves simultaneous consideration of a number of major factors:

> General economic trends.
> Political and international trends.
> Trends peculiar to the industry. (For example, forecasts prepared in the airplane industry must take account of such possibilities as a changeover from manned aircraft to missiles, changes in the government 'mobilization base' concept

with all that would mean for the aircraft industry, and
rising expenditures required for research and development.)

Estimates of the firm's competitive strength relative to other
members of the industry.

Estimates of improvements in the company performance which
can be achieved through market penetration, market development, and product development.

Trends in manufacturing costs.

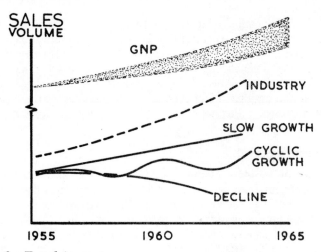

Fig. 2   *Trend forecasts*

Such forecasts usually assume that company management will
be aggressive and that management policies will take full advantage
of the opportunities offered by the different trends. They are, in
other words, estimates of the best possible results the business can
hope to achieve *short* of diversification.

Different patterns of forecasted growth are shown in Fig. 2, with
hypothetical growth curves for the national economy (GNP) and
the company's industry added for purposes of comparison. One of
the curves illustrates a sales curve which declines with time. This
may be the result of an expected contraction of demand, the obsolescence of manufacturing techniques, emergence of new products
better suited to the mission to which the company caters, or other
changes. Another typical pattern, frequently caused by seasonal
variations in demand, is one of cyclic sales activity. Less apparent,

but more important, are slower cyclic changes, such as trends in construction or the peace-war variation in demand in the aircraft industry.

If the most optimistic sales estimates which can be attained short of diversification fall in either of the preceding cases, diversification is strongly indicated. However, a company may choose to diversify even if its prospects do, on the whole, appear favourable. This is illustrated by the 'slow growth curve'. As drawn in Fig. 2, the curve indicates rising sales which, in fact, grow faster than the economy as a whole. Nevertheless, the particular company may belong to one of the so-called 'growth industries' which as a whole is surging ahead. Such a company may diversify because it feels that its prospective growth rate is unsatisfactory in comparison with the industry growth rate.

Making trend forecasts is far from a precise science. The characteristics of the basic environmental trends, as well as the effect of these trends on the industry, are always uncertain. Furthermore, the ability of a particular business organization to perform in the new environment is very difficult to assess. Consequently, any realistic company forecast should include several different trend forecasts, each with an explicitly or implicitly assigned probability. As an alternative, the company's growth trend forecast may be represented by a widening spread between two extremes, similar to that shown for GNP in Fig. 2.

Contingencies

In addition to trends, another class of events may make diversification desirable. These are certain environmental conditions which, if they occur, will have a great effect on sales; however, we cannot predict their occurrence with certainty. To illustrate such 'contingent' events, an aircraft company might foresee these possibilities that would upset its trend forecasts:

A major technological breakthrough whose characteristics can be foreseen but whose timing cannot at present be determined, such as the discovery of a new manufacturing process for high-strength, thermally-resistant aircraft bodies.

An economic recession which would lead to loss of orders for commercial aircraft and would change the pattern of spending for military aircraft.

A major economic depression.

A limited war which would sharply increase the demand for air industry products.

A sudden cessation of the cold war, a currently popular hope which has waxed and waned with changes in Soviet behaviour.

The two types of sales forecast are illustrated in Fig. 3 for a hypothetical company. Sales curves S_1 and S_2 represent a spread of trend forecasts; and S_3 and S_4, two contingent forecasts for the same event. The difference between the two types, both in starting time and effect on sales, lies in the degree of uncertainty associated with each.

In the case of trend forecasts we can trace a crude time history of sales based on events which we fully expect to happen. Any uncertainty arises from not knowing exactly when they will take place

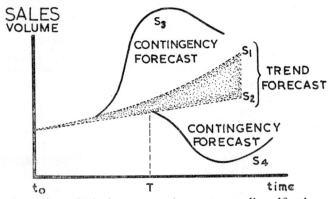

Fig. 3   *A hypothetical company forecast—no diversification*

and how they will influence business. In the case of contingency forecasts, we can again trace a crude time history, but our uncertainty is greater. We lack precise knowledge of not only *when* the event will occur but also *whether* it will occur. In going from a trend to a contingency forecast, we advance, so to speak, one notch up the scale of ignorance.

In considering the relative weight we should give to contingent events in diversification planning, we must consider not only the magnitude of their effect on sales, but also the relative probability of their occurrence. For example, if a severe economic depression were to occur, its effect on many industries would be devastating. Many companies feel safe in neglecting it in their planning, however, because they feel that the likelihood of a deep depression is very small, at least for the near future.

It is a common business practice to put primary emphasis on trend forecasts; in fact, in many cases businessmen devote their long-range planning exclusively to these forecasts. They usually view a possible catastrophe as 'something one cannot plan for' or as a second-order correction to be applied only after the trends have been taken into account. The emphasis is on planning for growth, and planning for contingencies is viewed as an 'insurance policy' against reversals.

People familiar with planning problems in the military establishment will note here an interesting difference between military and business attitudes. While business planning emphasizes trends, military planning emphasizes contingencies. To use a crude analogy, a business planner is concerned with planning for continuous, successful, day-after-day operation of a supermarket. If he is progressive, he also buys an insurance policy against fire, but he spends relatively little time in planning for fires. The military is more like the fire engine company; the fire is the thing. Day-to-day operations are of interest only insofar as they can be utilized to improve readiness and fire-fighting techniques.

Unforeseeable events

So far we have dealt with diversification forecasts based on what may be called *foreseeable* market conditions—conditions which we can interpret in terms of time-phased sales curves. Planners have a tendency to stop here, to disregard the fact that, in addition to the events for which we can draw time histories, there is a recognizable class of events to which we can assign a probability of occurrence but which we cannot otherwise describe in our present state of knowledge. One must move another notch up the scale of ignorance in order to consider these possibilities.

Many businessmen feel that the effort is not worthwhile. They argue that since no information is available about these unforeseeable circumstances, one might as well devote the available time and energy to planning for the foreseeable circumstances, or that, in a very general sense, planning for the foreseeable also prepares one for the unforeseeable contingencies.

In contrast, more experienced military and business people have a very different attitude. Well aware of the importance and relative probability of unforeseeable events, they ask why one should plan specific steps for the foreseeable events while neglecting the really important possibilities. They may substitute for such planning practical maxims for conducting one's business—'be solvent,' 'be light on your feet,' 'be flexible.' Unfortunately, it is not always clear (even to the people who preach it) what this flexibility means.

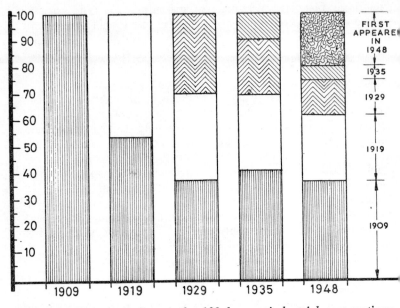

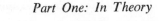

Fig. 4   *Changes in list of the 100 largest industrial corporations*

An interesting study by The Brookings Institution[3] provides an example of the importance of the unforeseeable events to business. Fig. 4 shows the changing make-up of the list of the 100 largest corporations over the last fifty years. Of the 100 largest on the 1909 list (represented by the heavy marble texture) only thirty-six were among the 100 largest in 1948; just about half of the new entries to the list in 1919 (represented by white) were left in 1948; less than half of the new entries in 1929 (represented by the zigzag design) were left in 1948; and so on. Clearly, a majority of the giants of yesteryear have dropped behind in a relatively short span of time.

Many of the events that hurt these corporations could not be specifically foreseen in 1909. If the companies which dropped from the original list had made forecasts of the foreseeable kind at that time—and some of them must have—they would very likely have found the future growth prospects to be excellent. Since then, however, railroads, which loomed as the primary means of transportation, have given way to the automobile and the aeroplane; the textile industry, which appeared to have a built-in demand in an expanding world population, has been challenged and dominated by synthetics; radio, radar, and television have created means of communication unforeseeable in significance and scope; and many other sweeping changes have occurred.

Planning for the unknown

The lessons of the past fifty years are fully applicable today. The pace of economic and technological change is so rapid that it is virtually certain that major breakthroughs comparable to those of the last fifty years, but not yet foreseeable in scope and character, will profoundly change the structure of the national economy. All of this has important implications for diversification, as suggested by the Brookings study:

'The majority of the companies included among the 100 largest of our day have attained their positions within the last two decades. They are companies that have started new industries or have transformed old ones to create or meet consumer preferences. The companies that have not only grown in absolute terms but have gained an improved position in their own industry may be identified as companies that are notable for drastic changes made in their product mix and methods, generating or responding to new competition.

'There are two outstanding cases in which the industry leader of 1909 had by 1948 risen in position relative to its own industry group and also in rank among the 100 largest—one in chemicals and the other in electrical equipment. These two (General Electric and Du-Pont) are hardly recognizable as the same companies they were in 1909 except for retention of the name; for in each case the product mix of 1948 is vastly different from what it was in the earlier year, and the markets in which the companies meet competition are incomparably broader than those that accounted for that earlier place at the top of their industries. They exemplify the flux in the market positions of the most successful industrial giants during the past four decades and a general growth rather than a consolidation of supremacy in a circumscribed line.'[4]

This suggests that the existence of specific undesirable trends is not the only reason for diversification. A broader product line may be called for, even with optimistic forecasts for present products. An examination of the foreseeable alternatives should be accompanied by an analysis of how well the over-all company product-market strategy covers the so-called growth areas of technology—areas of many potential discoveries. If such analysis shows that, because of its product lines, a company's chances of taking advantage of important discoveries are limited, management should broaden its technological and economic base by entering a number of so-called 'growth industries.' Even if the definable horizons look bright, a need for flexibility, in the widest sense of the word, may provide potent reasons for diversification.

Diversification objectives

If an analysis of trends and contingencies indicates that a company should diversify, where should it look for diversification opportunities?

Generally speaking, there are three types of opportunities:

1. Each product manufactured by a company is made up of functional components, parts, and basic materials which go into the final assembly. A manufacturing concern usually buys a large fraction of these from outside suppliers. One way to diversify, commonly known as *vertical diversification,* is to branch out into production of components, parts, and materials. Perhaps the most outstanding example of vertical diversification is the Ford empire in the days of Henry Ford, Sr.

At first glance, vertical diversification seems inconsistent with our definition of a diversification strategy. However, the respective missions which components, parts, and materials are designed to perform are distinct from the mission of the overall product. Furthermore, the technology in fabrication and manufacture of these parts and materials is likely to be very different from the technology of manufacturing the final product. Thus, vertical diversification does imply both catering to new missions and introduction of new products.

2. Another possible way to go is *horizontal diversification.* This can be described as the introduction of new products which, while they do not contribute to the present product line in any way, cater to missions which lie within the company's know-how and experience in technology, finance, and marketing.

3. It is also possible, by *lateral diversification,* to move beyond the confines of the industry to which a company belongs. This obviously opens a great many possibilities, from operating banana boats to building atomic reactors. While vertical and horizontal diversification are restrictive, in the sense that they delimit the field of interest, lateral diversification is 'wide open'. It is an announcement of the company's intent to range far afield from its present market structure.

Choice of direction

How does a company choose among these diversification directions? In part the answer depends on the reasons which prompt diversification. For example, in the light of the trends described for the industry, an aircraft company may make the following moves to meet long-range sales objectives through diversification:

1. A vertical move to contribute to the technological progress of the present product line.
2. A horizontal move to improve the coverage of the military market.
3. A horizontal move to increase the percentage of commercial sales in the over-all sales programmes.
4. A lateral move to stabilize sales in case of a recession.
5. A lateral move to broaden the company's technological base.

Some of these diversification objectives apply to characteristics of the product, some to those of the product missions. Each objective is designed to improve some aspect of the balance between the over-all product-market strategy and the expected environment. The specific objectives derived for any given case can be grouped into three general categories: *growth objectives,* such as 1, 2, and 3 above, which are designed to improve the balance under favourable trend conditions; *stability objectives,* such as 3 and 4, designed as protection against unfavourable trends and foreseeable contingencies; and *flexibility objectives,* such as 5, to strengthen the company against unforeseeable contingencies.

A diversification direction which is highly desirable for one of the objectives is likely to be less desirable for others. For example:

(a) If a company is diversifying because its sales trend shows a declining volume of demand, it would be unwise to consider vertical diversification, since this would be at best a temporary device to stave off an eventual decline of business.

(b) If a company's industry shows every sign of healthy growth, then vertical and, in particular, horizontal diversification would be a desirable device for strengthening the position of the company in a field in which its knowledge and experience are concentrated.

(c) If the major concern is stability under a contingent forecast, chances are that both horizontal and vertical diversification could not provide a sufficient stabilizing influence and that lateral action is called for.

(d) If management's concern is with the narrowness of the technological base in the face of what we have called unforeseeable contingencies, then lateral diversification into new areas of technology would be clearly indicated.

Measured sales goals

Management can and should state the objectives of growth and stability in quantitative terms as *long-range sales objectives*. This is illustrated in Fig. 5. The solid lines describe a hypothetical company's forecasted performance without diversification under a general trend, represented by the sales curve marked S_1, and in a contingency, represented by S_2. The dashed lines show the improved performance as a result of diversification with S_3 representing the curve for continuation of normal trends and S_4 representing the curve for a major reverse.

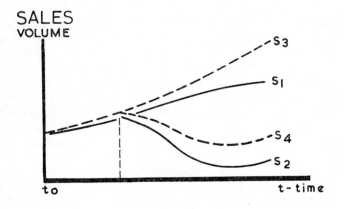

Fig. 5   *Diversification objectives*

Growth. Management's first aim in diversifying is to improve the growth pattern of the company. The growth objective can be stated thus:

Under trend conditions the growth rate of sales after diversification should exceed the growth rate of sales of the original product line by a miniumum specified margin. Or to illustrate in mathematical shorthand, the objective for the company in Fig. 5 would be:

$$S_3 - S_1 \geqslant \rho$$

where the value of the margin ρ is specified for each year after diversification.

Some companies (particularly in the growth industries) fix an annual rate of growth which they wish to attain. Every year this rate of growth is compared to the actual growth during the past year. A decision on diversification action for the coming year is then based upon the disparity between the objective and the actual rate of growth.

Stability. The second effect desired of diversification is improvement in company stability under contingent conditions. Not only should diversification prevent sales from dropping as low as they might have before diversification, but the percentage drop should also be lower. The second sales objective is thus a stability objective. It can be stated as follows:

Under contingent conditions the percentage decline in sales which may occur without diversification should exceed the percentage drop in sales with diversification by an adequate margin, or algebraically:

$$\frac{S_1 - S_2}{S_1} - \frac{S_3 - S_4}{S_3} \geqslant \delta$$

Using this equation, it is possible to relate the sales volumes before and after diversification to a rough measure of the resulting stability. Let the ratio of the lowest sales during a slump to the sales which would have occurred in the same year under trend conditions be called the stability factor F. Thus, $F = 0.3$ would mean that the company sales during a contingency amount to 30 per cent of what is expected under trend conditions. In Fig. 6 the stability factor of the company before diversification is the value $F_1 = S_2/S_1$ and the stability factor after diversification is $F_3 = S_4/S_3$, both computed at the point on the curve where S_2 is minimum.

Now let us suppose that management is considering the purchase of a subsidiary. How large does the subsidiary have to be if the parent is to improve the stability of the corporation as a whole by a certain amount? Fig. 6 shows how the question can be answered:

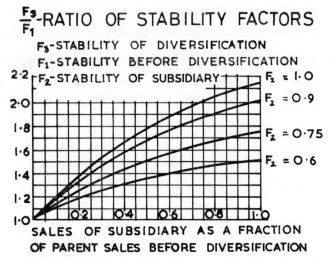

Fig. 6   *Improvement in stability factor as a result of diversification*
         for $F_1 = 0.3$

On the horizontal axis we plot the different possible sales volumes
of a smaller firm that might be secured as a proportion of the
parent's volume. Obviously, the greater this proportion, the greater
the impact of the purchase on the parent's stability.

On the vertical axis we plot different ratios of the parent's stability before and after diversification (F_3/F_1).

The assumed stability factor of the parent is 0.3. Let us say that
four prospective subsidiaries have stability factors of 1.0, 0.9, 0.75,
and 0.6. If they were not considerably higher than 0.3, of course,
there would be no point in acquiring them (at least for our purposes here).

On the graph we correlate these four stability factors of the subsidiary with (1) the ratio F_3/F_1 and (2) different sales volumes of
the subsidiary. We find, for example, that if the parent is to double
its stability (point 2.0 on the vertical axis), it must obtain a subsidiary with a stability of 1.0 and 75 per cent as much sales volume
as the parent, or a subsidiary with a stability of 0.9 and 95 per cent
of the sales volume. If the parent seeks an improvement in
stability of, say, only 40 per cent, it could buy a company with
a stability of 0.9 and 25 per cent as much sales volume as
it has.

This particular way of expressing sales objectives has two important advantages: (1) By setting minimum, rather than maximum, limits on growth, it leaves room for the company to take advantage of unusual growth opportunities in order to exceed these goals, and thus provides definite goals without inhibiting initiative and incentive. (2) It takes account of the time-phasing of diversification moves; and since these moves invariably require a transition period, the numerical values of growth objectives can be allowed to vary from year to year so as to allow for a gradual development of operations.

Long-range objectives

Diversification objectives specify directions in which a company's product-market should change. Usually there will be several objectives indicating different and sometimes conflicting directions. If a company attempts to follow all of them simultaneously, it is in danger of spreading itself too thin and of becoming a conglomeration of incompatible, although perhaps individually profitable, enterprises.

There are cases of diversification which have followed this path. In a majority of cases, however, there are valid reasons why a company should seek to preserve certain basic unifying characteristics as it goes through a process of growth and change. Consequently, diversification objectives should be supplemented by a statement of long-range product-market objectives. For instance:

(a) One consistent course of action is to adopt a product-market policy which will preserve a kind of technological coherence among the different manufactures with the focus on the products of the parent company. For instance, a company that is mainly distinguished for a type of engineering and production excellence would continue to select product-market entries which would strengthen and maintain this excellence. Perhaps the best known example of such policy is exemplified by the DuPont slogan, 'Better things for better living through chemistry'.

(b) Another approach is to set long-term growth policy in terms of the breadth of market which the company intends to cover. It may choose to confine its diversifications to the vertical or horizontal direction, or it may select a type of lateral diversification controlled by the characteristics of the missions to which the company intends to cater. For example, a company in the field of air transportation may expand its interest to all forms of transportation of people and cargo. To paraphrase DuPont, some slogan like

'Better transportation for better living through advanced engineering,' would be descriptive of such a long-range policy.

(c) A greatly different policy is to emphasize primarily the financial characteristics of the corporation. This method of diversification generally places no limits on engineering and manufacturing characteristics of new products, although in practice the competence and interests of management will usually provide some orientation for diversification moves. The company makes the decisions regarding the distribution of new acquisitions exclusively on the basis of financial considerations. Rather than a manufacturing entity, the corporate character is now one of a holding company. Top management delegates a large share of its product-planning and administrative functions to the divisions and concerns itself largely with co-ordination, financial problems, and with building up a balanced 'portfolio' of products within the corporate structure.

Successful alternatives

These alternative long-range policies demonstrate the extremes. No one course is necessarily better than the others; management's choice will rest in large part on its preferences, objectives, skills, and training. The aircraft industry illustrates the fact that there is more than one successful path to diversification:

(a) Among the major successful airframe manufacturers, Douglas Aircraft Company, Inc., and Boeing Airplane Company have to date limited their growth to horizontal diversification into missiles and new markets for new types of aircraft. Lockheed has carried horizontal diversification further to include aircraft maintenance, aircraft service, and production of ground-handling equipment.

(b) North American Aviation, Incorporated, on the other hand, appears to have chosen vertical diversification by establishing its subsidiaries in Atomics International, Autonetics, and Rocketdyne, thus providing a basis for manufacture of complete air vehicles of the future.

(c) Bell Aircraft Corporation has adopted a policy of technological consistency among the items in its product line. It has diversified laterally but primarily into types of products for which it had previous know-how and experience.

(d) General Dynamics Corporation provides a further interesting contrast. It has gone far into lateral diversification. Among the major manufacturers of air vehicles, it comes closest to the 'holding company' extreme. Its airplanes and missile manu-facturing operations in Convair are paralleled by production of sub-marines in the Electric Boat Division; military, industrial, and consumer electronic products in the Stromberg-Carlson Division; electric motors in the Electro Dynamic Division.

Selecting a strategy

In the preceding sections qualitative criteria for diversification have been discussed. How should management apply these criteria to individual opportunities? Two steps should be taken: (1) apply the qualitative standards to narrow the field of diversification oppor-tunities; (2) apply the numerical criteria to select the preferred strategy or strategies.

Qualitative evaluation

The long-range product-market policy is used as a criterion for the first rough cut in the qualitative evaluation. It can be used to divide a large field of opportunities into classes of diversification moves consistent with the company's basic character. For example, a company whose policy is to compete on the basis of the technical excellence of its products would eliminate as inconsistent classes of consumer products which are sold on the strength of advertising appeal rather than superior quality.

Next, the company can compare each individual diversification opportunity with the individual diversification objectives. This pro-cess tends to eliminate opportunities which, while still consistent with the desired product-market make-up, are nevertheless likely to lead to an imbalance between the company product line and the probable environment. For example, a company which wishes to preserve and expand its technical excellence in design of large, highly stressed machines controlled by feedback techniques may find consistent product opportunities both inside and outside the industry to which it caters, but if one of its major diversification objectives is to correct cyclic variations in demand that are char-acteristic of the industry, it would choose an opportunity that lies outside.

Each diversification opportunity which has gone through the two screening steps satisfies at least one diversification objective, but probably it will not satisfy all of them. Therefore, before subject-ing them to the quantitative evaluation, it is necessary to group them into several alternative over-all company product-market strategies, composed of the original strategy and one or more of the remaining diversification strategies. These alternative over-all strategies should be roughly equivalent in meeting all of the diversification objectives.

At this stage it is particularly important to allow for the unforeseeable contingencies. Since the techniques of numerical evaluation are applicable only to trends and foreseeable contingencies, it is important to make sure that the different alternatives chosen give the company a broad enough technological base. In practice this process is less formidable than it may appear. For example, a company in the aircraft industry has to consider the areas of technology in which major discoveries are likely to affect the future of the industry. This would include atomic propulsion, certain areas of electronics, automation of complex processes, and so forth. In designing alternative over-all strategies the company would then make sure that each contains product entries which will give the firm a desirable and comparable degree of participation in these future growth areas.

Quantitative evaluation

Will the company's product-market strategies make money? Will the profit structure improve as a result of their adoption? The purpose of quantitative evaluation is to compare the profit potential of the alternatives.

Unfortunately, there is no single yardstick among those commonly used in business that gives an accurate measurement of performance. The techniques currently used for measurement of business performance constitute, at best, an imprecise art. It is common to measure different aspects of performance by applying different tests. Thus, tests of income adequacy measure the earning ability of the business; tests of debt coverage and liquidity measure preparedness for contingencies; the shareholders' position measures attractiveness to investors; tests of sales efficiency and personnel productivity measures efficiency in the use of money, physical assets, and personnel. These tests employ a variety of different performance ratios, such as return on sales, return on net worth, return on assets, turnover of net worth, and ratio of assets to liabilities. The total number of ratios may run as high as twenty in a single case.

In the final evaluation, which immediately precedes a diversification decision, management would normally apply all of these tests, tempered with business judgement. However, for the purpose of preliminary elimination of alternatives, a single test is frequently used—return on investment, a ratio between earnings and the capital invested in producing these earnings. While the usefulness of return on investment is commonly accepted, there is considerable room for argument regarding its limitations and its practical application.[5] Fundamentally, the difficulty with the concept is that it fails to provide an absolute measure of business performance applicable to a range of very different industries; also, the term 'investment' is subject to a variety of interpretations.

But since our aim is to use the concept as a measure of *relative* performance of different diversification strategies, we need not be concerned with its failure to measure absolute values. And as long as we are consistent in our definition of investment in alternative courses of action, the question of terminology is not so troublesome. We cannot define profit-producing capital in general terms, but we can define it in each case in the light of particular business characteristics and practices (such as the extent of government-owned assets, depreciation practices, inflationary trends).

For the numerator of our return on investment, we can use net earnings after taxes. A going business concern has standard techniques for estimating its future earnings. These depend on the projected sales volume, tax structure, trends in material and labour costs, productivity, and so forth. If the diversification opportunity being considered is itself a going concern, its profit projections can be used for estimates of combined future earnings. If the opportunity is a new venture, its profit estimates should be made on the basis of the average performance for the industry.

Changes in investment structure

A change in the investment structure of the diversifying company accompanies a diversification move. The source of investment for the new venture may be: (1) excess capital, (2) capital borrowed at an attractive rate, (3) an exchange of the company's equity for an equity in another company, or (4) capital withdrawn from present business operations.

If we let i_1, i_2, i_3, i_4, respectively, represent investments made in the new product in the preceding four categories during the first year of diversified operations, we can derive a simple expression for the *improvement* in return on investment resulting from diversification:

$$\Delta R = \frac{(p_2-p_1)(i_2+i_3+i_4)+(p_2-r)\,i_1-i_2r+(p_1-r)(i_2+i_3)i_1/I}{I+i_2+i_3}$$

where p_1 and p_2 represent the average return on capital invested in the original product and in the new product, respectively, and quantity I is the total capital in the business before diversification.

We can easily check this expression by assuming that only one type of new investment will be made at a time. We can then use the formula to compute the conditions under which it pays to diversify (that is, conditions where $\triangle R$ is greater than zero):

1. If excess capital is the only source of new investment ($i_2 = i_3 = i_4 = 0$), this condition is $p_2 - r > 0$. That is, return on diversified operations should be more attractive than current rates for capital on the open market.

2. If only borrowed capital is used ($i_1 = i_3 = i_4 = 0$), it pays to diversify if $p_2 - p_1 > r$. That is the difference between return from diversification and return from the original product should be greater than the interest rate on the money.

3. If the diversified operation is to be acquired through an exchange of equity or through internal reallocation of capital, $p_2 - p_1 > 0$ is the condition under which diversification will pay off.

A comprehensive yardstick

The formula for $\triangle R$ just stated is not sufficiently general to serve as a measure of profit potential. It gives improvement in return for the first year only and for a particular sales trend. In order to provide a reasonably comprehensive comparison between alternative over-all company strategies, the yardstick for profit potential should possess the following properties:

1. Since changes in the investment structure of the business invariably accompany diversification, the yardstick should reflect these changes. It should also take explicit account of new capital brought into the business and changes in the rate of capital formation resulting from diversification, as well as costs of borrowed capital.

2. Usually the combined performance of the new and the old product-market lines is not a simple sum of their separate performances; it should be greater. The profit potential yardstick must take account of this non-linear characteristic.

3. Each diversification move is characterized by a transition period during which readjustment of the company structure to new operating conditions takes place. The benefits of a diversification move may not be realized fully for some time, so the measurement of profit potential should span a sufficient length of time to allow for effects of the transition.

4. Since both profits and investments will be spread over time, the yardstick should use their present value.

5. Business performance will differ depending on the particular economic-political environment. The profit potential yardstick must somehow average out the probable effect of alternative environments.

6. The statement of sales objectives, as pointed out previously should specify the general characteristics of growth and stability which are desired. Profit potential functions should be compatible with these characteristics.

We can generalize our formula in a way which will meet most of the preceding requirements. The procedure is to write an expression for the present value of $\triangle R$ for an arbitrary year, t, allowing for possible yearly diversification investments up to the year t, interest rates, and the rate of capital formation. Then this present value is averaged over time as well as over the alternative sales forecasts. The procedure is straightforward (although the algebra involved is too cumbersome to be worth reproducing here[6]). The result, which is the 'average expected present value of $\triangle R$,' takes account of conditions (1) through (5), above. Let us call it $\triangle Re$. It can be computed using data normally found in business and financial forecasts.

Final evalution

This brings us to the final step in the evaluation. We have discussed a qualitative method for constructing several over-all product-market strategies which meet the diversification and the long-range objectives. We can now compute $(\triangle R)e$ for each of the over-all strategies and, at the same time, make sure that the strategies satisfy the sales objectives previously stated, thus fulfilling condition (6), above.

If product-market characteristics, which we have used to narrow the field of choice and to compute $(\triangle R)e$, were the sole criteria, then the strategy with the highest $(\triangle R)e$ would be the 'preferred' path to diversification. The advantages of a particular product-market opportunity, however, must be balanced against the chances of business success.

Conclusion

A study of diversification histories shows that a firm usually arrives at a decision to make a particular move through a multi-step process. The planners' first step is to determine the preferred areas for search; the second is to select a number of diversification opportunities within these areas and to subject them to a preliminary

G

evaluation. They then make a final evaluation, conducted by the top management, leading to selection of a specific step; finally, they work out details and complete the move.

Throughout this process the company seeks to answer two basic questions: How well will a particular move, if it is successful, meet the company's objectives? What are the company's chances of making it a success? In the early stages of the programme, the major concern is with business strategy. Hence, the first question plays a dominant role. But as the choice narrows, considerations of business ability, of the particular strengths and weaknesses which a company brings to diversification, shift attention to the second question.

This discussion has been devoted primarily to selection of a diversification strategy. We have dealt with what may be called *external* aspects of diversification—the relation between a company and its environment. To put it another way, we have derived a method for measuring the profit potential of a diversification strategy, but we have not inquired into the *internal* factors which determine the ability of a diversifying company to make good this potential. A company planning diversification must consider such questions as how the company should organize to conduct the search for and evaluation of diversification opportunities; what method of business expansion it should employ; and how it should mesh its operations with those of a subsidiary. These considerations give rise to a new set of criteria for the *business fit* of the prospective venture. These must be used in conjunction with $(\triangle R)e$ as computed in the preceding section to determine which of the overall product-market strategies should be selected for implementation.

Thus the steps outlined in this chapter are the first, though an important, preliminary to a diversification move. Only through further careful consideration of probable business success can a company develop a long-range strategy that will enable it to 'run twice as fast as that' (using the Red Queen's words again) in the ever-changing world of today.

REFERENCES

1 Carroll, Lewis J., *Through the looking glass,* Heritage Press, N. York, page 41.
2 Kaplan, A. D. H. (1954), *Big enterprise in a competitive system.* The Brookings Institution, Washington, p. 142.
3 Kaplan, A. D. H., *op cit.*

4 Kaplan, A. D. H., *op cit*, p. 142.
5 Schwartz, Chas. R. (1956). The return-on-investment concept as a tool for decision making. *General Management Series No. 183. New York, American Management Association, 42-61*; Drucker, Peter F. (1954) *The practice of management*. Harper and Brothers, New York; and Barnet, Edw. M. (1956) *Showdown in the market place*. HBR July-Aug. p. 85.
6 Ansoff, H. Igor (1957) *A model for diversification*. Burbank, Lockheed Aicraft Corpn.; and Williams, John Burr. (1938) *The theory of Investment value*. The North-Holland Publishing Co., Amsterdam.

11 | Programme for Product Diversification

by THOMAS A. STAUDT

PRODUCT diversification is currently the centre of widespread executive interest as a means of market adjustment. Product development and innovation have always been major facets of competitive rivalry, but the present dynamic quality of the economy is particularly characterized by an expanding frontier of new products, acquisitions, and mergers.

Management today must be unusually alert in finding effective strategy adjustments to keep pace with fluctuations in the business cycle, changes in demand, and an ever-increasing rate of technological development. These conditions have been manifested in an accelerated rate of product displacement and less resistance to change on the part of consumers and industrial purchasers. Product diversification has consequently been called upon successfully by

THOMAS A. STAUDT is Director of Marketing for the Chevrolet Motor Division of General Motors. His responsibility includes marketing research and planning, advertising, and passenger car merchandizing. Prior to his present position, Mr Staudt was Chairman of the Department of Marketing and Transportation Administration at Michigan State University, and administratively responsible for the largest faculty of its kind in the country. Earlier, he was on the faculty of the School of Industrial Management at M.I.T. and before that, at the School of Business at Indiana University.

Mr Staudt has been both an officer and director in both the American Marketing Association and Sales and Marketing Executives-International. He was appointed by the Secretary of Commerce to the National Marketing Advisory Committee in 1967, and was appointed on the 11th February 1970, by President Nixon to the President's Advisory Council on Management Improvement.

A continuing author, Mr Staudt's most recent publication is *A Managerial Introduction to Marketing*—second edition, Prentice Hall 1970.

Author's note: I wish to acknowledge the assistance of Mr. Robert F. King in the preparation of this chapter.

This chapter is reprinted with permission from: *Harvard Business Review*, Vol. 32, No. 6, pp. 121–131, November/December 1954.

many executives to meet the challenge of a changing industrial environment. This article is a discussion of some aspects of the planning, analysis, and methods useful to management in programming diversification.

Lessons from experience

Unfortunately, the experience of many firms with diversification has not been particularly gratifying. A recent study showed that 80 per cent of the new products placed on the market by 200 leading packaged goods manufacturers failed—for reasons other than insufficient capital.[1] This extremely high rate of failure is evidence in itself that diversification required more careful planning, selection, and control than had been anticipated, and it suggests that diversification may not have been the most appropriate means of achieving corporate objectives.

Product diversity should rarely, if ever, be entered into for its own sake. This is one of the lessons from experience—experience of companies that avoided such a mistake and diversified successfully, and experience of companies that through pressure of circumstances or unawareness of the difficulties involved in diversification made expansion moves that were regretted afterwards.

In fact much of the unsuccessful, ill-advised diversification in recent years might have been avoided if a careful analysis had been made of the problems which superficially seemed to warrant diversification. Problems such as a declining market share, unused plant capacity, or shrinking profit margins, while frequently amenable to diversification, may often be better resolved by more conservative methods. Relief from such pressures might be accomplished alternatively, for example, by greater efficiency in present operations, more productive use of current resources, more intensive market cultivation, or expansion of some present facility.

Empirical evidence ought to caution thoughtful administrators to at least consider the appropriateness of alternative courses of action for achieving objectives before proceeding with diversification that may lead the enterprise into relatively unknown areas with greater risk. The burden of proof should be placed on diversification as the optimum solution to the particular problems involved.

Executives likewise would be well advised not to regard diversification as a short-term tactical expedient, capable of resolving this year's operating problems or achieving the preferred rate of profit in the next fiscal period. A more prudent viewpoint holds diversification as an effective weapon of longer-term strategy.

Many of the most successful ventures have been characterized by the selection of growth product fields which were closely related to principal corporate strengths and long-range company objectives. To achieve such gratifying results, however, usually requires carefully formulated plans in advance of the search for new products.

Why companies diversify

A. SURVIVAL

1. *To offset a declining or vanishing market*—A traditional example of this was Studebaker's move into the automobile field from its previous carriage manufacturing business.

2. *To compensate for technological obsolescence*—With the advance of technology, a producer of a part for battery sets found it necessary to manufacture electric radio sets in order to stay in business.

3. *To offset obsolete facilities*—Entering the industrial lubricants field was the response of a company engaged in filtering operations, when the methods of refining oil changed, making filtering plants obsolete.

4. *To offset declining profit margins*—The meat packers, for example, have made every effort to develop by-products in order to enhance profit margins.

5. *To offset an unfavourable geographic location brought about by changing economic factors*—Some northern non-integrated paper mills have found it necessary to add speciality paper lines and convert their operations in order to meet the competition of southern integrated rivals.

B. STABILITY

1. *To eliminate or offset seasonal slumps*—A mechanical toy producer, motivated by a desire to offset a seasonal slump, began making electric fans.

2. *To offset cyclical fluctuations*—'The average machine tool builder has over a period of years investigated and actually undertaken diversification projects, with the object of flattening out the peaks and valleys in the demand for regular machine tool products,' says the president of a large machine tool company.

3. *To maintain employment of the labour force*—In 1943 when a $4½ million government parachute order was cancelled with a request to 'please stand by,' Textron began the production of shower curtains, draperies, and negligées in order to maintain employment of 3,500 people.

4. *To provide balance between high-margin and low-margin products*—Housewares and soft goods have been added by super-markets in part to achieve higher margins alongside low-margin food products.

5. *To provide balance between old and new products*—A food products manufacturer diversifies so no product gets more than a third of the company sales.

6. *To maintain market share*—A stove company, known for a low-price promotional line, purchased a company making a larger medium-price stove in order to capture a strategic share of the stove market.

7. *To meet new products of competitors*—The production of the Thunderbird by the Ford Motor Company may be presumed to stem from a motive to meet the competition of Chevrolet's new Corvette.

8. *To tie customers to the firm*—An ink manufacturer brought out a desk pen and ink stand which only his uniquely shaped ink bottles would fit.

9. *To distribute risk by serving several markets*—As a women's garment brand name became known in the consumer market, management believed it less dangerous to expand in several lines rather than to build up any one line to too large a percentage of the market, and added blouses and men's wear.

10. *To maintain an assured source of supply*—Olin Industries has combined diversification with integration, aiming at independence from outside suppliers.

11. *To assure an outlet for the sale of the product*—This has been an important reason for oil refineries entering the gasoline service station business.

12. *To develop a strong competitive supply position by offering several close substitute products*—A recent example of this was soap companies diversifying to include detergents in their lines.

C. PRODUCTIVE UTILIZATION OF RESOURCES

1. *To utilize waste or by-products*—A paper company added fibreboard to its line in order to make use of waste screenings and tailings.

2. *To maintain balance in vertical integration*—A canning company which had integrated backwards to manufacture cans for its own use decided to sell cans produced in excess of its requirements.

3. *To make use of basic raw material*—This is an important objective, for example, for rubber companies, who have become engaged in producing a wide variety of products made from rubber.

4. *To utilize excess productive capacity*—In one instance the manufacturer of plastic light fixtures was able to convert idle equipment to the production of plastic dishes.

5. *To make use of product innovations from internal technical research*—The research department of a petroleum company developed a medicinal oil for its own use, then began to manufacture it commercially.

6. *To capitalize distinctive know-how*—A company manufacturing hearing aids found its production skills adaptable to inter-office communication systems and subsequently diversified along these lines.

7. *To make full use of management resources*—The production of electric and coin weighing machines was undertaken by a manufacturer of sound-transmission equipment, in order to make the best use of an overbalance of production executives skilled in managing products requiring precision work.

8. *To utilize excess marketing capacity*—The J. M. Smucker Company has added such products as jams and jellies; i.e., products which are sold through the same channels as apple butter.

9. *To exploit the value of an established market position, trade name, or prestige*—The Globe-Wernicke Company believes diversification is an opportunity for greater recognition of brand names on a national scale than is possible from concentration on just one product line.

10. *To keep pace with an ever-increasing rate of technology*—Office machine companies have diversified into high-speed electronic digital computers.

11. *To capitalize on company research with existing techniques as well as its advances in technology*—Experimentation by a manufacturer of electrical goods led to the discovery of air cleaning by electrostatic precipitation of dust particles and concentration by ultraviolet radiation. Cleaning machines and sterilizing lamps were consequently added to the product line.

12. *To capitalize on a firm's market contacts*—A manufacturer of glass bulbs entered the production of glass tubing because of its uses by the same customers.

D. Adaptation to changing customer needs
1. *To meet the demands or convenience of diversified dealers*—As a result of a number of dealers' requests, a manufacturer of auto lubricants and chemicals began to produce tyre-patch kits.

2. *To meet the specific requests of important individuals and/or groups of customers*—In order to avoid the danger of loss of an

important customer's business in tin containers, a producer of tin cans, at the customer's request, began making a container of paper which incorporated tin ends.

3. *To meet government requests for national security*—The Packard Motor Car Company has been engaged in the defence production of airplanes and marine engines.

4. *To improve performance of existing products* (*equipment*) *through adding accessories or complementary products*—The United Shoe Machinery Corporation found it desirable to add auxiliary products such as eyelets, lasts, brushes, and others, in part to assure the successful performance of its machines.

E. GROWTH

1. *To counter market saturation on present products*—This has been a strong motive for radio manufacturers moving into the air-conditioning field.

2. *To reinvest earnings*—A games manufacturer is currently undergoing diversification for the sole reason of reinvesting earnings rather than paying exceptionally large dividends.

3. *To take advantage of unusually attractive merger or acquisition opportunities*—The president of a steamship company gave this as a reason for entering the outdoor advertising field.

4. *To stimulate the sale of basic products*—An example of this is the sale of electric appliances by utility companies in order to increase the consumption of their basic commodity, power.

5. *To encourage growth for its own sake or to satisfy the ambitions of management or owners*—A large national publisher of magazines follows the policy of adding a new magazine every seven years.

F. MISCELLANEOUS

1. *To realize maximum advantage from the tax structure*—A chemical company with a good excess profits tax base purchased a smaller company with outstanding earnings and a very poor tax base, to the mutual tax advantage of both companies.

2. *To salvage or make the best of previously acquired companies or products*—This is likely to be the case with companies which, in pursuit of specific products to bring about vertical integration, have purchased firms producing other commodities.

3. *To maintain a reputation for industrial leadership*—The president of the Otis Elevator Company recently stated that his company's policy is to seek only such diversification as is necessary for reasonable stability and will preserve the company's reputation for technical leadership in its field.

4. *To comply with the desires (or whims) of owners or executives*—Chief among the factors for a particular product addition in one firm was the fact that the owner of the company was an inventor who had developed a new type of sled for his children.

5. *To strengthen the firm by obtaining new management and abilities*—Some companies have been known to buy a firm in order to get an outstanding executive to add to their management group.

Role of planning

Some executives presume that nothing need be done before proceeding with the search for 'profitable' diversification opportunities. Available products are brought to the attention of management and examined individually as they are discovered. The decision-making process takes place without the benefit of planning to provide guides for executive judgement.

Of course, 'try it and see,' if carried far enough, may be one way of ultimately arriving at an acceptable solution. Or the right product may emerge if management is presented with a likely-looking opportunity on a provisional 'hunch' basis and then conscious attempts are made to come closer to what is wanted with succeeding product candidates. But why forego the advantages of a more organized and systematic approach from the beginning?

What is urged here is selective exploration of opportunities in the light of the special character and problems of the particular enterprise. This procedure often saves time, money, and effort in locating products that closely match the requirements and resources of the organization. Even if unusually attractive expansion opportunities come unexpectedly and demand hurried action if they are not to be lost, they can be more quickly and effectively appraised by executives who have a careful diversification policy planned well in advance of need.

What, then, are the basic elements of a sound programme of product diversification? In the light of the successful experience of a number of companies, these five steps should be useful:

1. A clear definition of objectives.

2. An analysis of the diversification situation in the light of present operations.

3. An audit of the tangible and intangible corporate resources for diversification.

4. Establishment of specific criteria for new products in line with the three preceding points.

5. A comprehensive search for products and their evaluation against the criteria.

Definition of objectives

Long-run profit maximization may be thought of as the primary goal of diversification. So general an objective, however, is too broad for short-run analytical purposes, since alone it provides no real guide for those evaluating the relative merits of various product opportunities.

A well-defined product strategy is often more useful—as, for example, the policy of a large electric motor manufacturer that all new products should serve to increase sales of its basic line of fractional and small integral horse-power motors (in effect products which incorporate its motors as components). But even this kind of objective, definitive as it is, can be superficial unless it expresses the fundamental need which leads the company to want to increase sales by diversification—e.g., to even out cyclical demand or to make up for obsolescence of existing products.

The underlying motivation must be crystallized and made explicit if it is to have any constructive effect on product decisions. The list of 'reasons' for diversification shown above indicates how great the range of motives is in actual practice.

The clue to successful formulation of objectives is to think in terms of what the company can *accomplish* through use of its resources rather than in terms of what products it may happen to find. Here the concept of convergence can be very useful.

Convergent production

When unused plant capacity is a major motive for diversification, products may be added that are suitable for manufacture with present facilities but not necessarily for distribution by the existing marketing mechanism. In contemplating this type of diversification, caution should be exercised in determining whether an adequate over-all marketing programme can be developed that will ensure effective and profitable market cultivation. The importance of this decision is exemplified by the fact that the greatest single cause of failure in the product additions of the 200 largest manufacturers of packaged consumer items, mentioned earlier, was the lack of a well-conceived and detailed marketing programme.

The International Paper Company once undertook to manufacture and sell a mulch paper to farmers, only to discover that small home gardeners were the sole realizable market; accordingly, different distributors were needed from those used for the company's other products. Ultimate marketing expenses were magnified, and no significant portion of the company's excess production capacity was utilized.[2]

Product expansion of this kind has often been followed by companies whose primary orientation was to production and whose top management tended to be dominated by personnel with manufacturing backgrounds.

It should be noted also that unused plant capacity—or even specialized production knowledge—is oftentimes at best a temporary or short-term source of competitive strength. Machinery and equipment, as well as production skills, often are readily accessible to potential competitors, whereas established market positions are characteristically much less transient.

Convergent marketing

Conspicuous success has often been enjoyed when product additions utilize the company's existing marketing structure and perhaps trade on its established reputation in the market, even though such products may require new and different manufacturing facilities. (Costs of market entry or initial investment can sometimes be minimized by sub-contracting or by securing the needed machinery on lease.) Diversification of this type is frequently most feasible and desirable when the company has a single or clearly dominant distribution mechanism as in the case of the multiplant or branch-plant firm whose production functions are decentralized but whose sales organization is closely knit through centralized management.

A well-organized and established marketing organization often constitutes an unusually effective competitive force. Capable sales personnel and a loyal dealer organization may be a company's most valuable assets, and ones which potential competitors would find hardest to duplicate. Established dealer priority is frequently a major barrier to market entry; hence, the addition of products that more fully serve those dealers can help to strengthen the company against competitors' inroads.

Actually, diversification into dissimilar but complementary lines often provides an opportunity for *greater* recognition of brand names on a national scale, and helps to establish a reputation of more far-reaching importance, than is possible with concentration on one product line.

The Globe-Wernicke Company, for example, has found product diversification to be a strong competitive advantage by fabricating not only complete lines of metal business equipment such as desks, tables, chairs, and modular equipment, but also distinctly different items in the paper goods field, such as filing folders, guides, index cards, and celluloid tabbing items.

Product expansion with convergent marketing is not always feasible, however, in that there is an outer limit to the breadth of product line for efficient and productive sales operations—a limit to the number and variety of products that a salesman can efficiently sell, as well as a limit to the number and different types of customers that he can profitably serve.

Full convergence

When existing (or similar) production and marketing facilities may both be used for the new product, the company has what might be called the ideal type of diversification. Full benefits of economies of scale should be realized as a broader base is provided for the spreading of overhead costs in both production and sales. The firm continues operations in closely related fields, with the maximum opportunity to take advantage of management skills and an established market position.

Thus, the Giddings and Lewis Machine Tool Company successfully added planers, vertical boring mills, and planer-type milling machines to an existing line of horizontal boring, drilling, and milling machines. In discussing these product additions, the president of the company emphasized that they were 'not in the nature of getting into someone else's business.' He also stated his belief that 'diversification should not be attempted unless the existing lines are already in a high state of development and standing up well competitively . . .'[3]

Because of the relative simplicity of adapting to this type of diversification, thoughtful management should thoroughly explore such opportunities before proceeding to any of the other types. Having both production and marketing convergence does not necessarily mean that the product additions will be successful, of course; nor is this to deny that some venturesome firms have achieved enviable results from completely divergent diversification. Technological advance and the product innovations of unusually creative or resourceful research departments often account for moves into fields completely new to the firm. No apparent rationale accounts for others—e.g., a steamship company's entrance into the outdoor advertising field.

Venturesome diversification seems to hold an alluring appeal for many executives. J. S. Knowlson, President of the Stewart Warner Corporation, said recently, 'Willingness and eagerness of American businessmen to tackle the problems and reap the profits of new fields, after they have proved their abilities in the ones in which they started out, is as traditionally a characteristic as is their belief in free enterprise.'[4]

The proportion of failures in divergent diversification none the less far exceeds that in convergent diversification. For this reason, product expansion which does not capitalize on company resources should be resisted until a thorough search has been conducted for more promising products; and in the event that divergent diversification is nevertheless undertaken, it should not be without the realization that the risks are greater.

Situation analysis

Once objectives have been determined, they must be appraised against the specific circumstances surrounding the diversification problem by what can be called a situation analysis. The need for this procedure, and what it involves, can best be demonstrated by an illustration:

Company X produced a product whose market was made up predominantly of young single men from the lower income groups, without college education, and ranging in age from 17 to 23. The company's growing idle productive capacity seemed to stem directly from a declining demand. Consequently, one of the important objectives established for diversification was to utilize an increasing amount of excess productive capacity.

When the problem was studied in some detail, it became evident that a low point in the market for the product had been reached because the number of potential customers had diminished. This market shrinkage was primarily a natural consequence of the low birth rate in the economically depressed 1930s. Other contributing factors included the large number of men in the age group in military service (unavailable for consumption of the product) and an abnormally high marriage rate for the age group.

A forecast of sales for several years in advance showed that rather sizeable sales increases could be expected as a larger number of potential customers became available from countering trends. Moreover, it was apparent that opportunities for additional sales were good as a result of slight, but important modifications in the marketing programme. In view of this situation analysis, a substantially smaller percentage of productive capacity was committed to diversification than had initially been anticipated. The company was able to achieve its over-all objectives with a limited diversification programme tailored to the actual situation.

The principal purpose of the situation analysis, then, is to permit weights or measures to be attached to objectives so that specific goals can be established for diversification—for example, to utilize a given percentage of plant capacity, to consume a given quantity of waste product, or to establish specific economic characteristics for product additions.

As a valuable by-product of the analysis, some alterations of present operations can frequently be prescribed to bring about improvement in the current position of the enterprise. Quite important, too, a final sharpening of the reasons for additions to the present line is brought about so that either they come out stronger and hence can be followed more confidently; or else they show up as untenable, and expensive, wasteful action is avoided.

Resource audit

Next, it is important to audit and appraise the tangible and intangible corporate assets which can be capitalized on. The principal diversification strengths (and limitations) of the several functional groups within the company—procurement, production, marketing, research, and so on—should be evaluated both individually and collectively, and compared to competitors' resources in these areas.

The audit should proceed first with the measure of the tangible factors involved, including such things as financial strength, the nature of the manufacturing process, the type and quality of machinery and equipment used, the number and versatility of research personnel and facilities, the size and character of the marketing organization, and the nature and type of staff service available. This type of corporate resource is usually readily susceptible to appraisal and often can be measured with a relatively high degree of precision.

The intangible assets of a company, unfortunately, are not usually so readily apparent. Moreover, the value judgements involved in what must be largely a subjective appraisal are open to controversy and difference of opinion. Yet oftentimes the intangible strengths of the enterprise are the most important competitive advantages for diversification.

Important intangible considerations include the quality of engineering skills, the resourcefulness of technical research personnel, the flexibility or adaptability of the management, the character of thinking and centres of interest of individual management members, the recognizable attributes by which the firm is known in the trade, and the unusual know-how or dominant orientation which provides

a quality of lasting distinctiveness for the enterprise. An appreciation of the consequences of these intangibles may be gained by
noting several cases:

(a) A large watch manufacturer chose for diversification a line
of ladies' compacts, which initially appeared almost ideally suited
to the company's operations. The firm was known for the quality
of its product, had a well-recognized brand name, and enjoyed
special standing in the jewellery trade. Ladies' compacts, however,
proved to be out of character with the distinctive know-how of the
company. The continuous but unexpected mark-downs which were
traditional for this class of product and the importance of style
which called for frequent design changes proved to be incompatible
with the firm's traditional operations.

On the other hand, the company's long experience in the manufacture of high-quality precision watches had provided almost
unique competency in the field of miniaturization. Even though the
company had no previous experience in the industrial market, later
events indicated that an unusual opportunity for successful diversification existed in the field of small scientific precision instruments.

(b) A second illustration involves a closely held corporation
with a long history in the manufacture of a high-price sports product. All members of top management had for many years been
sporting enthusiasts. For more than a decade the company had
considered diversification but was reluctant to do so except on
the basis of absolute necessity. In these circumstances, additions to
the product line probably needed to be characterized by a quality
of 'glamour', on a par with its existing products; otherwise, they
would not secure the necessary managerial interest and attention to
assure a high probability of commercial success.

(c) Finally, an extreme example of the influence of intangibles
is provided by the case of a proposed merger. The smaller company
being considered for acquisition seemed ideally suited as a diversification opportunity in view of the competitive position and principal resources of the larger firm. Negotiations proceeded on the
basis that the management of the smaller firm would continue to
operate the business as a division of the acquiring firm: Not only
was such an arrangement demanded by the owners of the smaller
firm as a part of any agreement to sell their equity, but also it was
desirable from the larger firm's point of view because of the need
for specialized management.

Yet, once personal contact had been established between the two
management groups, the president of the larger firm discontinued
negotiations because the president of the smaller firm was of differ-

ent racial origin and in his judgement not likely to fit in as a member of a combined top management. In this situation psychological considerations were determining.

In sum, diversification appears most likely to be successful when it capitalizes on the unique know-how or special qualities which provide the firm with lasting distinctiveness as against perishable distinctiveness. In this respect, final judgement should weigh heavily the human capabilities available for the venture.

Product criteria

The fourth step in programming diversification involves establishing specific criteria or specifications for products or product fields in accordance with the findings from the preceding analysis. Here, the purpose is to set forth in detail the characteristics of a model product, which can then be useful in providing direction to the search for product candidates and in helping to evaluate them, once found.

Two classifications of criteria can be established: (a) *required* characteristics, and (b) *ideal* characteristics. The *required* characteristics derive from the primary strategic objectives which were established for diversification; these are the criteria which must be met if the diversification is to accomplish the ends which were orginally intended. The *ideal* criteria, or desired specifications of the model product, result from the analysis of the particular situation faced by the company and the resource audit of the major strengths of the company to be capitalized on in diversification.

For example, the criteria established for Company Y, a manufacturer of internal combustion engines, were as follows:

Required characteristics

Will use excess tool capacity.
Requires minimum additional investment in production equipment.

Ideal product characteristics

Similar to internal combustion engine in customer performance requirements.
Requires medium precision production.
Medium bulk size.
Broader market than now served.
Minimum investment for sales, service, distribution.
Will support the sale of present products.

Uses existing service organization.
Complements existing seasonal sales pattern.
High value added by manufacture.
Basis for further diversification.
Capitalizes brand name.

Obviously, no individual product candidate could be expected
to meet all the criteria established by management. Nevertheless,
once relative importance has been attached to the individual characteristics, a meaningful basis exists for evaluating potential additions to the line.

Search and selection

Executive judgement and participation are vitally important in
carrying forward the planning for diversification through these first
four stages, which may account for as much as 40 per cent of the
total activity in finding new products. From this point on, with
such a blueprint to guide them, specialized personnel can carry on
the product search, subsequently reporting back to top management for final review and decision.

Experience indicates that a productive search for diversification
opportunities has these four requisites:

1. Able personnel to conduct the search and appraise and
screen candidate opportunities.

2. An economical basis for uncovering an adequate number of
candidate products which appear to dovetail with the diversification
planning.

3. A rational basis of allocating expensive research in depth to
the most worthy candidates.

4. Effective follow-up to insure decisive action.

Screening process

In searching for candidate products which closely match the
diversification criteria, it is often wise to employ a funnelling process by starting off with as many new product ideas as possible
and then narrowing the field successively through (a) initial screening, (b) preliminary market audit, and (c) research in depth.
(Sources of new product ideas include field survey of users, prospects, and distributors; analysis of company sales experience; research department; marketing and production executives, salesmen,
production workers; analysis of competitive offerings; and industrial designers.)

The initial screening process is designed to eliminate product areas that do not compare favourably with the required and ideal characteristics of the model product—solely on the basis of readily distinguishable factors. Thus, the products meeting the criteria of Company Y set forth above included: garden tractors, outboard motors, motor generator units, motor compressor units, motor pump units, industrial trucks, materials handling equipment, refrigeration machinery, air conditioning equipment, engine accessories, compressed-air drilling equipment, industrial engines, measuring and dispensing pumps, and blowers and ventilation equipment.

The list of candidates surviving the primary screening can often be further narrowed by management judgement. A modest field investigation can usually provide the basis for quickly and convincingly discarding some products which at first appear to meet the desired critieria. For example, research was unnecessary to determine that a particular company with long experience in hand-blown table glassware was not capable of producing magnifying lenses, but a short, economical market audit was needed to reveal that the company was also very poorly situated for the manufacture and sale of hand-blown laboratory-type glassware. This type of approach enables the analyst to use rational discrimination for allocating expensive research in depth to the more promising candidate products.

The final screening is characterized by thorough research of the three or four products that have stood the test of preliminary research appraisal. A penetrating investigation includes an analysis of at least the following factors: industry growth, industry structure, competitive environment, important features and characteristics of existing products, potential technological obsolescence, characteristics of the market, purchase requirements and factors influencing the choice of suppliers, the effectiveness and costs of appropriate channels of distribution, methods and cost of demand cultivation, opportunity for market entry by a firm new to the field, requirements for market entry, and of course the general suitability of the product field in the light of the established criteria.

Quantitative evaluation

An attempt to quantify the degree of fit of various candidate products within the diversification blueprint is a helpful supplement to research in depth. The use of product profiles is one approach to this problem.

Fig. 1 is a visual presentation of a diversification opportunity matched to the criteria established by Company Y. The relative

Required Diversification Criteria (in order of importance)	No fit	Degree of Fit			Full fit
		25%	50%	75%	

Use excess tool capacity
Minimum additional production equipment

Ideal Diversification Criteria (in order of importance)

Similar to present production know-how

High value added by manufacture

Support main product sales

Minimum investment for sales, service

Counterseasonal to present sales

Medium precision production

Utilize present service organization
Broader market
Capitalize on firm name

Medium bulk size
Basis for further diversification

Fig. 1 *Product profile: evaluating extent to which product X meets established diversification criteria*

importance of the criteria (qualitatively) is reflected by the descending order of rank, and a gradient of fulfilment (quantitative) is shown by the horizontal bars. By matching product x (an actual product) to the criteria in this manner, a quantification results which facilitates comparison, thus aiding in the selection process. Estimations must be on the basis of the best evidence available and necessarily cannot be precise.

Fig. 2 compares corporate resources with the important entry requirements for any firm seeking to compete in the market for product x. Entry requirements have been classified as primary and secondary and are ranked in order of importance. The horizontal bars again provide a picture of how well the company resources dovetail with these entry requirements. Factors which register a poor fit or no fit should be viewed in terms of their availability and cost from outside the firm.

Throughout, of course, potential profit and return on investment must be the paramount consideration. Quantitative evaluation of the type just described makes no sense except in that light. Cost and profit analysis, together with the other research findings, should provide a reliable factual base for the judgement and vision of top executives who must make the final decisions.

The procedure outlined here might appear to discourage creative thinking to the exclusion of 'imaginative' product candidates that might not be born of an orderly and logical search. On the contrary, experience indicates that such candidates are more likely to be discovered when some parameters have been given to the problem. Selective exploration is an important aid to insight. A new view

	Degree of Fit				
Primary Entry Requirements (in order of importance)	*No fit*	*25%*	*50%*	*75%*	*Full fit*
Plant for line production					
Technical sales					
Engineering development skills					
Secondary Entry Requirements (in order of importance)					
Production skills					
Specialized production equipment					
Financial investment					
Reputation for quality of product					
Geographic location					
Raw-material supply source					

Fig. 2 *Product profile; evaluating extent to which company Y meets requirements of market entry*

of the situation which will lead on to a valuable solution may burst on the analyst in the midst of his explorations. Furthermore, random imagination is not as reliable in itself as the more orderly system proposed.

Case example

The following case demonstrates the general approach to diversi-fiction outlined here and its potential application by business execu-tives to their own individual companies:

The First Paper Company, a northern non-integrated mill, pro-duced a variety of fine and coarse paper products. As was true with other similar northern mills, the company had suffered serious inroads from the competition of southern mills. Although a number of products were distributed through both fine and coarse paper merchants, the bulk of the sales were made to a relatively limited number of direct mill accounts which had been built up over a number of years through the personal efforts of company executives.

The mill's declining competitive position was abruptly magnified with the loss of one large and important customer who accounted for approximately 25 per cent of the gross sales of the company. In view of the critical condition of the mill it was concluded by management that additional product diversity was essential.

Several strategic objectives were established by management for new products. To improve the mill's position materially, additions to the line should (a) be suitable for production on present equipment with no more than minor machine changes and modest additions of accessory equipment; (b) be of a character which precluded efficient production by southern mills; and (c) allow a minimum profit of $40 per machine hour.

The situation analysis indicated the characteristics of products that would be unsuitable for competitive southern mills which enjoyed four principal advantages: (a) newer, bigger, faster equipment, (b) lower wage rates, (c) lower raw material costs, and (d) economics of operation from combining pulp and paper mill operations. Hence the new products of the First Paper Company should have a particularly high value added by manufacture to offset or minimize the lower raw material costs and cheaper labour of southern mills, a particular quality of pulp not readily accessible to the South, relatively frequent short production runs to offset or minimize the superior size and speed of southern equipment, and also, if possible, a market allowing a considerable potential sale within a relatively small radius of the mill to take advantage of freight differentials.

When the resource audit was made, it revealed that the First Paper Company held a distinguished reputation in the trade as a quality mill, was known for its business integrity, and was particularly competent in the production of intricate grades of paper with close tolerances. This study also revealed that a number of areas in the present marketing operations of the company could be substantially improved. For example, inadequate market coverage existed and sales territories were badly out of alignment. Some of these problems were thus subject to short-term corrective action on the part of management. Plans for diversification were then made which reflected the desired goals, the situation analysis, and the resource audit.

Next, a preliminary market audit was made of a wide range of grades, falling in the lightweight paper field. As a result, several particular grades were selected for comprehensive market appraisal. One of the products surviving the final screening and selected by management to be introduced to the market was a technical reproduction paper used in a variety of business machines. The product dovetailed closely with the blueprint for diversification and appeared to be an especially suitable competitive opportunity for these reasons:

1. The market for the product was growing at a rate appreciably more rapid than the field of lightweight papers as a whole.

2. A sufficient market potential existed for sales substantially in excess of the idle capacity on machines suitable for the production of this particular grade of paper.

3. The market was not dominated by integrated mills; on the contrary, the smaller mills were capable of effective and aggressive competition. Buyers typically purchased in reasonably small lots, which mitigated the long runs required by southern mills.

4. The product had a particularly high value added by manufacture to minimize the raw material and labour advantages of southern rivals.

5. The number of potential customers provided a reasonably broad customer base to minimize the possibility of a large reduction in sales occurring through the loss of one account.

6. The majority of dominant buyers were located in close proximity to the mill, providing excellent opportunity for market penetration.

7. The product was particularly suited to the technical knowledge and excellent quality characterizing the operations of the company. Precise manufacturing specifications had to be met.

8. The product was compatible with the present or contemplated production and marketing facilities of the company. Only modest operational changes were required prior to the introduction of the product. Finally, substantial evidence was available to indicate that adequate opportunity existed for market entry by a new firm.

The case is described here merely for the purpose of indicating the feasibility of the application of planned diversification to the peculiar problems of individual firms. Executives can be expected to make appropriate adjustments to reflect their own circumstances.

Conclusion

Diversification as a means of market adjustment is now the centre of widespread executive interest. Administrators should recognize however, that product diversity has substantial elements of risk. The burden of proof should be placed on diversification, in the light of alternative courses of action, as the optimum solution to the economic problems confronting management. If the grounds for diversification are really tenable, comprehensive planning in the spirit of an orderly problem-solving process is particularly important. This requires a careful selection of objectives, an analysis of present operations and competitive environment, and a thorough audit of the tangible and intangible resources to be capitalized in diversification.

These procedures, manifested in a diversification blueprint, provide the basis for selective exploration of product opportunities and simplify appraisal and decision making. Selective exploration proceeds through initial screening, preliminary market appraisal, and research in depth. This analytical task is likely to be most productive when delegated to a full-time specialist instead of relying on committee action or on executives already burdened with functional responsibility.

In the past, aloofness to the requirements of the market place has been a major reason for misfortune in product diversification. In this respect special production facilities or unusual manufacturing know-how should be recognized as a temporary source of competitive power, while entrenched market positions are characteristically much less transient. Selection of the most appropriate means of market entry is therefore of special importance to policy makers; so also is careful organizational planning for integrating the added product or enterprise into the existing operations of the firm.

By recognizing diversity as a longer-term strategy move and insisting on a tailored programme for action, executives can contribute much to the successful diversification of their companies.

REFERENCES

1 — *The introduction of new products.* Survey done by Ross Federal Corpn. for Peter Hilton Inc.
2 Malcolm, P. *et al.* (1949) *Problems in marketing.* McGraw-Hill, N. York, p. 174.
3 — (1953) Top management forum. *Industrial Marketing,* Sept. 6. p. 102.
4 — *ibid,* p. 10.

12 | Planned Product Diversification
by W. E. HILL

MANY companies in New England and throughout the US are asking some very searching questions regarding the future development of their sales and profits and in turn, their organization and facilities.

Long-range sales and profit forecasts for each of its ten divisions have been formulated by one company. In another case, a company is determining the proportionate share of management time, effort and imagination and corporate investment required by each of its four major product lines for the next five years. Still another company has a new products committee examining the future prospects of existing products in each of three major divisions and the requirement for new products to replace, supplement and complete these lines.

Inevitably, in each of these companies the question of diversifying beyond its present products has arisen. These are the questions most often raised in such cases:

1. What are the general advantages of diversification, as experienced by other companies?
2. What are the specific advantages of a planned and organized programme of diversification?

WILLIAM E. HILL is President of William E. Hill and Company, and William E. Hill International. The firm maintains offices in New York, Brussels and London. A graduate of Yale University, Mr Hill has been active in the management consulting business approximately 30 years. He is recognized for the development with his associates of original management practices in long range planning, corporate strategies, organization planning, and management development.

Mr Hill is a director and trustee of a number of industrial and banking companies and institutions.

This chapter is reprinted with permission from: *Industry*, official publication of Associated Industries of Massachusetts, April 1954.

3. Have we the qualifications to diversify, particularly in our management and in our management outlook on the future?
4. Have we legitimate objectives for diversification, such as an increased return on investment stability of operations and others?
5. How do we lay out a 'blueprint' or programme for diversification?
6. How do we organize our activities to successfully carry out the programme?

It is not unusual that management should ask these questions. The planned approach to product diversification is only twenty years old as a corporate concept. While it is now an established practice with a number of highly successful companies, as evidenced by the William E. Hill Company recent survey of fifty companies engaged in product diversification, it is only recently that it has become recognized as a new and specialized tool of management. Even today there are a hundred companies chasing new products unsuccessfully for the one that is using a well-organized and planned approach.

Principal advantages of diversification

Historically, we are all familiar with the fact that an analysis of companies with unbroken dividend records usually discloses continuing and sound new product development as the underlying basis responsible for their progressive growth and prosperity. DuPont forecast that in 1970 at least 60 per cent of their income would be derived from products either unheard of at the time or only then in their infancy.

Many an industrial company is organizationally and financially capable of making the transition through sound product diversification from an old or single-product company in an unstable and static industry to a growing, highly profitable corporate organization. Other companies in a growth industry find that participation in one or more additional new fields is beneficial to their operations.

The odds on the success of this major transition are excellent—companies which have incorporated continuing programmes of sound diversification into their basic operating policies have achieved remarkable results. With astute management of an organized plan of diversification, a company can enjoy advantages today which even some of the most successful diversifying companies in the accompanying table and charts did not have when they first launched their programme.

Some of the more significant advantages of product diversification are illustrated by the results, shown on the charts, of four companies selected from many known to our firm.

1. Higher return on investment. Pre-tax earnings of successful growing companies often range from 20 per cent to 50 per cent annually on invested capital. Money reinvested and compounded at these rates grows very rapidly.

   American Machine & Foundry Company, with newly acquired companies accounting for 31 per cent of total sales

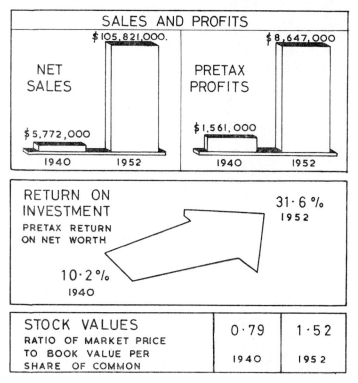

Fig. 1

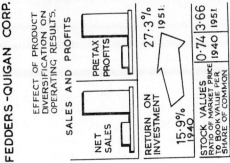

FOOD MACHINERY AND
CHEMICAL CORPORATION
EFFECT OF PRODUCT
DIVERSIFICATION ON
OPERATING RESULTS.

SALES AND PROFITS

NET SALES

PRETAX PROFITS

RETURN ON INVESTMENT
20·4% 1940
30·3% 1952

STOCK VALUES
RATIO OF MARKET PRICE
TO BOOK VALUE PER
SHARE OF COMMON.

0·61	1·44
1940	1952

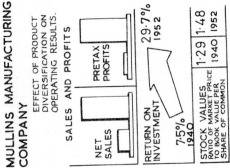

MULLINS MANUFACTURING
COMPANY
EFFECT OF PRODUCT
DIVERSIFICATION ON
OPERATING RESULTS.

SALES AND PROFITS

NET SALES

PRETAX PROFITS

RETURN ON INVESTMENT
7·5% 1940
29·7% 1952

STOCK VALUES
RATIO OF MARKET PRICE
TO BOOK VALUE PER
SHARE OF COMMON

1·29	1·48
1940	1952

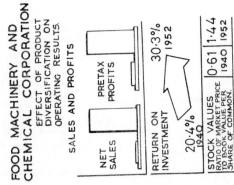

FEDDERS-QUIGAN CORP.

EFFECT OF PRODUCT
DIVERSIFICATION ON
OPERATING RESULTS.

SALES AND PROFITS

NET SALES

PRETAX PROFITS

RETURN ON INVESTMENT
15·9% 1940
27·3% 1951

STOCK VALUES
RATIO OF MARKET PRICE
TO BOOK VALUE PER
SHARE OF COMMON

0·74	3·66
1940	1951

Fig. 2

in 1952 and with a sizeable and permanent defence products programme, is illustrative of the four companies. Pre-tax return on AMF's net worth increased from 10.2 per cent in 1940 to 31.6 per cent in 1952. This is the real measure of management.

2. Enhancement of market value of stock. A recent inquiry of a number of industrial companies disclosed only one-sixth with a market price greater than book value per share of common stock.

   Entrance of Fedders-Quigan Corp. into air conditioning field has changed its ratio of market to book value from 0.74 in 1940 to 3.66 in 1951. Each of the other three illustrations have benefited by diversification.

3. Stability of sales and profits. Rapidly growing product fields do not reflect the sharp instability in operations suffered by cyclical and many mature industries.

   Mullins Manufacturing Company is not solely dependent on its industrial contract work but has tapped the growth kitchen products market, supported by the revolution in consumer housekeeping habits.

EXAMPLES OF SOUND DIVERSIFICATION

Expansion in sales and profits

	Sales (millions)			Pretax Profits (millions)		
	1940	1952	Per cent Increase	1940	1952	Per cent Increase
American-Marietta Company	$ 2.9	$ 76.7	2529	$ 0.1	$ 6.5	4641
Borg-Warner Corporation	75.2	353.9	371	7.5	60.0	700
Harnischfeger Corporation	9.3	60.2	543	0.8	9.2	984
McGraw Electric Company	8.3	104.9	1170	2.2	15.4	596
Minneapolis Honeywell Regulator Co.	15.9	165.7	940	3.8	20.6	442
Minnesota Mining & Manufacturing	21.0	785.2	783	6.8	41.4	507
Rheem Manufacturing Company	10.4	144.5	1296	0.8	7.2	831
Rockwell Manufacturing Company	9.3	85.9	820	1.4	10.2	621
All Manufacturing (billions)	70.3	276.5	293	5.8	25.3	336

4. Expansion in sales and profits. Diversification is not limited to large companies. The four examples on the accompanying charts were not large companies in 1940, ranging in sales from $5.8 million to $10.4 million. Yet their growth in sales and profits in the 1940-52 period exceeded the comparative average of all manufacturing's 293 per cent increase in sales and 336 per cent increase in profits. Sheer expansion in size, however, is not the principal motive of sound diversification.

Taxes have changed the historical New England approach to capital accumulation. Money made in profitable years was put away and used to offset periods of economic recession. This particularly applied to machinery and other capital goods companies. The tax structure today practically prevents the continuance of this practice. It is therefore necessary in many cases to consider product diversification as the means of offsetting unstable operations.

A major programme of planned product diversification was announced in the *Worcester* (*Mass.*) *Gazette*, on February 3, by Crompton & Knowles Loom Works, one of the oldest and most respected names in the textile machinery field. Under the progressive leadership of its new president, Frederic W. Howe, this 120-year-old company is planning to acquire companies in one or more of three growth industries. These fields are new to Crompton & Knowles, but capitalize on the technological skills and other corporate strengths of the company.

Advantages of the planned approach to diversification

Planned product diversification provides more certain results by attaining specific objectives in the expansion of a company and by reducing the time and risk inherent in such an undertaking.

Diversification is an essentially difficult job to accomplish successfully. It may not be achieved for two to four years. Because there is no easy or quick method of achieving it, proper planning and organization are vital requisites in launching a new programme of diversification.

There has, of course, been the occasional company without a purposeful programme which has 'struck it rich' with an opportunistic acquisition of a new product or company. Odds against such a situation are heavy. In contrast to a few successes of this sort are the hundreds of costly failures and frustrations experienced by companies which have attempted to diversify without properly organizing for it. Most of the aircraft manufacturers, and many of the shipbuilding and railroad equipment companies, particularly after World War II, failed in diversifying their operations by haphazard and unplanned methods.

By 'blueprinting' the factors involved and the steps to be taken, common agreement can be reached by the management and Board of Directors on exactly what they should and should not do and why. Planned diversification avoids all the frustrations resulting from various members of the management and director group having different interpretations of the Company's needs and different ideas of what should be done.

Among the advantages to a company of such a programme are:

1. Specific objectives or goals can be established and achieved for the future development of a company.
    Everyone involved (management, directors, stockholders) will know what these objectives are and where the company is headed.
2. The advantages of various methods of obtaining new products can be predetermined—acquisition of companies, product development, or other practices best suited to the company.
3. A company can capitalize on its unique strengths by entering specified fields requiring the company's particular abilities and character. Random entry into product fields where the company has no peculiar advantages offers far less opportunity and can often damage the future of the company.
4. Workable specifications prevent costly frustrations experienced by many companies in attempting diversification without knowing exactly what they are looking for and as a result rarely finding it. They also permit quick identification of desirable prospects and prompt elimination of unsuitable situations.
5. Concentration in specified growth fields enhances the prospects for long-term future benefits to the company. Diversification in the favourable environment of a growing industry greatly increases the company's opportunity for future growth and profits, and avoids acquisition of miscellaneous companies and products based solely on appraisal of their past records.
6. Organization of diversification efforts in a special department prevents management diversion from their regular duties,

and permits economies based on professional and specialized techniques.

7. Planned diversification points out what a company has to work with in its diversification programme, and what the company must do to sharpen its 'financial trading weapons' for most effective results.

Donald C. McGraw, the new president of McGraw-Hill, in his recent editorial, 'Business is Building a Foundation for Future Prosperity', underlined well the case for planning in diversification and expansion programmes.

'Business plans for 1954 do not represent a haphazard expansion, such as those that marked our earlier and more speculative booms. In the great majority of cases, the 1954 plans for plant improvement are in line with carefully worked-out long-range goals that the companies have developed by many months of planning. These expenditures are connected with plans to enter new markets, diversify production and modernize facilities.'

Does every company qualify for diversification?

At present there are two very strong schools of miscellaneous thinking regarding the desirability of product diversification. One group is all for it, with the extremists loudly proclaiming, 'Oh sure, we'll consider new products. What have you got to suggest?' This group also includes the 'lip-service' type, illustrated by the 70-year-old chairman of a single-product company saying, 'Yes, our directors are interested in diversification and, if I only had the time, I'd carry it out myself.'

The other group is on the other side of the fence, crying 'Everyone is getting in everyone else's field. Diversification is not for us; we're going to stick to our last. After all we are specialists in our own field.'

In between these two extremes are the companies seriously exploring the desirability of diversification. They realize that not every company should undertake the diversification of its existing product lines. Nor can every company carry out a planned programme even if they have one. If this is so, how does a company qualify?

First of all, J. S. Knowlson, President, Stewart-Warner Corporation, made this statement in the September, 1953, issue of *Industrial Marketing* that specialization and diversification are compatible.

'While it is true that accomplishment in a given field can lead to recognition of a company as a specialist in that field, it does not follow that the company's interests or future must be solely or primarily in that direction. Successful specialization does not rule out diversification.

'I believe then, that the ideal situation is one in which a company is recognized for both diversification and specialization. Such a company can enter new fields with the advantages inherent in public acceptance of its name, and without creating the impression that is has found competition too tough in the old field.'

To determine objectively whether it qualifies for diversification, a company should ask itself four basic questions.

1. Is it unable, due to conditions beyond its own control, to meet its objective in its own fielid? Four important objectives of corporate development are listed below.
2. Is it just seeking 'greener grass' or the easy way out of its own management ineptitude? Mr Knowlson puts its nicely. '. . . that diversification is only for companies after they have proved their abilities in the fields in which they have started out.'
3. Is the organization free of 'corporate arteriosclerosis'? This is the term used by Morehead Patterson, President, American Machine & Foundry Company, to describe the type of management, including officers and directors, which is unable to adopt to new types of thinking required in building a sound corporate position in a new product field. The William E. Hill Company will not take on an assignment in product diversification planning unless it first feels that the management has the all-important will and capacity to carry out the programme.
4. Is the management fully appreciative that a diversification programme is usually for long-term company development? Results will not show up in a financial statement in a matter of a month or two. Diversification should not be a matter which management talks about when business is poor and sidetracks when business is good.

The principal management decision is to have legitimate corporate objectives which can be accomplished by diversification. Among the sparse literature on the subject of product diversification is an article in *Harvard Business Review*, by Kenneth R. Andrews.[1] It is

H

an excellent source of information on the relationship of corporate objectives to diversification. The William E. Hill Company uses it as reference material in its training of individuals selected to manage new product departments in industrial companies.

Four corporate objectives of diversification are worth commenting on:

1. Increased growth and earnings. The Elgin National Watch Company, which announced its diversification programme in 1953, found that intense competiton in its industry limited the attainment of certain important corporate objectives. In Elgin's brochure, 'A Programme of Diversification', J. G. Shennan, President, states as a matter of company policy:

   'Basically these objectives are a higher return on investment and sizeable additional sales in new and fast-growing fields.'

   W. R. Grace & Company, the well-known shipping and trading organization, is rapidly becoming one of the largest chemical producers in the United States. In a brilliant address before the Newcomen Society on November 19, 1953, J. P. Grace, Jr., President, outlined his company's diversification objectives:

   'The picture therefore (in 1945) was one of about equal distribution of our assets between North and South America, but with the South American business enjoying far wider geographical distribution and much sounder diversification than our United States enterprises . . . Without diminishing the pace and force of our development programme in South America . . . we set forth on a parallel course of diversification and industrial expansion in the United States.'

2. Increased stability of sales and earnings. Diversification can offset seasonal instability such as A. C. Gilbert Company adding fans to its Erector sets. It also can offset one industry instability with Crompton & Knowles Loom Works exploring three non-textile machinery product fields. American Brake Shoe Company has achieved major success in its diversification beyond the railroad equipment field. William B. Given, Jr., Chairman, has pointed out that in 1952 general industrial sales of Brake Shoe amounted to $70 million or 51 per cent of total shipments.

3. Further utilization of company assets or resources. Besides rounding out a product line, this can include use of manufacturing capacity, use of an established marketing organization or distribution systems as pointed out by John A. Carter, President, Oakite Products, Inc., use of laboratory developments as B. F. Goodrich Company has done with Koroseal, exploration of an established trade mark or reputation, or simply putting to work corporate fat in the form of liquid assets to provide a greater turnover of capital.

4. Other objectives. By acquisition of companies certain types of management can be obtained to supplement the present organization. Also, by this means patents, established distribution systems and other ready-made objectives can be realized often at less cost than by development from within.

Diversification has contributed to the growth and stability of Rockwell Manufacturing Company, Willard F. Rockwell, Jr., President, made this statement in the June, 1953, issue of *Industrial Marketing*:

'The diversification programme has had to meet many tests . . . The comparisons . . . show we were much better off than our competitors who operated in narrow market areas . . . Our competitors' net profits have dropped considerably. One of our major competitors has dropped from 6.11 per cent to 3.76 per cent. Another from 5.84 per cent to 3.02 per cent. A third from 6.23 per cent to 2.38 per cent. We consider 1952 a disappointing year, yet we were still able to maintain a 6.78 per cent ratio after taxes.

'We realize that diversification alone isn't a cure-all. It is not the magic word that opens the door to success. But it can be made to work and the results are worth while. What makes it work is pre-planning.'

How to plan and organize a diversification programme

Three activities are most important to a company in successfully carrying out a major product diversification programme. The first is the imaginative layout or 'blueprint' of the programme. The second is the skilful organization and conduct of this specialized work. The third is to get the company's financial and corporate 'trading weapons' in shape to develop or acquire new products and companies.

The planning and layout of the programme is essential to guide, direct and budget the company's efforts and investment in diversifying its operations. It formalizes the company's new product activities and reduces the time and risk inherent in entering new product fields. There are six principal parts in the development of the 'blueprint'.

1. Determine the objectives of diversification and establish goals in sales, profits and other corporate requirements to be achieved through the establishment of this programme. If it takes an average of seven years to complete the engineering and development of an automatic machine, a company may find non-machinery products will more quickly realize growth in sales and profits.
2. Evaluate the company's corporate strengths, tangible and intangible, as a base on which to build the new products programme and to capitalize on the existing abilities, skills, assets and character of the organization in entering related fields. A company can be evaluated as well as a person, and William E. Hill Company has adapted psychological techniques in this type of analysis.

    Mr Grace describes corporate character as follows:

    > 'A business that has lived a hundred years acquires inevitably a flavour and a character that is unique. More important, it also acquires, whether the individual actors at the time realize it themselves or not, a distinctive business philosophy which guides it and runs as a common thread through the decades and across the diverse business situations it encompasses.'

3. Set up specifications for the selection of new product fields based primarily on the corporate objectives of the diversification programme and the corporate strengths of the company.
4. Select broad but well-defined product fields with sound future prospects that fit the objectives of the programme and capitalize on the corporate strengths. Mr Grace again is specific, this time on the selection of the chemical industry, not only as a growth field, but because it capitalized on a corporate strength:

    > 'Studies convinced us that for growth purposes the United States chemical industry was unrivalled, and particularly petrochemicals and chemicals related to agriculture. You are mindful of the fact that we had know-

how in this field gained by almost a century of experience
with Peruvian guano and Chilean nitrate of soda.'

5. Determine if product development, product acquisition, or
company acquisition, or a combination of all three is most
suited to the company's needs. These methods are listed in
ascending order of desirability for speed and low-cost in
achieving results. Even companies with somewhat limited
capital resources have achieved successful diversification by
acquisition. Charles F. Adams, Jr., President, Raytheon
Manufacturing Company, has a policy in the electronics field
that at this time is primarily product development, based on
the engineering and productive know-how of the company.
Basically, this is the policy of DuPont and Minnesota Mining
and Manufacturing Company. American Machine &
Foundry is dedicated to company acquisition but at the same
time maintains a large engineering staff for its automatic
machinery development. American Home Products' diversification has been primarily by acquisition of companies.

6. Establish a specialized organization. Concentrate the search,
appraisal, negotiation and integration activities under one
man, usually reporting to the president. This provides a
continuity of operation, and prevents diverting other members of management from their regular duties.

Train this man in the established practices of commercial
research and commercial development so that he gets a continuous flow of new product ideas for screening and appraisal
in line with the established specifications.

There are now a number of specialized commercial development managers in leading companies, concentrating on
diversification programmes. The William E. Hill Company
holds meetings of a number of these men throughout the year.

Organization of the product diversification activities is a full-time
and continuing task. They include the selection, appraisal, acquisition and integration of new companies and products. This is
specialized work and is no part-time job for one or more other-
wise-occupied executives.

The paramount principle in a comprehensive programme is to
diversify into product fields that will be a commercial as well as a
technical success. This requires the predetermination of the commercial prospects of new product fields. Rockwell's Facility Purchase Formula is a particularly well-developed guide for this type
of pre-determination.

Without this approach, diversification can be a sorrowful business.

There are many examples of companies that have done an outstandingly excellent *financial* job in acquiring new products. Most companies have the means and the time to get their corporate and financial 'trading weapons' in shape. A programme may be exceptional but without the cash, credit or stock to use for acquisitions or development, the plan is solely a plan. Financial public relations play an increasingly important part in this part of a diversification programme.

The planned approach to product diversification achieves maximum results in company expansion and development. A well-thought out and organized programme, avoids diversification becoming solely diversion in time, effect and capital.

Mr Knowlson states the current situation in regard to diversification in these words:

'I do not believe that diversification—which has resulted from a balanced blending of imagination, self-confidence, and ability —has even reached a plateau. Nor do I believe that any corporation, unless it is resigned to a static future, can afford to close its eyes to opportunities to diversify.

'Willingness to tackle problems and reap profits of new product fields is as traditional as belief in free enterprise.'

REFERENCE

1 Andrews, Kenneth R. (1951) Product diversification and the public interest. *Harvard Business Review*, July.

13 | Merger Objectives *and* Organization Structure

by H. IGOR ANSOFF and J. FRED WESTON*

WHEN a firm is merged into another its organizational structure may undergo far-reaching changes. New top management may be brought in. There may be changes and consolidations of physical plant; certain staff functions, such as accounting and industrial relations, may be consolidated into the parent organization. Thus, the management function after integration is quite certain to be different from the management organizational-policy framework before diversification.

This raises an important question: What degree of management integration should accompany diversification? The answer depends upon the merger objectives, which in turn determine the kind of merger activity that will take place. To establish this proposition, our analysis will cover three major points. First, we shall examine the nature of some of the objectives for diversification or merger. Second, we shall investigate kinds of mergers related to objectives. Third, the organization implications of the differing objectives and types of mergers will be explored.

Objectives of mergers

Among the motives for diversification and merger are the three objectives of growth, stability, and flexibility.

Growth
The basic motive for growth in sales and profits is that a firm,

---

* Empirical studies upon which the generalizations in this chapter are based were aided by research assistance provided by the Bureau of Business and Economic Research, University of California, Los Angeles. We benefited from the help of Byron Weston.

This chapter is reprinted with permission from: *Review of Economics and Business,* Autumn 1962, pp. 49–58.

like a tree, must either grow or die. The most obvious need to find new product markets arises when an industry falls into secular decline. This was the motive for diversification which pressed upon the railway equipment industry because of the rise of the auto and the aeroplane. Backward integration by the auto manufacturers necessitated diversification by the auto parts companies.

The pressure to diversify for growth also exists if a firm faces prospects of an industry growth rate below that of the economy as a whole. If a number of other industries are growing faster, they will be able to attract the more able technical and managerial talent by virtue of more rapid promotions, higher salaries and benefits, and so forth. Thus, if the economy is to grow something like $3\frac{1}{2}$ per cent a year in constant dollars and 5 per cent a year in current dollars, a firm must set a target rate of growth of at least 5 or 6 per cent a year to compete successfully for the best resources in the economy. If the firm's existing product line does not offer such a growth rate, it may seek diversification as a method of entering product-market areas with more attractive growth potentials.

Stability

Instability in sales and profits may occur because of cyclical and seasonal shifts as well as secular changes. Cyclical and seasonal fluctuations imply a regularity of oscillations with which a firm may cope by building enough reserves to weather periodic adversity. However, a firm may seek to diversify into product lines which have complementary sales patterns.

A producer of industrial equipment such as fork-lift trucks may seek to add road-building equipment to its product line since the latter may be stimulated by public works programmes instituted to offset declines in industrial activity. Similarly, Gillette Safety Razor Company's purchase of the Toni Company was motivated in part by the desire to offset the depression-decline in razor blade sales by the rise in use of home permanents during a decline in incomes and employment.

It is doubtful whether it is feasible to establish a universal norm for stability as in the case of growth. The important consideration is the extent to which instability can be foreseen, for a firm can develop plans for dealing with periodic instability. It is the unforeseeable changes that pose the difficult challenges. Such instability leads to inefficient utilization of the company's resources and makes it non-competitive in its industry, as well as a poor investment prospect.

Flexibility

The unforeseeable contingencies represent the most important characteristic of the present-day economic environment. The problems posed take on characteristics of both instability and unfavourable growth prospects. What is distinctive is that within the product family of a growing and perhaps relatively stable (with respect to periodic fluctuations) industry, frequent and substantial shifts may take place in the manufacturing processes and the products or the demand patterns. These may be referred to as innovations, which have brought about product changes, new products, and changed techniques in the manufacturing processes.

Such changes are the consequence of the age of technological discovery which has penetrated every phase of American industry. The dynamics of changes in population composition and growth patterns and the rise of institutions such as common markets also fall into this category.

For these reasons, analysis of vulnerability to unforeseeable contingencies deserves special attention. A firm may have excellent apparent growth and stability prospects and still be vulnerable to sudden changes because its product line has a narrow technological and market base. To reduce this vulnerability, it may need to increase its *flexibility* by broadening this base to new markets and, particularly, to new areas of technology.

Types of mergers

The respective objectives of mergers may be related to the forms or types of mergers which may take place.

Vertical

Vertical mergers stay in the same product line, but take over more of the process. They may represent forward integration by manufacturers into consumer markets. An example of this is the purchase of Best Foods, Inc., by the Corn Products Refining Company. Diversification or merger may also represent backward integration. An example would be the acquisition of Universal Products by Chrysler.

Vertical mergers may improve stability by regularizing the supply of raw materials or parts or by movement towards the markets of the final consumer, thereby decreasing the fluctuations resulting from derived demands. Thus, vertical integration can improve stability of sales.

Vertical integration may also improve profit margins if combining the stages of production results in economies. However, such economies must offset the gains from specialization achieved by a firm which provides the same products to a number of other manufacturers. Vertical integration may, therefore, improve the stability or growth of profits, but will not necessarily improve the growth of sales unless final product prices are reduced appreciably.

Vertical integration also holds grave dangers. A firm which previously supplied semi-finished goods to a number of firms risks losing all but one of its customers if it is merged with a finished-product manufacturer. Dis-economies of scale may thus force it into inefficient operations which, in turn, will reflect on the price of the finished product.

Horizontal

Horizontal mergers move across product lines instead of up and down a given product line. Wide extremes of the degree of relationship between products may be encountered. Horizontal diversification may involve the same products as in the case of the acquisition of St Helens Pulp and Paper by Crown Zellerbach, or it may involve products that substitute in consumption such as tin cans and jars as in the acquisition by Continental Can of Hazel-Atlas Glass.

A very important type of horizontal merger rounds out a product line. It puts together a spectrum of products which, though different, are sold through the same distribution channels. It therefore offers opportunities for joint economies of selling and advertising efforts.

Concentric mergers

Both vertical and horizontal mergers appear to be sub-groups of the broader class of what may be termed concentric mergers. Concentric mergers involve a common thread in the relationships between the firms. The existence of a common thread in their relationships will produce two-plus-two-equals-five effects. To achieve these multiplicative rather than merely additive effects requires a complementary relationship which, in turn, reflects the degree of fit between the operations joined. The measure of fit may be explained both in concept and illustration.

The criteria for the measure of fit are basically three in number. One is the increase in each company's product-market strength as a consequence of the merger. This may be measured by reciprocal technological contributions or by diverse experiences in manufacturing or marketing.

A second criterion for measure of fit is the potential for joint product development. This will suggest the number and kinds of new products that potentially may be developed by the two firms requiring combination of the two companies' skills. Technological considerations, however, are not the only factors to be taken into account. The potential market demand for the new skill combinations must also be analysed.

The third criterion is operational compatibility. It refers to the existence of related technologies which may condition management's attitude towards change and product development. It may also involve similarity of marketing tasks. For example, in marketing industrial machinery, availability of a strong service organization as an adjunct to the sales organization is of central importance. In the marketing of consumer non-durable items, such as cigarettes or soap, highly developed skills in advertising and promotion campaigns are of central importance.

Common-thread mergers may involve emphasis on research capabilities, as in the Sperry-Rand merger, or production economies as in the American Motors or Studebaker-Packard mergers. An example of aiming at more effective marketing is provided by the Ford-Philco merger. Bringing together complementary products is illustrated by Allis-Chalmers' acquisition of Baker Manufacturing Company and Tractomotive Corporation in order to combine agricultural equipment with road-building equipment.

Conglomerate mergers

Conglomerate mergers combine unrelated product lines. They are usually characterized by a distinct strategy of investment. The acquisitions of the Philadelphia and Reading Corporation were primarily in situations that were regarded as 'undervalued'. The mergers of W. R. Grace represent an emphasis on entering new growth areas. In the initial phases of its merger operations, H. K. Porter and Company is said to have sought what is termed 'disaster situations'—companies that had relatively poor management records. Their objective was to improve the management and perhaps obtain some of the liquid funds of the corporation. Many of Textron's early mergers involved tax-loss situations. The mergers of Olin Mathieson Corporation appeared to aim at the objective of diversification flexibility.

All of the objectives of growth, stability, and flexibility of sales and profits may be achieved through conglomerate mergers. But in conglomerate mergers, mainly additive effects of opportunities already possessed by the other firm in the merger or consolidation are achieved. For diversification or merger to produce a net increase in benefits to the combined firm, over and above those contributed by the individual firms, and thereby produce a net increase in social product, more than additive effects must be involved.

It is only when a complementary relationship exists between the activities joined that multiplicative effects are achieved. The common-thread relationship based on a good fit between the firms joined will product more than the sum of the individual parts joined. Some evidence on this proposition can be examined.

Limited test of the hypothesis

Our generalizations about the importance of the two-plus-two-equals-five effect are supported by examples from our own experience and direct observations. An approximation to an objective test is provided by comparing results for two samples of firms, one group representing concentric mergers, the other conglomerate mergers.

This test must be regarded as a relatively weak one. In the first place, disagreements would arise over placing a firm in one category rather than another. Second, a wide variety of factors could

Table 1

STABILITY UNDER CONCENTRIC AND CONGLOMERATE STRATEGIES

Concentric strategy	Recession drop in sales	Recession drop in profits	Conglomerate strategy	Recession drop in sales	Recession drop in profits
Norm for all manu-facturers	8%	23%	Textron, Inc.	8% 4	23% None
Warner-Lambert	None	1	National Distillers & Chemical Corp.	3	14
Food Machinery & Chemical	None	2	W. R. Grace	6	36.7
Union Carbide	7	7	Borg-Warner	12	38.6
B. F. Goodrich	5	10	Curtiss-Wright	35	38.7
Rockwell Manu-facturing Company	12	23	H. K. Porter	11	48.6
			Olin Mathieson Chemical Corp.	None	73.4
Average	8%	9%		12%	42%

Sources: Department of commerce for all manufacturers and Moody's *Investment Manuals*

affect the results. The trends of the particular industries involved might be more important than the type of diversification followed. In conglomerate mergers, the investment policy followed would greatly influence the performance results. Nevertheless, the test has some limited value. Since conglomerate mergers achieve only additive results and concentric mergers attain multiplicative results, we would expect the latter to perform somewhat better as a group. Also, we would expect conglomerate mergers to present more diverse results than concentric mergers since the former are more dependent on the correctness of investment decisions in a highly dynamic environment.

Since flexibility is reflected in both stability and growth, the tests involve measurement of performance with respect to stability in Table 1 and growth in Table 2. Table 1 presents the comparative performance on stability during the recession of 1957-58 for a group of firms which appear to have followed the concentric strategy as compared with a group of firms which appear to have followed the conglomerate strategy. The recession drop in both sales and profits were substantially smaller for the firms following the concentric strategy. In fact, the recession drop in sales and profits was on the average lower than the norm provided by the results for all manufacturing corporations.

The results for firms following the conglomerate strategy were on the average less favourable than those following the concentric strategy. In addition, firms following the conglomerate strategy failed to perform as well as the norm provided by the experience of all manufacturing corporations. The diversity of stability experience among these conglomerate mergers was substantial.

Similarly, growth in earnings per share and in market price per share adjusted were calculated for the period 1952 through 1959. These data end with the year 1959 in order to examine results not too far removed from the major merger activities of the companies involved. The firms following the concentric strategy obtained an average growth in earnings per share and growth in market price per share over the period studied that was greater than the average achieved by the conglomerate firms. These firms also performed better than the firms in the Dow-Jones industrial average, which may be employed as a convenient standard.

The results for the firms following the conglomerate strategy are overstated somewhat in that negative results were treated as zero (since large negative numbers could distort the results even further). Nevertheless, the average results for these firms were somewhat less

Table 2

GROWTH RESULTS UNDER CONCENTRIC AND CONGLOMERATE STRATEGIES
(ANNUAL COMPOUND RATES)

Concentric strategy	Growth in earnings per share 1952-59	Growth in market price per share adj. 1952-59	Conglomerate strategy	Growth in earnings per share 1952-59	Growth in market price per share adj. 1952-59
Dow-Jones industrial average	5%	12%	Olin Mathieson Chemical Corp.	5%	12%
B. F. Goodrich	1	15	National Distillers & Chemical Corp.	NEG.	NEG.
Rockwell Manufacturing Company	6	12	W. R. Grace	10	2
Union Carbide	8	11	Textron, Inc.	3	7
Food Machinery & Chemical	8	10	Borg-Warner	5	8
Warner-Lambert	19	37	Curtiss-Wright	5	9
			H. K. Porter	8	18
				20	29
Average	8%	17%		8%	12%

Sources: *Barron's* and *Moody's Investment Manuals*

favourable than those following the concentric strategy. The growth in earnings per share thus measured was somewhat more favourable than the growth in earnings per share of the firms in the Dow-Jones industrial average. The growth in market price per share was about equal to the norm. Again, as our hypothesis had suggested, the results were much more diverse for firms following the conglomerate strategy than for firms following the concentric merger strategy.

As an interim summary, we may note that both conglomerate and concentric mergers may contribute to the growth stability, and flexibility of an enterprise. But conglomerate mergers will achieve only additive effects. Mergers that involve a common thread may achieve something more than the individual contributions made by the respective firms. However, we feel that another important principle must be observed if mergers in each category are to avoid failure and are to approach the achievement of their potentials. This principle involves the organization implications of different types of mergers.

Degree of carryover

The organization implications of the different types of mergers result from differences in potential carryover of management know-how and experience. By and large, a common-thread merger involves a carryover of some management know-how and experience between the two businesses. On the other hand, a conglomerate merger provides little opportunity for this carryover. This suggests an analysis of the degree to which a merger involves a common-thread relationship and the related organization implications.

A framework for this analysis is provided in Table 3, which presents a pattern of management carryover between industry groups. For illustrative purposes, the American industrial spectrum is divided into four broad segments, according to the nature of the managerial skills critical for success in each particular area. The defence area puts a premium on advancing the state of the art, new technological achievements, and reliability of performance. Buyers of producers' durable goods seek reliability of performance and availability of prompt service for maintenance and repair. Quality of product and low-cost management of process technology are of prime importance in the successful manufacture of producers' materials. In the consumers' goods fields, there is much less emphasis on research and development, with greater concentration on

Table 3

Carryover of Management Capabilities Between Industry Groups*

Industry group	Capability†	Industry group			
		Defence	Producers' durables	Producers' materials	Consumers' durables and nondurables
Defence	F	High	High	High	High
	G	High	High	Moderate	Moderate
	E	High	High	Moderate	Low
	M	High	Moderate	Low	Negative
	S	High	Negative	Negative	Negative
Producers' durables	F	High	High	High	High
	G	High	High	High	Moderate
	E	High	High	Moderate	Low
	M	Moderate	High	Low	Negative
	S	Low	High	Low	Negative
Producers' materials	F	High	High	High	High
	G	Moderate	High	High	Moderate
	E	Moderate	Moderate	High	Low
	M	Low	Low	High	Low
	S	Negative	Low	High	Negative
Consumers' durables and nondurables	F	High	High	High	High
	G	Moderate	Moderate	Moderate	High
	E	Low	Low	Low	High
	M	Negative	Negative	Low	High
	S	Negative	Negative	Negative	High

* The range is high, moderate, low, and negative.

† The management capabilities are F, financial management; G, general management; E, research and development and engineering; M, manufacturing; and S, Sales.

low-cost mass production operations; promotional advertising is of the greatest importance for a firm's competitive strength.

Thus, managements accustomed to emphasis on the close tolerances and rigorous performance requirements of the defence industry would find these qualities less important in the producers' industries and a handicap in the consumers' industries. Conversely, managements of firms in the consumers' industries would find their manufacturing and sales skills inapplicable in the defence industries. In general, the degree of fit between the industrial categories diminishes over the spectrum from defence industries to consumer industries.

However, some management functions have a substantial carry-over. Financial controls are equally applicable in all categories. The nature of the controls would vary, but their application would be generally similar. The general management functions of organization, staffing, direction, planning, and control have a carryover but require some knowledge of the technical problems of the industrial area for the most effective application. Research, manufacturing, and sales are more technically oriented management functions which require a background in the specific characteristics of the industrial area in which they are to be applied.

As we move in Table 3 from any one of the four industrial categories to another farther away in the spectrum of categories, the degree of carryover of the five management capabilities will vary. Financial management has equal carryover in all the categories. General management skills have a strong carryover, but are constrained if the technologies differ substantially. Research skills have still somewhat less carryover. Manufacturing and sales are highly technical operations oriented to the specifics of their product-market lines.

The relationships involved may be made concrete by describing the degree of carryover of management capabilities that would be achieved if a firm in the defence industries planned a merger with a firm in one of the other groups. An entry by a firm from the defence industry into a non-defence producers' durable goods industry would offer the greatest opportunity for carryover of management experience. This suggests a closely integrated divisional organization with a considerable amount of centralized market and product planning as appropriate for this type of entry.

In producers' non-durables, the management carryover would be less complete, particularly in the very important areas of sales and manufacturing. The appropriate organization appears to be a loosely federated structure, with top management exercising general policy control.

In the area of consumers' goods, the diversifying company has serious weaknesses in both manufacturing and sales management. The control should be very loose, limited to the establishment of basic financial policies and targets.

Forms of management control

The preceding analysis suggests a general principle: The level of management control to be applied by an acquiring firm to an acquired firm, or the degree of integration to be attempted in a consolidation of two firms, should reflect the potential degree of carryover of management capabilities. We have pointed out that, where there is a strong common thread between the companies in a merger, full integration of the managers will be called for. If the degree of integration is less than this optimum, some of the full potential advantages of joint operations will be lost.

Where a moderate degree of carryover is involved, there should not be full integration. Rather, a divisionalized operation will be carried on in which the top corporate level simply sets out general policies for the guidance of the individual operating divisions or companies.

Indeed, when the carryover of capabilities between the two firms is likely to involve negative elements because one is in producers' durables, for example, and the other in a consumers' non-durable goods industry, the degree of integration or control should be relatively loose. The control may be nothing more than financial tests of profitability of performance.

In the latter two cases, where only general policy control or general financial control is the appropriate degree of integration to be attempted between the merging organizations, the danger is in going beyond the optimum degree of control. If control exceeds the level of applicable management experience of the top-level officer group, this group may not be able to give effective guidance to the acquired business and may, in fact, retard its successful growth. There is evidence in diversification histories of a number of large companies in the United States both of 'over-control' and 'under-control' which have led to difficulties in utilizing the full potential of the joint resources of a merger.

The conclusion from a management-policy standpoint is this: in approaching diversification, a company can take two alternative points of view of the degree of integration of management control. It can arbitrarily select a level of control which it wishes to exercise in the new enterprise. In this case, it would be well advised to forgo certain diversification opportunities which are not compatible with this level of control. This may mean that companies which would be attractive when measured by the general objectives of the merger will become unattractive because of the lack of 'operational compatibility', in the light of the degree of integration and control that top management desires.

The alternative is to make no advance decisions with respect to the level of control, but to establish the additional criterion of the degree of fit. This will measure the operational or management compatibility of different diversification alternatives. On the basis of this determination, the appropriate level of control or integration can then be determined in each case.*

Thus, completely heterogeneous mergers can be justified if the latter approach is taken. The objectives of growth, stability, and flexibility can be attained. While there may be little carryover of capabilities or of fit, the probabilities of success of the joint enterprise can be enhanced by permitting a high degree of decentralized operations. But in concentric mergers where carryover of management capabilities appears to be substantial, sometimes integrated operations and centralization of strategic decision making is not carried out. To illustrate, for an electronics firm with systems capability to merge with a firm with computer or instrument capability and not to attempt to utilize the hardware of the acquired firm in systems applications would be to overlook opportunities of great potential magnitude.

Conclusions

The central thesis of this chapter is that assurance that a merger has potential for meeting the objectives of growth, stability, and flexibility may be insufficient to guarantee its success. The attainment of favourable external environmental opportunities may be a necessary, but not a sufficient condition for the success of a merger, since an internal relationship is also involved.

Where there is substantial carryover of management competences between the merging firms, a high degree of integration, control, and centralization is needed. Such a policy is likely to increase the reciprocal benefits which each of the constituent parts of the merged company may confer upon one another.

On the other hand, where the merged companies have been operating in hitherto highly diverse areas, there may be little carryover or operational compatibility. Operations with only general policy or control through financial targets may be all that is possible. To do more may impede the effective decision-making processes of the operating units.

In some situations the particular characteristics of the industries

* Another recently published study concludes: 'Our case studies indicate that from the point of view both of the acquiring management and of the acquired management, financial controls by themselves are not sufficient to enable the realization of the anticipated benefits of acquisition.'[1] We are confident that this conclusion would be altered if the authors had in their case studies been operating with a framework which included a distinction between concentric and conglomerate mergers.

or managements may explain the subsequent performance of the merged firms. Nevertheless, the generalization here developed suggests that it is plausible, and indeed likely, that despite favourable environmental conditions achieved by a merger, success or failure may depend upon internal organization policies followed.

There is an optimal degree of integration, control, and centralization related to the nature of the merger. Where there is little fit between firms in a merger, the optimal degree of integration is low, and exceeding this optimum will lead to failure of the merger. However, where the degree of carryover is great, the optimal degree of integration is large. Here the great danger is failure to marshal effectively the independent potential contributions that the constituent members of the merger have available, and which might react in a highly favourable fashion if the potential carryover is effectively exploited.

REFERENCE

1 Mace, Myles L. & Montgomery, George C. (1962) *Management problems of corporate acquisitions.* Harvard Univ. Graduate School of Business Administration. p. 255.

14 | Organization Structure for Innovation
by RODNEY LEACH

As the complexity of our industrial processes steadily increases, and the technological sophistication of many new products becomes even greater, management is being subjected to two major pressures.

First, it is constantly being exhorted to spend more in order to keep up with the technological hunt. This apparently irresistible pressure is clearly illustrated by the fact that, over the last decade, Britain's expenditure on R & D has grown by around 250 per cent, and now totals almost £1,000 million per annum. Second, and to some extent in conflict with the first, is the mounting pressure to exercise a tighter control over R & D expenditures, to make sure that resources are used wisely. Many executives report 'we're spending more and more on research but we still don't know much about managing it.'

How is management in the United Kingdom responding to these two powerful pressures? So far as scale of expenditure and percentage of resources devoted to R & D are concerned, it appears that we are in line with most of our major competitors. There are, however, growing fears in many places that in the *management* of R & D effort we may be lagging behind competition in the USA, Germany, Japan and elsewhere. It is hard to quantify these fears, but they all amount to a feeling that it should be possible to improve the productivity of the R & D pound. Evidence of this concern is widespread. Many companies are scrutinizing their R & D budgets and projects more carefully. Others are radically reorganizing their R & D staffs. While I think this feeling—that management technology in Britain is less effective than in other countries

Dr. LEACH, of McKinsey & Company, Consultants, first presented this paper to the *National Conference on The Management of Technological Innovation* sponsored by Mintech and *Management Today* at The University of Bradford Management Centre, March 1969.

—can be over-exaggerated, it is almost always possible to do better.

Scope of chapter

I want to focus attention on the management processes and guidelines that companies should have in mind when determining the 'shape' of their R & D organizations. The approach I shall take will be to outline a systematic way of analysing the key variables which in my view make up the 'technological profile' of a company. In taking this approach I shall be dealing more generally than might be assumed from a literal interpretation of the chapter's title. However, I believe one cannot be more definite, since an organization must be tailored to reflect the specific and individual needs of the enterprise it is meant to serve, in the light of the opportunites open to it.

The first point is that it is not possible to produce a 'package' solution to a problem of organization, whether it be in handling innovation or in any other business activity. Just as with most other problems of business, the solution can only be found by careful analysis of both the internal characteristics and the external environment of the company.

A second point which is important to bear in mind, is that we are talking about problems for which no completely satisfactory solution exists anywhere today. However, one thing I firmly believe is that we are talking of *business* problems and *not* narrow scientific or engineering problems. It is usually possible to go out and hire technical staff. The difficulty lies in using them effectively on problems of real concern to the business—and this is a problem for general management.

What are the features that make up the technological profile of a business? These can normally be reduced to the four or five essential variables shown in Fig. 1. The first of them is the 'R' and 'D' mix. To what extent is a given business focused on making basic discoveries as the source of new products, as opposed to developing commercial products from existing knowledge? The second is the amount of 'interaction' necessary between the R & D functions and the manufacturing and marketing functions, which are further 'downstream' towards the customer. Third is the product life-cycle. Is our business one in which new products must be introduced every few months, or do our products typically have a life of many years? Next, the R & D investment ratio. What proportion of the company's total investment is being committed to

THE PROFILE OF A TECHNICALLY-ORIENTED
BUSINESS MIGHT LOOK LIKE THIS . . . . .

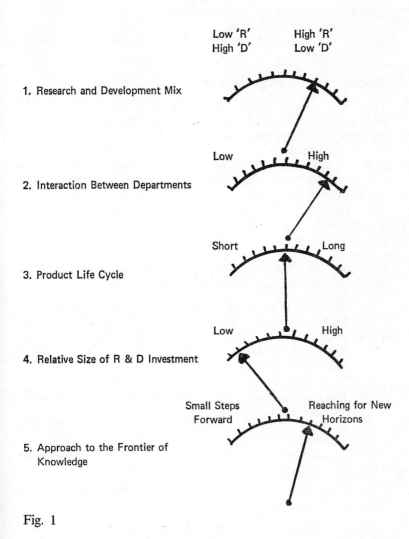

Fig. 1

the R & D effort? And finally there is the question of 'proximity to the frontier'. Are our technologists reaching for new commercial horizons or are they nibbling at the frontiers of knowledge?

Let us look in more detail at each of these factors to show the light they can throw on the broad type of organization that may be appropriate in different company situations. This approach can also give valuable insights into overall business strategy, as well as pointers towards the type of organization that may be appropriate.

Research and development mix

First is the question of the 'R' and 'D' mix. The words 'research' and 'development' are coupled together so frequently that important and basic differences between them are all too often confused by top management. Some successful research directors describe their activities as a type of gambling game which, if played skilfully and often enough, is bound to result in a few big wins that can more than offset the cost of the losses. This is in marked contrast to the role of the Development Manager, whose aim is to engineer a process or product that is known to be technically feasible, and to fit a given specification within defined time and cost budgets.

It generally turns out that the more efficient research-intensive organizations display six dominant characteristics:

(a)   Work tends to be carried out with rather indefinite specifications

(b)   Information on market or other objectives is often fed to the whole research group instead of being channelled to specific individuals

(c)   Work assignments tend to be relatively non-directive

(d)   Great value is attached to insight—the ability to spot the significance of research results

(e)   There is a tendency to value innovation more highly than efficiency

(f)   Research-intensive organizations usually employ a continuing process of project evaluation and selection.

In contrast, four quite different factors typify the successful development organization:

(a)   Design specifications are relatively complete

(b)   Supervision tends to be highly directive

(c)   It is often necessary to arrange tasks sequentially, since suc-

Characteristic	High 'Research' Content	High 'Development' Content
1. Type of organization	† Relatively 'flat' — with few tiers of management, high degree of 'mobility' of personnel	† Well-structured, clear lines of responsibility
2. Type of leadership	† Creative, intuitive — but with feet firmly on the ground	† Analytical, disciplined
3. Nature of work assignments	† Non-directive; except in the broad sense	† Objectives and work programmes precisely defined
4. Frequency of change	† Fairly great in response to changing technical insights	† Low, once objectives are spelled out
5. Performance measurement and control	† Relatively long term	† Well-defined programmes and frequent checks on performance

Fig. 2

cessive development stages are often dependent on the completion of an earlier one

(d)   The development organization is highly vulnerable to disruptions caused by changes in objectives or specifications from manufacturing or marketing.

It is clear from these distinctive characteristics that there are, in reality, marked differences between 'research' and 'development' functions. Management should therefore decide where its business lies in the R & D spectrum, and then bear these important differences in mind in choosing the form of organization to adopt. Fig. 2 summarizes the most important ways such differences can affect the choice of organization. There is plenty of evidence to suggest that the historic weaknesses of British industry in getting new products to market result, as much as from any other single factor, from applying to a development organization the loose long-term controls appropriate in research.

Interaction between departments

The second major variable in our technological profile is the degree of interaction, or 'coupling', between research/development departments and succeeding functions of manufacturing and sales. Management must be aware of the extent to which the company's success depends on tightly co-ordinating the activities of successive departments concerned with the flow of product towards the market. Obviously, there are significant differences between the needs of companies concerned with, for example, branded breakfast foods and basic chemicals. However, there are many companies where this problem has either not been recognized or has not been properly thought through, resulting in major friction between departments—and sometimes even in the development of products for which there is no market!

While the spectrum of interaction is, in reality, infinitely variable, it is useful to distinguish three degrees of coupling (see Fig. 3). In organizations with low coupling, activities of separate departments are relatively independent, and the flow of both product and information is generally in the forward direction only. Separate activities of different departments tend to be organized along clearly defined lines and conflicts should be minimal. However, most innovative companies tend towards the opposite end of the spectrum, where a high degree of interaction is required between technical, manufacturing and marketing functions. It is a characteristic of

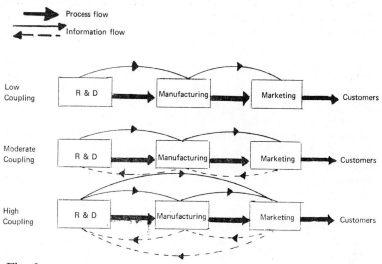

Fig. 3

these companies that detailed market information is essential for new product planning. Selection of research or development projects is heavily influenced by factors such as availability of raw materials, manufacturing costs, marketing effectiveness and competitive forces. Impact of new products on manufacturing facilities is often critical, careful quality control is frequently vital to marketing and time pressures are usually acute.

Some 'highly-coupled' companies have tried to achieve the required interaction by shifting the technical service group from marketing, to production, to product development, and on occasion back again, in the search to obtain effective co-ordination. In other companies management is constantly battling to maintain the right balance between development, production and sales/technical departments. If the development influence becomes too strong there is a tendency to force uncompetitive products forward into manufacturing. If, on the other hand, technical service is dominant, too much company energy is frequently devoted to the 'problem of the moment'—to the detriment of long-term development vital to the company's future. On occasion even manufacturing can assume too great an influence in overall strategy, and production schedules are based on achievement of the lowest unit costs, regardless of either market considerations or the possibility of improving the product at the expense of a short interruption in production.

While there is no single clear-cut solution to these organizational problems, there are a number of approaches which have been found valuable by companies that have consciously tackled this problem.

In some companies, for example, attempts are made to provide the necessary co-ordination by making senior executives responsible for certain facets of the activities of departments that do not normally come under their 'line' control. One possibility is to make the development manager responsible for training technical service engineers who form part of the Marketing Department. Another is to assign to a marketing manager responsibilty for co-ordination of all activities necessary to complete a specific project. However, there are the inevitable dangers of dual responsibility, or dual reporting relationships, and it is necessary to define very clearly where responsibilities begin and end.

Other companies have successfully employed the concept of 'matrix-management'. This is a rather grandiose way of describing what is basically a combination of project and functional organization. It employs cross-functional project teams which have full responsibility for all aspects of a given new product and act as a group with a single head. The important point, however, is that while team members act as a group they still draw on the resources of the individual departments of the company. Advantages that result when this approach is properly applied are that (a) the project team rapidly acquires a common identity of purpose, (b) responsibilities within the group are clearly defined and unambiguous, and (c) individual team members can more easily grasp the role of their function in the overall business concept.

A third, relatively informal, approach is for the research department to bring in development engineers and marketing specialists at regular intervals to review the progress of the research programme. The object is to ensure practical application of important discoveries at the earliest possible moment and to eliminate so far as possible the expenditure of effort on projects that clearly could never find a place in the company's product line.

However, since interaction between departments is, by definition, an inter-functional problem, in the last resort the necessary direction and arbitration between conflicting interests must come from general management.

Product life cycle

The next variable is the influence that product 'life-cycle' can exert on the shape of the company organization. Most executives in the marketing area are now familiar with this valuable concept, yet it appears that many companies do not make real strategic use of it when thinking through the evolving needs of their business. Obviously, life-cycles vary greatly from product to product, ranging between extremes of a few months for many fashion goods and years for the traditional products of heavy engineering. What then are the differences that should categorize the organization of companies whose products lie at opposite ends of the spectrum?

Looking first at the implications of short life-cycles, it is clear that here a premium must be placed on obtaining speedy management action and response. Many activities must take place concurrently, and good approximations must often take the place of absolute precision. The company organization exhibits most of the characteristics of the 'highly-interacting' company considered earlier, and short-circuited devices are inevitably required between functions. These can take the form of tightly-knit inter-functional committees. Alternatively, a system of product or project management may be found to produce the most effective results. Because of the need for rapid response, organizations may sometimes appear top-heavy. But this can, and should, be the result of a carefully judged balance between economy in the use of man-power and the need to provide a rapid response when required. Short life-cycles can also result in a need for managers to think broadly, outside the confines of their functional specialism. For example, marketing managers commonly need to be knowledgeable about the technology of their products, and production managers should have an understanding of the marketing factors that may cause production requirements to change.

In contrast, the focus of long life-cycle companies is on operating within well-established procedures and routines. Frequently their dominant need is to produce results at least cost, even at the expense of increasing the time interval between conceiving and marketing a new product. So the traditional form of functional organization tends to be the most effective; with clearly defined and non-changing responsibilties both between, and within, departments. Furthermore, their activities are usually highly sequential, with, for example, detailed R & D completed before manufacturing and market planning is begun. Paradoxically, however, some British companies manufacturing long life-cycle products fail to realize the importance of completing R & D effectively before embarking on costly manufacturing and marketing programmes. Much of their effort is devoted to reducing expenditure at the marketing end of the business, where the impact on total product cost may be quite small in comparison with the leverage obtained by designing thoroughly before embarking on manufacture.

While organizational problems may appear simpler for companies with long life products, things can, and do, change; as companies occasionally learn to their cost. A classic example was the case of the steam locomotive manufacturers, in this country and elsewhere, who failed to realize that the railway 'permanent way' no longer had need of their products, and so went out of business.

Increasingly, technology-based companies are finding a progressive trend towards shorter life-cycles, which can have significant organizational implications. This trend is very evident in the aerospace industry. Similarly, in the data processing industry the product life-cycle has shortened rapidly, and in some cases painfully, as we have progressed from punched cards to hard valve computers, to transistorized machines and now to integrated microcircuits. As these changes take place in the character of a business it is vital that top management recognizes and responds to the need to make the organizational adjustments that permit increased flexibility. On occasion, these necessary adjustments can be painful for the managers concerned, but they are none the less vital if the company is to remain competitive in its changing environment.

To summarize these conclusions, I think it is clear that a company's organization should reflect, in part, the expected life-cycle of its products. The well-structured, highly-functional organization which may be appropriate in a company manufacturing long-life products must give way to a looser cross-functional organization in a situation where there is rapid product obsolescence.

R & D investment ratio

The next question is the impact on company organization of the size of its investment in future technological innovation. A high ratio of R & D to total expenditure has, I believe, four important implications for the organization of a company.

The first is the need for top management constantly to evaluate alternative procurement strategies. Feasible alternatives include: developing the required skills internally by a continual training process; hiring technical group leaders from outside in order to bring in specific kinds of technical competence; taking over smaller companies that have demonstrated a high degree of technical competence; and acquiring technology through licensing, or where feasible from consultants. The first of these alternatives is usually only possible in industries with a low or moderate R & D ratio.

Where the amount of investment is high there is usually not time to wait for skills to develop slowly without being outpaced by competition. In choosing between the other alternatives there is a vital need for corporate staff to be adequately briefed on the pace of industry development and possible competitive moves.

The second implication of a high investment ratio is an acceleration in the tradional pace of product or process change. Therefore, there is all the need for adaptability that characterizes companies with a short product life-cycle. In this case, however, there is an even greater risk of life-cycles being abruptly terminated by a competitor's major leap forward.

Next, high investment ratios usually result in a highly dynamic market, with emphasis shifting rapidly from new product introduction to reducing unit costs, and back again. To respond to this situation a company must have a well-developed strategic planning system linked with an organization that makes it easy to see what resources are devoted to each project.

Fourthly, high R & D investment demands close top level supervision of technical efforts. Because of the importance of R & D to the company's future, senior managers must have the necessary breadth of understanding to evaluate research performance and problems.

At the other end of the investment ratio spectrum, organization requirements are generally the converse of those just identified. For example, technology can normally be developed internally, marketing is usually functionally well-separated from product development and resources devoted to individual projects do not have to be clearly identifiable in the short term.

Finally, whatever the ratio of investment, management must decide whether there is a threshold of investment in any project below which efforts are likely to be ineffective. Such thresholds are difficult to measure precisely, but an estimate can be made by critically assessing both the company's own past performance in introducing new products, and the record of competitors. Once the threshold of expenditure is recognized, however crudely, management is in a position to select specific areas in which it will aim to be a leader —accepting that it is better to hit a few things hard than to tackle a whole spectrum of problems half-heartedly.

Proximity to the frontier

The final variable is the degree of approach to the 'frontier of knowledge'. Approach to the frontier can, of course, mean either

of two things. On the purely technological side it can be the frontier
beyond which researchers are seeking for new fundamental knowledge: while on the development plane it can mean the frontier of
commercial exploitation. The degree to which a company's technology approaches the frontier of knowledge, or application, clearly
has important implications for the management of technology.

First, companies whose whole production falls on the frontier
tend to be relatively unstable. In many cases they must continually
strive to repeat the rapid advances by which they have attained their
position. At the same time they must be highly sensitive to threats
to their market position caused either by competitive emulation of
their efforts or by a break-through on costs.

Maintaining effective management control makes special demands
on the organization of such companies. It is absolutely vital that
top management should be personally involved in the problems
their researchers are trying to solve. They must have a clear understanding of at least the broad nature of these problems. Such involvement is particularly necessary because of the sheer impossibil-
ity of relying on the more formal control systems that are effective
in more predictable parts of the business. Perhaps because of this
difficulty of controlling the unpredictable, many large companies do
not have the same record of success on the fringes of knowledge as
other much smaller entrepreneurial enterprises. Instead they prefer
to move rapidly to 'buy in' new knowledge when it reaches the
development stage.

Next, working close to the technological frontier puts a premium
on adaptability and versatility, with the need to ensure that research
managers themselves do not become obsolete. In the larger companies there is frequently a definite policy of bringing in young
new 'thinkers' to the research department for a period of a few
years, then allowing them to move elsewhere in the company when
they feel their creative talents are drying up. In other companies,
it is recognized that most research technologists need to move to
different problems after periods of a few years. Sometimes, in fact,
it is found beneficial to replace an entire team by another group,
who will either continue to attack a problem on the same lines as
the first group, or perhaps attempt a new approach.

Finally, participation in a rapidly-moving technology places a
premium on management skills of a very special kind. Management
must be highly sensitive to activities of their competitors who may
introduce not just a slightly better, or cheaper, product but one
which could make an 'entire' product line obsolete. It is therefore
essential for top management to be able to react quickly; to know

when to terminate unproductive programmes or where to apply additional effort, perhaps on a crash basis. In this situation, manufacturing efficiency is frequently secondary to the ability to bring new products to market rapidly. Success demands a high degree of flexibility and the closest possible interaction between research, manufacturing and sales, to take maximum advantage of each newly-identified product opportunity. A frequent mistake of research oriented companies is to underestimate the time required for competitors to catch up with a new discovery that may have taken years of research to produce.

Conclusion

That completes the outline picture of the five key variables which I believe are of particular importance in a technology-based enterprise. I have not put forward any unique organizational solutions, but what I have tried to do is to outline a systematic framework that I believe can be of value in thinking through the special needs of a wide range of technically-advanced companies. While it will never be possible to allow, through organization alone, for all of the unique factors that characterize each separate enterprise, I contend that it is possible to identify and eliminate the major sources of potential conflict. It is imperative that any company that wishes to protect or expand its business through application of technology should devote the same care to creating the best possible form of organization as it gives to selecting the right plant and equipment.

I

15 | Conditions Favourable to Product Innovation

by DAVID ASHTON, RUSSELL GOTHAM & GORDON WILLS

THIS study constitutes an examination of the process of product innovation within the firm. It looks at the management problems of organization and control at each stage from pure basic research through to the marketing consummation of product ideas. In doing so it aims at examining relevant evidence and highlighting the techniques appropriate to ensuring that the most efficient use can be made of the resources deployed.

The major definitions adopted, now fairly widely accepted,[1] are as follows:

Pure basic research—carried out solely to increase scientific knowledge.

Objective basic research—carried out in fields of recognized potential technological importance.

Applied research—carried out with the object of attaining specific goals such as a new product or process.

Development—bridges the gap between research and production and includes the construction of pilot plants and prototypes.

Innovation—used throughout to mean the operational adoption of any development.

Macro context

At the macro level, there is little evidence[2] to suggest that Britain is under-spending on total research compared with other industrial nations. In 1961-62 it stood at 2.7 per cent of the Gross National Product, and has been growing at a real annual rate of 9 per cent over the last ten years.[3] This level is comparable in percentage

The authors were members of the Institute of Scientific Business Study Group which prepared this paper in 1963. It first appeared in *Scientific Business* (1964) 2, 1, 13-28.

terms with the United States, although it should not be forgotten that their GNP is seven times greater, and the proportion of research costs borne by any product selling in their larger market is also automatically less. Nowhere has this latter rider been more vividly brought home recently than in the British aircraft industry, and the moves towards an Anglo-French industry in this, and possibly the computer industry, are designed to achieve just such economies.

It is unfortunately not possible at the present time to distinguish how much of Britain's total annual expenditure on research goes to applied research and development work in industry. And even if it were possible there would be few so bold as to lay down a right allocation. However, although pure and objective basic research lay foundations for long-term advances, it is applied research which yields results in growth terms most speedily for the economy. Japan is reported to excel in applied research but to concern herself little with basic research,[4] and the USA has long been thought to tend this way. If the balance in Britain towards applied research and development is wrong, it could be one of the major reasons for an unsatisfactory growth rate. Its major causes would not be far to seek—the disincentive effects of a stop-go economy on investments dependent for their success on a sustained pattern of demand; the lack of qualified technical and managerial talent in industry, particularly amongst smaller firms; the emphasis on old skills engendered by our apprenticeship system, rather than a bias towards seeking new ones.[5]

In these areas the Government has now taken some major initiatives which can be expected to transform the pattern of activity in many industries by creating the right atmosphere for innovation and in doing so provide the stable economic framework for investment. The global research spending mentioned earlier is being examined and discussed in terms of specific industries via the network of Economic Development Committees, serviced by the NEDO and watched over by the DEA. The new Ministry of Technology has been given an overall brief to disseminate scientific knowledge throughout industry and specific sponsorship for the key machine tool, computer and electronics industries. It has inherited the late DSIR's wide range of technological research stations, and has expanded the NRDC. The Ministry of Public Building and Works, by establishing a Directorate-General of Research and Development, has put itself in a position to stimulate the introduction of new methods in the construction industries.[6] All these initiatives are shortly to be related to each other in a six-year economic plan under preparation at the DEA, and should go a long way towards directing the pattern of applied research effort to secure necessary economic growth.

At the same time, the advent of the *Industrial Training Act, 1963*, the rapid growth of facilities for management and business education, and the recently announced National Redundancy Fund, will all play their part in overcoming educational shortcomings and fears of change.

All these measures can leave no doubt that a determined effort has begun in Government to get down to the root causes of growth in the economy, and considerable powers are available, not least the use of civil development contracts. More may be added. One suggestion we endorse is that made by the PEP Broadsheet *Government's Role in Applying Science to Industry*[2] which proposes an extension of the compulsory levy for industry research associations, perhaps jointly with the levy now made by the Industrial Training Boards under the 1963 Act.

In summary, the role of Government in stimulating economic growth is increasing, and can be expected to continue to do so in conformity with the probable objectives of the forthcoming six-year national Plan. This should give stimulus to all stages of the innovation process from objective basic research through as far even as the use of market research,[7] particularly in industries lagging behind competitors overseas.

This is the context, albeit briefly sketched, which will provide a background for the main concern of this study, the process of product innovation within the firm.

Product innovation

Product innovations can be broadly classified into laboratory oriented and market oriented. Which area will be of the greatest significance in any particular firm, at any one point in time, will depend largely on historical factors. There can be little doubt, however, that the greatest steps forward have occurred from laboratory oriented programmes of research. New products emerging from a marketing oriented programme are normally evolutionary. Both programmes can bring success to the firm which organizes its search for, and development of, opportunities.

No matter what balance a firm's new product programme may have, however, there is a continuous urgent need to examine the process involved in order to ensure that at every stage the appropriate personnel work in the most favourable environment under the right degree of supervision.

We look in turn at the four main stages of product innovation in the firm—basic research (relevant only for laboratory oriented programmes), applied research, development and marketing consummation. Finally, we will examine the patterns of overall control of product development programmes throughout the firm.

Although this subject has been dealt with before in business literature, it has mainly been in the United States.[8] We attempt here to discuss it in terms of British industry today.

The firm and basic research

By its very nature basic research, either in its pure or objective form, is unlikely to improve the profit position of the firm engaging in it in the short term. As such the allocation of resources to it is usually seen as an act of either faith, hope or charity. Only the very large firm is in a position to absorb the costs of its own basic research department in its overheads, but even some of these prefer to make different arrangements, perhaps with universities. The medium-sized and smaller firms, if participating at all, usually organize their basic research on an industry co-operative basis often with Government backing via the Ministry of Technology (formerly the DSIR). In addition various Government departments maintain fifteen of their own Research Stations which disseminate their results widely.

The main advantage accredited to research at a university or in any other academic environment is the freedom to seek new knowledge for its own sake, without the need to justify the usefulness of research activity in the short term. At the same time, however, a great deal of basic research at universities, when aided by grants from the Government and industry, is objective. The grants naturally aid projects which are more likely to provide developments in technology of ultimate use to the specific industrial sponsor.

It would seem probable that the academic environment is the most favourable context for the development of new ideas in pure basic research because it is not expected to resolve short term problems related to existing technological processes, nor does it have to justify the nature, direction and costs of its activities within a profit oriented administrative framework.

Research departments in industrial organizations generally face many problems which do not occur in the university. They must be able to justify their existence, both in the long and short term, by their contribution to the effectiveness of their firms as profit-making organizations. This context would seem to make this environment most appropriate for objective basic research when a firm has the necessary size to carry the cost alone.

The management of basic research teams presents a special problem in industry. Whilst the academic context automatically stresses the importance and value of basic research, the head of a firm's research department often has to work hard to justify its activities to other sections of management and to ensure that his research workers feel their work is important. Researchers in firms also lose a certain amount of contact with other scientists and their isolation in industry might ultimately affect both the quality of their work and their attitude to it. Their behaviour patterns are known to be different from those of other employees, and it is essential that management both recognizes this and makes allowances for it.[9]

These problems of basic research have often led to the establishment of laboratories right away from any productive location of the firm, which gives them an environment very similar to that obtained when an industry or trade sets up a research association on a co-operative basis.

Generally, however, whether or not a firm participates in basic research will depend mainly on its size and the nature of the industry's technology. The location in which it is undertaken will largely be the result of historical circumstances. Although there is always a need to review such historical patterns to see how they apply for present and foreseeable future circumstances, the major focus of attention must be on the procedures by which basic research workers are selected, and the pattern of their immediate management.

Before any selection procedure can be devised, however, a definition of the work of the basic researcher must be attempted. Essentially he is required to make discoveries, or to develop new ideas by the alignment, or re-alignment, of facts into fresh, significant patterns which enable totally new products or processes to be developed, or overcome problems in existing products or processes. The re-alignments may involve the alteration of elements in existing patterns or the separation of single elements to make distinct sub-elements not previously considered as separate entities.

The tests which have now been developed in the United States for the selection of research staff, however, admit that the scientific criteria of good researchers are as yet restricted in use.[10] The good researcher as a general type has not yet been identified, and the large amount of work on the nature of genius has produced no general agreement on the psychological structure of the research innovator. Indeed, some evidence suggests that the creative process is best stimulated in a group. Gordon in *Synetics* claims that informal group meetings of specialists and non-specialists and the use of free analogy can be more effective than the individual in producing new ideas.[11] It is a claim similar to those made for brainstorming sessions to shake participants out of stereotyped thought patterns, and has been proved of value at certain stages in the emergence of new ideas.

The importance of a background of security in both psychological and job terms is also often emphasized. Only a man who is personally secure can deviate from the group and suggest a novel approach.[12] It must be stated, however, that any research presupposes either dissatisfaction with the limits of present knowledge and/or unwillingness to accept the present alignment of facts in a particular context. The second attitude will so often flow over into the researcher's attitudes outside the context of his work that it has important implications for the management of basic research.

The patterns of the immediate management of basic research workers have often been dealt with at length.[9] They must be managed without rigidity. Full allowance must be made for the special nature of their work. No hierarchical organization is practical in such laboratories. Furthermore, general management, which provides the research funds, is required to take an understanding attitude towards barren years with no major break-throughs.

The relationship of basic research with many general managements is an uneasy one; they can see the value of it in theory, but tend to feel it is the job of someone else. And the larger companies tend to suffer from poaching by smaller firms of ideas which cannot be protected by patents. It is a situation akin to that reached in industrial training, which led to the establishment of Industrial Training Boards financed by a compulsory levy. Such a step might well be appropriate now for basic research.

The time is also surely appropriate for extensive work, in Britain, on selection procedures designed to identify the good basic research worker, as well as further objective study of the research environment of the firm, both in location and management. Industry as a whole has tended to neglect the social sciences in its policies towards research; it is a policy which can only be continued at peril.[13]

Applied research

Any new product at the basic research stage has a long distance to travel before any firm can use it. The crucial link is the applied researcher. He is the man who must remain in touch with the main stream of basic research, whilst at the same time showing the necessary appreciation of its possible commercial applications. He is alternatively called the engineer and the technologist. It is he alone who is in a position to bring to the attention of his management the potentialities of new basic research findings—unfortunately there are all too few such people in decision-making positions themselves.[14]

Applied researchers are members of a distinct group by virtue of their tested ability to speak and understand the languages of basic research and production, and by virtue of their ability to translate information from basic research into information usable in commercial production. Their function in terms of product innovation is to carry the research idea through to the stage where a rough and ready *bread-board* model is produced.

Firms possessing their own basic research organizations, or participating in Industry Research Associations, will receive a regular

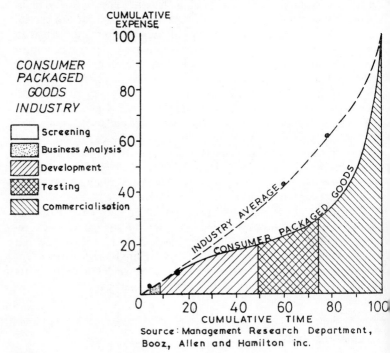

Source: Management Research Department, Booz, Allen and Hamilton inc.

Fig. 1

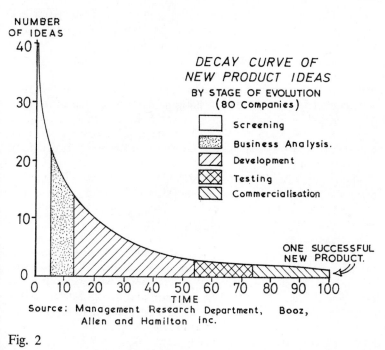

NUMBER OF IDEAS

DECAY CURVE OF
NEW PRODUCT IDEAS
BY STAGE OF EVOLUTION
(80 Companies)

☐ Screening
▒ Business Analysis.
▨ Development
⊠ Testing
◩ Commercialisation

ONE SUCCESSFUL
NEW PRODUCT.

TIME

Source: Management Research Department, Booz, Allen and Hamilton inc.

Fig. 2

Figs. 1 and 2 *indicate the curves of decay of new product ideas and cumulative growth of costs, against time, in a sample of U.S. firms. The general pattern undoubtedly applies in Britain. They emphasise the need for an abundance of ideas and for adequate evaluation as early as possible before major expenses are incurred.*

supply of research findings to evaluate. This should not prevent them from conducting a much wider continuous search for ideas, particularly in foreign literature and reports and also university and professional papers.[15] Ideas will also often come in the reverse direction, in the form of production and particularly marketing feed-back. Rather than the applied researcher pioneering new ideas of his own, he may frequently be asked what solutions he can offer to particular problems.

The development of thixotropic (jelly) paints resulted in this way from a demand for a non-drip paint; knowledge already available on jelling agents at the basic research level was able to provide the answers.

A similar example was the use in the Xerox Copier of photoconductive selenium, a scientific fact known for many years but only developed when one man saw its potential for reducing a major restraint on office reproduction technology.

The applied researcher relies for his success on understanding and talking two different languages. He must operate in a completely flexible environment in the same way as the basic research worker, but he has a different pattern of research. He is engaged in a continuous review of basic research with a view to possible applications for his firm. As such he has a somewhat tighter brief than the basic researcher, but to make a real success of it demands rare skills on his part.

The problem in most firms in Britain today is that the function of applied research is either insufficiently done or not done at all. It is a function which firms cannot afford to ignore if they intend to live by creating their product opportunities.

It is also a function which management must endeavour to integrate fully with the mainstream of development, production and marketing activity. It is from these areas that much feedback will come. It is also to these areas that ideas must be passed once the *breadboard* model has emerged. No hard and fast rules can be laid down for a precise system for communication; each firm simply needs a system that works. Two common devices for achieving such co-ordination are the co-ordinating department and the cross-functional co-ordinating committee. For both devices a balance of interests is essential, and the staffing must be by those closely allied to technical problems in their work rather than administrative heads.[16]

Co-ordination at this stage must also include the first major appraisal of the new product in commercial terms. Doubts normally arise as much from the competing advocacy of supporters and detractors as from the possible market size. To overcome this problem a technique of evaluation known as *qualitative product screening* has been developed.[17] Essentially it involves determining whether the firm is in a position to endow the new product with the necessary features that would result in profits, and what type of advantage the company can most readily provide. Against an inventory of all the company's resources are set all the various demands and contributions that the product will make. These include the permanence of its market, growth prospects, product marketability, the extent to which the firm's existing production and development facilities will be adequate or, indeed, impart special advantages. As many as thirty or forty factors will enter such a consideration. Each factor is then ascribed a numerical weight against which the new product is scored, and a product profile emerges which can be compared with the min/max or average scores, alternative products under consideration, or competitive products.

The great merit of this screening is that it brings all functions in the firm into the co-ordinating process in a positive way, and ensures that their contribution is made at the earliest possible moment. It has, furthermore, the effect of focusing attention on problem areas and getting a product's priority right compared with alternatives for development in the firm.

It must be emphasized that this review should take place as soon as a *bread-board* model has shown that a given product idea is technically feasible, but before development work begins. It must be applied to both the evolutionary product ideas from marketing feedback as well as to the creative ideas fished from basic research by the applied researcher.

Products passing this screening process can proceed to the development stage.

Development

Development is the province of the designer and his team, who have to carry the *bread-board* model of the applied researcher to the pilot production of a final prototype. The outcome of their work will then be submitted to a sample of its intended users for testing and evaluation. It is a costly and extremely dynamic phase where some practical difficulty can necessitate considerable shifts in the total approach at various prototype stages. It is also a time when the inputs of all relevant disciplines must be thoroughly co-ordinated. None is more important than that of marketing, which must rapidly establish the price objectives towards which all must work, and prepare a product plan which sets commercial specifications on the basis of detailed examination of user needs and motivations.

Within the price area adopted, the co-ordination of design is often effectively undertaken by a Development Committee staffed by experts familiar with the thousand and one minute details which enable new products to meet price objectives at maximum profitability.

Design for function and use is naturally of great significance if a product is to secure repeat sales. The contribution which ergonomics can make in this area is not generally utilized, and offers considerable scope for further exploration in British industry.[18] It will ensure that design of machinery, for example, will maximize effectiveness whilst minimizing fatigue. Its basis is usually on the various body dimensions of the human operator, his or her muscular power and vision.[19]

At the same time, the law has various requirements as in relation to fabric for children's night clothes and oil heaters; all motor cars must have automatic windscreen wipers and brakes on four wheels. There are also BSI and International Standards to be observed.

Design for production focuses attention on the over-riding aims of the production group—to produce a product of a desired quality, at a required rate, within the price objectives, at a minimum cost. The design must enable this to be accomplished. Accordingly, estimates of the desired rate of sales off-take and the investment in capital equipment to be envisaged must be available.

The design must take into account the need to minimize labour costs incurred in the production by reducing the skilled element involved and minimizing the number of transmissions and activities required. Considerable savings will also be effected by thus reducing the occasions for error. Component part standardization also has considerable economies to offer. The use of Brisch references to ascertain which existing components available to a firm can be used rather than specials is sadly lacking in many instances. Instead, design and then stock-holding costs increase, reducing profit margins or even rendering many new products unprofitable. The extent of savings which are possible was well illustrated by the belated use of value analysis techniques on the TSR 2 reported to be able to save £250,000. Lavatory door bolts have also been specially designed for the Vanguard at a unit cost of £17.[20]

Various raw materials and their sources of supply will also need appraisal to see what lead times will be required for ordering, the quality levels which can be expected, the relevant cost of alternative supplies and any price breaks at different quantities.

Ease of inspection during production to ensure that requisite quality is being maintained should also be borne in mind in the consideration of design for production.

There are certain assumptions which will have to be made at this stage concerning the type of tooling which will be used. Without actually purchasing any new tools, or disrupting any existing runs in the production shop, the optimum tooling procedures for a range of possible volume off-takes must be established. These will, of course, be among the factors considered in design for production.

Finally, there are two aspects of marketing which must be given attention at the development stage by the designer. The first is the question of design for maintenance—both in terms of avoiding all that is possible and facilitating that which has to be done by ensuring easy access.

Secondly, the special requirements of distribution must be borne in mind, including ease of handling, storage and transportation; the role of packaging in protecting products should be also be considered.[21]

The outcome of all these interacting elements will be a set of drawings for pilot production of a prototype, normally with improvised, *knife-and-fork* tooling. Within the firm a series of internal tests will normally necessitate several modifications before the eventual production of a small batch of the final prototype. Prototype production may take place either in the main production shops or in some cases in separate pre-production prototype shops established for this purpose. The former has the advantage of full-scale trials under actual production conditions, whilst the latter provides additional flexibility for the incorporation of changes with minimum paper-work, and also avoids disruption of the main production facilities.

In practice, laboratory development occurs continuously throughout the development phase and sometimes also beyond pilot production. This almost invariably leads to late improvements and developments, being incorporated either during the pilot run or as a *retrofit* programme. As a generalization, the more competitive or complex the item, the greater is the likelihood of this type of activity. In highly competitive conditions these changes are usually required to improve the performance of the article in order to gain additional last-minute advantage over competing lines on the market. Complex products usually require prolonged acceptance testing, which may only reveal inherent weaknesses in design at a very late stage in development. Such weaknesses, when revealed, will then necessitate the rapid reshaping of the area affected, which may in itself require additional applied research or development in order to overcome the difficulties encountered.

On completion of the production of acceptable prototypes, drawings and production documentation will then be brought into line and the production department will be ready for the go-ahead which is dependent upon successful market and end-user tests.

User acceptance tests

At last those responsible for the processes of decision-taking in the firm can look to the end-users for some indication of whether their enterprise is likely to be rewarded. A quantitative basis can at

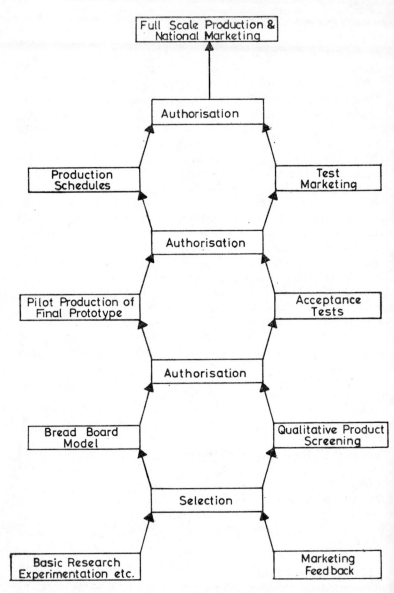

Fig. 3   *A sequence for new product development*

last be ascribed to the new product's performance *in user terms* against competition.

It is therefore essential that the evaluation of the prototype should take place as far as possible in a realistic user situation. To this end, placement should be made with a small but highly representative sample of user situations, with particular attention paid to those circumstances which will most frequently occur. This research phase is the last opportunity the development technologist will have to evaluate his prototype before the company commits its resources to its marketing and distribution. Faults which still go on undetected can damage company goodwill, as well as incur considerable additional expense.

Two key facets of the product to be closely examined are its performance/reliability, and the user's price expectations for it. The product must live up to general user expectations and to any claims that are held to make the new development in some way unique. So many new technical developments or improvements introduced are too sophisticated for an unsophisticated user (this is of course more so in consumer markets than with industrial products). It is also valuable to conduct such tests *blind,* i.e. without any brand name indicating who has manufactured the product. If a new product can stand up well on its own performance without any corporate or brand image support, then it augurs well for its eventual success.

The assessment of the price expectations of the people who have tested a new product has particular significance when sales forecasts and profitability calculations come to be finalized, should the product succeed in its user trials. It is not always too straightforward to unearth precisely the relevant replies. Inevitably they are conditioned by respondents' existing ideas, and will be based in the main on comparisons with existing materials or products.

This, however, is not so great a disadvantage as may seem apparent at first, since it provides not only a basis for sales forecasts and profitability calculations; it also gives a measure of the superiority, or lack of it, which the new product is seen to have over competitive products the user sees it superseding.

At this stage it is relevant to mention that in such user tests, it is helpful practice where the product does not break away completely from conventional designs and uses, to test against one or more existing, successful products, after all means of identifying them have been removed. Most fields into which new products are introduced can provide such yardsticks. It is also advisable to conduct a *series* of tests which can measure the extent of stability of preferences for the new development against the yardstick.[22] This is particularly necessary for taste tests. When such testing has been completed the development team in the firm can be confident that the technical assessment of their product's users in comparison with competition, provides a realistic marketing assessment of the situation. But it takes no account of the existing corporate or brand images of the manufacturer concerned, because up to this time the user has no idea who the manufacturer is.

At this stage, once again, the manufacturer will need to decide whether the results constitute a sufficiently favourable reception for work to proceed on a full scale evaluation of the capital investment involved, and the likely returns to be anticipated. Two major pieces in the commercial appraisal jigsaw now begin to fit into place—an appreciation of whether or not the price objective in the market is likely to be acceptable in users' eyes and a first broad indication of the likely level of sales based on product performance.

Investment appraisal

At every stage in the process of applied research and development the commercial factors, as interpreted by the marketing experts on co-ordinating committees, have been taken into account. Numerous rough drafts, constantly revised, have been prepared by the financial members of the team. On each occasion to date, however, it has been a question of does this look feasible commercially? The calculations have been based on qualitative rather than quantitative assessment of the user's behaviour. At last, however, the user acceptance tests have provided some preliminary quantitative data on which the financial men can bring their calculations down to fact-based sales and price predictions; and with them they can proceed to the overall appraisal of the investment in the new product. Skeleton ideas of the extent of new productive capacity required, of the stock-holding and space costs, and of the development of channels of distribution, all begin to take on flesh.

Forecasting all the costs likely to arise and determining the time cost of capital tied up as a result of any given product investment decision is a complex task which has only been understood by even the most progressive managements or economists in recent decades. More and more evidence has come to light, since the famous Oxford studies just prior to World War II on investment decisions, to indicate that far from subjecting possible investments to scientific evaluation by proven techniques, haphazard factors are largely responsible. As Merrett and Sykes remark, what many firms suffer from is not a lack of investment but a lack of the right *quality* of investment.[23]

The essence of any appraisal of an investment in industry lies in an evaluation of the cost of the money to be tied up in the project which is set against the returns anticipated. Provided all other resources in the firm are available, all investment opportunities which afford a satisfactory margin between cost and return should be adopted and actioned. But assessing cost and return is hazardous, for both involve uncertainty.

No full-time production of a product will have been undertaken at the time of making the investment appraisal; no full-scale marketing will have been undertaken either. Production cost estimates must be based on material prices over which one often has no long-term control; sales forecasts have to be based on the scanty user trials referred to earlier, and the acceptable price to consumers for a forecast level of off-take has to be surmized on equally uncertain findings. This is not to minimize the value of pilot production nor of user trials of prototypes, but merely to point out that their value has certain limits. Indeed, the greater the technological stride being taken, the less reliable the early experiments can be expected to be.

Inevitably, final investment decisions in the best firms will be choices between several alternatives, many of which could reasonably be expected to afford adequate returns. Here it is important to bear in mind the product strategy of the business. Peter Drucker distinguishes three major types of product investment—additive, complementary and breakthrough.[24] The first more fully exploits what resources are already employed by better allocation, or by development of new potential in a market, for instance. The complementary investment is self-explanatory. The break-through is the sort of investment which, even with great risk, a firm just cannot afford to take. For many firms, entry into atomic power generation at a time when no realistic appraisal could see any real chance of its becoming economic was just such an investment.

To get the right balance between these three types is no easy task. It will never occur unless the emphasis is on maximizing opportunities rather than minimizing risks, and on the joint evaluation of all major opportunities open to a firm in both the short and the long term.

So crucial is the taking of the correct investment decisions in the individual firm to the health of the national economy, that the National Economic Development Council directed its Office to prepare and publish an examination of the topic.[25] Its findings indicated that there was reason to conclude that many businessmen were unaware of the effects of tax incentives available via invest-vestment and initial allowances and tax-free depreciation, and that many of the methods of evaluation of investment decisions were widely unreliable.[26] The outcome of this state of affairs was firstly, a reluctance to undertake investment and secondly, a demand for an unnecessarily high rate of return.

The NEDC paper comes out firmly in favour of the discounted cash flow (DCF) method of appraising the cost of various invest-ments. Its particular advantages are summarized as:

(a) it takes appropriate account of differences in the time-stream of net earnings over the expected life of the pro-ject and the fact that £100 today is worth more than £100 a year from now;

(b) it easily takes tax liabilities and allowance, and their timing, into account.

DCF establishes the difference between receipts and expendi-tures for each year, termed the net cash flow from the investment. This is then discounted in order to arrive at the true cost of the capital locked up now. If the capital cost is seven per cent per annum under the discounting procedure, £100 invested today requires a return of £107 in a year's time. This procedure, applied throughout all the investment's forecast life, indicates the total cash flow to be anticipated. Provided this is no less than the initial cost, the implication is that the project can earn at least seven per cent per annum on capital, in addition to repaying the initial invest-ment during its life.[27]

We have given an extended consideration to investment appraisal in this section because the success of investment policies is obvi-ously critical to the firm's willingness and continued ability to in-troduce new products. It is also vital to ensure that the maximum number of investment opportunities are taken and that resources are, therefore, most effectively utilized. It is an area which is destined to attract more and more attention from marketing men as they attempt to forecast sales and consumer acceptability on the basis of prototype products, and from production men and cost accountants as they grapple with the problems of cost projection from their pilot operations.

Within the individual firm, however, the go-ahead from invest-ment appraisal means the preparation of detailed production schedules first to meet the sales forecasts for a test marketing opera-tion and later to meet demand in the total market.

Production schedules

The preparation of detailed schedules will be affected by the type of production, e.g. flow line or batch, the volume or batch size, and the anticipated product life. Other factors affecting scheduling and control include a firm's overall existing product-line diversity, the programming of the various product mix factors where customer options are given, and the cycle times of critical items. Where conditions are such as to make its application economical, PERT or similar critical path techniques often prove valuable, particularly in establishing optimized lead times.[28] APD or EDP techniques offer considerable advantages in production control and material provisioning. Not only does this enable comprehensive assembly schedules to be developed incorporating sufficient lead for lower generation sub-assemblies to enable priorities to be established for procurement and production of these items; it also integrates individual parts requirements into the total parts population for the production area concerned. The adoption of a regular routine of data processing gives several fringe benefits. A discipline is enforced which necessitates the regular receipt of sales forecasts, which if correctly examined will provide many useful pointers to product movement. In addition, by regular, say monthly, action a full review of parts availability, on-order position, production status, and shop capacity may be obtained.[29] This in total will lead to optimized utilization of all resources. If scheduling and the breakdown of material requirements is performed as a purely clerical function, then action must be taken in preparing full lists of the parts required, together with as detailed a list of priorities as possible in order to meet production target dates. Obviously, as a manual exercise, much duplication of effort will occur due to inability to correlate material requirements by part number, which means that the advantages of scale will not be obtained either in manufacturing sub-assemblies or in obtaining price breaks from external suppliers. Procurement authorization having thus been established, the accent will shift to the purchasing department, where firm endeavours are made to obtain parts to the given specifications at best prices within the required lead time. It will be apparent that the work of this department will be greatly facilitated by periodic consolidated requirements for given items rather than many partial requests for what would ultimately be the same gross quantity. Concurrently, production control must examine the forward load position and brief purchasing departments as far in advance as possible of any likely requirements for sub-contract capacity. At this time the production department put the finishing touches to specialized installations on the production line, whilst chasing special purpose tools and appliances, and finalizing the visual aids.

The foregoing is all part of the integration process of a new product into an established production facility which is the most likely eventuality with product innovation. This phase of the process often demands little in the way of innovation, success being achieved by adherence to a planned pattern of events. The major scope for possible innovation is in the way in which the events are planned.

Now is not the time for value analysis or alterations to the product design; the full details of such matters must have been settled before full-scale production began. Attention must now concentrate on ensuring that the production programme is fulfilled at the required rate of output and at the requisite quality. Volumes and quality control are the final elements to watch.

Presenting the product to the market

The time will eventually arrive when all the contributions which design and acceptance testing can make to product innovation will have been made. An appraisal of the return anticipated on the investment involved has been calculated for given levels of sales, and production is prepared to meet such demands on its capacity. Management must now present its new product to the market as yet one more product to compete for purchasing power. Even now, however, except in abnormal market circumstances, it will be inadvisable to jump directly into the national market as a whole.

There are a large number of factors in the marketing situation other than the product itself which we have so far largely been considering. These are ignored only at great peril. The most obvious are the advertising approach, brand name selection, the package design, the buying of media space, sales representative and retailer/wholesaler briefings, the sell-in, distribution arrangements and so on. Not only has the marketing mix to be decided but the launching itself is a major organizational activity. PERT systems can prove of great assistance.[30]

For any specific product some of the factors involved will be less of a problem than others. One more product added to an existing range will not normally encounter particular problems in distribution, since *entrée* into appropriate outlets already exists. If, however, the product is in a new area, not only new salesmen with differing technical background may be required, but new outlets of a different type altogether may need to be sold into.

It is as a result of the many complexities which a major product launch involves that the techniques of test marketing and area marketing have evolved. Both seek to commence selling on a limited basis, often just a single TV region, or a few counties.

Test marketing, on balance, is to be preferred. It sets out to mount a marketing operation in a microcosm of the total market which in all possible respects will simulate what should occur nationally. What happens is carefully examined by continuous research procedures, checking the distribution levels achieved, the effect of any advertising campaigns and the reactions and off-take by consumers, particularly repeat purchasing.

Area marketing, on the other hand, is markedly less scientific, and as such is unable to give the more accurate estimate of likely effects if the new product goes national. It does, however, in the event of failure, enable one to withdraw a product without a great loss of face or resources. Area marketing is best regarded as merely phase one of a plan to market a product nationally, which is tackled in stages when the full effort of a national launch would overtax the firm. It is a policy of confident, some would say over-confident, management, for if sales levels are unsatisfactory there is no re-search base to indicate what the deficiencies might be, and it is of course too late to discover what consumers thought before they were informed of the product or were exposed to its promotions. Nor is there any qualitative measure of the distribution obtained in relation to the universe of outlets in the area.

Test marketing, therefore, is to be preferred because it consti-tutes a controlled experiment of the eventual national activity. If it is to provide the necessary accurate results (a) for projection to the total market in respect of sales achieved and their quality, and (b) of the level of repeated purchasing to be expected, then great care must be taken in the selection of the location for test marketing and the way it is conducted.[31]

It is quite crucial, once the product is put into a test market, that alternative courses of action are ready in the event of strong com-petitive reaction. Particularly where a new product is tackling a firmly entrenched market, fierce competitive counter measures should be anticipated. Marketing any product is a dynamic pro-cess, and it is not sufficient for the research man to plead that he needs six months before he can really evaluate the outcome of the test when a new product is being undersold to kill by giant competitors. The outcome of the test is already obvious.

Statistics on new product failures in the United States from the Federal Bureau of Commerce indicate that they stand as high as 90 per cent after four years. Well over half the products test marketed in Britain are thought never to get beyond their test area. This second statistic focuses particular attention on the criteria by which a test marketing operation is to be judged.

The British Market Research Bureau has recently released a tentative evaluation of forty-four test operations for which it has been responsible.[32] The evidence available deals with new grocery and chemist lines, and shows clearly how sales build up in tests to a peak and then stabilize at a lower level. The valuable statistic which has emerged is the relationship between the peak and the stabilization level, known as the *drop factor*. This has been found to remain more or less constant when test markets are extended to a national operation. There does not yet seem to have been much success in predicting the actual peak level or stabilized level of sales. The average drop encountered is about 40 per cent from the peak sales reached, however, which enable two rules of thumb to emerge:

1. If at any stage during the initial sales build-up, sales exceed twice the rate of the stable target level, there is a three to one probability that the product has made it.
2. Unless peak sales exceed the target stable level by at least 50 per cent, there is a three to one probability that the product will fail to maintain its target.

Although this recent addition to generally available knowledge of test marketing represents a substantial advance in the planning of new product innovations, it does not cover many qualitative aspects which such tests must seek to understand. The product may prove to create for itself on test a small minority market, for example, which is devoted to it, rather than a mass market with a level of sales off-take originally envisaged. This minority market could transform the entire marketing approach, making it possible to reduce, perhaps drastically, the original estimate of sales costs and minimum distribution. A new marketing synthesis could emerge which makes lower sales off-takes quite economic at an increased price.[33]

On the other hand, high off-take and an absence of repeat purchases could indicate a serious defect in the product, or advertising, in that it failed to square with expectations which had been aroused. User attitude research can help to pin down particular shortcomings.

In any interpretation of test marketing results, management must always remember that the product with which they have grown so familiar is quite fresh to its user. We all, as consumers, have an existing set of values with which a new product idea may be incompatible. We may be slow to try and even slower to accept; we may be slow to understand the complexities involved. We need sympathetic understanding, and the marketing man needs an intelligent appreciation of that need if he is to fully evaluate the results he obtains.

At the end of the test marketing stage, the firm can have a clearer picture of just how the new product has fared in obtaining a sustained level of sales, what distribution it has obtained and what users' attitudes towards it are. Furthermore the production departments have had experience of producing the product at the requisite quality level and rate. If, once again, the test procedures give the new product the go-ahead, the blueprints in all sectors will be ready and tried. The new product will stand its best chance of success in the national market.

(It is perhaps appropriate at the present time to draw specific attention to the use of the word *national* market in our discussion. Many products have an international appeal which differs no more than product appeal can between Scotland and South-East England. But it is as well to be over-wary of radical differences and to approach *foreign* markets with respect. This often implies further experimentation.)

The overview

Our ultimate justification for this lengthy and discursive examination of the procedures of product innovation in the firm, set in the current national context, is that it tries to give the overview which the general manager should have. Naturally there will be times when he will have to short circuit the process or where a new product idea is not of sufficient value to justify some of the procedures outlined. But this having been said, nothing can shake our fundamental certainty that product innovation, which is the life blood of almost every enterprise, must be kept continually under planned control. Only by such planning can it be ensured that the complexities are mastered and all relevant inputs are made early enough on to reduce costs for optimum results.

Organizations which operate in such a way create the atmosphere in which voluntary feed-back from all areas adds further strength. Dynamic innovative organizations of this type have a crucial role to play in the British economy; they also ensure the optimum return to the shareholders and those who devote their time and labour to the business.

It is appropriate, in conclusion, to mention briefly the type of overall organization which firms have established to ensure that they do not fall short in their development of new products. Naturally, evidence comes mainly from the United States. Many have set up separate product development departments charged with supervising all plans from applied research within the framework of company objectives through to launching full-scale on to its market. S. C. Johnson & Son report that particularly in the area of co-ordination between research, development and marketing, such a department has a vital role to play.[34] It also necessitated clarification of company product objectives and strategy in a way not appreciated before. A special new products department is by no means universally accepted, however, since it naturally adds further problems of communication. Others place greater emphasis on the actions and re-actions of management rather than organizational forms. Nevertheless, it is conceded that, in companies with strong departmental barriers, a specialist corps of new product developers may well be the only way to ease product innovations over the various barriers.[35]

Quite obviously the problem of overall organization can only be resolved on an individual firm basis. It is our final observation that it deserves attention by every firm.

REFERENCES

1 — (1961) *Management and control of research and development* (HMSO) (The first four definitions abridged).

2 — (1963) *Government's rule in applying science to industry.* P.E.P. broadsheet, July.

3 — Advisory Council on Scientific Policy: Annual reports. (HMSO).

4 — (1963) Prosperity without science. *Economist* (June 23).

5 Williams, Gertrude. (1963) *Apprenticeship in Europe* (Chapman & Hall).

6 Wooster, Clive. (1965) Management and design in the building industry. *Scientific Business,* Feb.

7 Wilson, Harold. (1964) Address to Market Research Society.

8 Berg, T. & Shuchman, A. (1963) A programme for new product evolution: *Product strategy and management* (Holt, Rinehart & Winston).

9 Burns, Tom & Stalker, G. (1961) *Management of innovation* (Tavistock Pubns).

10 Taylor & Barron. (1963) *Scientific creativity* (Wiley & Sons).

11 Gordon, W. J. (1961) *Synetics* (Harper & Bros.).

12 Becker, S. W. (1964) The innovative organization. Selected Paper No. 14, Chicago Graduate School of Business.

13 — (1964) Evidence of Tavistock Inst. of Human Relations and others to Heyworth Committee on Research in the Social Sciences.

14 Leach, G. (1964) Essential engineer. *New Statesman* (Dec. 25).

15 Hughes, Ifan. (1965) Introducing and applying technology. Institute of Scientific Business Research Tract No. 1, March.

16 Lorsch, J. & Lawrence, P. (1965) Organizing for product innovation.

17 Wilson, Aubrey. (1963) Selecting new products for development. *Scientific Business*, Nov.

18 — (1964) Ergonomics: designing the driver's work-place. *Design*, Aug.

19 McCormick, E. J. (1957) *Human engineering* (McGraw Hill).

20 — (1965) *The Guardian* (April 2).

21 Buck, G. Hearn. (1963) *Problems of product design and development* (Pergamon).

22 — (1964) Applications report No. 5. Research Services Ltd.

23 Merrett, A. & Sykes, A. (1964) *Finance and analysis of capital projects* (Longmans).

24 Drucker, P. (1964) *Managing for results* (Heinemann).

25 — (1965) *Investment appraisal*. N.E.D.C. (HMSO).

26 Williams, B. R. (Sept. 1964) Information and criterion in capital expenditure decisions. *Jour. of Management Studies*.

27 Alfred, A. M. (1964) *Discounted cash flow and corporate planning*.

28 Woodgate, H. (1964) *Planning by network* (Business Publications).

29 Foster, F. G. (1963) Automatic control by turnover. *Scientific Business*, Nov.

Woolwich Economic Paper No. 3.

30 Rawle, L. J. (1964) The right order of things. *Progress*. March.

31 Day, R. (1964) The use and abuse of test market research. *Commentary*.

32 Davies, J. (1964) Sales curves of new products (*Research in marketing*), Market Research Society.

33 Tate, B. & Rothman, J. (Aug. 1964) Researching for maniple markets. *Scientific Business*.

34 Johnson, S. C. & Jones, L. C. (May/June 1957) How to organize for new products. *Harvard Business Rev.*

35 McCarthy, E. J. (1959) Organization for new product development. *Jour. of Business*, April.

16 | Technological Myopia

by GORDON WILLS

IT is my purpose to explore the ways in which the imperatives of modern technology interact with the marketing concept; with the idea that the customer is in some sense sovereign in the determination of what will be produced and how it will be marketed in our economic system.

I have selected a title which is intended to be quizzical and provocative, and which was first suggested to me as I was reading Reynolds's paper on 'Research and the Marketing Concept'.[1] Galbraith,[2, 3] however, must take the blame for having awoken my interest as a marketeer to the conceptual problems posed in the fundamental oversimplification which *le client-roi* implies. Technological myopia is a widespread disease amongst the marketing fraternity and particularly, one might add, the teachers of marketing. It is most acute when we are under persecution by either the sales oriented executives we have superseded or by the research and development scientists and engineers who have produced a technically beautiful product which is not selling too well. It is a condition which requires careful handling, for reputations and status are involved. None the less, it is probably an unavoidable counter-condition to marketing's attempts to scan the distant horizon, to avoid charges of marketing myopia.

Marketing's conception and early childhood with 'mother' selling and 'father' production, necessarily meant a swing in adolescence towards a thorough-going independence. The onset of maturity, however, can only be manifest in a proper relationship between the customer's interest and the intelligent use of research and development. One particular adolescent belief was that marketing's role was to plan and co-ordinate the development of the company's

Professor GORDON WILLS is Professor of Marketing at The University of Bradford Management Centre. This paper was first presented to the National Conference on the *Strategic Analysis of Customer Behaviour,* sponsored by the Institute of Marketing at The University, December 1969.

future unaided and independently of other functional interests. Such a viewpoint reached its most subtle, if extravagant, exposition in Levitt's much discussed paper on Marketing Myopia.[4] His strictures for instance, on the buggy whip and the petroleum industries are now enshrined in our mythology. Reynolds points out that they need to be desecrated if we are to arrive at any currently valuable working relationship between these two, mutually dependent, founts of new product ideas. No company is a slave to any definition of the business it is in, nor even to its current pattern of resource allocation. The whole rationale of the corporate planning backlash towards marketing is to demonstrate that a company has a wide range of resources, each, some, all or none of which can form a basis for successful growth, maintained performance, or whatever other objective we might pursue. Successful innovation, however, will normally require both marketing and technological innovation and marketing and technological critique. The two are so closely inter-related that there cannot be work in one area without assumption and consequence that bear on the other. Production/Market characteristics mutually determine one another. Schon[5] has spotted that much of the problem stems from the professionalism of the division of labour between marketing and technology. Each tries to make true, safe statements within its professional territory, leaving the uncertainty inherent in the situation to the other. The problems of institutionalization once again rear their heads; once again we are faced with the need for a dynamic sociology if the problem is to be conquered. Burns[6] has described the problem as sclerotic, one of the major challenges facing the social sciences today.

Galbraith's revised sequence

What has been suggested here is something greater than Galbraith's 'revised sequence' which he develops fully in *The New Industrial State*.[3] The synergy, which Schon, Reynolds and I feel results from the interaction of technology and marketing, is not a sinister social conspiracy, as Galbraith is tempted to imply, by a small technostructure, but a more satisfactory, less wasteful deployment of business resources in the service of the customer and hence of society.

Galbraith's thesis is worth re-stating here to demonstrate his synergistic myopia:

'We have seen that the accepted sequence i.e. customer sovereignity does not hold. And we have now isolated a formidable apparatus of method and motivation causing its reversal. The mature corporation has readily at hand the means for controlling the prices at which it sells as well as those at which it buys. Similarly, it has means for managing what the consumer buys at the prices which it controls. This control and management is required by its planning. The planning proceeds from use of technology and capital, the commitment of time that these require and the diminished effectiveness of the market for specialized technical products and skills.

'Supporting this changed sequence is the motivation of the technostructure. Members seek to adapt the goals of the corporation more closely to their own; by extension the corporation seeks to adapt social attitudes and goals to those of the members of its technostructure. So social belief originates at least in part with the producer. Thus the accommodation of the market behaviour of the individual, as well as of social attitudes in general, to the needs of producers and the goals of the technostructure is an inherent feature of the system. It becomes increasingly important with the growth of the industrial system.

'It follows that the accepted sequence is no longer a description of the reality and is becoming ever less so. Instead the producing firm reaches forward to control its markets and on beyond to manage the market behaviour and shape the social attitudes of those ostensibly, that it serves. For this we also need a name and it may appropriately be called The Revised Sequence. I do not suggest that the revised sequence has replaced the accepted sequence. Within the industrial system the accepted sequence is of diminished importance in relation to the revised sequence.'

Galbraith does, of course, go on to agree that the two can exist side by side, and I for one have no wish to deprecate the direction of his argument. None the less, he fails to explore the significance of the two-directional sequence. Some aspects of demand satisfaction do indeed require a long planning period with concomitant high risks, and a need to manage demand if at all possible. But there are, equally, a wide range of technological improvements and innovations which do not. Furthermore, the corporate need for managed demand (from the firm's viewpoint) can arise from planned marketing investment as well as from planned industrial investment. Marketing investment can often be substantially higher than its manufacturing equivalent.

That a technostructure exists in industry is beyond doubt, and the reasons Galbraith enunciates for its emergence are surely right. Most industries today employ the widest possible range of knowledge to meet the complex technological demands that are made upon them. This knowledge is shared amongst many individuals and must be reconciled. In addition, the forward commitment implicit in the gestation of new technology makes the forecasting and/or creation of specific demand fundamental to corporate success. Team reconciliation is accordingly unavoidable, but Galbraith again strays when he suggests this is exclusively the task of the techno-structure. There are are least two readily identifiable counter-trends which are restraining the entrepreneurial/business policy function in business. The first has already been alluded to as the corporate planning backlash. The corporate planning function provides the 'toppermost' management with its own specialist skills in the integration of technologies and functions—it could perhaps be termed a techno-superstructure, but it is scarcely ever allied to the techno-structure, which continues to exist but at a lower level. A second more problematic development is in terms of the increased potential for entrepreneurial decision making to be re-established with the advance of computing power. It is apparently now beyond all reasonable doubt that within the next two generations of computers we shall be able to restore our individual mastery of the complex organizations to at least that level formerly enjoyed by the dominant figures of the 19th century.[7]

None of these comments is intended in any sense to contradict the self-evident fact of which the marketeer is aware—that specific demand can be managed in much the same manner as the level of aggregate demand is managed within the total economy, along Keynesian lines. Institutional advertising in many sectors has borne witness to this, so has the acceleration of consumption in response to educational campaigns during the early stages of product diffusion. Equally however, we are aware that unless the product does strike a chord, the sustained level of specific demand will not be maintained. We are all persuasible but not infinitely so. The most successful commercial activity seems normally to be that wherein a company identifies and/or creates a need which is perceived as worthwhile by the customer. Whilst it is always possible to argue that what is worthwhile can be an opinion induced by the manufacturer himself, there are probably many more examples where such an argument has failed than has been substantiated, and there are certainly many better ways of making good returns on investment.

There is a more perplexing and complex situation that is often encountered in process industries which Galbraith's preoccupation with the car industry perhaps led him to overlook. It is common to all industries which produce by-products in the course of manufacturing something perhaps totally in line with the accepted

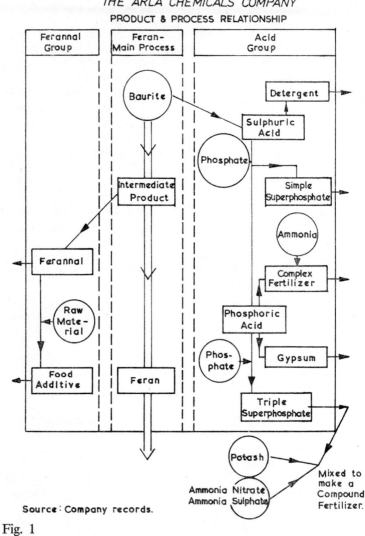

THE ARLA CHEMICALS COMPANY
PRODUCT & PROCESS RELATIONSHIP

Source: Company records.

Fig. 1

sequence, and for such organizations it would seem necessary, if possible, for the revised sequence to operate in respect of by-products. Alas the evidence is that this is seldom the case.

Arla Chemicals

A classic illustration of the problem to which I refer is to be found at Arla Chemicals.[8]

As Fig. 1 illustrates, the company's operations centre around the production of feran. All the other products which the company sells were introduced in an attempt to make a profit from feran by-products. The by-products emerge in a fixed relationship to the volume output of feran. The problems within this complex industry are further aggravated by the ever-present danger of losing the supply of raw material—baurite—altogether.

Until 1937 Arla had disposed of all its by-product sulphurous material simply by producing and selling sulphuric acid. The introduction of fertilizer products at that time was made largely because of adverse conditions in the sulphuric acid market. Since sulphuric acid had always been difficult to store or transport, other producers had had repeatedly to dump their output in the local market as supply temporarily exceeded demand. Consequently, the price for sulphuric acid traditionally had fluctuated greatly. Furthermore, as the world demand for feran increased substantially in the second half of the 1930s, Arla increased its production of feran and found itself faced with a greater supply of sulphurous material than ever before. At the same time, the general supply of sulphuric acid had outgrown the demand within the marketable area.

Under these circumstances, Arla began to process the sulphuric acid into simple superphosphate fertilizer, phosphoric acid and triple-superphosphate fertilizer. These new products permitted Arla profitably to dispose of its sulphuric acid excess in new markets and also alleviated the problem of storage. Up to 1962 Arla had been the only feran manufacturer in its geographical area that processed sulphuric acid into derivative products—in this case, fertilizers. After World War II the local pattern of industrial chemical requirements changed, and the demand for sulphuric acid greatly increased until it far exceeded the supply available from feran by-products in the area. Consequently, by 1962, Arla was producing one-third of its sulphuric acid production from free sulphur to meet these needs.

Although the acid group consisted of ten products by 1960, only four of these were sold in any substantial amounts. Of these, sulphuric acid and triple-superphosphate fertilizer accounted for 80

per cent of the acid group sales. Simple superphosphate and complex fertilizers represented another 12 per cent, while the other six
products accounted for the remaining 8 per cent. Phosphoric acid,
one of these six products, was actually produced in great quantities,
but it was primarily used as an internal intermediate product because no significant demand existed for it outside the company.

The markets for these products were diverse. The sulphuric acid
was sold direct to industrial users within a 100/150 kilometre
radius. The fertilizers were sold to farm supply distributors. Transportation costs limited this market to a radius of 150 kilometres.
The other products were normally sold through agents in Europe.

The other major by-product, ferannal, was sold mainly to the
food processing industry for use in the production of additives.
However, Arla's customers had recently introduced a new process in which no ferannal additive was required. It is not at all clear
how Arla can ensure that the philosophy inherent in the revised
sequence would work itself out in such circumstances as these. But
I concede I have taken an extreme example.

It is perhaps helpful if this examination of Galbraith's revised
sequence is concluded by restating the manner of synergistic effect
that is potentially available if technology and marketing can work
sympathetically together. The cost of innovation can be reduced
because the risks which separation between marketing and technology necessitates that each must take, can be reduced; the cost
of innovation can be reduced because the time scale of innovation
can be telescoped; the invoiced price to the customer can be reduced because the cost of innovation has been lessened. But *none*
of this synergy can result unless both marketing and technology
work together, each on the understanding of where its professionalism ends and where the professionalism of the other begins. The
company wishes to embrace the inventiveness of both professions
and to judge not the source of the ideas but their customer-worthi-
ness. There is more respect for the intellect of customers in industry
than Galbraith gives credit for, although that respect has sometimes
had to be learned the hard way. Once again Galbraith has omitted
to develop the full implications of the customer backlash, but he did
not fail to note it was inherent in the system he described.

The educational and scientific estate

Modern technology's basis in current knowledge and its desire for
further development contain the basis for avoiding the worst consequences of Galbraith's technostructure, even assuming it to exist

in its most sinister form as a conspiracy against customers. The educated and knowledgeable members of the very technostructure itself rebel against any social straitjacket inspired by the techno-structure. They influence the determination of technological objectives, the pattern of organization to implement them, and the manner of demand management in specific sectors as shown in Fig. 2. Furthermore, as discretionary incomes rise they express their individuality by contracting out of the industrial system's mass market approach in favour of segmented modes of behaviour. Galbraith has identified this as no more than a possible method of protest—it could perhaps be more aptly observed as the most significant pattern of the future. As more and more join the educational and scientific state and more and more enjoy rising dis-

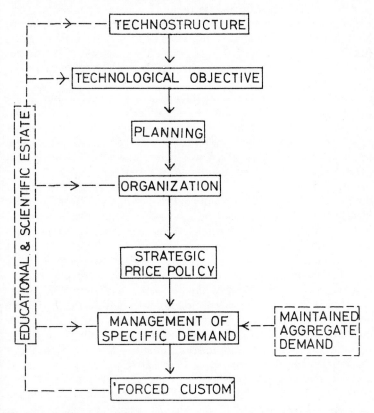

Fig. 2 *Galbraith's 'Revised Sequence' with its leakage through the 'Educational and Scientific Estate'*

K

cretionary incomes, the creation and satisfaction of widely differentiated patterns of demand, as well as aesthetic and cultural objectives, can certainly be expected to become increasingly necessary. This is not a pattern of technostructural managed innovation but of customer expectations. Of course what can be conceived and created will remain the province of the creative mind, be it in research and development or marketing or customers' letters of complaint or suggestion boxes.

Spurious differentiation of demand is and will continue to be cynically received by the educational and scientific estate. The most violent critics of detergent and petrol advertising, for instance, can be found in the advertising companies and agencies themselves. Indeed, the spuriousness has reached such a pitch that many customers are now treating a wide range of heavily branded products as no more than commodity goods—flour, petrol, detergent, beans, biscuits. This is one of the prime reasons for the massive burst (the last gasp perhaps of the spurious differentiators) in below-the-line promotion and 'own label' brands in the past ten years. Customers are not tempted into a new pattern of loyalties in such commodity markets. They merely take the marginal purchasing advantage proffered and move to any other national brand or own label which next offers an advantage in its turn. As so many interviewed customers in these fields have remarked, a price cut would be preferable to them, and it looks increasingly as if its effect would be no different from the manufacturer's viewpoint either.

One can surely not be surprised that the human mind should develop an immunity to bamboozlement. In face of it, we may identify our referent to fend off innovative indigestion. Stravinsky[9] has neatly expressed these anxieties and the classic response: 'As far as I am concerned, I experience a kind of terror as I am about to go to work and before the infinite possibilities offered to me, I feel that everything is permitted. If everything is permitted, best and worst, if nothing offers any resistance every effort is inconceivable. I can't base myself on anything and from then on every enterprise is in vain. . . . Nevertheless, I will not perish. I will conquer my terror and will take assurance from the notion that I have the seven notes of the scale in its chromatic intervals, its strong or weak beats are within my reach, and that I hold in this way solid and concrete elements which offer me as vast a field of experiment as this vague and vertiginous incident which has just frightened me . . . What pulls me out of the anguish caused by unconditional freedom is that I always have the faculty of concentrating on the concrete things which are in question here and now.'

We could opt out altogether, using neo-luddite or hippie approaches to contemporary problems or nostalgic escapism as we go '. . . lumbering back to the clever tools (we) do not love and do not understand'.[10]

Contracting out will not be necessary, however. Salvation lies within the industrial system itself, even as described by Galbraith 'In contrast with its economic antecedents, it is intellectually demanding. Men will not be entrapped by the belief that apart from the production of goods and income by more progressively advanced technical methods, there is nothing important in life . . . The industrial system brings into existence to serve its intellectual and scientific needs, the community that, hopefully, will reject its monopoly of social purpose.'[11]

Social planning of technology

Galbraith describes a contemporary market place where technology has replaced the customer as sovereign, technology not only in the shape of what can be achieved but also of what cannot. Although he hopefully sees salvation around the corner, he does not examine the powerful tools which society as the representative of customers has at its command today. They go under the collective title of technological forecasting (TF) and although as yet by no means perfected, they show the way forward to a methodology for anticipating and hence shaping our technological environment. This is not the place to explore the range of techniques which have been developed (I have done that elsewhere [12, 13, 14]). Nor do I wish to suggest that TF is a totally new approach either in Britain or North America. Managements have traditionally, albeit perhaps intuitively, kept a cautious eye on the pace of technological change in those sectors which they thought likely to impinge on their business interests. But as is so frequently the case in management, it was a defensive eye more often than a purposeful one. The problem was often construed as lying in the danger of being overtaken by new technologies before an adequate return had been obtained on a particular investment.

That this view is changed and in many industrial sectors is now mere history, is reflected in a series of international, national and corporate events which have characterized industrial technology in the sixties. The issues have been pinpointed by the journalistic presentation of Servan-Schreiber,[15] with his catch-phrase, *le défi americain;* in the more sober thoughts of John Duckworth, Managing Director of our greatly expanded National Research Development

Corporation, (interviewed by Beer *et al*[16]), through countless political and ministerial pronouncements from the Wilson Labour Government, beginning with the Prime Minister's own 'white-heat of
technology' speech, and its constant echo first from Frank Cousins
and, since his departure from Mintech, from Anthony Wedgwood
Benn. The movement forward, *la sensibilisation* of senior management to a positive role for technology in our industrial prosperity,
has been institutionalized not just in our own Ministry of Technology but in our educational system through the eleven new technological universities and the enhanced status of the polytechnics.
It also become the major basis for our flanking strategy in the
face of the Gaullist veto on British entry into the European Community.

This positive deployment of national resources as the basis for
our industrial structure has entailed the abandonment of intuitive
thoughts about technological futures. A new technology for the
mastery of technology has been spawned, not based solely on the
extrapolation of existing trends in functional capabilities but on
normative demands about the sort of future we wish to create; and
as a vitally important corollary to that, a realistic understanding of
the sort of role we as a nation can play in the totality of world
technology, either from the British industrial base or the wider industrial base of the European Economic Community.

The normative approaches inherent in much of the new field of
technological forecasting are equally exhilarating from the individual, social and commercial viewpoints. They provide a rigorous
opportunity for all to participate more meaningfully in the development of the environment in which we and our heirs shall need to
live. They provide the basis for the democratic management of the
technostructure.

Within Britain already the purposeful structuring of our technological initiatives is beginning to pay off, although there are as many
instances where the failure to take the initiative in technological
change has led to catastrophic decay, both commercially and
socially. The pattern of our trade with other nations, however, emphasizes some of the success we have achieved. Fred Catherwood,[17]
Director-General of the NEDO, has pointed to the transformation
of the structure of our exports. From the situation in 1959 where
39 per cent of exports went to the sterling area, the comparable
proportion in 1968 had fallen to 28 per cent. The shifting balance
has been occasioned by the growth in our trade with the major
advanced industrial economies in the world. We are moving towards a situation where we must increasingly 'live and cope with

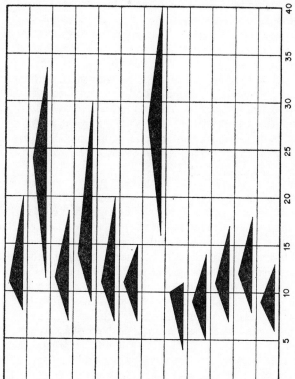

YEARS AFTER 1968

USE

National UK Data Bank with central record of whole population—Income Tax, National Health, etc.

Chequeless Society in UK

Cheques used only by private individuals

Computer-aided teaching in over 50% of UK comprehensive schools

Complete control of London's underground railway system

10 fully integrated management information systems operational in UK

1% residential houses in UK with terminal linked to information service computer

National economic forecasting and planning by computer

Large-scale information retrieval system
    (a) Science & Technology

    (b) Patents

    (c) Law

    (d) Medical Diagnosis

Fig. 3 *Delphi timescale for computer applications*

the rigorous competition of advanced high-technology, high-wage, capital-intensive economies rather than the closed-trading system inherited from the Empire'. Britain can no longer afford to cover the whole industrial waterfront. We must concentrate further in those areas of our greatest expertise. When this is done, we can be seen to be succeeding, for example in aerospace, computers, electronics and chemicals.[18] In each of these industries the techniques of technological forecasting are in action. The Programmes Analysis Unit, jointly established in the AEA and Mintech at Didcot is also playing an important role in promoting their use, both in strategic government planning and more widely throughout British industry.

TF gives us the ability to fight the future if we do not wish to become a victim of some particular facet which might otherwise be in store for us. Through TF, society can lay bare the alternative futures and choose between them. *The Guardian*[19] put the view succinctly, if in a somewhat pessimistic manner: 'But as always, there is a ray of hope. The ideas germinated in the think tanks may serve as an innoculation against the real thing. If we concentrate our thoughts now on 100,000-ton hovercraft, Mach 10 airliners, brains directly linked to computers, controlled longevity, and intelligent animals bred for low-grade labour we may be able to resist them when they become practicable, as assuredly they will. It is bountiful of Nature to provide us with this defence mechanism. Caught unawares by concrete proposals to inflict such things upon us we might be unable to say no. And in that case the future of mankind would be nasty, brutish, and everlasting.'

Hall's[20] description of possible computer applications using the Delphi technique perhaps gives a clearer indication of the futures in store for us (see Fig. 3). It also gives society an opportunity to accelerate, by the deployment of additional resources in support of particular applications, their fruitful development. The gross delays currently inherent in our legal system might well not be acceptable if continued for the period implied by this forecast. Legislation to prevent a National UK Data Bank ever becoming a reality has already been prepared.

Technology transfer and balance

Two major problems remain as yet unmentioned. Positive optimism about a mastery of technology, based on our ability to forecast and plan, must return to the opening issues which were raised in the notion of technological myopia. Only a closely integrated re-

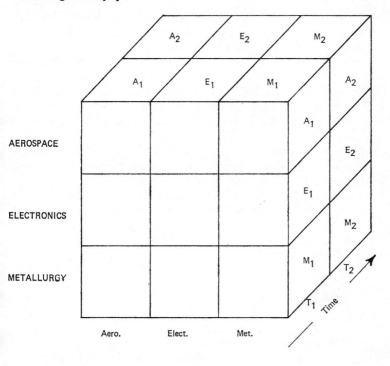

For these three sectors, two balanced technologies exist:

	T_1	T_2
Aerospace	Pre-Satellite	Satellite
Electronics	Vacuum Tubes	Transistors
Metallurgy	99.99 % Metals	99.999 % Metals

Fig. 4 *Technological capability/market requirement balance*

lationship between technology and marketing can ensure effective technology transfer and a profitable balance between market requirement and output technology. Gruber and Marquis[21] have focused attention on the variety of elements making for successful transfer, and suggested as a model:

Magnitude of transfer = f (source, nature of item to be transferred, structure of channels for transfer, potential recipients i.e. customers, of item to be transferred)

Each element of this transfer structure needs careful examination, both separately and as elements in the total transfer process.

Equally Hetrick[22] has focused attention on the problems inherent in achieving a balance between market considerations and technology. He goes further, however, to examine the problems of an aggregated technology and the balance necessary between each of its component technologies if successful, least-cost output is to be achieved. Fig. 4 demonstrates balanced aggregated technologies T_1 and T_2.

Both these issues—of technology transfer and the balance of technologies (especially aggregated technologies) with market considerations, go beyond the normal scheme of TF. Allied to TF, however, they provide a powerful way forward to an intelligent restatement of the marketing concept in the overall corporate context, which avoids the technological myopia which has at times looked like becoming hereditary in the marketing family.

REFERENCES

1 Reynolds, W. B. (1961) Research and the marketing concept, Pt. 2, 14-21 in *Marketing innovations*: Proceedings of the 8th Biennial Marketing Inst. American Marketing Assn., Minnesota.

2 Galbraith J. K. (1958) *The affluent society* (Hamish Hamilton).

3 Galbraith, J. K. (1967) *The new industrial state* (Hamish Hamilton).

4 Levitt, T. (1960) Marketing myopia. *Harvard Business Rev.*, July/Aug.

5 Schon, D. A. (1967) *Technology and change: the new Heraclitus* (Pergamon).

6 Burns, T. (1969) *Models, images and myths*, Ch. 1 in Gruber, W. H. & Marquis, D.G. (see ref. 21).

7 Hayhurst, R. *et al.* (1970) *Organizational design for marketing futures* (Nelson). (These ideas are explored more fully in Pt. 1 of this book, entitled 'Marketing futures'.)

8 Arla Chemical Co. (1962) Case study from I.M.E.D.E., Lausanne. (The name of this company has been changed to conceal its identity; the facts have not.) Written by Learned, E. P. & Aguilar, F. J.

9 Stravinsky, I. (1945) *Musical poetics*, La flute de Pau, 98-99.

10 Peters, L. (1964) Poem in Mphahlele E. (ed.) (1967) *African writing today* (Penguin Books) 243.

11 Galbraith, J. K. (1967) *The new industrial state* (Hamish Hamilton), 399.

12 Wills G. S. C. *et al.* (1969) *Technological forecasting and corporate strategy* (Bradford Univ. Press/Crosby Lockwood).

13 Wills, G. S. C. (1970) The development and deployment of technological forecasts. *Jour. of Long Range Planning*, 2, 3, March.

14 Wills, G. S. C. & Wilson, R. M. S. (1970) The managerial implications of technological forecasting. Roles and Parker Occ. Paper, reprinted in Wills, G. S. C. (1971) *Exploration in marketing thought,* Ch. 19 (Crosby Lockwood).

15 Servan-Schreiber, J. J. (1968) *Le défi Americain* (Hamish Hamilton).

16 Beer, S. & Wills, G. S. C. (1969) Government money for the inventor. *Management Decision,* 3, 2, Summer.

17 Catherwood, F. (1969) The planning dialogue. *National Westminster Bank Rev.,* May 2-9.

18 British Industry Week (1968) Special survey: Technology in Britain —a test of strength, 233 May 3.

19 Guardian (1967) Think tanks, Sept. 26.

20 Hall, P. D. (1968) Technological forecasting for computer systems, Ch. 12 in Wills *et al.* (see ref. 12).

21 Gruber, W. H. & Marquis, D. G. (eds 1969) *Factors in the transfer of technology* (M.I.T. Press).

22 Hetrick, J. C. (1968) The impact of technological forecasting on long range planning. Ch. 3 in Wills, G. S. C. *et al.* (see ref. 12).

17 | Long Range Planning and Creative Marketing

by RAY WILLSMER

DEFINITIONS of marketing habitually confuse techniques with philosophy. The philosophy is an extremely simple one, namely that all marketing activity should start with the consumer in mind. Thus the role of marketing in long range corporate planning is absolutely fundamental. Resource planning with no regard for what customers may buy in the future is extremely dangerous and futile. However it does not take a specialist marketing man to pursue this marketing philosophy. Therefore I want to consider what the marketing man can contribute in long range corporate planning.

The place of the brand

The well-known product life-cycle of introduction, growth, maturity, saturation and decay governs the life of a brand (see Fig. 1). Very simply, the place of any brand in long range corporate planning depends upon its position on the life-cycle curve at any given time. What will be of crucial importance to the company will be identifying the various stages and maximizing profits throughout the total life-span. This entails keying all the resources of the enterprise to the forecast life-cycle of the brand and not, for example, planning to put in a new production unit at the time when growth is likely to stop.

No successful marketing man lives only for today. He is accustomed to looking forward to maximize his profit opportunities. He continually deals with the situation where he has to decide between bread and jam today and only today, or bread—and only bread—for a good few years to come. He is no stranger to long range

RAY WILLSMER was Marketing Manager with the Tea Division of J. Lyons and Co. Ltd. when he first presented this paper to the *First Annual Conference of the Marketing Society*, April 1967.

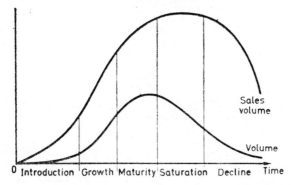

Fig. 1 *The product life-cycle of introduction, growth, maturity, saturation and decay governs the life of a brand, and the place of the brand in long range planning depends on its position on this curve at any moment in time.*

planning, but the period of the plans and their comprehensiveness has varied according to the situation of the company, the business it is in, the attitude of his chief executive, his own outlook and that of his colleagues.

He should be glad that the rest of the enterprise is going to march in step with his long-term marketing plans. The introduction of long range corporate planning means that the commitments the marketing man makes today will be accompanied by a much greater awareness of their implications on the rest of the enterprise in the future. The best description of corporate planning I have heard is that 'It is not . . . a process of making tomorrow's decisions today, but rather a process directed towards making today's decisions with tomorrow in mind and a means of preparing for future decisions so that they be made rapidly, economically, and with as little disruption to the business as possible'.[1]

How long is 'long-term'?

From the marketing man's viewpoint the problem of long range planning hinges on the length of the time scale, since the lives of products are becoming shorter and shorter. With the pace of technology and fashion leading to rapid product obsolescence, profit plans tend to be restricted to periods which offer the best possible chance of accuracy. My own division operates five-year plans and expects to achieve a high degree of success with its forecasts for year one, and rather less for year five. By the time year five has become year one, it is usually unrecognizable! If our five-year plans are so inaccurate—we are not alone in this—why plan for longer periods?

To answer this we need to look further ahead simply because the profitable life of the results of all kinds of management decision —whether it concerns a product, a factory or an investment policy —is becoming shorter yet the complexities surrounding decision taking are becoming greater. The brand manager's five-year plan can be positively dangerous for his company if his absorption with accurate prediction leads him, as it must, to merely project what was and what is, without taking account of what could be. To take the product life-cycle concept to its ultimate, he will eventually succeed in telling his chairman when his company will go out of business!

This is where life gets difficult for the company marketing man. Of course, we all know that the conventional response to the plateau on the life-cycle is to find new markets for the product, to produce product variants, improvements or new sizes and so create a new growth period above the plateau. But somewhere he will have to think of a completely new product, or perhaps even a new market.

Now we really do have corporate problems. From where is the technical expertise for the new market to come? How long will it take to site, build, equip and staff a new factory? Is there sufficient capacity in the sales force? Do we need to call on different types of outlet? What distribution system do we need? These, and many more, are the corporate complications of a new product/new market recommendation and they are often difficult for people to take. They seem so remote from day-to-day reality and so much in conflict with the normal operations of the successful business, that they often become spare time planning jobs or are relegated to the people who can best be spared.

There is no simple solution to the problems of 'how long is long-term?' It will vary from company to company and from product to product. In my own case, I prefer to define by landmarks rather than simply by years. The *short-term* is my current operating plan for the next five years—the projection of current business. The *mid-term* covers a period beyond that, five to ten years, when the balance of profitability will in all probability swing between the basic product areas in which we operate in such a way that deployment of resources and especially production and labour could change dramatically. *Long-term* ranges from ten to twenty years, when we could find ourselves right out of some current markets and deeply immersed in different ones. If you are to encompass this sort of period, you have to make up your mind what your particular business skills are and whether you are in business to earn an adequate return on the resources employed or simply, for example, to sell tea. The latter is dangerous.

I particularly favour this landmark approach because to talk solely in terms of years can be meaningless. The short-term in producing a new car may seem insufferable to a brand manager who can put a new product on the market in thirteen weeks from the word 'go'. It is ironic that fashion changes seem to occur with much greater rapidity in products with a long gestation period. I suspect that product obsolescence varies in an inverse ratio to development time! It is strange, too, that product changes are often so much more traumatic to those companies with short development time and low capital intensity!

I deduce that Esso uses this landmark approach in its corporate model. It is quoted[2] as having set 1975 as its *horizon year* on the basis that a ten-year period was 'short enough to permit reasonably accurate forecasts about technology and costs, but long enough to get away from the company's existing pattern of business and existing pattern of equipment'.

Reverse profitability analysis

It is one thing for the marketing man to decide to plan ahead for much longer periods than are usual in his company, but often quite another to secure the willing co-operation of other functions who are probably less familiar with even relatively short long-term plans, and these people feel the day-to-day pressures of business most. The marketing man can make a really significant contribution here by projecting the present business to emphasize both the need for effort and the timing of effort. I call this method *reverse profitability analysis*.

If the forecast sales of the enterprise are plotted over a really long period (see Fig. 2), the likelihood is that profitability (P) will be shown to fall below the company objective (O), here defined as an adequate return on capital employed. Thus we can find from the graph that point in time when profit performance is only just satisfactory (X) and therefore when a gap (g) will appear which can only be filled by the profit of products we do not have. We can refine this simplified model with a more realistic one. On the last graph we saw the profit objective increasing on a straight line pro-

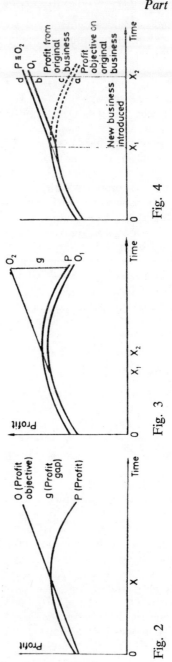

Fig. 4

Fig. 3

Fig. 2

gression. A sophisticated company ought to have two sets of objectives. One will be the minimum acceptable profit objective defined in terms of return on capital employed, while the second will be an acceptable growth rate over and above the minimum. Thus a company may express its objectives as: 'to earn an adequate return on the capital employed and increase profits by a minimum of 5 per cent per annum'.

This is sensible because a good marketing man will arrange things so that he nearly always achieves the minimum objective, even though volume and profit are declining. I say 'nearly always' because, when sales of a product fall very low, fixed costs and overheads assume increasing proportions and make it difficult if not impossible to attain profit objectives. This situation is illustrated on the refined model (see Fig. 3). O_1 is the minimum objective, O_2 is the growth objective. On this model, the company falls behind its growth objective from X_2 in time, but on the ratio of actual profit to growth objective shown here the warning shot is fired at point X_1.

Reverse profitability stems from the need to work backwards. Using this sort of analysis, you give your product development team the following type of brief: 'By time X_2 produce with not more than £C capital expenditure products yielding £P profit.'

The effect of achieving such a brief is seen by the third graph in this series (see Fig. 4). From the point where a line drawn from X_1 meets the minimum objective curve O_1, profitability (P) increases and coincides with the old line O_2. Similarly O_1 increases in proportion to the extra capital employed. The whole business is on a new course. If we look along the line X_2, the distance ab is the measure of the extra profit to be earned upon the extra capital employed in the business: the distance cd is the extra profit attributable to the new business. The margin represented by bd is the extent to which the enterprise succeeds in bettering its new minimum profit performance requirements.

My model is of course very stylized. The relationship between profit achieved and a profit objective based upon the capital employed in the business is not as constant as my graphs show, even in a highly successful business. Capital is employed in real assets such as plant and property, in stocks of raw materials and finished, unsold goods and in net debtors (debtors less creditors). Expenditure on real assets progresses as a series of plateaux, as new plant is put in and new factory sites are purchased. Stocks and the net debtor/creditor position are much more directly variable with output. Thus the distance bd will vary at different points in time as the proportion of fixed assets employed in the total capital structure varies.

The great value of this analysis should be in high-lighting the need to achieve certain ends by specific dates. I have talked about products, but the objective could just as well be to achieve, say, certain production cost savings. It is this sense of urgency, involvement and commitment that the corporate planner tries to create. The difficulty of creating his sense of urgency is, historically, one of the greatest problems of marketing management.

However, many companies have invested money in machinery and bricks and mortar on the pipe dreams of a brand manager! But whether capital is invested in new plant at a point on the life-cycle where a product is in decline, or in machinery for making a product that is not going to succeed, the financial outcomes are similar. Long range brand plans can lead to unnecessary investment in management time if not in plant, if no review procedure exists. While other functions need the longest possible notice that something dramatically new may happen, they need even more urgently to receive swift notice that a project is not coming to fruition. It is this area that needs network planning with clear 'Go/No Go' check points.

My own division is moving towards making greater use of the computer for reviewing long range plans for existing business. For some while now, the computer has produced our budgeted sales and profit forecasts by four-week periods. These may be amended at any time. Every fourth week, however, *actual sales* are fed in and the forecast for the *year* amended. This enforced amendment is an invitation to the brand manager to reconsider the rest of the year. He may, for example, decide that high sales now may be compensated for by low sales later and decide to write out the upward, enforced amendment. We are using this system on our five-year plans and this will obviously increase the accuracy of our reverse profitability analysis.

However, as far as the long term goes, this automatic review will do no more than define the likely contribution from existing products. The projection of what different markets one might be in or what new products might exist will be revised by continually examining economic and sociological conditions, by using the new product research techniques available, and backed up with some form of network plan review procedure for all the likely runners.

Thus the long range corporate plan for my division, which is similar in size to many companies, combines the long-term projection of present business with the projection of the likely contribution from new products. This latter projection is backed up by a series of network plans, one for each product under development, in which the truly critical points are the decision dates when resources normally employed on the day-to-day business and not on new product development are diverted and where new investment costs are incurred in those areas.

Problems of the planner

Very human problems of real, creative, long range planning face the marketing man. Since he has to predict what will sell, when, and in what quantities, his head is seen as being clearly on the block! Faced with a sickening responsibility and experienced enough to know that his predictions will probably be wrong at least as often as they are right, he will be inclined to find reasons why longer range planning than he is used to should stay near the bottom of his work pile! However, it is the very uncertainty of prediction that makes some form of long range preparation all the more necessary. After all, your prediction that your present product will go on selling for twenty years is only a little more probable than the surmise that you might be selling a completely new product in an entirely new product field in twenty years' time! Any good corporate planner will tell you that it is the *process* not the *plan* that is important. The detail of the plan could well be obsolete almost as soon as it is written, but the process which created it should not be obsolete. Hence the importance of review techniques.

Another very real problem is that of day-to-day pressures—a profit is to be made now, a television advertisement devised by next month and a new premium offer found. A very healthy company may find less problems in devoting a high proportion of marketing talent time to the very long run plan. Companies with problems today need to solve them quickly—tomorrow if not today! To paraphrase Peter Drucker: the first task of management is to run the business it has; the second is to ensure its future[3]. There is no reason why the two should not run closely together.

More and more companies practise *management by objectives,* usually short-term objectives. Most of his plans will not come to fruition—witness the many confusing statements on the very small number of new product ideas which ever reach the market, let alone succeed. So the company judges him by the quality of his plans—which could produce a completely ivory tower detachment.

Another problem is whether a man heavily involved with a going brand should handle completely new ideas with all the problems this involves, or should a separate brand manager, long range planning (new product development) be appointed. If the company decides on the latter, as mine has, it runs into the problem of a man doing all the donkey work and then handing over just when the product gets really exciting. And who will everybody remember when the brand is a success? However detached he tries to be, the planner is only human and a time will come when he wants to grow up with his plans, to see them to fruition. He wants promotion, and he is only too aware that results are more often judged by profit, volume and brand share. In terms of management appraisal he must be assessed by the quality and practicability of both his plans and the process he creates to achieve them.

My own experience is that it takes a good deal more time to effectively introduce longer-term plans than the management of the business realizes. I do not really find that surprising. It is probably less than ten years since many of us first convinced our boards to think in terms of three-, four- and five-year plans and there are still many companies which have nothing but the very sketchiest idea about their overall plans for more than a year ahead.

Once a marketing man has convinced everyone that a longer-term plan for the business is meaningful and has secured their involvement and commitment, much spadework remains to be done. The longer the planning period, the more rigorously must he examine the conventions used. He may, for example, be able to ignore the possible effects of inflation in the short run but this may be a vital factor in a ten-year plan. A company cannot set up a rush programme by putting all its top brand managers on the job for six months.

The creative role of the marketing man

The marketing man can make his most useful contribution in this area by being both the creative and practical antidote to the necessarily theoretical thinking involved in long range corporate planning. Some companies may feel that they must have corporate planning in the same way that ten years ago they were saying, 'We must have a market research'—and with as much idea of the meaning! Corporate planning has attracted first-class experts from all disciplines, but this almost invariably means that it will become heavily technique orientated. In particular, corporate planning will encompass much greater use of operations research techniques and computers. One vital function of the marketing man lies in his contributing a large part of the input and assessing the practicability of the models that are being built to ensure that they offer the best possible chance of meeting the ultimate test of profitability. The whole process will otherwise quickly fall into disrepute.

Many marketing men seem to fear corporate planners. They perhaps see the planners as becoming the guardians of the long-term success of the enterprise, a role which has been rapidly assumed by the marketing director. I have already shown that this fear should be an unreasonable one and that corporate planning is something the marketing man should welcome, but much will depend on the way top management uses corporate planning. It is not a means of supplanting the marketing role in long range profit planning, but a means of ensuring the success of those plans.

However, the marketing man must fulfil one absolutely fundamental role. The more *programmed thinking* there is in forward planning and the more companies make use of mathematical prediction, the greater will be the need for creative thought. The computer enables a far wider range of likely variables to be considered at great speed. This, combined with a growing conventionality in the responses of large companies to certain stimuli, inevitably increases the chances of different companies coming up with the same idea. You can see evidence of this growing, week by week. In consequence it is becoming much more difficult to make the sort of breakthrough that gives one's company a healthy solo spot in a new field. This is where the questing mind of the marketing man comes in.

The greatest contribution the marketing man can make to the long range plans of his company is the use of real creative marketing.

REFERENCES

1 Warren, E. Kirby. *Long range planning—the executive viewpoint* (Prentice-Hall), 18.
2 Owen, Geoffrey. (1967) How Esso studies the far horizon. *Financial Times,* March 30.
3 Drucker, Peter, *Managing for results* (Heinemann).

Part 2
IN PRACTICE

18 | Some Management Lessons from Technological Innovation Research

by JAMES BRIGHT

THIS chapter presents some research conclusions as a number of *propositions* about technological innovation. The word, 'proposition', has been chosen since these conclusions are not 'laws', for one can certainly cite exceptions. And to present them as 'hypotheses' is to neglect the support of repeated observations found in studying xerography and some thirty other recent technological innovations. The work of other researchers also supports some of these propositions. Finally, 'proposition' was chosen to convey an assertion of some force, with a modest level of confidence.

The propositions are directed at management, for it is the managers of business and government institutions that are the directors of society's technological and economic efforts. A second intended audience is the students of economic and social progress —the academicians and their industrial and governmental counterparts whose theories and ideas influence the policies and actions of management. They are, however, in no sense offered as being final, complete, or universally valid. Some of them are only the starting point for further research. I intend that they be regarded as concepts, observations, and points of view that deserve consideration by the decision makers as they make choices relative to new technology.

DR. JAMES BRIGHT is Professor of Business Administration at the Harvard Business School, and currently Visiting Professor in The University of Texas at Austin. This paper was first presented to the National Conference on The Management of Technological Innovation, jointly sponsored by Mintech and *Management Today* at The University of Bradford Management Centre, March 1969. It was reprinted in the *Journal of Long Range Planning* (1969) 2, 1, September.

Proposition 1

Technological innovation: the process of translating technical knowledge into economic reality, involves four major functions, (usually but not always in the following sequence): the *scientific* (search for knowledge), the *engineering* (reduction to practice), the *entrepreneurial* (introduction to society), the *managerial* (optimization of usage). Each of these functions requires a different type of skill and knowledge, may involve some change of attitudes and values, and requires the manipulation of very different resources. Technological innovations are delayed or may fail because the person or group involved lacks the skill, the knowledge or the resources to carry out some portions of one or more of these functions.

MacLaurin pointed out that, in the case of radio, no one man ever carried out this full process (Armstrong, with FM radio, might possibly be an exception).[1] Dr. Edwin Land of Polaroid fame is an unquestioned exception to this proposition. Doubtless there are a few more such individuals, but one must search long and hard to find them.

Conclusion: Management must realize that an innovation requires these four types of activities, roughly in the sequence mentioned. In proceeding with a radical technological innovation, management must continually assess the current leadership needs of the innovation process, and it must nurture the project by providing the necessary skills and leadership at the right times.

Proposition 2

The full process of technological innovation usually takes upwards of ten years; and a quarter of a century is not an uncommon time. Although it is frequently stated that the time to innovate is much shorter today, these statements usually turn out to be based upon erroneous data or applicable to only a portion of the innovative process. To understand this proposition we must break down the process into its chronological stages. While the process of technological innovation can be divided in as few as three or as many as fifteen stages, I find the following eight-stage division most usefull. It uses identifiable points, which facilitate measurement and comparison. These particular stages also reflect transitions of the innovation to the next of the four basic functions. Of course, I do not mean to imply that these stages can always be rigorously or sharply defined. I shall identify some exceptions to these sequences after reviewing them.

Stage 1—Scientific Suggestion, Discovery and Observation, or Recognition of Need. Most innovations seem to begin with the latter, but there are notable exceptions, such as atomic power, the laser, and penicillin.

Stage 2—Development of Theory or Design Concept. While early theories or designs are usually imperfect, their definition leads to a focus of effort along certain lines. In many technical innovations, new scientific theory is not necessary or may be late in coming. Then a combination of known science and/or technology—a design concept—is the goal of this stage.

Stage 3—Laboratory Verification of Theory or Design Concept. This is the laboratory experiment which simply confirms the validity of the principle suggested in Stage 2.

Stage 4—Laboratory Demonstration of Application. Here the concept is first embodied in a *bread-board* model of the device, a sample material, or a laboratory model of the process, as it would be used (hopefully) by society. In other words, the concept is demonstrated in application form.

Stage 5—Field Trial or Full-scale Trial. The innovation next is developed to a level where it can be tried under operating conditions. Usually, it has passed the prototype stage but is short of being the marketable, commercial version. The stage is defined as the achievement of *technical success under normal operating conditions*.

Stage 6—Commercial Introduction. This stage is marked by 'first sale' (or operational use for the military) as distinct from experimental use. The line between Stages 5 and 6 is sometimes far from clear, and may be shifted simply by intent. I mean to imply, in Stage 6, that the innovation has been purchased in the belief that is is now applicable and reliable enough for everyday requirements.

Stage 7—Widespread Adoption. A subjective judgment is required to mark this stage, and I have been unable to pin down a single common measure of accomplishment. Therefore I include several notions: (a) that the innovation is widely recognized as a practical device and not as experimental, (b) that the innovation has enough usage so as to achieve profits for the innovating firm, (c) that substantial numbers are in use. To a British audience I suggest that the hydrofoil boat reached Stage 7 in, perhaps, the late 1950s, but that the ground effects machine (Hovercraft) is not quite at this stage (although I maybe wrong on this judgment).

Stage 8—Proliferation. The innovation is used in a number of devices and its principle is adopted for other purposes. The innovation spreads in two ways: (a) the original device is applied to a number of new uses (on more than an experimental scale), and (b) the technical or scientific principle is applied to other machines, processes, or materials. (For example, (a) consider how radar spread from military uses to commercial planes, ships, air traffic control, police cars and private boats; (b) consider how the microwave technology of radar was applied to commercial heating, to home ranges for cooking purposes, as well as to microwave communication systems.)

Obviously, these stages are not always sharply defined, false starts are made, and some stage may be rapidly by-passed. Most important, we must realize that though the main thrust of the innovation can be identified as having achieved a certain point, some components may be in very different and much earlier stages. And even when the basic innovation is clearly well along (as in the case of, say, the computer or television), the research and engineering development stages are filled with new technological elements (such as solid state circuitry today), which lead to further drastic changes in the device or performance. Nevertheless, the fundamental notion of a 'process of technological innovation', with identifiable stages, remains extremely useful.

Take the statement that 'the time to innovate has been greatly reduced'—a statement that is frequently made and often supported by selected data offered by very competent technologists. However, when one applies these definitions carefully, a much more accurate picture emerges with significant managerial implications. It is true that the period from Stage 4, *Laboratory Demonstration of Use* to Stage 6, *Commercial Introduction,* can be, and is, shortened by the use of new management techniques such as parallel development, PERT and related concepts. However, can we identify formal procedures that have been widely applied to speed the first three stages of innovation? By what means has industry speeded the last three? Only Governments have speeded progress from Stage 5 through Stage 7, for some innovations deemed socially desirable, such as agricultural, health, and environmental safety needs. Governments also have shortened the T/I process time by providing funding of R & D costs, by providing availability of the innovation, by education of users, and by legislation or taxation to speed adoption. But commercial equivalents generally do not exist. In practice, the concept of leasing and otherwise financing use by the customer may well speed Stages 6 and 7, but I doubt that leasing to speed diffusion is a conscious policy in more than a handful of cases.

Of course, Governments have speeded many innovations by funding the entire process. The classic case probably is atomic weapons, in which the US Government picked up the innovation after Stage 2, *Development of Theory,* and carried out multiple approaches to development through Stages 4, 5 and 6, and on a massive scale. Note, however, that in the case of nuclear power for civilian use, Stage 7 has been reached only recently. Nuclear power has been *over 20 years* in going from Stage 2 to Stage 7! I suggest that the manager dealing with a radical innovation presented to him in the *Laboratory Application* (Stage 4), must think of supporting it for roughly a decade to reach significant profits.

The manager can confirm this 10 year minimum for himself by simple estimates based on his own experience. Let us suppose that his technical people show him a laboratory model of the new technology, which successfully serves a promising and useful purpose. How long will it take to achieve a prototype for full-scale or field trial? 1 to 4 years? *Assume 2 years.*

Then how much longer until a commercially saleable product, with necessary adjuncts in the form of maintenance, user training aids, promotional support, etc., is ready for sale? 1 to 4 years? *Assume 2 years.*

Once first sale is made, how long will it be until the number of sales recovers costs and achieves a profitable position for the firm, or until the innovation is in widespread use? 3 to 10 years? *Assume 6 years.* Using these rough assumptions on the optimistic basis, the total time is about 10 years! Now allow for the fact that we may be lucky in shortening some of these phases, but are more likely to have under-estimated at least one of them. Then a 15 year time span is a strong probability.

But notice that we ignored Stage 1, the birth of the concept, Stage 2, the achievement of a theory or concept on which we would work, and Stage 3, the verification of theory or concept and time to reach Stage 4, Laboratory Demonstration. Surely this must usually involve 5 years or so. Therefore, our likely time span for the full process has extended to 20 years. (Although Carlson carried xerography through Stages 1 to 3 in three years, six more years went by until the innovation reached Stage 4. It took xerography around 5 to 7 years (1950 to 1955-57) to move from first sale to wide adoption. It is thought-provoking to realize that Carlson began his work on xerography in 1934, so 20 years passed before this innovation achieved Stage 7. If we consider his original goal—the office copier—another 5 years was required and a quarter of a century went by.)

Of course, management is usually confronted with a proposal already in Stage 3 or 4. Also I recognize that 'success' may be adequately present long before the achievement of Stage 7—*Widespread Adoption*. But, at the very best, this leaves management dealing with a process taking in the order of a decade! How does this fact sit with conventional management goals, resources, aspirations, and innovative procedures, and even management reward systems (based on last year's profits)? Not very well!

More seriously, the present value theory which we teach our management students is totally inadequate for this spectrum of management decisions. If present value theory is applied to radical innovations, it will discourage progress and will cause management to reject magnificent opportunities. It is only proper to agree that it will probably also forestall some painful errors for firms and individuals, and it will preclude those failures that inevitably apply to some percentage of attempts to deal with radical innovation.

Conclusion: Management decisions about radical technological innovations need to be made with an entirely different value system to that applied to most business problems. We are dealing with a 10 to 25 years process, and it is wrong to use conventional business wisdom when relating oneself to this long process of *radical* technological innovation.

Proposition 3

Radical innovations often originate outside the traditional supplier-user sources. I pointed this out in earlier writings, and find only further confirmations of this widespread phenomenon. Consider:

Innovation	*'Logical' Originators (Traditional Supplier and/or Users)*	*Actual Origin of the Commercially Prominent Concept*
Diesel locomotive	Steam locomotive builders and railroads	Automotive firm
Kodachrome film	Photographic industry	Independent inventors (two musicians)
Xerography	Business machine industry	Patent lawyer from electrical components firm
Polaroid film	Photographic industry	Independent inventor
Phototypesetting	Printing machine industry	Independent inventors
Computer	Business machine industry	Universities and U.S. Army Ballistics Laboratory
Ground effects	Aircraft, automotive industry, or transportation industry	Private inventor supported by British Government
Transistor	Electrical component manufacturers	Bell Telephone Laboratories

In late 1968 I studied two current and little known innovations, and found the same phenomenon:

1. The *Rolligon* is a vehicle operating on very low pressure (2 psi) barrel-like bladders (tyres). Its rough terrain capability is now finding success as a 'swamp buggy' for oil exploration and construction work in jungles and swamps of the Gulf Coast and South-east Asia. The idea originated in 1951, when a US school teacher in Alaska observed the Eskimos' handling of whale boats on soft rollers made of inflated sealskins.

2. After a dozen years of work the world's first all-plastic aeroplane is about to be certified by the FAA (in Midland, Texas). This four-place plane has a unique construction, based upon a stiff fibreglass shell filled with a cellular plastic core. The construction leads to outstanding strength to weight performance and manufacturing economies, plus numerous other advantages. The entire project was the brain child of a dentist, Dr. Windecker, who applied his knowledge of bone structure to achieve strength and light weight. He has been supported by the Dow Chemical Company and a group of oilmen and ranchers in the Midland area. I submit that these two examples are further evidence of this peculiar and fascinating proposition.

Conclusion: Firms and Governments should develop and exhibit more interest, respect and methodology in *searching* for technological opportunity and threat outside the traditional and logical sources, and among people who may have little in the way of conventional technical credibility.

All managers, particularly older, senior men who have built great enterprises around new technology, should be given periodic reminders that the technology which will replace theirs may well originate outside their industry.

Proposition 4

The most important application of a new technology is not always that which was visualized first; and a corollary: **Technological innovations frequently gain their first foothold for purposes that were originally not thought of or were deemed to be quite secondary.**

This proposition is of utmost significance to management, and especially to market research inputs to management decisions. We are indebted to Rupert MacLaurin, whose classic study of radio led him to state that Marconi's shift from attempting to exploit applications of radio on land to ship communications: 'illustrates the principle that the most profitable outlet for an innovation is frequently not the one which is explored first.'[2]

My study of contemporary innovations is replete with more confirmation of this phenomenon. I have re-defined MacLaurin's observation because it has two quite different aspects—one dealing with that *first use,* which is so desperately needed to launch an innovation; and the second, with the *ultimate major use.* As examples of the first aspect: radio got its start at sea, rather than in replacing the land telegraph, as Marconi had intended. Xerography failed initially in office copying but was rapidly adopted to make master plates for multilith duplicating machines. Its second major adoption was to make enlarged reproductions of engineering drawings that had been stored in micro-film.

And as examples of the second aspect: radio was conceived as a means of communication for private messages, but its great use was in sending public messages (broadcasting). The computer was originally thought of by many as a business machine that would mechanize much office paper work. However, it is clear that the computer is far more than that, and its great importance lies in the storage and manipulation of data and in problem solving and machine control capability. Indeed, I believe that we still do not know the ultimate importance of the computer, which is diffusing through society and performing hundreds of once unimagined services. And who will be bold enough to now predict the ultimate most important use of the laser, or of holography?

Conclusion: The sponsors of a radical technology should adopt a policy of searching for applications, with an open mind toward new uses and a readiness to support trials in unexpected fields. The strategy should be one of exploration, rather than of single-minded commitment to one pre-determined usage. Therefore, market research studies should be taken with a very large grain of salt, for it is dubious that any one small group can imagine or discover the potential uses of a radical innovation that all of society will uncover. This is particularly true because other new technology and social developments create future needs that were unimagined when the early market studies were made. The market we can foresee today is likely to be drastically altered by changes during the decade in which the innovation grows to reality.

Proposition 5

Technological capabilities and para-meters (such as power, speed, strength, etc.) advance in an exponential manner over time.

The fact that progress is of exponential nature is of utmost significance to decision makers. Consider the sketch, Fig. 1. Because the early part of the curve is relatively flat we tend to project 'straight line' progress and minor gains. But, in fact, once certain troublesome features are surmounted, a technological capability increases at a rate that can only be described as explosive. This phenomenon can be seen in the speed of manned aerial vehicles, the computation time of computers, the miniaturization of solid state circuitry, and many other devices. Judgments made about technical progress may be wildly off the mark, due to failure to appreciate this curve or to estimate its exponents.

Conclusion: In estimating future achievement the nature of this exponential progress curve must be remembered. 'Straight-line' progress can be anticipated initially, but when the crucial technical breakthroughs are made, progress will explode.

Proposition 6

Advances in technological capabilities often reach points of diminishing economic returns. This is due to the cost of achieving the last incremental advance, or to inability to use the gain for economic purposes. For example, as transport speeds cut travel time from US to Europe to, say, three hours, the relative advantage of a further cut to two hours is less. At some point the value of time saved is dissipated by other requirements of the system, such as waiting for baggage, or checking in. Or consider overnight air freight coast-to-coast. Over-night service has value to many firms, but a five to six hour service arriving, say, at four o'clock in the morning, has little or no additional economic value.

Conclusion: The immediate application of every additional technological gain may not have much economic value. However, the reason for this seems to be that other parts of the system (or society) are not yet in a position to benefit from the gain. In addition to the need for proper timing of the introduction, this proposition points to new opportunities in improving the ends of the system that are reducing the advantages of the advance.

Proposition 7

Accelerated and often unexpected progress comes about due to the impingement and convergence of one technology on another. Thus solid state electronic circuitry provided the cost reduction, size reduction, and reliability gains essential for computer progress.

Numeric control of machine tools was extremely limited until the generation of control tapes by computer became practical.

Conclusion: Many erroneous rejections of new technical possibilities or their markets occur because we tend to hold all other technology constant. We must always examine the possibility that other technological elements are also subject to exponential progress, and so may rapidly change the merits or feasibility of a particular technological innovation.

Proposition 8

The demonstration of a new technological concept is a most critical point to the progress of an innovation.

Demonstrations must be planned with great care because they can easily discourage support:

(a) Very few people can grasp the economic significance of a demonstration of a *scientific principle*. Few people can translate 'principle' into 'hardware'.

(b) Failure in a detail is readily judged by observers to be a failure in basic concept.

(c) Successful demonstration of laboratory application or prototype easily causes one to underestimate the time needed to achieve commercialization and profits.

Conclusion: We need greater skill and thoughtfulness in appraising demonstrations.

Proposition 9

The mode of financing usage of the innovation is of utmost significance to the rate of diffusion and to the financial returns to the innovating firm.

Few technological innovators have paid much attention to the design of the system by which users or consumers will pay for the use of their innovation. The importance of this area can be illustrated by the case of xerography. From 1960 to 1965 Xerox Corp installed about 65,000 Model 914 Copiers in the USA. If these units had been sold for twice manufacturing costs, the gross revenue would have been about $330 million. If the units had been leased for $300 per month, as was considered at one time, the gross revenue would have been about $360 million, with the advantage that further annual lease fees would continue to accrue *and* the company would gain the cash flow advantages of an enormous depreciation charge. However, using the charge-per-copy pricing system that was actually installed, the gross revenue was about $660 million with the same advantages of continuing revenue and cash flow from depreciation. Roughly, the additional revenue over these five years was at least *$300 million more* than the first two plans—a decision equivalent to doubling the value of the innovation!

Furthermore, there is no doubt that the very low cost of the charge-per-copy plan greatly encouraged adoption and speeded diffusion. Consider how slowly the computer would have spread had IBM only sold the machines.

Conclusion: The design of the method of charging for the use of the innovation deserves far more attention that it normally receives.

Proposition 10

A major weakness in our national support of the innovative process is the financing of innovation during progress after Stage 3—verification of theory up through Stage 5—full scale or field trial.

Universities, the US Federal Government and Foundations have policies and funds to support technology in Stages 1 to 4; (and sometimes even further if they have sponsored the first portion of the process). There are also many financial and industrial institutions that will readily support an innovation that has reached Stage 5. But in between there is no formal, effective support procedure by government or society in the USA.

Notice that scientific research is readily funded as an act of national faith and intellectual respectability, but the development of inventions and their launching into society as technical innovations are not often nationally supported. We do not fund this activity as an act of faith; and the private agency or individual who does so is not regarded as doing something particularly socially desirable and important. Instead, he is regarded as gambling on a long shot for personal gain, if not as a fool pouring money into a 'crackpot' idea!

Furthermore, we leave this search for financial support of the innovation in the hands of the inventor. During this crucial time, in effect, society expects the inventor to drop his real *forté* (invention), and to become a promoter, entrepreneur and financier. Why should the inventor, dedicated to a technological struggle and probably already under financial stress, be expected to be an effective fund raiser? Psychologically and intellectually he is not (usually) a

L

good candidate for this job. Is it any wonder that social and economic progress is delayed?

The point is badly missed by American society. A panel convened by the United States Government, and with the help of distinguished industrialists and technicians, in January 1967 went on record stating that 'In view of present information on the potential availability of venture capital, the Federal Government should take no action with respect to the establishment of new federally supported programmes for the furnishing of venture capital.'[3]

The Panel showed a puzzling tender concern for inventors, for they made a number of excellent recommendations to help the inventor's financial position by allowing various tax exemptions and adjustments. They explicitly recognized the need to encourage invention and inventors. But they missed the point that *venture capital agencies support inventors with only slightly more risk-taking propensity than do conventional financial sources.* They missed the point that *no venture capital agency takes on an underwriting programme unless they are highly confident that it will be a profitable venture.*

The Panel jumped right past the fundamental distinction made above—that we presently do not have a good way of financing technological innovation from Stage 3 through Stage 5, as we do for basic research. The venture capital schemes now in existence leave the inventor right where he was—searching and begging for supporters to help him move his invention from the laboratory to commercial introduction. These venture capital agencies use the same old judgment criteria—'Can *we* make a profit out of this, and in a reasonably short time?' Thus the inventor does not receive the support that society gives to the researcher. If we are to have more innovation we must give the inventor more support to invent, and not expect him also to be a financier and promoter.

Nothing above is intended to deny that inventors have a better chance today than did Carlson (xerography) of getting support from the same source. The whole nation—government, industry, and financial leaders—are far more conscious of the opportunities in new technology. The point is that we in the USA do not yet have a good system of financing this critical portion of the innovative process. Indeed, as a national policy, we do not even recognize that there is an inconsistency in our support of the innovative process.

It is my impression that the National Research and Development Corporation is an imaginative governmental step to correct this gap in support. I speculate that it will receive some criticism from those who fail to realize the long time span of the innovative process; as well as from those who assume that the agency must only support 'sure winners'.

I hope that these 'propositions' will help to persuade society that such a screening in the early stages of innovation is impossible, as well as undesirable, for it will cause the loss of some great opportunities.

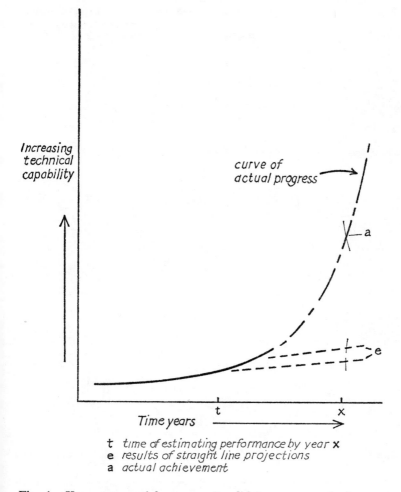

t *time of estimating performance by year* **x**
e *results of straight line projections*
a *actual achievement*

Fig. 1 *How exponential progress invalidates some projections*

REFERENCES

1 MacLaurin, W. R. (1949) *Invention and innovation in the radio industry* (Macmillan Co., New York).

2 MacLaurin, W. R. The process of technological innovation. Reprinted in Bright, J. R. *Research development and technological innovation.* Homewood, 111, 78 (Richard D. Irwin Co.).

3 *Technological innovation: its environment and management.* (1967). Report to the Dept. of Commerce, Washington, D.C. See page iii, also 41-43. (Because the Panel deemed that venture capital was 'available', they assumed that the inventor can readily get support. But he cannot get money on the same basis as the scientist. The inventor must 'prove' potential profitability.)

19 | Developing a Product Market Strategy as part of the formal Corporate Planning Process—I.T.T.

by GERHARD SIMONS

THE objective of ITT may be summarized as (1) to develop, on a sound analytical basis, short and long range financial *performance objectives* for each ITT company, and to obtain ITT top management approval of these goals; (2) to develop *business plans* for achieving these objectives that provide a clear expression of the company's operating plan for achievement of financial performance objectives for first plan year, and that show product development, market development and capital investment plans for achievement of the company's long range financial performance objectives; (3) to develop means for sensing and anticipating changes in production and sales volumes from those planned, and to provide sound plans for profit assurance in the event of a decline in volume; (4) to provide means of direct communication between company and ITT top management; and (5) to insure that company and area managements work as teams in the development of objectives and business plans, and continue so during execution of plans.

To quote from ITT's 1968 annual report:

'This growth, this building, is a consequence of well-managed planning—for example our two five-year plans—which has re-

DR. SIMONS is Area Planning Director, ITT Europe, Inc. (Brussels). This paper was first presented to the National Conference on *Long Range Planning for Marketing and Diversification* sponsored at The University of Bradford Management Centre by the British Institute of Management, June 1969.

sulted in a highly product-diversified but strongly-unified operating company.

'The success of the company's programme for quality growth through diversification into areas of high earnings potential, attests to the economic soundness of the management's basic philosophy. The overriding responsibility of management is to direct the course set for our diverse operations, to anticipate obstacles to the fulfilment of these goals, and to take prompt effective counter-action against them—in short, to ensure profitable results by participation.'

ITT's ten planning principles are: (1) profit oriented plans, (2) actions, no numbers, (3) long range and short range plans, (4) planning by responsibility, (5) integrated planning, (6) realistic objectives, (7) simple goals, (8) flexibility, (9) continuity, and (10) alternatives, and its annual planning cycle consists of:

Steps	Timing
Up-date long-range plans	Continuous
Establish objectives	January to March
Develop full plans	April to July
Screen and consolidate plans	August, September
Review and approve plans	October
Modify plans	October to November
Establish monthly budgets	November to December
Approve budgets	December
Measure results	Monthly

The Plan, if properly organized, becomes a central management tool, where management prepares a plan, communicates it to operations with instructions to begin operating according to plan. Management monitors operations; compares actual results with planned results, identifies significant deviation and its causes, provides direction and guidance designed to rectify deviations.

If deviation is due to the fact that the plan is no longer valid, guidance is issued to change the plan. If the plan is still valid, guidance is issued to operations to modify activities so that they conform to the plan.

This relationship between management, plan and operations exists at all management levels, in all business functions, and on all time scales.

Preparatory steps for developing a business plan

Clearly, new product ideas or new marketing concepts need pre-screening, feasibility studies, evaluation and management approval at least in principle, before they can be used as building blocks for a business plan. Our tools to do this: (1) a European Business Opportunity Planning Group, and (2) a formal Product Planning and Evaluation Process.

The *European Business Opportunity Planning Group,* which is to serve as a focal point throughout Europe for all activities associated with new product or market opportunities, is the major instrument—and the first step—to developing a product or marketing strategy as part of the formal corporate planning process described earlier. The scope of this small and fairly informal group is:

to project the possible economic-political scenario for Western Europe ten to twenty years ahead:

to collect, review and communicate all ideas related to new business opportunities;

to analyse—on a broad scale—economic, market, technical, financial and other data pertaining to potential business opportunities for ITT in Europe;

to assist product line managers in the evaluation of new business or product opportunities; and

to initiate appropriate follow-up activities for the pursuit of identified opportunities.

New business or product opportunity proposals submitted to ITT by the Group (which means asking for approval to spend additional time and money on more detailed market research or feasibility studies) normally covers the following points:

description of opportunity

market data (size, growth, competition)

proposed strategies (product and marketing strategies)

targets (introduction data, cost objectives)

ITT's strength and weaknesses related to the new opportunity in marketing, technical and manufacturing areas

investment requirements and, as appropriate, special programme requirements (staffing, training, etc.).

A proposal by the Business Planning Group, if approved, leads to first feasibility studies and to the *risk classification* of the new idea.

The two key dimensions of a new product are:

the market: to whom and how the product is to be sold, enabling profitable distribution; and

the technology: the fund of knowledge, technical or otherwise, enabling the product to be economically produced.

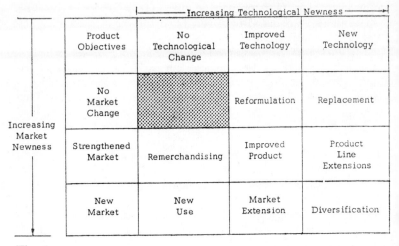

Fig. 1

The risk to the company increases with increasing marketing and technological newness, to its maximum at the extreme diagonal 'diversification'.

New market or product development can be broken down into manageable stages for planning and control. In a simplified manner the life-cycle of a product can be considered in the following steps:

New product proposals
Search proposal and screening of new product ideas to meet company objectives with respect to identified markets and profit opportunities.

Preliminary evaluation
Early assessment of product potential which might include preparation of a product plan, to provide first detailed analysis of all aspects of the proposed programme and, where necessary, provide technical or marketing feasibility through further specialized studies.

Development
Turning proposal into a working model committing significant technical resources and funds.

Full production and sales
Launching the product into full-scale production and sales, fully committing the company's resources.

Phase-out and termination

Timetable and plan for phase-out of further sales and production of the product, concentrating on maximizing profit contribution of a declining product and initiating planning for replacement products.

ITT's product planning and evaluation procedures

These have been developed to translate the needs of the market (giving the customer the right product at the right place, time and price) into meaningful and useful product plans which provide means for marshalling and integrating all company functions to achieve:

- expansion of the product and market base to development of products that satisfy market needs in terms of price, performance and timing
- control of expenditures required for development of new products and services; and
- maximum profits and return on investments in accordance with company objectives.

Business plans are then keyed to and made up of product plans. Projection of sales, costs, profits, forecasts of requirements for facility and personnel, without clear product plans can only reflect broad targets and no specific programmes. Profits generally can be sustained in the long run only by the continuing flow of successful new products, not only to maintain sales volume but also to sustain and increase profit margins. Product planning is thus a significant tool for management to achieve objectives.

Tie-in of Corporate Planning and Marketing at ITT

The chief executive of each company is requested to submit—as the first pages of his company's annual business plans—his 'business overview' which is a narrative concentrating on the long-range outlook for current product lines, and business development plans including new market developments, new products to expand current product lines, and introduction of new product lines.

The marketing function's contribution to annual business planning efforts can best be described by showing the elements of the marketing plan as listed in the ITT Business Planning Guide.

Mission

Assignment made to Marketing Function.
Services to be performed; recipients of such services.

Profit plan

Committed contribution by marketing group in response to needs expressed by product lines—to reach objectives.

Major premises, environmental factors upon which plan is based.

Principal problems encountered; strategies and requirements to overcome such problems.

Supporting information

Product improvement efforts (RD & E)

Pricing policies and techniques

Discontinuation of unprofitable products

Discontinuation of unprofitable product lines

Building up profitable products

Adding revenue producing products or services

Developing new product line businesses

Capturing added market shares

Improving customer or distribution channel mix

Export expansion efforts

Securing favourable franchises

Analysis of sales and distribution organization

Are they adequate? What changes are required to improve them? When? By whom?

Marketing expense analysis

Is money spent adequate? Or too high or too low? Or wrongly spent?

What changes are required? When and by whom?

Sales financing

If this is a critical point in any product line, what sources are available: what are plans to utilize these sources?

Advertising and sales promotion

Are they adequately organized? Are changes required? When and by whom?

Marketing research efforts and plans

Is market research activity adequate? Are efforts and plans responding to product line needs? What changes are required? When and by whom?

Some comments on long range planning and its influence on developing product or market strategies

Long-range planning is an assignment to each company's Managing Director, but also to the European Business Opportunity Planning Group. This Group, as stated, is concerned with longer range projections up to ten and twenty years. In addition, it is their job to:

  identify those developments which present biggest opportunities or biggest dangers for ITT's businesses;

  convince managers that the future might bring something different; and get them to plan and act today to be ready for these developments of tomorrow;

  secure that long range considerations form the basis for current planning efforts;

  see to it that all marketing and product development concepts used in business planning are based on the same assumptions about future developments.

A number of examples for basic assumptions developed by the Business Opportunity Planning Group, and their probable influence on long range marketing concepts will be given.

Developing a product and marketing strategy as part of the formal corporate planning process is done in the following sequence:

  Developing long range economic/political scenarios.

  New business/product ideas channelled to Business Opportunity. Planning Group for screening and evaluation.

  Approval or refusal by ITT management of proposals submitted.

  Feasibility studies.

  Product planning: screening and approval of product plans.

  Product plans form building blocks for business plans.

20 | Increasing Penetration in Industrial Markets—Rank Xerox

by MICHAEL HUGHES

MY title begs a question. Does it mean penetration at all costs or, alternatively, profitable penetration? I would suggest that the distinction is important, and worth closer examination than that accorded by many companies for whom increased penetration has not led to success. I believe there is a place for both approaches, provided that each approach lies at the heart of a comprehensive plan and that the difference is understood within the business. It is essential that managers know which strategy they are embarked on and the difficulty of successfully bringing about changes between the two. At any one time, of course, different strategies may be being followed for different products or different geographical areas or market sectors.

Rank Xerox owes much of its success to the ability that has been developed to address its opportunities, using at any one time the better of these alternatives. It has developed an understanding of the weakness of only acting when a plan demonstrates that the proposed action *must* be profitable at every step. It has developed too an understanding of the need for measurement and for control. Let me try to indicate some of the features that made Rank Xerox unusual.

In 1960 the market was introduced to a revolutionary reprographic device—the 914. There were some notable features:

1. Its manufactured cost was between ten and thirty times that of its competitors.

MICHAEL HUGHES is Assistant Director, Product Programme, Rank Xerox Ltd. This paper was first presented to The National Conference on *Long Range Planning for Marketing and Diversification* sponsored at The University of Bradford Management Centre by The British Institute of Management, June 1969.

2. It required some seventy feet of operating space against perhaps nine square feet of competitors.
3. The 914 weighed 700 lb, required a higher than usual power loading and was being sold by a company whose first name meant films and whose second name meant nothing and was unpronounceable anyway.

In spite of these unusual features it has been described as the most successful single product ever brought to any market. The success, in product terms, was due to two main features. The copies were made on to ordinary untreated bond paper; the quality far exceeded that of any rival process. In terms of timing and performance, never perhaps has any product arrived to meet a need so directly—a need that was known to exist but in the event proved much larger than the most optimistic forecast.

Decisions that led to success

In marketing terms success was founded on one major decision, from which stemmed a number of subsidiary decisions. Pre-eminent, the decision to exclusively rent the device. There were two main motivations for this decision:

1. It would give the customer protection against obsolescence in an area likely to be responsive to technological development.
2. The machine would have been so expensive no one would have bought it outright.

The subtendent decisions were:

1. To meter usage and charge a flat rate above a minimum; rather like a telephone system, the more you used it the more you paid. By this means it was possible to finance the service necessary to maintain rented equipment of considerable complexity whilst covering a range of customer requirements from 2,000 to 20,000 copies per month.
2. That customer relations where machines were placed on rental were paramount.

Initially care was taken to ensure that equipment, which was in short supply, went to customers likely to be most profitable. This approach was soon seen to have problems. Many customers underestimated their needs and so a less cautious approach of massive expansion was employed. Facilities and resources were increased and the development of overseas markets accelerated. We therefore planned to increase penetration, but with increased risk.

A number of interesting events then began to have an effect. Rank Xerox launched another product which in a rental business usually means an element of self-impact. This was a smaller copier and we were concerned that all the metered copies made on the smaller machine might merely be the redistribution of copies currently being made on our existing equipment. In addition, we were realizing that our growth potential lay in two simultaneous directions; the winning of new placements of machines, obviously, but also the increase of usage on existing equipment.

Specialized services to customer

To increase throughput on machines already placed we set up a team of specialists in either the documentation and reprographics or in the needs of a particular market sector.

Information was fed to them from the sales forces where they found either particular problems or particular success. I will quote an example. The Council of the Stock Exchange were seeking to introduce uniform modern paper-handling techniques. We were permitted to give some assistance in this and as a result produced a system which simplified and streamlined the paper-handling in stockbrokers' offices. The system involved the organized collection and distribution of brokers' slips and the use of coloured copy paper for signalling the destiny of some of the prints. We held a number of demonstrations in the City to show the advantages of this system to stockbrokers and other interested parties, and the result was a considerable increase in our total business with stockbrokers.

We published numerous reports designed to help the customer take advantage of the features of Rank Xerox equipment. Techniques were developed of adding, deleting and substituting information on documents, using simple templates and screens. We have to this day maintained a large number of specialists to render this kind of service to our customers. Advice on reprographic problems and the choice of equipment is therefore available to any Rank Xerox customer, although it is surprising and sometimes discouraging to note the suspicion in which a free service of this nature is often held. In this way the development of sales volume on existing equipment has gone hand in hand with aggressive expansion in terms of machine placements. This demonstrates that aggressive plans to increase penetration can have the risk element cushioned by more measurable expansion from existing revenue sources.

Customer relationships

We have tried to maintain close relationships with our customers at several levels. Not just the 'order-signer' but the users and operators of the equipment. This stems in part, of course, from motivation other than undiluted altruism. Such contact is used to constantly monitor the need for new features, the importance of speed, of quality; the ever-changing nature of competitive pressure. It is plain that an organization with virtually all its revenue coming from equipment which is the subject of a thirty-day rental agreement has to know how it stands with its customers. This essential relationship exerts two main pressures. The first is a structure which enables the relationship to develop and to operate as a sensitive indicator.

During its first years Rank Xerox had a simple sales structure:

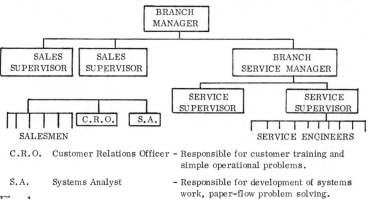

C.R.O.   Customer Relations Officer – Responsible for customer training and simple operational problems.

S.A.   Systems Analyst   – Responsible for development of systems work, paper-flow problem solving.

Fig. 1

The objectives of rapidly increasing penetration have led to several changes, particularly in the job of the salesman and his motivation.

We tried to ensure that a salesman prudently divided his time between the placement of new equipment and the development of already leased equipment. This endeavour met with mixed success only. A top line salesman wants to sell—he needs the stimulus of challenge—the laurels, and money, of success. Increasing by, say 15 per cent the output of one machine by developing systematized documentation is not as satisfying. The systems analyst, on the other hand, is too specialized, too expert to be satisfied by such successes. In his turn he looks for integrated systems, marrying several functions for several processes with time-saving forms design and the methodical use of sometimes complex software.

To answer this dilemma, Rank Xerox introduced a customer sales force whose prime function was to increase penetration within existing customers, leaving the mainline salesmen to seek further penetration in new accounts. Similarly, to meet the customers' needs we have developed a sales force to deal exclusively with our largest customers. Behind this lies the belief that the larger customer needs better service in terms of expertise. His problems tend to be more complex; the availability of alternative processes, usually not practical for the smaller company, leads to difficult decisions in which expert advice may be needed. And so, the need for growth has brought a three-tiered sales force. The major account salesman, the customer salesman and the mainline salesman.

This demonstrates, in a simplified form, an attempt to match human resources to customer needs, one avenue of pressure from our belief in close customer liaison. The other significant pressure from the same source is, of course, product development and market extension.

Product improvement

Product development takes on a different emphasis in leased or rented products. Improvements to the equipment have to be designed so that they can be retro-fitted to existing installations, by the service force more normally engaged in routine maintenance. In the main, Rank Xerox product development takes one of two main forms:

1. Improved reliability.
2. Improved speed or quality.

Improved reliability has been a constant aim since the very first machines were installed. This is brought about by closely monitoring the details of all service calls, whether they arise as an emergency or a routine maintenance call. These details are tabulated and processed to see what areas within the machine system are leading to breakdown or unsatisfactory service, and this analysis is followed by effort to redesign the component to give a longer or more reliable life and for this redesigned component eventually to be retro-fitted to the existing machine population.

Improved speed and quality have been brought about by redesign of a much larger order and have led to a new marque of machines with a substantially increased performance. This process, which is really no more than the application of standard product life extension techniques, has enabled us to keep pace with current change on equipment whose basic design is now several years old.

This policy of product improvement does, of course, bring a train of problems with it. It can be very expensive in terms of materials and labour to fit new machine systems or major components where the existing field population is numbered in tens of thousands. There can be surprising customer resistance to having his equipment out of action for even a short time, in spite of the assurances one can give that the results of this inconvenience will be an enhanced machine.

Pricing for increased penetration

At least as significant in Rank Xerox marketing terms has been penetration increase brought about by pricing innovation. Copying can be defined as taking up to, say, five prints from an original. Some years ago it became apparent that the growth rate of the market for copies was such that Rank Xerox's growth rate would have to level out. This was unacceptable and we looked for ways of extending our market with the equipment we had and envisaged having in the medium term future.

The answer seemed to lie in encouraging customers to take copies beyond five from an original and move into what we termed 'short-run' duplicating. However this needed pricing changes because of the lower cost of duplicating, and so we extended the viability of equipment by putting additional meters on machines that enabled a reduction in price as the number of copies from an original increased. In this way our total volume of prints from our equipment increased but the average price for the increase declined. By employing this approach, we have been able to penetrate a market which gives us considerable scope for growth, largely using the equipment we already have.

Pricing presents many problems on rented equipment where the effect of price changes works quite differently from price changes on equipment offered for sale. The telephone is a simple analogy. Let us suppose that a telephone company decided on an aggressive expansionist programme and wished to offer permanently reduced terms to new customers to gain new business. This is a quite usual business custom but cannot easily be applied in a rental situation, since existing revenue is reduced overnight if the reduction is applied to all, or a set of privileged customers appears. The dangers of such privilege are obvious when the bulk of one's customers has a standard price and a short-term rental contract.

There is a difficult balance to be struck in selecting the levels of minimum return and on rented products where there is a continuing charge for usage. It is all too easy to be ultra-cautious and demand a minimum commitment that guarantees an adequate return, but this commitment will also operate as one of the main factors controlling the size of the market that the product addresses. If the level is set too high, then opportunities may be missed; too low, and the return may dilute revenue to an unacceptable level.

Let me illustrate this. The 914 was launched at a metered charge of threepence per copy and a minimum total commitment of £30. It would have been safer to have made the minimum £50 or £100 but this would have restricted the market. A figure lower than £30 would have yielded a larger market but the average return would have declined, possibly to unacceptable levels.

Need for experiment

To be able to expand within a planned framework the advantages of knowing with some accuracy the real size of the market is obvious. The methods of determining the parameters of opportunity are somewhat more obscure. Market research is the most commonly used tool for such measurement but frequently gives coarse answers, and I would suggest that more sophisticated information is available from marketing research designed to stretch conception, to call to question and examination traditionally held views of the opportunity. Why not experiment with pricing, with structure, with sales targets, compensation, philosophy—indeed with the whole gamut of the address to the customer?

This is a technique used a good deal in Rank Xerox and has largely been developed by a management prepared to listen to suggestions and ideas, prepared to experiment, prepared to accept that a rapidly growing and changing company needs rapidly growing and changing ideas. If a suggestion is made by an overseas operating company suggesting a way in which they would like to vary their selling approach, there is an attempt to go with the suggestion provided that a suitably designed monitoring activity runs concurrent with the test. We experiment with pricing techniques and levels and in the manner in which price is stated to the customer.

We continually test structure and compensation, seeking to ensure that the direction in which the field forces' terms point them is not at odds with the direction required by the overall plan.

Experiments have been carried out with numbers of salesmen; expressed crudely in the statement, 'what happens if you double the sales force?'; with the more normal tests into promotion methods and the value of machine features.

Summary

The decision to increase penetration needs careful planning and definition; the element of risk must be measured and progress fully monitored. Every factor that affects the customer needs to be assessed and the maximum advantage extracted from every turn of the business. Real energy has to be devoted to determining what services the customer wants; there is nothing new in saying this, but one feels that many companies pay lip service to the principle without allowing it to affect their plans or activity. The application of product-life extension programmes and pricing techniques have a central part to play in any expansion programme. Lastly, experiment, test and develop trials; anything to ensure that the frame of penetration is not artifically constrained.

21 | Increasing Penetration in Consumer Markets—Cleveland and T.B.A.s

by WILFRED SMOLDEN

WHATEVER product an organization is marketing—whether it be detergents, ladies' lingerie or motor fuels—all have common problems and often similar marketing objectives. For each there is a constant struggle for optimum profits and market share in a competitive environment, related to supply/demand factors, price, quality and costs. Each is irrevocably linked to the consumer and his changing needs. Many people have written text books about marketing, but the shortest and best definition I have heard is this: 'Marketing is where the customer is, and it is the customer who ultimately determines the fate of any business.'

This is the crux of the whole thing and in my opinion it follows that the top management of any successful trading company must be marketing (or customer) orientated and not solely product orientated.

Outward looking

The marketing functions must always look outside the company and keep pace with changing needs. I think this thought is summarized well by Professor Levitt, who writes: 'We sit on a volcano of potential change. It has colossal power to alter the course of events, tastes, immemorial custom, and established ways of doing things. It has the power to immolate even the most prosperous com-

WILFRED SMOLDEN is Sales Director, Cleveland Petroleum Company Ltd. This paper was first presented to the National Conference on *Long Range Planning for Marketing and Diversification* sponsored by the British Institute of Management at The University of Bradford Management Centre, June 1969.

panies, companies full of outward appearance of awesome invincibility.'

This idea often runs through one's mind when reading the balance sheet of a company whose business is centred on one main product which could easily become obsolete.

All of us are concerned with the anticipation of potential change. The old order changeth, and if we are not to be swept into the backwash of progress we, our concepts, and our practices, must change too. Our customers are changing—today they are no longer in a definite social class. They may be of any age from 17 to 70. They are better educated. Where in the past we were perhaps concerned largely with the man of the household, now we find the woman increasingly important. Decisions are shared, the woman plays a part in influencing purchasing decisions in the choice of a car, insurance policy, holiday, in a way that was not true in the past. In the retail petrol market we now find that almost 10 per cent of our customers are women. Children are increasingly important in deciding what is bought. The married woman who goes out to work provides additional discretionary income, as does the increasing high level of earnings available to youth. With this increased power to spend comes a developing confidence, a willingness to experiment, and ability to be critical of products and advertising claims. Shopping habits are changing too—there is an inclination to self-service, and more people shop by car.

All these trends and changes are linked by the customer's desire to choose. This desire is of crucial marketing significance. It means a greater need for investment in research, a clearer definition of one's market, an acceptance that the increasing range of incomes and tastes represents a continual fragmentation of a market.

It has been estimated that half of what we know today will be obsolete in ten years and that half of what we will need to know a decade from now still remains to be discovered. A sobering thought.

I have dwelt just briefly on the changing environment which concerns us all. To the marketing man the message that rings out loud and clear is simply: 'You can't focus on tomorrow's market with yesterday's concepts.'

Future opportunities

Against this background, what has been the development of the motor fuel market, and what are the future opportunities for the marketing man of a petroleum company to make more profitable use of its assets? Let me give you a brief review of the size and

shape of the UK retail petroleum motor fuel market. First a look at
the vehicle population growth rate:

Table 1

VEHICLE POPULATION GROWTH

U.K. Car Population		*Growth*	
1955	3 600 000		Annual growth rate of
1960	6 000 000	35%	between 7% and 14%—
1965	9 000 000	50%	or 444% increase over
1969	11 000 000	24%	20 years from 1955-75.
1975	16 000 000	27%	

Car population has almost doubled over the last decade from six
million in 1960 to some eleven million today, and by 1975 it may
be approaching sixteen million. Based on today's road system, this
would be seventy-five cars for every single mile of roadway.

This pattern is confirmed by the ratio of cars per head of population:

In 1955 there was one car for every eight people. Today there is
one car to 5.4 people, and in 1975 it is expected that there will be
one car for only 2.5 people.

UK petrol sales through the dealer market have moved in step—
more than doubling in the 1955-65 decade; they are forecast to increase again by more than 50 per cent from $2\frac{3}{4}$ to $4\frac{1}{2}$ thousand
million gallons by 1975, although average purchase per motorist
has remained fairly constant at approximately three gallons per
purchase.

Table 2

UK PETROL SALES GROWTH

	gallons, millions	Growth per cent
1955	1 323	
1960	2 040	46.5
1965	2 763	34
1969	3 520	28
1975	4 500	26.4 (estimated)

Looking at motor lubricant sales, which have not risen as fast
as motor fuel, the likely increase in the next decade is only $7\frac{1}{2}$ per
cent. The motor oil to petrol ratio has actually declined from $2\frac{1}{2}$
per cent in 1955 to under 2 per cent today, and may fall to 1.2 per
cent by 1975. The reasons are greatly improved quality of motor
oils with longer periods recommended by manufacturers between
oil changes, smaller sump capacities and more new cars, of improved engine design. Nevertheless, the market is still expanding in

volume, and there is a big sales opportunity. The trend is away
from the forecourt to the lubrication bay, and some main dealers
and car distributors have already anticipated this and installed
really comprehensive lubrication and service facilities.

Table 3

UK MOTOR OIL SALES

	gallons, millions	Growth per cent
1955	33	
1960	41	25
1965	46	12
1969	48	2.4
1975	50	3

When we hear that there has been an uncontrolled growth in the
number of service stations in this country, it is worthwhile to recall
that there were 35 000 outlets of one type or another back in 1938!
The current figure will probably remain fairly static, with inferior
stations going out of business and new replacement stations, with
improved standards, being developed.

Table 4

NUMBER OF RETAIL OUTLETS

1955	32 174
1960	34 704
1965	35 820
1969	36 959
1975	37 000

That then is roughly the profile of the petroleum market over
the past fifteen years, with pointers for the future.

A cosseted market?

Certainly, until the early sixties it was in many ways a cosseted
market, with a UK vehicle explosion of 300 per cent and ten years
producing a 6 per cent average increase in motor fuel consumption.
During the 1950s the major petroleum marketers were certainly
unembarrassed by dramatic changes in the marketing pattern or
by new entrants to the market. But during the late fifties and early
sixties there were several events which had a major impact in the
reshaping of the retail petroleum market, although their significance
was not always recognized at the time.

First, in the early fifties, the introduction of solus trading,
whereby a filling station became exclusively contracted to sell one
petrol brand only, made the retail outlet of greater significance to

the petrol company. In my own group's case, this followed heavy investment in refinery development. It was, therefore, a logical follow-on to invest by loans and other means in retail outlets and to encourage the dealer to plan and redevelop, thereby improving his profitability. It also provided an assured outlet through long-term contract to the company.

At much the same time the petrol companies started to buy and lease their own service stations. Ownership of a chain of company-owned stations, together with supply agreements at privately owned stations, offered a degree of control over distribution hitherto unknown.

Another landmark was the introduction of stamp trading. Green Shield started operations in the UK in 1958, and for several years they and their competitors concentrated on the franchising of grocery outlets.

However, by 1963 stamp trading was making major inroads into motor fuel retailing. This obviously successful form of sales promotion produced additional sales volume, but as dealers vied with each other to give more stamps—offering multiple stamp promotions—so their profit per gallon began to fall. Stamps also introduced a new factor into consumer choice which had hitherto been largely determined by brand or station loyalty.

There is no doubt that the increasing introduction of stamp trading by the service station has, over the years, caused a sharp increase in the overall level of promotion. The man without a stamp franchise has been encouraged by the suppliers to fight back with premium offers, give-away promotions or price cuts.

But perhaps the most significant individual development during this period was the abolition of Resale Price Maintenance in 1965, which gave added impetus to the previously mentioned changes. Prior to its abolition the gallonage potential of any filling station could be quite accurately assessed by its location and its physical attributes alone. After 1965 and the abolition of RPM, flexibility in pricing and much more aggressive promotion upset these benchmarks. From then on the motor fuel market became more fluid (if you will pardon the apparent pun), more aggressive and less profitable.

In spite of the developing pressure on margins, the UK market was still regarded by the oil companies as lucrative. This and a world surplus of crude oil and surplus refining capacity at continental channel ports encouraged new entrants into the market. Between 1965 and 1969 the number of companies retailing petrol under various names has more than doubled.

Table 5

NUMBER OF COMPANIES IN THE MARKET

	International Majors	UK Minors
1955	8	6
1969	17	25 plus

In addition, government activity played its part in influencing market planning. The Monopolies Commission recommendations that franchise agreements be limited to five years resulted in the petrol companies restricting the amount of finance they were prepared to invest in an outlet where the security of tenure was much reduced. In many ways this had a determined effect on the people it was intended to protect. Certainly, there was a delay in the development of the service station as a merchandising centre through lack of capital investment.

It is interesting to see what was happening to the development of the product while all these other influences were at work. Technical improvements in petrol quality had been continuous and had more than kept pace with engine requirements. The research expenditure of the oil industry provided a continuous stimulus to the engine designer. Looking back over the fifteen years, car compression ratios had increased on average from about 6.7 to 1 to around 8.7 to 1, as octane ratings had been progressively increased and other quality improvements introduced.

Table 6

QUALITY RESEARCH OCTANE NUMBERS

Approx. Average All Companies

	Regular	Premium	Super
Pre 1955	84	91	—
1960	88	96	101
1965	90	98	101.5
1969	91	99	101.5
1975	94	101	102

It is interesting to note that the research octane number of 'Premium' pre-1955 is the quality of 'Regular' today.

Impressive record

In spite of substantial quality upgrading, as far as price is concerned, the industry's record is quite impressive. During the 1955-

69 period the price of 'Regular' fuel increased by only 1d, or 5 per cent, and half of this was accounted for by the surcharge resulting from the closure of the Suez Canal at the time of the 1967 Middle East war. Of course, the increasingly high incidence of duty resulted in a fairly steep increase to the motorist as these figures show.

Table 7

PRICE CHANGES: RETAIL

	Regular	Premium	Tax	Nett Regular
1955	4 1	4 3	2 6	1 7
1960	4 2	4 8	2 6	1 8
1965	4 10	5 3	3 3	1 7
1969	6 2	6 5	4 6	1 8

The introduction of yet another factor, in addition to brand, grade name, and price at the point-of-sale, appeared in 1966. This was a Board of Trade recommendation that a system of star grading should indicate the research octane number bracket of each grade —and there is now a high public awareness of this star system.

All these influences:

The Monopolies Commission restrictions on long-term agreements and numbers of company owned stations;

The growing use of trading stamps, and point-of-sale promotions;

The abolition of Resale Price Maintenance;

The introduction of the star grading system; and

Product improvements, heavy duty increases, and increasing operating costs,

all amounted to a requirement for changed policies and new marketing strategies.

This need became even more urgent as the market share of a number of established companies was eroded by the entry of new competition, both in the form of large international companies, and local companies cashing in on a world-wide product surplus situation and able to sell cheaply because they did not have national distribution.

How then is the petrol marketer achieving the greater penetration of his market essential to the maintenance and increase of corporate profitability? The answer lies in the fundamental redefinition of the petrol companies' role in marketing. No longer completely product orientated, they have widened their scope. Their market has expanded to provide a composite service to the motorist. In accepting this we have, perhaps a little belatedly, become far more consumer orientated in our thinking. We recognize the service station as being a retailing complex capable of selling a wide range of products and services to every motorist, 85 per cent of whom have in the past only purchased motor spirit.

For the petrol companies the solution lies in the following:

A stronger identification of their company with composite service to the motorist—as a specialist in motoring in its widest concept as opposed to being specialist in motor fuels only.

The redevelopment of outlets to reduce operating costs, increase productivity and maximize usage of every square foot of land and buildings; and

The development of a range of new products and services to the motorist merchandizable through existing outlets.

Implicit in these policies is the recognized need to actively assist dealers to operate more profitably, whether independents or tenants, as well as to help them recognize and exploit a wider market and continue to sell the company's base products (i.e. petrol and oil) in the required volume.

The petrol marketing man now has to project himself not just as a supplier of petroleum products, but as a professional specialist in the business of car care and service to the motorist. Advertising and public relations now concentrate on projecting these wider images. I may add that as far as my own company is concerned we have taken the opportunity to fundamentally re-image every aspect of the company's outward appearance, designing and promoting a completely new company symbol and new livery, and re-identifying every outlet.

Drastic reviews

As in many other industries, there has had to be a drastic review of the economics in operating the very small outlet. The high cost of deliveries related to low volumes, the limited potential of some sites for development and the exploitation of products other than petrol have created a continual pressure on the achievement of an increase in the average output volume per outlet.

It is worth noting that the average gallonage per outlet has increased from 41 000 in 1955 to 54 000 in 1960, to something approaching 90 000 currently. With the construction of more motorways and the redevelopment of so many towns, it is more than likely that there will be a small decrease in the total number of motor fuel retail outlets. However, the average throughput per station should rise to approximately 150 000 gallons per annum in a few years, and steadily increase after that.

Petrol companies are to some degree in the real estate business. Increasing cost of land and property, particularly in well-populated areas, makes it essential to develop and exploit sites to the fullest potential.

Substantial capital investment will be needed to help develop and convert sites to different usage. Some of this will be channelled into stations of a new and comprehensive nature associated with multi-storey car parks, motels, restaurants, shopping precincts and other developments. However, a very large part will go into the modernization and redevelopment of existing stations.

Existing outlets can be made more productive, more economic, more pleasing to the customer by the employment of new, more advanced, selling techniques; as for instance, self-service and grade blending equipment. With these new possibilities it still remains true that each outlet has to be evaluated in its own right. Every station operates within its own marketing area and as such the critical analysis of product and services range is essential. What is successful at one station is by no means an assured success at another.

These figures help to illustrate the rapid development and potential of consumer motoring expenditure.

Table 8

UK Family Expenditure

Increase in National Expenditure

	Percentage increase in Spending 1958-1968	Percentage increase in Prices 1958-1968
Food	41	22
Alcoholic drink	86	32
Tobacco	53	42
Clothing	55	16
Cars and Motor-cycles	135	(14)
Furnishings	65	30
Radio and Electrical Goods	57	3
Books and Magazines	73	68
Chemist Goods	72	17
Recreational Goods	82	76

During the ten year period 1958-68 the percentage of national expenditure on cars and motor-cycles increased dramatically by 135 per cent, with an equally dramatic reduction in cost of 14 per cent. The trend that these expenditure figures reflect, in addition to increased vehicle population, is the rapid development of the market for tyres, batteries and accessories. It has to be admitted that the service station was slow to recognize this potential. Continuing to concentrate on and adequately cater for the average annual 6 per cent increase in motor fuel, the normal service station had not exploited or perhaps even fully recognized the profit potential of this additional market.

Table 9

DEVELOPMENT OF CAR AFTER MARKET

| 1967 | Retail Sales Potential | £197 million |
| 1969 | Retail Sales Potential | £240 million |

Forecast growth 10% per annum.

As the distribution breakdown shows, a large share of this important market had been captured by the more aggressive merchandizing techniques of supermarkets, departmental stores and specialist high street shops.

Table 10

DISTRIBUTION BREAKDOWN

High Street Accessory Shops	30%
Mail Order	20%
Garage Trade	17%
Other Outlets	33%

'T.B.A.' development

Tyres, batteries and accessories represent a developing and profitable market. It is a market with a large potential—both for expansion and profitability. It is a thriving market. The existing TBA wholesalers, who have been showing healthy sales increases in the past few years, found it easier to deal with the high street ties to maintain sales to their traditional customer—the service shops, and have been perhaps a little lethargic in their responsibilities to maintain sales to their traditional customer—the service station—by effective sales promotion, such as their counterparts offer in other sides of the UK consumer market. The type of service given to the grocer was born out of fierce competition, but it has made the grocery trade one of the most efficient retail organizations in the UK, surviving and thriving on small margins and quick stock turnover.

Whilst since the end of World War II the numbers of independent car manufacturers have decreased, there has been no marked reduction in the number of models. In fact they might well have increased in name, but in many instances this merely amounts to a small change in 'trim' to a basic design. This sameness of the finished product offers a fundamental reason for the existence of the motor accessory trade. Certainly, within the UK, the motorist likes to have some choice in the appearance, specification or performance of his vehicle. It is almost true that he can now only achieve this by the personalization of his vehicle with accessories.

With a current market value of £240 million per annum, and an annual development rate of 10 per cent, rapidly drifting to the high street shop, it is hardly surprising that petrol companies' own brands are now appearing. In this situation the greatest challenge is the retraining of company sales personnel and dealers in the merchandizing and marketing of fast-moving packaged goods.

We are continually researching new customer orientated areas for improvement of efficiency and income at retail outlets. For instance, the development of car wash facilities, automatic or self-service, reflects a changing motorist attitude. Fewer and fewer motorists are now content to wash their cars with bucket and sponge on a Sunday morning. The car has rapidly moved from a luxury to an accepted means of everyday travel, and the consequent demand for fast, economic cleaning has in itself opened up a whole new service area for the retailer with sufficient forecourt space to accommodate this activity.

Improving the flow

Workshop and lubrication bays are being designed to improve the flow of vehicles going in and out for service and repairs. There is also an increasing development of specialist services, tune-up bays, diagnostic centres, tyre replacement services, wheel alignment and balancing, specialist replacement services for exhaust systems and shock absorbers and carburettors. Again the relevant planning of these particular services is dependent on the location and clientele of any particular site.

In certain areas there is also a definite demand for 'Do It Yourself' car maintenance facilities, where bays and specialist tools and equipment can be hired by the hour.

Vending machines, in addition, offer a wide range of possibilities and profit opportunities. Confectionery, drinks, even instant meals, are all relevant to the development of a wider service to the motorist.

And to indicate the extent and opportunities for service to the motoring public my own group is well advanced in the development of an international chain of motor hotels aimed at providing the ultimate in convenience and comfort to the motorist and composite service for his motor car.

New strategies and attitudes

I referred at the beginning to the volcano of change on which we are perched. I have tried to illustrate how the changes in the automotive market are producing new corporate strategies and attitudes, and how the petrol company has redefined its market and has become more strategic in the use of its assets and resources. However, I hope I have not given the impression that the solutions which we are currently applying to our marketing problems are necessarily the ultimate. The truth is that there is very little about Cleveland's management thinking that is static. We simply cannot afford to assume that our past or current successes offer any guarantee of smooth sailing in the future.

Think a moment of the revolutions that will engulf all of us fifteen years hence:

There will be a wide-scale revolution in energy supply. The gas drawn from the North Sea will turn the consumer durable industry upside down. What will this do to the markets for electricity, oil and solid fuel? Change them out of recognition. Atomic energy will follow almost immediately. This fuel source could be available in the foreseeable future almost anywhere on an inter-continental scale.

Nearly every major consumer industry can expect some major revolution. The food industry will see the introduction of the domestic microwave oven. The microwave oven, already in use in parts of the catering industry, offers instant cooking in a matter of seconds for prepared food. A vast market will appear for complete meals in packs—a market which perhaps only the giant manufacturing organizations will have the resources to develop. In its turn the liberation this development will offer the housewife in freedom from cooking chores will reflect in the leisure markets. We shall have more people with time to travel, to use their cars, to need them serviced, repaired, fuelled, personalized.

The pressures to which we have to be prepared to react, remind me of those with which the Queen of Hearts was confronted in Alice in Wonderland:

'It takes all the running you can do to keep in the same place: if you want to get somewhere else you must run twice as fast!'

22 | Planning a Future Product Market—Rolls-Royce R.B.211

by KENNETH BHORE

Preliminary market research

WE began our market research planning by an investigation of airline traffic growths. In terms of world production air transport has, over the past decade, exceeded other major industries (Fig. 1). This historical growth will continue and, in fact, increase. Reputable forecasts indicate that the 1965 traffic will have doubled by 1970 and trebled by 1975 (Fig. 2). There will therefore be a demand for greater aircraft capacity. This can be provided either by more aircraft of existing types or by new and larger aircraft. Two factors indicate that development of capacity will be through the latter rather than the former solution:

1. Advances in technology, particularly engine technology, which will lead to more efficient aircraft, and
2. the heavy growth in traffic which is causing airport and airway saturation.

A subsidiary reason for the new types of aircraft is the general acceptance that passenger comfort on board must be increased, i.e. fuselages must be bigger and each passenger allowed more space without adversely affecting economics.

An analysis of the historical past and projected future demand for different aircraft types is show in Fig. 3. This indicates that, starting in 1971/72, there will be a growing and very substantial requirement for a type of aircraft which has been labelled an 'Airbus'. In terms of value over the years 1972 to 1977 this aircraft will exceed that of any other. There will also be a growing require-

---

KENNETH BHORE is Sales Manager, Civil Engines, Rolls-Royce Ltd. This paper was first presented to The University of Bradford's one week programme *Marketing Technological Products to Industry*, March 1968.

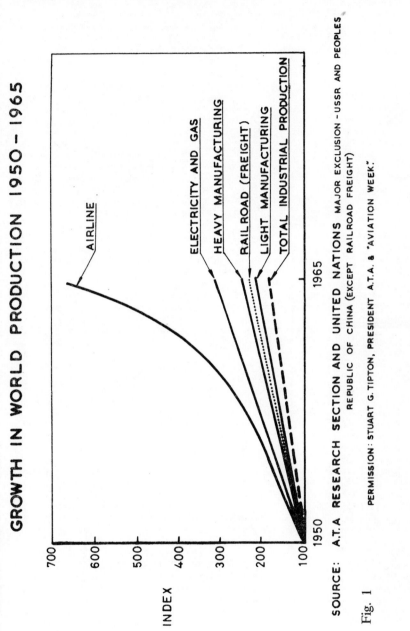

GROWTH IN WORLD PRODUCTION 1950-1965

SOURCE: A.T.A RESEARCH SECTION AND UNITED NATIONS MAJOR EXCLUSION - USSR AND PEOPLES REPUBLIC OF CHINA (EXCEPT RAILROAD FREIGHT)

PERMISSION: STUART G. TIPTON, PRESIDENT A.T.A. & "AVIATION WEEK."

Fig. 1

M

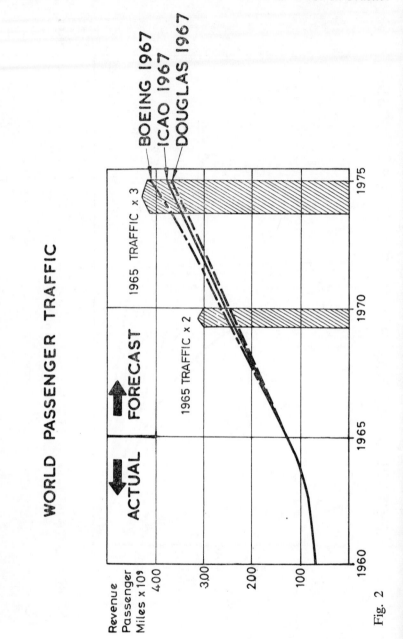

WORLD PASSENGER TRAFFIC

Fig. 2

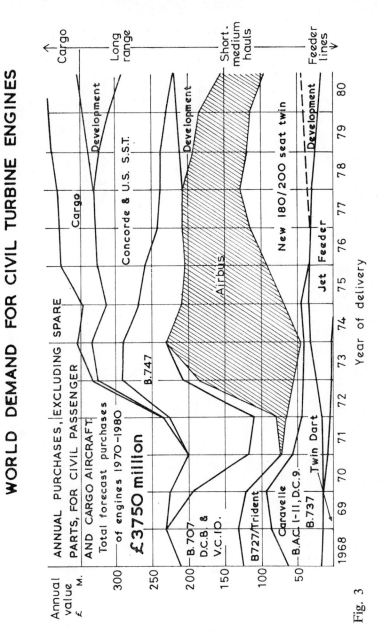

Fig. 3

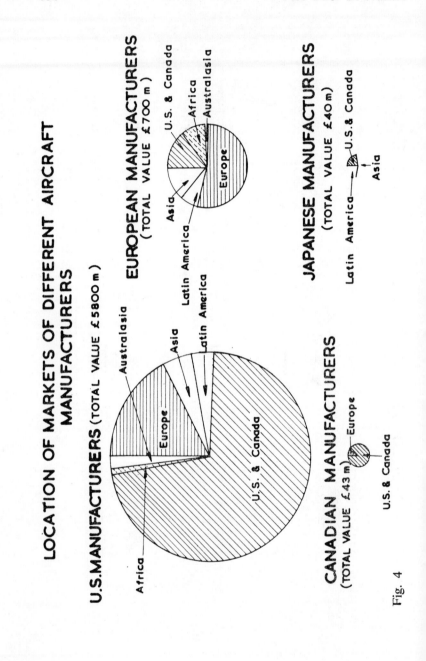

LOCATION OF MARKETS OF DIFFERENT AIRCRAFT MANUFACTURERS

U.S. MANUFACTURERS (TOTAL VALUE £5800 m)

EUROPEAN MANUFACTURERS (TOTAL VALUE £700 m)

CANADIAN MANUFACTURERS (TOTAL VALUE £43 m)

JAPANESE MANUFACTURERS (TOTAL VALUE £40m)

Fig. 4

ment for another new, but smaller, aircraft having a capacity of 180-200 seats. It was obvious that for any manufacturer seeking a new project the 'Airbus' represents the biggest share of the business for the 1970s.

Geographical distribution of markets

A survey of the potential market for the 'Airbus' indicated that the USA will absorb more than 50 per cent, Europe 25 per cent with the balance distributed through the rest of the world. (This excludes Russia, China and their associates.)

Historical sales pattern

The projected location of markets is shown (Fig. 4) and is very similar to that which has happened in the past. It shows that US aircraft manufacturers, partly because of their large domestic market and partly for other reasons, have dominated the world market and will continue to do so, leaving only a small share to European manufacturers and even less to Canadian and Japanese manufacturers.

Technical product investigating

The market survey outlined above led inevitably to the conclusion that Rolls-Royce should aim at:

(a) The 'Airbus' market and
(b) get their engine into an 'Airbus' manufactured by a US Company.

Since it takes a good deal longer to develop an engine than the airframe in which it will be used, and since both of the major US manufacturers already had engines embodying advanced technology under development, one for military and one for civil purposes, it was necessary for Rolls-Royce to develop a project which would enable the delivery requirement (i.e., service by end of 1971) to be met before the aircraft manufacturers had finally decided what form the 'Airbus' would take. Rolls-Royce had, therefore, to anticipate the aircraft manufacturers on this point.

Mission requirements

The first item requiring decision was the mission for which the aircraft would be designed. There was at the relevant time fairly close agreement on the passenger capacity required (250 passengers in a mixed first/coach configuration), but the range requirements varied from operator to operator and no clear pattern was available.

Type of aircraft

As mentioned earlier it was necessary for Rolls-Royce to anticipate the aircraft manufacturers in deciding the type of aircraft which would finally evolve for the 'Airbus' and particularly the number of engines. The great majority of thinking at that time was in favour of a big twin-engined aircraft on the basis that its economics were better than that of a three-engined or four-engined aircraft. However, for the US market we in Rolls-Royce felt that there was a strong case for a three-engined aircraft, operational and other considerations outweighing the theoretical economies possible with a twin. Further, the traditional engine arrangement of three jet engines at the aft end of the aircraft could, we felt, be improved by mounting only one engine there and the other two under the wings in a conventional manner.

Having decided that the three-engined formula would be finally accepted, the operational flexibility of three engines led us to believe that when the various proposals were studied by the major US carriers, they would opt for a US trans-continental non-stop operation rather than the one-stop which was then the current fashion. Therefore, in our opinion the US 'Airbus' would develop as a three-engined aircraft (one at the aft end of the fuselage and two under the wings) with a mission capability of carrying 250 passengers plus some 5 000 lb freight non-stop across the US at not less than mach. 85 speed.

Engine specification

The advances in engine technology (which will not be itemized here) had primarily resulted in the ability to offer an engine with a fuel consumption some 20 per cent to 25 per cent less than engines now in service and with better thrust/weight ratios. Having decided on the aircraft mission, it was possible to optimize an engine for it and this produced the RB.211 with the following basic characteristics:

By-pass ratio		5	:	1
Pressure ratio		27	:	1
Take-off thrust—sea level static—40 600 lb			

As stated above, our two US competitors both had engines which were not optimized to this aircraft configuration and mission but which could nevertheless be utilized. Furthermore, both these engines were committed and, in order to compete in their own market, it was necessary to better their technical specification. The RB. 211 was, therefore, designed with two unique features, in addition, of course, to the advanced 'state of the art' common to all the competitors. These two features were:

1. The use of a three-shaft arrangement instead of the conventional two-shaft, and
2. the use of composite materials instead of metals for parts of the engine.

These two features produced an engine which was basically more simple, without loss of efficiency, and somewhat cheaper to manufacture. This latter enabled the price in the US, after paying transportation and US duty, to be competitive with the US manufactured engines.

Sales planning

The engine specification resulting from the technical product investigation was available early in 1967, though at that time the aircraft specification (and indeed its mission) was still the subject of much conflicting opinion from both the US manufacturers and air-lines. The Rolls-Royce sales plan therefore involved keeping in close touch with the aircraft manufacturers likely to be successful in the competition, as well as with the US Airline operators.

During the first half of 1967 the aircraft specification and mission became firm, almost exactly as we had anticipated. Technically, and in regard to engine size, therefore, we were well placed for the final competition.

In August 1967 we anticipated that the real competition would start about October and a decision would probably not be made before the end of March 1968.

Allocation of staff

Staff allocations were made on the basis of this timetable. Rolls-Royce already had in the US a basic sales organization and an extensive service coverage. This was reinforced by the allocation of three senior people from Derby, one each being attached to the principal aircraft manufacturers in the competition (this was desirable in order to avoid, as far as possible, unwittingly giving away information of one manufacturer to another) and a third responsible for coordinating these activities and with the sales organization as a whole. In Derby a special group comprising representatives of all the departments concerned was formed specifically to action requests and problems transmitted from the US. Because of the importance of this business to the future of Rolls-Royce and in order to achieve the necessary high level contacts, the Managing Director of the Aero Engine Division virtually took up residence in New York. In addition, responsibility for the day-to-day contact with the US Airlines was that of our existing Sales Organization in the US under the VP Sales of our US Company.

Sales techniques

Apart from its scale, the sales plan for the RB.211 did not differ in basic concept from our normal practice though, because of the impact on the US Industry, we anticipated many more problems than usually occur. The first step, a perfectly normal one, was to convince potential airline customers that the RB.211 was technically and economically superior to its competitors. This involved detailed engineering and commercial discussions; as and when the sales staff in the US considered it appropriate, teams of specialists were called up from Derby to visit the individual airlines. The technical liaison with the aircraft manufacturers was continuous and intensive; however, I believe it is fair to say that all the major US airlines and both of the principal manufacturers concerned eventually accepted that the Rolls-Royce engine was superior in technology and economics to its competitors.

Of the problems we had foreseen, the following were most important:

1. Production capability.
2. Ability to meet the promised programme.
3. Political interference.
4. Balance of payment problems.

One and 2 were closely allied. The US aircraft industry has an excellent record for meeting its production schedules, a reputation which, I am afraid, is not shared by the European industry. The US doubts (which I believe would apply to any major contract of this nature which is let in Europe) centred round:

(a) the belief that European industry is not organized sufficiently to react promptly to problems arising during large quantity production.

(b) the belief, fairly widespread in the US, that the labour situation in respect of strikes in the UK was unsatisfactory and could easily disrupt a programme, even though the prime and sub contractors were not in themselves affected. The effect of strikes in the transport industry and docks was a particularly vulnerable point.

(c) There was a surprisingly widespread ignorance in the US of the manufacturing capability in the UK and Europe.

The answering of these problems involved preparation of very intensive and thorough brochures illustrating, for example:

(a) The machine capacity available to Rolls-Royce in the UK and Europe over and above existing and other possible commitments.

(b) Similar data in respect of design, development and production man-power.

(c) Data on industrial relations and man-hours lost in various sections of the UK industry.

In the end, I believe, these satisfied the doubts except perhaps on the labour situation which remained, and still remains, as our most vulnerable point.

We anticipated considerable political activity against us; in fact, apart from a minor effort by one of our competitors and a few politicians, this did not occur. I think all of us concerned were particularly impressed with the very fair hearing which we got from the US politicians, and this could well have been due largely to the help given behind the scenes by the British Embassy in Washington.

The balance of payments problem was an extremely delicate one, particularly as the height of our sales campaign coincided with the height of the US steps taken to cure their adverse trade balance. Here again we were particularly impressed by the statesmanlike attitude of the US Government officials, but it was necessary to take positive steps to forestall propaganda on this point.

A major problem at the height of the campaign was caused by the UK devaluation. Though this had the immediate effect of reducing the price of our engine in the US, there was widespread apprehension that this devaluation would cause runaway inflation in the UK and that prices of engines delivered after the initial contracts and of spares supplied during the life of the engines would far offset any immediate advantage derived from devaluation.

Our results

The result of the preliminary market research, technical specification and the sales campaign was that the RB.211 was chosen by the Lockheed Aircraft Company and, initially, by four major US Carriers to power the Lockheed L.1011 aircraft. The competitor to the Lockheed L.1011, the Douglas DC.10, was selected later by three of the remaining US operators, two of whom chose the GE engine and one the P & W. It is believed that the reason Rolls-Royce failed to secure the order for the DC.10 aircraft was doubt by the Douglas Company whether, within the time scale, we could do two competitive engine installations and the suspicion that the Lockheed Aircraft Company would have preference in the event of such a problem arising.

23 | Strategic Planning in a Dynamic Technology—The Electronics Industry

by SEYMOUR TILLES and RONALD R. McFARLAN

Electronics: A case study of a classical problem

FOR anyone interested in corporate strategy the electronics industry represents an unusually fertile field of study. All of the classical problems of strategy determination exist with particular poignance in this industry.

The broad question of 'where do we go from here?'—which is the fundamental issue of corporate strategy—arises with particular vehemence wherever a company's environment changes. Few industries have seen as many, and as drastic, environmental changes as has the electronics industry in its relatively brief history. A look at what some of these changes have been and the strategic issues they posed forms the focus of this chapter.

The major cause of the continual upheaval in the electronics industry has been its extremely dynamic technology. This has created whole new segments of the industry—and then brought them to both maturity and to obsolescence in a very short period of time. Because technology has been so important as a strategic consideration for electronics companies, the approach taken in this chapter has been to first trace the technological evolution of the industry and then to examine its implications.

It is quite clear, however, that additional factors have contributed to the radical change of the industry's environment—for example, changes in government spending plans, and increasing internationalization of both markets and sources of supply, Also,

---

This chapter is reprinted, with permission, from a Boston Consulting Group Special Commentary, 1964

the persistent tendency of companies to broaden their product lines has steadily changed the industry's competitive structure. This has made it necessary for electronics companies to develop management methods which would permit them to deal with increasing diversification.

Having to deal with an environment made increasingly unstable by these factors is by no means a problem unique to the electronics industry. But the issues posed are so sharply focused in this industry that we believe they can be readily identified and their implications fruitfully explored in this context. It is our firm conviction that the lessons to be learned from the history of the electronics industry are relevant to many other industries.

New technology: promise or pitfall?

It is one of the most dangerous of oversimplifications to assume that corporate success is guaranteed if one can only direct product developments towards the exciting new technical discoveries that are emerging from the labs. A brief look at the history of the electronics industry proves quite conclusively that more companies have got into serious difficulties by pursuing the latest technical trends than have made money by doing so. On the other hand, staying out of the technical race is no guarantee of survival either. It may not produce the dramatic catastrophies which result from too avidly pursuing some particular technological will-o'-the-wisp, but it may result in the more protracted agony of being mired in a slowly obsolescent product line.

In retrospect, those in the electronics industry who were successful in converting technical developments into solid profit opportunities all had several things in common.

1. They took advantage, either knowingly or unknowingly, of conditions under which specific technical developments became major commercial opportunities. Either through skill or luck, they were in the right place at the right time.
2. They acted as if they understood the dynamics involved in the characteristic evolution of growth products from technical curiosities to mature industries. They were aware that a shake-out inevitably takes place.
3. They were able to identify the critical attributes necessary to achieve long-term profitability in a specific area of opportunity. They were then either able to develop and exploit these; or to sell out because they appreciated their inability to do so.

From the events occurring in the history of the electronics industry, it is easy enough to state the essential problem of corporate strategy. It is simultaneously to assess both environmental change and potential competitive performance. While easy to state, it is exceptionally difficult to do. How difficult may be seen from the record which follows. But this record also demonstrates how important it is to try.

From radio to radar

There is always some doubt as to where one should begin a historical account, for things logically flow from the antecedents. Certainly in speaking of electronics one may properly include the development of the telegraph, the telephone, and the teletype during the nineteenth century, as well as the numerous important experiments in physics conducted during that period, as an essential part of our historical narrative. However, we will arbitrarily begin our account at the turn of the century.

The early years

In the early days of the twentieth century, the electronics industry was radio, and radio summarized most of the major segments into which the industry may still be divided; entertainment, including both transmission and home receivers; military; components—both to manufacturers and to hams; and mobile—including marine.

Around 1910 a radio receiver could be built consisting of a tuner, a detector, and a pair of headphones. Resistors were used only for adjusting the bias of silicon carbide detectors, and these resistors were usually air-supported turns of resistance wires. The radio of that day was the 'Model T' equivalent of today's radio—but it had many of the 'Model T's' advantages: it was simple, inexpensive and it changed the lives of all who owned it.

The new technology and the simplicity of the early models attracted a large number of basement operators. Some of these went on to become great enterprises; others fell by the wayside. Still others branched off into still newer areas where technological developments offered the promise of another bonanza for those who were skilful enough to mine it. This has since become a characteristic pattern for the industry.

The period 1910-1915 saw the recognition of the fact that the thermionic triode was capable of providing amplification. This led to the realization that the real function of a tube filament was to provide electrons, and that high vacuum in the tube envelope was not only desirable but necessary.

This development was a key factor in the evolution of the industry's structure. In the early twentieth century, the great specialists in the art of making a combination glass envelope, filament, and high vacuum, were the producers of electric light bulbs. Thus it was perfectly natural that both General Electric and Westinghouse should be among the early entrants into the new industry. RCA was subsequently formed through a spin-off of certain GE and other radio patents and properties.

World War I

The period 1915-1920 was a period of rapid technological development due to the demands of World War I. Transcontinental wire telephony was made possible by the use of triode repeaters. Speech was transmitted to Honolulu and Paris from Arlington by means of a tube transmitter, and it was demonstrated that the telephone land wire could be coupled directly to the transmitter, and used to talk to ships at sea.

The impact of these improvements in communication was similar to that which was to occur 40 years later with the advent of the electronic computer. There was a direct increase in the degree of communication possible between far-flung entities—and consequently an increase in centralization. In the Department of the Navy, for example, the Office of the Chief of Naval Operations was created at this time, because it was now feasible to have such an office.

The 'twenties

In the decade 1920-1930, the radio part of the electronics industry grew substantially from one of infant proportions to one having a significant impact on the economy. In addition, this decade marked the birth of both radar and television. In 1922 Taylor and Young in Washington at the Naval Research Lab made the accidental observation that a ship interrupted some experimental high-frequency radio communication across the Potomac River when the ship intercepted the propagation path between transmitter and receiver. In 1927 the Bell Telephone Laboratories set up a system for transmitting television from Washington DC to New York City. The system used mechanical discs.

While both these technological advances did little more than suggest what the future possibilities of the industry would be, the source of these advances is significant in that it foreshadowed where many of the future advances in the industry would come from: the military research activities, and Bell Labs.

Radio: boom and bust

The roaring 'twenties saw a series of developments which resulted in radio becoming a commonplace home appliance. One of the important contributing causes was the introduction of receivers capable of operation from electric power lines. The great advantages which this provided in terms of convenience and economy of operation helped to increase the sale of home sets. More sets brought more radio broadcasting stations. This was made possible, technically, by the development of receiver designs capable of much sharper tuning so that station interference could be eliminated. It was made possible, economically, by a sharply rising standard of living up to 1929, which gave people both the desire for such new-fangled luxuries and the ability to pay for them. The combined effect was to create a burgeoning industry in ten years. Factory sales of electronic products went from $11 million in 1921 to $180 million in 1925 and $465 million in 1929.

With this kind of growth, it might be anticipated that a lot of new companies would try to share in the wealth. They did. According to one source, 'Between 1923 and 1934 some 1,070 firms entered the radio set business and 960 failed.'[1]

This early phase of the radio industry provides an exact preview of what was subsequently to take place in the television industry twenty-five years later. First, a major growth industry is spawned by a combination of technical development and social change. Then a combination of a large unsatisfied demand for the new product and a rapidly expanding economy raises the market volume rapidly, and attracts numerous new entrants. As demand becomes filled, or economic conditions shift, a shake-out occurs, leaving only a small minority of the companies originally in the industry. This has happened in radio, television, computers, semi-conductors. There are clear signs that it may now be going on among defence products, although this will be discussed later.

The 'thirties

The period from 1930 to 1935 was one of major technological progress, and there were a number of sources of motivation for these advances. To begin with, a consent decree issued under the Clayton Act resulted in the superheterodyne patents being released for licence, and there was a frantic scramble on the part of companies not formerly part of the patent pool to produce and merchandize superheterodyne sets. Second, the depressed condition of the home radio market resulted in the introduction of a combination radio and two-speed phonograph in an effort to bolster sales, and it also led to the introduction of automobile radios. Third, military necessity was leading to the development of radar at the Naval Research Lab. And fourth, working in their industrial research labs, Farnsworth and Zworykin demonstrated all-electronic television.

The fifteen-year period from 1920 to 1935 covers the establishment of the commercial foundation of the industry. Not only were the technical developments being brought about that would serve as the basis for major changes in the industry, but the structures of the companies themselves were emerging to form the pattern that the industry would follow in the future. The essential element of this pattern was size as a competitive advantage. The manufacture and distribution of radio sets to the many people who wanted them could best be done by very large companies who could develop the national marketing network required and who had the financial resources to build the plants and keep them running.

Surge in components companies

From 1935 to 1940 the electronics industry continued to experience a series of major changes. Changes occurred in components section of the industry. The nature of the commercial market changed substantially: in the military field, the collaboration between Great Britain and the US led to major advances in radar, FM radio appeared, and television sets were offered for sale. Many of these developments were related to one another.

In terms of industry structure, one of the significant developments of this period was the emergence of companies specializing in limited aspects of the components field. This was brought about by two contributing trends. One was the increase in the number of radio receiver manufacturers. The smaller manufacturers of radio receivers had no way of supporting the research and development necessary for individual component parts, nor could they afford the mechanization necessary to compete with the component manufacturer who specialized in a limited product area. Another contributing factor was the steady expansion in the number of applications of electronic technology outside the home radio field due to the emergence of TV, Microwave, and FM. Some of the companies which were started at this time were Eitel-McCullough, Varian Associates, and Amperex.

Effect of thinking small

One significant event in terms of components was the development of the small low-drain electronic tube. This tube—combining low power and space requirements—had major repercussions throughout the industry. It was a precursor of the major upheavals that the quest for miniaturization would bring again and again to the industry.

One result of this low-drain tube was the introduction of the portable radio, which was a rapid success in the entertainment field. This was an extension of a trend that was already going on, as table-model radios were increasing rapidly in sales at the expense of the larger, more expensive consoles and combination radio-phonographs. It is an interesting sidelight that GE, which sparked the introduction of the table model in the early 'thirties, would do the same thing in the television market in the 'fifties. In both cases it made life difficult for the people concentrating on large and expensive consoles.

The smaller companies who were alert to the trend towards smaller, less expensive radios did well—even during the depression. Emerson Radio and Phonograph Corporation, founded in 1924, really got its big start in the early 'thirties, when it successfully promoted a compact radio selling at a retail price of $25.[2] This success of Emerson's is illustrative of a strategy that small companies have used repeatedly in competing successfully against the giants of the industry.

> Pick a market that is outside the main field of interest of the large firms, especially one below its existing line in terms of performance and cost. Do a good technical job in terms of providing performance per unit of cost, and a good marketing job in terms of tailoring an approach to the specific group of customers most likely to be prospects. Husband financial resources carefully, and hope that by the time the market has grown large enough to interest the major firms in the industry, toe-to-toe competition will be possible.

The smaller firm has proven time and time again that in an area of primary interest to it, it can do very well against a large, diversified company which may be many times its size, but which may have only a limited interest in that particular product line.

The small tube had not only a major impact on the commercial market; it had a major impact on the military market as well, for as military equipment became more and more complex, and mobile installation of higher and higher priority, the ability to pack a complex circuit into a small space became more and more important.

One of the major developments in the military field that generated a need for a whole new family of components was the development of radar which, between 1935 and 1940, emerged from the lab and became a military technique of critical significance. After 1940, electronics would be associated at least as much with military requirements as with home entertainment.

Development of radar

In 1931 a project had been established at the Naval Research Laboratory for the 'detection of enemy vessels and aircraft by radio'. A major breakthrough occurred in 1934 when a proposal was made that the pulse method, as opposed to the use of CW 'beats', be tried. Work on this proposal was started in March, 1934. This proposal combined for the first time all the requirements for modern radar. The first requirement was to develop an indicator to display the outputs of transmitter and receiver. The second was to minimize the ring, or oscillation, time of tuned circuits from the high signal level induced by the transmitter pulse. The third requirement was the development of fast response to amplify the shortpulse echoes. The fourth requirement was complete absence of regenerative feed-back in the presence of high gain. The spectacular success of this set of experiments was followed by a greatly intensified effort aimed at reducing the size of the equipment so as to permit its use on ships.

A separate stream of radar development was conducted under the aegis of the Royal Air Force. This was completely independent of the American developments until 1940, at which time the two countries pooled their resources. In the technological trade, the US gained the uniquely British cavity magnetron, and Britain the uniquely American duplexer. The pooled resources formed the technological capital for the newly established National Defence Research Committee. This resulted in the superb development of micro-wave radar by the Radiation Laboratory of the Massachusetts Institute of Technology.

Handwriting on the radar screen

Radar exemplified what the Second World War would mean to the electronics industry: a growing dependence on government expenditure for military use; a sharp split between the military and commercial parts of the business, which would create increasingly difficult problems for companies with one foot in both; and a grossly uneven rate of growth, depending on the military situation and the pace of technical change.

Radar also foreshadowed what is now becoming an increasingly common feature of the industry: close international collaboration in the development and production of important advances in hardware. The international exchange between the governments of the US and Great Britain with respect to radar, have their current counterparts in the international collaboration currently prevailing with respect to computers. GE's relationships with Bull of France and Olivetti of Italy, RCA's relationship with Siemens of Germany, and Honeywell's relationship with Nippon Electric of Japan are current illustrations of the extent to which the industry has truly become world wide.

The evolution of the radio companies: some corporate profiles

The concept of the radio as a home appliance was the first one that dominated the industry. It did much to fix the future of those who embraced it, and the opportunities of those who didn't. Thus, at an early date, the major diversified companies in the radio business were heavily in the home appliance business as well: Philco, GE, Westinghouse, RCA.

RCA

General Electric, Westinghouse, and RCA were closely related in the 1920s. RCA was originally incorporated with General Electric as a major stockholder. It also had cross-licensing agreements with Westinghouse and AT & T as well. In addition, it started its distribution of home radio receivers as a sales agent for GE and Westinghouse. RCA did not become a separate entity until a consent decree in 1932 stipulated that both GE and Westinghouse spin off their RCA stock.

Despite its close affiliation during that period, with both General Electric and Westinghouse, RCA was from its inception a different kind of company from its two partners. General Electric and Westinghouse early in their evolution became widely diversified companies interested in all things electrical. RCA was much more narrowly focused, and a careful consideration of that early focus shows an unbroken line of development from its original interest in long distance radio communication in 1919 to its proposed merger with Prentice Hall in 1964.

One common thread running through all of RCA's activities has been a continuing interest in long-distance and mass communications, whether through radio, motion pictures, television or records. This makes its various investments hang together logically—its purchase of Victor Talking Machine Company, its formulation of the National Broadcasting Company, its stock interest in Radio-Keith-Orpheum Corporation. Printed matter is a logical extension of that concept, and consequently its proposed merger with Prentice Hall may be said to fit the pattern.

Computers do not fit the pattern—yet. However, if we project a future in which the relationship between the central processor and the input-output consoles will be analogous to that between a transmitter and a TV receiver, then RCA may indeed have a completely consistent product policy.

Motorola

Most of the major firms were primarily concerned with the home radio. Motorola got its start by making radios for automobiles at a time when this was a radical new idea.

The advent of the automobile radio is a classical case of the dynamics of innovation. The main thought for the car radio came not from the large, established radio companies, but from a hungry young upstart—which is what Motorola was in 1930. And it got started because its main business at the time—home receivers—was not doing very well.

Motorola's entry into the automobile radio market in the 1930s has a striking analogy today, thirty years later, in the entry of Mad Man Muntz into the market for automobile-installed stereo tape units. Having been squeezed out of Muntz TV, Inc. as a result of its financial difficulties, Earl Muntz is trying to repeat with stereo-players and tapes what Motorola did with car radios; take a product originally developed for home use and adapt it to the automobile. Moreover, do this with a product which may have significant growth as technology and the economy expand, but whose present potential is too small for a major company to get involved in it.

Actually, Motorola is of interest for several other reasons. One of them is that it actually began as a components manufacturer making plug-in attachments for battery sets. Its switch from these attachments to car radios is an early illustration of two phenomena that have been common in the electronics industry. The first is that components manufacturers frequently moved from components up into equipment. This switch is currently exemplified by the number of companies currently producing specialized computers that started in the business of logic modules. The second phenomenon is that a manufacturer could start out making one thing, discover another and develop wholehearted commitment to it instead.

This shift in product emphasis away from the original concept on which the firm was started deserves special mention. It is this skill at recognizing the main chance that successful companies are based on. In small companies it can often remain intuitive. In large companies, it must be organized into a formal planning process. Increasingly, in small companies as well, the nature of the industry puts a high premium on more rigorous planning concepts.

Zenith

One additional corporate experience is worth mentioning: Zenith's entry into FM. As described in a recent article:[3]

'When FM's inventor, Major Armstrong, broke with RCA, he worked with Zenith to design sets. For a time, Zenith was among the few in championing FM against considerable opposition, much of it from RCA, and in 1940 Zenith built an FM station in Chicago, which is the oldest in continuous operation. Now that FM has finally become a success, Zenith has reaped the rewards of its early and persistent drive. This year (1960) about 40 per cent of the estimated 550,000 sets sold will be Zenith's.'

This incident is of interest because it demonstrates the very long lead time that may be involved when a company decides to pioneer a technological advance. In this sense, Zenith's entry into FM and RCA's entry into colour television are similar. In both cases the companies involved pushed a technical development despite the indifference or opposition of the remainder of the industry—and after a long lead time, saw their foresight pay off handsomely.

The issues this raises for strategic planning in the electronic industry are rather fundamental ones: (1) what time horizon is necessary in order to do effective strategic planning: and (2) how should the continued feasibility of supporting a long-term project be assessed? Who should decide whether it merits continued support, and on what basis should they make their decision?

Pulsed circuits and continuous change

The history of the electronics industry since World War II can probably best be told in terms of the evolution of three specific product clusters: television, computers, and transistors. Television and computers are closely related to each other, and both are related to radar, since all of them depend heavily on pulsed circuit technology. A direct path can be traced back through circuitry development in computers, television, and radar, which reveals how developments in one led directly to developments in the other.

Television

The history of television follows the classical pattern for new products: (1) An enormous commercial opportunity created by science attracts a large number of technically competent firms. (2) Demand increases rapidly, and most firms make money—some make a great deal of money. (3) The key to successful competition shifts from development to production, as capacity is rapidly increased to keep pace with steadily rising demand. (4) Production capacity exceeds demand and in the glut that follows, it is marketing capability and financial strength that determine who survives the shakeout.

Although the first television set was offered for sale in the US as early as April, 1938, the coming of the Second World War postponed the real commercial context in TV until 1946. Once the production of civilian goods was again under way, the rate of increase of production of television sets was impressive, as shown by the following table:

Year	Total Sets Produced (*thousands*)
1947	179
1948	975
1949	3 000
1950	7 464
1951	5 385

Source: EIA *Electronic Industries* 1962 Yearbook.

The year 1951 was significant in the evolution of the industry, because it was the beginning of the shake-out. In that year, consumer demand fell off from the year before—always an ominous phenomenon in a 'growth' industry. The fact that it occurred so soon after a major effort to expand capacity caught a lot of firms off-base. In that year, for example, Du Mont lost $4 500 000. After that, the race went rapidly to the large, well-established companies with strong financial resources and marketing capability—especially those with a distribution network established in the days of radio.

During this post-war period the strategies pursued by several companies are especially noteworthy. GE entered the market fairly early in its development, and had sets for sale in 1938. But it did not make its serious bid for the market in TV until 1949, when its share jumped from around 2 per cent to around 7.5 per cent. It was subsequently to demonstrate a similar pattern in the computer field, making its real bid well along in the evolution of the competitive contest but coming in strongly at that time.

Du Mont had technical leadership in the early days of the industry. It had a quality product, but was faced with the task of having to create a distribution network to sell it. As competition become increasingly severe, its market share steadily declined. In 1958, it sold its television division to Emerson.

The computer

The military requirements of the federal government created the need for the computer. The necessity for calculating firing tables at Aberdeen, the necessity for improved fire control and missile guidance, and subsequently the necessity for rapidly interpreting the outputs of radar devices were important needs which justified the expenditures of large sums of money by the government.

Many companies saw the great value of the computer to the commercial world, and went after the government contracts which would make possible their entry into the computer market. Electronics companies, such as Raytheon, GPL, AIL, were engaged in computers for fire control as a natural outgrowth of their World War II activities. However, it was the makers of office machines rather than the producers of electronic equipment who first saw the great commercial opportunity that the computer represented. Both Remington Rand and Underwood were early entrants into the computer field. Remington Rand bought both the Eckert Mauchly Corporation and Electronic Research Associates, two of the pioneering technical firms in the early days of computer development. This major commitment was in keeping with Remington Rand's concept of itself as being in the office *systems* business, rather than in the field of office *equipment*.

All of the early entrants into the computer field were quickly outdistanced by IBM, which dominated the industry completely following its successful bid on the computers for the Sage Contract. The Sage programme, a vast network of radar and computers, gave IBM a substantial lead in computer technology. This, together with its commanding position in accounting machines, its control of the basic input device (the punched card), and its superb marketing skills have given it a dominant position in the computer field.

A look at several other companies that came into the computer industry offers some contrasting experience. First is Royal McBee, which had a go at the small computer field via a joint venture with General Precision. It had the marketing contacts, General Precision had the technical ability. The venture was very successful at first, but subsequently Royal sold its half of the venture to General Precision at a loss.

Underwood got into computers, had to give it up for lack of cash, and subsequently sold out to Olivetti. Ironically, Olivetti was subsequently itself forced to sell its computer operations to GE because of its great cash requirements.

General Electric entered the computer field in its characteristic fashion. It came on the scene relatively late, but committed substantial resources to gaining a position. As the competitive contest in the computer field settles down to one requiring vast financial resources and marketing capability, there is little doubt that GE will get an increasing share of the business.

RCA got into the computer business as an extension of its capability in industrial electronics. In fact, computers were a part of RCA's industrial electronics division when they were introduced. It was only several years later that the company established a data processing division. In entering the computer field, RCA was betting that it could develop a marketing capability that would do justice to its very real technical strengths. It remains to be seen whether this will indeed be the case.

It is to RCA's credit that it could carry on two technical development programmes simultaneously of such scope as colour television and electronic computers. However, while colour television represented an area which was clearly compatible with the company's basic strengths, computers were much more of a diversification.

The entry of Honeywell into the computer field represents an extension of a capability which was not even electronic. It was a familiarity with controls, and an ability to efficiently manage technologically oriented companies, that has been the basis of Honeywell's success in the computer field.

As the function of the computer has broadened from business data processing and scientific computation to centralized process control as well, the combined capability of Honeywell in both fields may give it an advantage in the forthcoming shakedown in computers.

An account of competitive strategies in computers would be incomplete without some mention of Control Data. Control Data was formed in a manner characteristic of the electronics industry, by a group which broke off from Remington Rand. Its strategy was a good illustration of how a small company may compete successfully against a large one. To be successful, Control Data had to play against IBM. It chose to do so with a completely well defined corporate strategy, and has done well.

It correctly assessed IBM's competitive strength as an overwhelming degree of customer service and assistance. It therefore decided to go after those customers who would not need such service. This meant, at first, going after the market for large computers, with an efficient machine and low price. The users of the large scientific machine would be sophisticated enough to appreciate the merits of the hardware, and the real value it represented. They would not need the kind of expensive hand-holding that other segments of the computer market would require. The strategy was admirably chosen for a small company having superior technical strength, and wishing to take advantage of a price umbrella.

The development of the computer suggests some interesting hypotheses about the development of major technological innovations. Among these are:

1. The firm which is most successful in profiting from a particular innovation is the one best able to match the innovation and the end use, rather than the one best able to develop the technical product. Du Mont in television and Remington Rand in the early days of the computer are the classical refutations of the 'better mousetrap' theory.

2. A major decision facing companies considering a new technical opportunity is whether they have the money to stay in the game. In fields such as computers, it frequently takes so much money to stay with a major innovation through several product generations, that a company may find itself facing a sharply rising ante with no reduction in risk.

3. Entering a new field through either acquisition or joint venture appears to be a particularly high risk method of entry.

4. Entry into a new product area involves both a commitment to particular types of hardware, and an expression of a particular business strategy. The appropriate business strategy is as important as the proper product design.

The transistor

The history of transistors as a segment of the electronics industry is a vivid illustration of how very rapidly events may move with respect to a major product group. In about fifteen years the transistor went from a scientific innovation so radical that it earned for its developers a Nobel prize to a mature industry suffering both from foreign competition and technological obsolescence.

Transistors came originally from Bell Labs. They were a direct result of A. T. & T's realization that the switching networks projected for future telephone systems would require something both less expensive and more reliable than tubes.

These requirements typify what still remain the major trends with respect to components: enhanced reliability and lower cost. The rapid strides made and the additional trend towards miniaturization have made economically feasible major systems of a much greater degree of sophistication than would have been possible only a few years ago.

As a group, transistor companies have had a difficult time. At one time the darlings of the stock market, they have had a rugged time in the shake-out. Competition forced many companies out of the business entirely, suggesting their failure to appreciate the shifting requisites for survival as the environment changed.

Competiton in the components industry hinges primarily on a combination of technical capability and manufacturing skill. When the component is young, technical skill in the development of improvements is the key. Technological obsolescence is too rapid to permit serious investment in manufacturing facilities. But as the technology matures—and this may occur from one year to the next —the key competence shifts from development to manufacturing, and competition begins to hinge largely on price and reliability.

As this shift occurs, the nature of the industry also changes. Anyone coming in late has to be prepared for a very large investment—but this is not really a deterrent to major companies who feel they want to be in the business. It does mean, however, that the small firm who came in early has only a limited time to develop some specific and clearly delineated advantages by which it can either make unattractive, or withstand successfully, competition in its markets from the larger firms.

Marketing in the components part of the industry is not the critical area that it is in selling either consumer electronics, such as TV sets, or electronic systems such as the computer. As a result, in the components sector, size is far less of an advantage. One has only to compare the early records of Texas Instruments and Transitron with that of RCA and Raytheon to show that a little company can do very well against a big company in the component field.   ·

In the components area perhaps the most critical strategic skill is a sense of timing: timing in terms of entry, commitment to mass-production machinery, and to either exist or amalgamation.

A second lesson which emerges from a study of the transistor portion of the electronics industry is the critical importance of deciding what the 'main stream' of technical development will be.

With respect to transistors, this was the decision as to whether germanium or silicon would be the material on which future developments hinged.

The significance of this decision can be seen in terms of two companies with a heavy early commitment to germanium—Raytheon and Germanium Products—and one with an early commitment to silicon—Texas Instruments. In early 1953, Raytheon and Germanium Products Corporation were numbers one and two in the production of junction transistors. Four years later, Texas Instruments was a clear first, Raytheon was far down the list, and Germanium Products had disappeared.

Conclusions based on history of the industry

The famous remark that 'those who do not study history are condemned to relive it' is particularly true of the electronics industry. Today, the industry stands at the threshold of a number of basic decision points. Almost without exception, every company in the industry faces fundamental choices with respect to its R&D policies, its product policies, and its financial policies. These decisions are typical of the kinds of choices that have faced companies in the industry since its inception. Therefore, some analysis of what may be learned from the past concerning the identification of critical strategic issues, the methods used to resolve them, and the outcomes of the strategies chosen may be a valuable platform from which to consider the future.

The nature of growth

The first generalization to be drawn concerning the evolution of the electronics industry is that the industry has been formed by the interaction of major forces in the fields of technology, economics, and political science. The evolution of the industry from a technological point of view is a familiar tale to those within it. What is less appreciated is that the pace and direction of the industry's evolution were as much a product of the state of the country's economy and its international policies as they were of developments in the state of the electronic art. The boom in radar and computers owed as much to the Cold War as to pulsed-circuit techniques.

A second point to be emphasized is that the industry has traditionally had a very uneven rate of growth. This has been true not only of the industry as a whole, but even more importantly of segments of the industry. The unevenness in growth rate is also directly related to the factors mentioned above. At times when there was rapid economic development or major military necessity, the parts of the industry which specialized in the revelant product lines thrived. At times when the economy did not advance, or slumped backward, or when military requirements diminished, parts of the industry specializing in serving those needs could be badly hurt.

The electronics industry has ridden several great technological trends upward. The first was radio, which made it an industry; the second was radar and micro-waves; the third, television; and the fourth, missile guidance and defence. The current trend is the computer which, while already of significant magnitude, will undoubtedly become even more important.

Pattern of success

One interesting conclusion that emerges from the history of the industry is that there are no recorded instances of companies which got into difficulty because they *refused* to get into one of these major technical fields. However, there are countless illustrations of companies who got into difficulty because they *did* get into one of these fields.

The conclusion can therefore be drawn that the ability to identify the major technical trends in the industry is fairly widespread. However, the ability to translate a particular observable trend into a valid opportunity for a particular company represents a skill which is much less widely distributed. Royal McBee tried computers, but couldn't make it last. Philco had computers, transistors, television—all the growth products, but was forced into a merger with Ford. Du Mont was a pioneer in television, but had to sell out. Raytheon had both computers and television for a time, but got out of both. And yet Control Data, Texas Instruments, and Zenith could make these same products yield very handsome returns.

A study of the industry suggests that it is not just the identification of a particular product as a growth product which determined the company's success, but a wide range of more sensitive discriminations. The most important of these are: (1) the ability to appraise more profoundly the nature of the opportunity offered by a new product; (2) the ability to appraise more perceptively the real strengths and weaknesses of the particular company; (3) the ability to choose a particular course of action which represented an acceptable match between environmental opportunities and corporate characteristics.

The necessity for companies improving their skills along these dimensions cannot be over-emphasized. Many industry analyses directed towards top management are little more than projections of the growth rates that can be anticipated by various parts of the industry. But it is misleading to assume that the fortunes of a particular company will necessarily be related to the overall growth of its industry segment. The relationship is more subtle than that—it requires an assessment of the match between the company's specific attributes, and those of the limited areas of the industry where it is attempting to compete.

Most companies in the electronics industry can be said to have some 'distinctive competence'—a particular set of skills that in some way makes them better than their competitors. At North American Aviation, it is the ability to determine what the military services and NASA will need, and to develop it economically. At IBM, it is the ability to provide superior customer service, together with an excellent technical competence. At Motorola, it is a superior skill in the design and production of mobile communication equipment. At Honeywell, it is a combination of capabilities in both data processing and process control.

Companies which have been successful in the industry have been those which have pursued new product opportunities in a manner consistent with their distinctive competence. For example, Control Data chose to focus on large users of computers who were already sufficiently sophisticated to appreciate the technical merits of a lesser-known brand, and who had enough in-house capability so that they did not require extensive customer service. It has done extremely well.

Companies have been very successful over the long run where environmental changes have given particular value to their distinctive competence. For example, Motorola chose automobile radio as its special field in the 1930s. As the automobile industry grew, it grew. With the advent of World War II, and the tremendous demand for mobile communications, it thrived. With the coming of the post-war suburban sprawl and the decline of public transportation, the increased use of cars and car radios have enabled it to continue to do well despite the steady decline in the annual volume of home radios.

Companies which did not perceive this shift in the radio market fared badly. This was repeated when television first appeared. In the beginning the television set was primarily a console, and perceived by the manufacturers as furniture. It soon became clear, however, that the market was more interested in television as portable, personalized entertainment than in television as furniture. Those who did not perceive the shift were hurt by it.

In the field of television programming itself, ABC presented an interesting contrast to NBC. NBC had been in radio broadcasting, and saw the television programme as essentially a visual radio programme. Upstart ABC-Paramount had been in motion pictures, and saw television as motion pictures of short duration to a mass audience. Within a few years it was challenging both NBC and CBS for first place.

An even more interesting illustration is the computer. When the computer first appeared, there were wide discrepancies in the way its capabilities were perceived. RCA assumed at first that the computer was merely an electronic device; and since it had considerable skill in electronics, it could also handle computers. Underwood assumed that the computer was merely an electronic business machine, and since it had considerable familiarity with business machines, it could handle computers as well. It failed. Royal McBee assumed that the computer was merely a large and complex office machine; and since it had considerable capability in the typewriter field, it could sell computers too. It was unable to stay in the race. The fatal flaw was to assume that the computer was merely an extension of what the producer could already do well, without exploring the validity of this concept.

The needed attributes

It is still a subject of controversy as to which concept of the computer most validly relates to the particular distinctive competences of the various companies in the industry. However, it would appear to be a safe generalization that those companies which do not carefully examine that match in their own particular case are without any real competitive strategy in an area where the penalties for not having one are very great.

Up to now we have emphasized that companies in the industry who have done well shared the particular skills of validly assessing their own particular competence and environmental opportunities. We should add that successful companies in the industry shared another important attribute: the ability to achieve strategic co-ordination. Strategic co-ordination involves the relationship of various organizational components to one another, and the total effort to a set of long-term objectives. Less successful companies either were pulled at cross-purposes by the people within them or failed to achieve any real understanding of where they were heading.

In this regard, it is interesting to contrast the experience of

Zenith with that of Philco. Zenith has been extremely profitable as a company, and has increased its share of the intensively competitive television set market because of its unusual ability to make reliable market forecasts, and to co-ordinate its production and inventories with its marketing. Philco, on the other hand, prior to its merger experienced great difficulty in getting its various groups all pulling together towards a coherent and consistent set of objectives. The situation has been described in an article in *Fortune* as follows: [4]

'The divisions seem to be competing harder with each other than with the company's competitors. Says Henry Bowes, who was running the television divisions at the time: "My job was to get all I could for TV; I was strictly for the buck, and so was every other general manager. Nobody was thinking about Philco." '

Perhaps a way of summarizing the history of the industry is that those companies which were successful had the capacity for consistent evolution. Recognizing both the strengths and weaknesses they had at a point in time, they could relate these both to threats and opportunities in the environment. They could then decide what they had to do so as to either enhance their own capabilities, or exploit them in additional fields.

This has been as true of the smaller companies that entered the industry as of the larger companies that dominate it. It has perhaps even greater importance for the smaller companies, since they did not have the financial strength which permitted them to make the kind of mistake their larger competitors did and stay alive.

One of the managerial dilemmas posed by the history of the electronics industry is that management must attempt to cope simultaneously with both mature products and growth products. To an increasing extent, more and more of the companies in the electronics industry have product lines which encompass both products which are quite mature, such as radios and black-and-white TV sets, and products which are growth products, such as semiconductors.

The simultaneous management of such disparate product philosophies is an increasingly common challenge in the industry, and one which few companies have really thought through. In the mature product, the penalties for mistakes are very high, and the major potential for innovation is in marketing. In the growth products, the major potential for innovation is the product itself, and errors can be compensated for.

These two modes of thought are so different that growth companies have tended to be formed by small groups which split out of large firms dealing in relatively mature areas.

As Alfred P. Sloan says in his retrospective look at General Motors,[5] '. . . companies compete in broad policies as well as in specific products.' The success of companies in a rapidly changing technology depends as much on their ability to keep their policies up to date as it does on their ability to keep their products modern. For policies to be evaluated in a context where the environment is changing rapidly, it is essential for a company to understand what the relationship is between its own capabilities and the changing requirements of a particular market.

If there is a single lesson of primary importance to be learned from a study of the electronics industry, it is the necessity for companies to back away from the product details enough to gain some perspective on the principles underlying their competitive position and to express them explicity in a carefully thought out strategy.

REFERENCES

1 Miller, Rogers, *et al.* (1964) *Manufacturing policy*. Electronics Industry Reference Notes. Richard D. Irwin, Inc. p. 456.
2 Miller, Rogers, *et al.* (1964) *Manufacturing policy*. Emerson Radio and Phonograph Corpn. (A). Richard D. Irwin, p. 497.
3 — (1960) Zenith bucks the trend. *Fortune*, Dec. p. 133.
4 — (1959) The upheaval at Philco. *Fortune,* Feb. p. 115.
5 Sloan Jr., A. P. (1964) *My years with General Motors*. Doubleday & Co. Inc. p. 65.

24 | Expansion into an Allied Market—
Massey-Ferguson

by JOHN HOUSTON

Development of Massey-Ferguson group

MY plan is to review the growth and development of the Massey-Ferguson Group, particularly over the last few years. Growth strategies available to a company have been summarized by Ansoff as:

1. Market penetration
2. Market development
3. Product development
4. Diversification

—the latter, of course, being divisible into vertical diversification, where the company makes more of its product, and horizontal diversification, where the company makes new products. In both cases it means the involvement of the company in new technology. Developments in technology and in market are of course inter-related.

Product changes may involve related or new technology, and the improved or new products may in turn open up similar or even new markets. In reviewing the growth of Massey-Ferguson it is possible to identify at one stage or another all of these growth strategies, and see how they have contributed to the overall growth of the group.

From its founding in 1847 when Daniel Massey opened his workshop to build and repair simple farm equipment, MF quadrupled its production every decade during the nineteenth century. Massey's

JOHN HOUSTON is Director, Industrial & Construction Machinery Division, Massey-Ferguson (Export), Coventry. He first presented this paper to The National Conference on *Long Range Planning for Marketing and Diversification* held at The University of Bradford Management Centre and sponsored by The British Institute of Management, June 1969. It was reprinted in the Journal *Long Range Planning,* March, 1970.

N

first export order came from Germany—before the German Empire and Franco-Prussian War—in 1867, for twenty mowers and reapers. This type of equipment had been exhibited earlier in the year at the International Exposition in Paris, where the company won two Gold Medals. The next impetus to exports was the International Exposition in Antwerp in 1885. The Canadian Government invited Massey to exhibit agricultural equipment, and Canada's present huge export trade in manufactured products stems from this time.

Because of the orders received at this Expo and because of the high US tariff barriers which kept it out of the lucrative US Market, the company raised its exports sights beyond the seas. Market penetration alone was not sufficient to sustain the growth objectives of the company—market development was also necessary. By 1888 the company had organized distribution of its products in England, Scotland, Ireland, France, Germany, Belgium, Russia, Asia Minor, South Africa, South America, the West Indies and Australia. Turnover was $30 000. In 1890 it had become $125 000. Twenty-five per cent of the business originated in Paris!

In 1857 Alanson Harris had started a workshop, also to make farm implements, and sales of these had developed steadily. Amalgamation of Massey and Harris took place in 1891.

Massey-Harris Limited prospered in the farm machinery industry, primarily manufacturing grain harvesting equipment. Total turnover world-wide in 1892 was $3 600 000; in 1897 it topped $4 000 000. This was fifty years from the time when Daniel Massey first opened his workshop.

From the 1880s to 1900 the company's export business grew to the point at which it represented 40 per cent of production. By 1911 it represented 52 per cent and by 1913, 60 per cent, 40 per cent for Canada.

When the war broke out in 1914 the company was operating separately incorporated companies in Great Britain, France, Germany, Hungary and Russia, with numerous agents in each of the other countries. From being a Canadian company, Massey-Harris Limited had expanded into a world-wide operation. The first World War was a serious set-back for the company, but it quickly recovered, and by 1920 foreign sales accounted for over 50 per cent of the business.

In 1926 the company entered the tractor field in order to keep its position as the leader in the industry. It lacked the capital resources to manufacture and looked around for a tractor to market. Secret negotiations with J. I. Case resulted in an agreement to market this company's well-known Wallis tractor. As a result of these negotiations, the company now had a full Farm Machinery line to meet the greatest-ever demand for agricultural machinery. In 1927, after eighty years, a new sales record of $31 000 000 was established, reflecting the company's new strength.

Merger with Ferguson

The thirties saw the continued growth of Massey-Harris as producers of grain harvesting machinery, and this was to culminate in the late 1930s in the manufacture of the first successful self-propelled combine. The success of this new product range confirmed the dominant position of Massey-Harris in grain harvesting. Meanwhile, in 1936, on this side of the Atlantic, Harry Ferguson had introduced the forerunner of what was to become probably the best known tractor in the world. Without going into details, this was a tractor which, by a system of hydraulics and linkage, transferred weight from the implement to the rear wheels of the tractor and hence permitted a light weight tractor which did not compact the soil to the extent of a heavy one, but did an amount of work equal to that which hitherto could only be done by a much larger unit.

The system became known as the Ferguson system and it was a technical breakthrough on tractors in the same way as the combine harvester had been a technical breakthrough on grain harvesters. It is interesting to see that today, thirty years later, no less than some 85 per cent of all tractors produced in the world embody some of the basic principles of the Ferguson system.

So we had in the late 1940s and early 1950s, Massey-Harris leading the grain harvesting segment of the farm machinery market and Ferguson leading the tractor segment of the same market.

It was not illogical—although it took the world by surprise—that in 1953 these two organizations should merge to form Massey-Harris-Ferguson Limited. This was an unwieldy name which some years later was changed to the present Massey-Ferguson Limited. Following the merger there was a massive restructuring of the organization and, despite the dominant marketing position of both the components, it was evident that there was considerable room for growth in Massey-Ferguson.

This growth came from three main areas:

Firstly: the market for farm machinery was still growing at a relatively rapid rate;

Secondly: there were very many market penetration possibilities, if improved marketing distribution techniques were adopted;

Thirdly: there was a profit growth opportunity if the company could move to producing a greater proportion of its product, as opposed to purchasing it from outside suppliers. In other words, vertical diversification.

From the mid 1950s, therefore, growth was available from these three sources and the company's action moved along all three paths. With the full product range, it was possible to benefit greatly from the growth in demand. Improved distribution was also possible as a result of being able to choose the best out of two world-wide distribution systems. Simultaneously, in the process of producing more of our own products, we purchased, in addition to the plant that was making Ferguson tractors under contract, Perkins Engines Limited and so by acquisition we diversified into the engine business.

Towards the end of the 1950s, there were signs that the growth in the free world agricultural tractor market was slowing down. However, several small companies around the world were starting to take agricultural tractors and add hydraulically operated shovels on the front and hydraulically operated diggers on the back to make a piece of light industrial digging and earth-moving equipment. This equipment was growing in popularity amongst the small building and public works contractors, and Massey-Ferguson decided that there was an opportunity for further growth through new application of its basic product—the tractor.

In terms of product development with consequent growth possibilities, this step was most significant because it moved Massey-Ferguson into one sector of the huge market for industrial and construction machinery. However, we will see the full significance of this later.

So, during the early 1960s, we were growing by increasing our penetration of agricultural tractors and implements, and of combine harvesters, by getting a greater share of the favourable engine business and by basic market growth of light industrial machinery. By the early 1960s we had reached a position where we were the world's largest producer of wheel tractors, of combine harvesters, of diesel engines and of light industrial equipment, and we took stock of our position.

Let us spend a minute now looking at the MF position at that time and the world market of each of the product groups I have mentioned.

Market survey

Agricultural tractors

The free world agricultural tractor market was virtually static at something between 580 000 and 630 000 tractors per annum. Was this market going to take off and expand? What about the world food shortage? Surely that would promote total market growth? A closer inspection showed that there was not a world food shortage. There was a world food distribution problem, and as emerging countries produced more of their food and used more tractors— in itself a slow process because of the availability of cheap labour —developed and sophisticated countries were becoming more efficient and were producing the same or a greater quantity of foods with larger but fewer tractors.

Therefore, our appraisal of the situation was that there would not be any significant growth in the world tractor market. It is interesting in hindsight to see that this has proved correct, because in 1963, 599 000 tractors were sold and the equivalent figure for 1968 was 594 000.

What about tractor penetration? In 1964 we were obtaining about 20.2 per cent of the free world market and it was extremely questionable whether we could economically achieve a great deal more than that.

Combine harvesters

On combine harvesters the world market was between 95 000 and 110 000 units per annum, and again there was no evidence to show that there would be any significant growth. The sophisticated territories were if anything over-populated with combines, which would offset increased demand in the developing countries. Again, our penetration was in the order of 20 per cent and it was questionable whether we could make significant increases on our economic basis.

Diesel engines

On diesel engines, the size of the total market depended to a very large extent on the size of the agricultural tractor and combine market—both using diesel engines—the world truck market and the industrial and construction equipment market. Although some movement was possible in the size of certain market sectors, its significance was reduced in any event because our potential market was limited to those producers of an end product who did not manufacture their own engines.

Light industrial equipment

In the light industrial field, whilst the increasing cost of labour was increasing the size of the market, the same rising cost of labour was moving the size of machinery out of this sector into the medium and heavy industrial field. We were getting something like a third of this market, so again our chances of economic penetration increases were remote.

Share of the market assessed

In summary, therefore, as a corporation we were faced with a situation in which, in our four main areas, significant market increases were not expected and our market share position was such that we were going to be the target for attack by competition and would probably have to fight hard to hold on to what we had got, let alone increase it. So, in the early 1960s, having taken stock of our position, we asked ourselves the question 'Where do we go from here?' From a world-wide sales volume of $89 million in 1947 our group sales had grown to $686 million in 1963 —a remarkable rate of growth, which it might be difficult to sustain.

The question we were really asking was: Had Massey-Ferguson come to the end of exploiting its inbuilt strength which had been developed as the result of the businesses they were in by that time, or could they exploit these assets for future growth? If the answer to that question had been that we could not exploit these strengths any further, then obviously future growth could probably only have come from radical diversification. We took stock of these assets:

We had a strength in design and manufacture of transmissions and axles, and were already manufacturing a wide range of diesel engines.

We had a strength in the area of hydraulics through the inherent hydraulic requirements for tractors, combines and light industrial equipment.

We had a knowledge and expertise in the manufacture of track equipment, having purchased a company called Landini in Italy, who had been for a number of years manufacturing crawler tractors for agricultural applications.

Last, but by no means least, we had an immense strength in our world-wide distribution. In our field we were probably the envy of the industry in the distribution structure with the calibre of distributors and dealers that we had around the world.

In the industrial and construction machinery field, as with farm machinery, it is vital that the user should have ready access to first-class service facilities and to reasonably priced spare parts with a high degree of availability. The world-wide leadership of MF in farm machinery stems in no small way from the availability of this kind of customer support, and it seemed that this strength could readily be adapted to the needs of the new potential market.

By our entry into the light industrial equipment market, we had moved into one sector of the earth-moving market. This was an immense market of $6 000 million annually, and a preliminary study showed that we could use the assets I have mentioned if we expanded into other sectors of the earth-moving market.

At the same time it was evident that there were certain other markets into which we could move that would use some of our assets. In most cases, however, these were areas without which we knew very little or in which, if they were likely to provide synergistic effects during the start-up phase, synergy was unlikely to occur in operation.

Earth-moving machinery

Therefore, the decision was taken *in principle* that the next stage of Massey-Ferguson growth would come from a move into other sections of the earth-moving market. It was evident that if we were going to break into this highly competitive market, where there was no shortage of equipment, we would have to plan and ultimately implement those plans with a degree of undivided attention that was going to be difficult to achieve with the company organization existing at that time and based to a large extent on farm machinery.

Therefore, in 1965, the structure of the company was changed and three product groups were set up directly under the President. One was for farm machinery, one was for engines and one was for industrial and construction machinery. Each of these in effect was a separate business. Each consists of a group vice-president, a group staff, a number of geographical operations units, and (within the farm machinery and engines groups) a separate, world-wide export activity. Because of their world-wide responsibilities, both the group vice-president and his staff are part of corporate management, and actively contribute to, or participate in, the formulation of the overall company strategy. While responsible for the success of their own product businesses, they must also consider the impact (financial and otherwise) of their plans and operations on other groups and the company as a whole.

Having got the company structure in a position to move forward, the industrial and construction machinery group set to work to plan the fulfilment of the decision to enter other segments of the earth-moving market.

In broad categories, the earth-moving machinery market was made up of eight sectors. They were:

1.   The industrial wheeled tractor market, in which we already competed.
2.   Crawler tractors.
3.   Hydraulic excavators.
4.   Wheel loaders.
5.   Motor graders.
6.   Motor scrapers.
7.   Off highway trucks.
8.   Rubber tyred dozers.

A look at these sectors, together with their projected growth over the next ten years, showed that in unit terms, of the seven sectors in which we did not compete, crawler tractors were the largest, followed by wheel loaders and hydraulic excavators.

Why were we interested in units and not just the value? We considered we had a greater chance of success by achieving sales by high unit volume than we would by trying for the same value of sales with a lower unit volume of higher priced more specialized products. The reason for this consideration was that a major factor in our ability to achieve a certain sales level was our world-wide distribution structure. However, our ability to maintain and improve that sales level, once it was achieved, would depend on our spare parts and service record.

In world-wide markets the distributors are the prime providers of parts and service to the customer and, if they don't stock adequate parts, the non-productive time of very expensive machinery will increase, with a very adverse customer reaction to the product. However, distributors are interested in economies and many of their actions are dictated by this. It is much more economical for a distributor to carry parts stock for fifty machines worth, say, £5 000 each than it is to stock parts for ten machines worth £25 000. For the same value of parts turnover the capital commitment for parts stock may be 25 per cent or even less.

To revert to the seven sectors of the market, the industry practice in the earth-moving market has been for manufacturers to concentrate on one or two sectors with a large degree of vertical product integration. By vertical integration, I mean that by having a very wide range of, say, crawler tractors, the manufacturer covers 95 or 100 per cent of the crawler tractor market. Our planners had to decide whether MF was going to follow the industry practice because, if so, perhaps acquisition was the right way to enter the selected market segment.

Because machines of many different sizes would have to be produced, vertical integration into one sector of the market would mean that many different sizes of components would be required for an effective coverage of the market sector. For example, many different engines, many different transmissions, many different axles and many different hydraulic pumps.

A closer look at the industry practice in this area of vertical integration showed that it has evolved more than been planned. In the early days one crawler, or one wheel loader, had covered the market sector but as each sector had grown and sizes had increased, a second, and then a third or even fourth model had been required. Therefore manufacturers' vertical product integration had evolved one model at a time.

However, to reach virtually in one step such a level of vertical integration relative to the market that existed by the mid 1960s would have meant a very expensive programme, with high design costs, high tooling costs and low production runs of the components. This would have slowed down and made much more expensive the Massey-Ferguson entry into the earth-moving market. Similarly, acquisition was not an answer because of the enormous problems of rationalizing components with MF current products. There would also have been the problem of rationalizing distribution—a vital factor.

Deeper investigation showed that with many of the same components—the same engines, the same transmissions, the same axles —we could in fact cover a large part of each of the three biggest sectors of the earth-moving market: the crawlers and hydraulic excavators and the wheel loader market. The advantages of this approach would be a greater coverage of the total earth-moving market and a relatively lower design and tooling cost, a speedier market entry and, very important, a much more valuable franchise to offer our distributors.

Furthermore, recognizing that to penetrate the earth-moving market, which was already well served by industry, would be extremely difficult, the value of a 1 per cent market share achievement would be much greater by covering three sectors of the market than by covering one.

This then was the direction we decided to take—contrary to industry practice. Using existing Perkins engines and incorporating many transmission and other components already in production by MF, it was found possible to produce product ranges to compete in each of these three sectors. With four models of crawler tractor we would compete for 78 per cent of the crawler market. With three models of loader we would compete for 85 per cent of the wheeled loader market. And with two models of excavator we would compete for 74 per cent of the total hydraulic excavator business. Together with our products in the industrial wheel tractor sector, these nine new products (which would have a considerable degree of interchangeability of components—in itself an enormous advantage in production and world-wide service) could give us coverage of 87 per cent of the unit volume of the entire $6 000 million earth-moving market.

Entry into new business

This became the programme. The engineering group was formed and design criteria established. In setting the design criteria, we had to remember that the market was already well served. Contractors were not waiting for Massey-Ferguson to produce machines before they could get what they wanted. Therefore, our design criteria not only had to provide performance at least equal to competition, but also had to have product features not offered by other manufacturers. An analysis of user preference trends established a number of factors in which more and more operators were interested. Ease of maintenance was one of the most significant of them because of the production lost when the machine is out of service. Similarly, operator comfort is important if the machine is to be highly productive through a long day. Safety was a matter of great importance to most contractors, and indeed has been the subject of legislation in many countries. Finally, it was important that the machines should have a functional appearance, and should look like a family of machines.

A detailed competitive review showed that no one manufacturer had paid real attention to all four of these aspects. Therefore, our design criteria required, in addition to competitive performance, a concentration on all four at once.

Many factors had to be considered before it was decided where we would manufacture these products. Apart from logistical considerations, such as the availability of materials, labour and proximity to the main markets, consideration had to be given to taxes, tariffs and government attitudes towards investment. Then factory plans were produced and manufacturing facilities were built.

From a design and manufacturing point of view, therefore, the ball was rolling and the marketing organizations were in a position to prepare the ground work for what was going to be the biggest introduction into the earth-moving machinery market that had ever been attempted.

In all Massey-Ferguson's operations units, including Massey-Ferguson (Export) Ltd, organizational changes were planned in order that the required amount of attention and expertise could be devoted to this new construction equipment we were to produce. We were not going to be able to market successfully these products with a farm machinery sales force, and separate ICM divisions had to be set up.

The distribution structure had to be prepared and organized for entry into this new business, because we were not going to succeed by having farm machinery distributors and dealers selling into this new market with their existing organizations. While synergistic effects were to be expected in the service and spare parts functions of the business, distributors and dealers had to reorganize their sales functions, and in some cases had to divest themselves of franchises which would have been competitive with the new Massey-Ferguson equipment. Sometimes, quite reasonably, distributors were unwilling to do this and alternative distribution had to be found without diminishing the standards of customer support established by MF.

March 1968 saw the formal launch of the new product range, although many other aspects had to be worked out before then—marketing strategies, advertising and sales promotion programmes and the many other factors that go to make up a product launch. Seldom has a launch been carried out on such a scale and certainly never before in the construction machinery industry.

During the last year or so, our new machines have been introduced in many countries of the world. The response from all who have seen and used these machines has been most encouraging. Indeed, we now have reason to believe that the confidence that inspired the important decision we took some five years ago was well founded.

Other factors, such as the development of construction techniques as well as the global human problems—the population explosion and the population shift into the cities, that create the pressing need for more and more construction, convinces us that the years ahead will bring an unprecedented demand for machines used for building. We see an exciting future for our company in this field, a future that will fully justify our decision to channel our expansion into an allied market. It was Archimedes who said: 'Give me a firm spot on which to stand and I will move the earth'. We seem to have found a spot that's pretty firm, and we're going to move an awful lot of earth.

25 | Organizing for Profit and Growth— I.C.I. Plastics

by DOUGLAS OWEN

ORGANIZATION, in my view, can be discussed much more sensibly in terms of a specific business. Some of the background to the plastics industry and the part which the relevant Division of ICI plays in this, may therefore be of interest.

Our business is broadly that of plastics materials for conversion by its customers into useful articles, either in their own right or as components in consumer or capital durables. The Division also includes, however, the manufacture and marketing of films in the packaging, reprographic and other industries and associate companies and subsidiaries are involved in the manufacture of packages themselves. Indeed one of these companies is the largest single manufacturer of plastics sacks in the world.

Plastics as part of the petrochemicals industry are, along with bio-chemicals, electronics and food, regarded as likely to be one of the great growth areas from now to the end of the century. World production in 1950 was some two million tons: by 1965 it was eighteen million tons and by 1980 it is forecast that the world total will be increased to 100 million tons. In the UK, production of plastics last year was about 1.2 million tons and it is forecast that by 1980 this figure will reach $4\frac{1}{2}$ million. Thus from the single criterion of market growth there is no prime urge for diversification in the sense of entry into entirely new business areas. However, within the plastics polymer business itself, considerable diversification has taken place in the past and will continue to take place in

DOUGLAS OWEN is Vice-Chairman of Plastics Division, I.C.I. Limited. This paper was first presented to The National Conference on *Long Range Planning for Marketing and Diversification* held at The University of Bradford Management Centre and sponsored by The British Institute of Management, June 1969.

the future in the sense that new grades of existing polymers will need to be developed, and there will be new plastics and combinations of plastics materials aimed at extending temperature resistance and strength into fields hitherto regarded as the realm of metals. To get the plastics business into perspective perhaps a single statistic will suffice. It is estimated that on a volume basis present world production of plastics equals that of all the non-ferrous metals put together and that by 1985 their volume production will rival that of steel itself.

Along with the explosive increase in use has been a period of technological innovation in the manufacture of the materials and the primary materials from which they are derived resulting from developments in the petrochemicals industry. Thus there has been a considerable reduction in costs in an intensive internationally competitive situation resulting naturally in very large reductions in price, as illustrated below for several typical materials.

		£/ton		
	1955	1960	1965	1968
Polythene	380	240	150	130
Polypropylene	—	400	230	200
P.V.C.	190	150	115	104
Retail Price Index	100	114	136	151

It is widely agreed that the profitability record of many of these polymers has for varying periods and at different times been far from satisfactory over the last decade. This has been due primarily to periods of very heavy over-capacity with inevitable pressures on price but also to unduly optimistic anticipation of technological advances in the manufacture of the basic raw materials.

Development

The development of the plastics industry depends on the expansion of existing and the development of new outlets. The usage at the present time between various applications in the United Kingdom is estimated to be as in the table on page 399.

If forecasts are to be realized it is expected that polymer producers will in future, as in the past, continue to play a major role not only in adapting the materials to give the required effects in processing and in the final article but also in the development of fabricating techniques and effects.

I have mentioned our own film activities which continue to present profitable opportunities for diversification, although the basis of our being in films stemmed originally from what we judged to be a necessity to stimulate the manufacture of plastics films primarily for packaging. The business took on almost another dimension with our development of an expertise in the manufacture of what are known as 'bioriented films' now extensively used in the packaging, photographic and drawing office industries and of course in the manufacture of recording tapes.

The Plastics Division of ICI itself manufactures around 25 per cent of the basic plastics materials made in the United Kingdom. Since the capital cost per ton/year of plants for manufacturing these types of materials is £100 or above and the market is expanding at the rate of 10-15 per cent per annum, it will readily be seen that we are involved in a significantly large investment programme. About 30 per cent of our product is exported and is sold overseas to a large extent through our associate companies and in some cases through agents. The ICI group manufactures plastics in a number of overseas territories including Canada, India, Australia, USA, Holland, South Africa, Denmark, Spain and the Argentine, and the Division is regarded as the main centre for research on many of its plastics products. The Division's research and development budget runs at about 5 per cent of turnover, a high proportion of which is devoted to the development of new processes for the manufacture of existing polymers and new variants of them. The Division is also an important exporter of 'know-how' to other organizations. Thus our operations are truly international.

So far as entirely new plastics are concerned, it is generally accepted that the cost of their development to a rewarding commercial scale is likely to be so great that they really can only be exploited internationally, the UK market not being sufficiently large. It has to be remembered that the development to full maturity may take as long as ten to fifteen years. We manufacture a

Sector	Percentage of Total Consumption
Packaging	21.7
Building	20.9
Electrical	7.8
Automotive	4.3
Housewares	4.1
Other transport	3.5
Furniture	3.5
Clothing (including footwear)	3.0
Toys, fancy goods, etc.	3.0
Mechanical engineering	2.8
Consumer durables	2.0
Agriculture	1.6
Miscellaneous and unidentified	21.8
	100.0

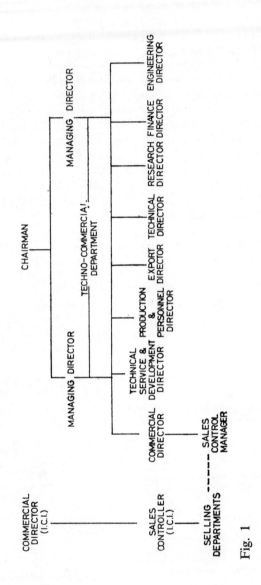

Fig. 1

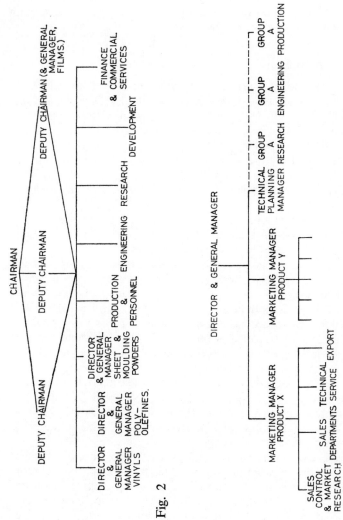

Fig. 2

Fig. 3

very wide range of plastics materials based on widely differing technologies, used in a huge variety of end products—in fact, our total business can be and is regarded as a number of separate businesses at the vital marketing stage, although further back there are a number of common functions which gather considerable strength from being part of a large organization.

Reorganization

These basic thoughts are not very different from those which resulted in a major reorganization of the Plastics Division in 1964. Until that time the Division had been organized on a functional basis, the broad lines of which were as shown in Fig. 1. This was changed to that shown in Fig. 2.

The essential feature was the setting up of four business areas covering all the Division's products in commercial production.

The typical organization of one of the Product Groups is shown in Fig. 3.

As will be seen, the whole of the marketing function and the responsibility for the total viability of the business area was delegated to the Product Group General Manager.

It will be noted immediately that the Product Group General Manager does not have direct responsibility for a number of activities which obviously have a considerable bearing on the viability of his business, notably personnel policy, research, engineering and production. There are also several others of a service nature—accountancy, management services including computer services, office services, operational research and mathematical techniques, relationships with overseas sales companies and agents and the servicing of licensing and other agreements. The underlying reasons for this were partly to avoid losing the undoubted advantages of the corporate nature and size of the Plastics Division in a national and international context and partly to ensure the most economic use of scarce and expensive expertise.

On research, for example, the Product Group General Manager determines the research objectives of his product group, the priorities to be adopted and the size of the research budget; he does not presume, however, to dictate how the research is to be carried out. He has, however, the right and duty to comment on the effectiveness of the research. The Research Manager responsible for the product group's research definitely regards himself as a member of the product group team under the Product Group General Manager.

In the intervening period the production organization has been changed, the Personnel and Production Director having become the Personnel and Production Services Director. The various Works Managers report to him for the running of their factories and for carrying out personnel policy, but the section managers of the individual product plants have a direct responsibility to the Product Group General Manager for their efficient occupacity, and the cost of running of the plants within the constraints imposed by the Marketing Managers.

Similarly the project engineers in the Engineering Department assigned to the individual capital projects regard themselves as being very much identified with the product group.

Planning and a good accountancy system

A prime requisite for planning—be it short or long term—is a meaningful, sensitive and speedy accountancy system. This has been developed to what we consider to be a high state of perfection within the Accounts Department at the Division's headquarters, working extremely closely with the Computer Services Department and Operational Research and Mathematical Techniques responding to the same Director.

Once again, however, within the Accounts Department are accountants whose livelihood is closely associated with the product groups, and they also regard themselves as being very much part of the product group team.

The Accounts Department is expected to play an important part in the development of methods of investment appraisal in connection with the Division's heavy capital programme. Of course, these are an important part of the Division's corporate long-term planning, and in turn the Division plans have to be reconciled and co-ordinated with those of ICI, both nationally and internationally.

It will be readily appreciated that since we market a whole range of plastics materials there will be occasions when there is more than one candidate for a specific job and therefore there could be difficulties in deciding which is the best and which should be promoted. This happens much more rarely than might be expected at first sight and is often resolved under the pressures of the marketplace. Whether or not to pursue a possible outlet is a product group decision taken by the marketing manager. Nevertheless we deem it essential at the present stage of development of the plastics industry to establish a nexus between the various materials which we manufacture, and this is achieved by the Development Department. This department is responsible for surveying, commenting upon and promoting the use of plastics across major outlets, for example the motor vehicle, packaging, building, agricultural and furniture industries. It is also responsible for evaluating new polymers as massive plastics and for taking new products from the Research Department and being responsible for their development in the widest sense up to the stage where a fully-fledged commercial production unit would normally become the responsibility of one of the product groups.

So much for our organization. There are, of course, many other aspects of it which could be discussed but we must ask ourselves what has been achieved. We have set up a highly integrated business organization which in our view enables identifiable business areas to operate with a reasonable degree of autonomy, but how reasonable is always a matter of debate, while at the same time recognizing the corporate objectives of both the Division and of the company itself.

What makes a business work?

What has been developed to a high degree and to a considerable depth among our 10 000 employees is a lively appreciation of what makes a business work, paving the way for a less highly mechanistic and more organic approach. The disciplines required for successful capital investment both in the short and long term are widely understood. Against this background it has been possible to tackle all other aspects of the profitability gap including cost reduction, withdrawal from unpromising lines and the simplification of existing ones with a widespread feeling of personal involvement.

The Division operates an annual Financial Plan and a four-year investment operating plan against the backgrounds of seven- and ten-year forecasts.

In building up these plans and forecasts, account has to be taken of the economics of plastics on a national and international manufacturing scale in relation to other materials—in particular, natural materials, competition with plastics materials themselves, competition by other plastics producers and new entrants into the field, the likely future groupings of the consumer industry, the improvement of existing plastics materials to increase their area of application and the development of new processes of fabrication.

The sheer size of the economic units of production, particularly of the raw materials—250 000 to 500 000 tons/year for the production of ethylene, 150 000 to 300 000 tons/year for the production of vinyl chloride, and, say, 100 000 tons/year for the production of polyvinyl chloride—bring with them big problems of the cycle of surplus and shortage with accompanying instability in price. Transition from speciality products to almost bulk commodities in some cases is well under way and mistakes will prove exceedingly costly if not catastrophic.

In the plastics industry, as I see it, the potential for diversification is inbuilt because the materials themselves, the routes and methods of their manufacture, the methods by which they are formed into useful articles, are all capable of immense further development and innovation. Plastics are materials for construction as are wood, concrete, steel, and find application in almost every industry. Their virtues are that they can be readily formed, replacing in some cases a number of fabricating operations in a traditional material by a single operation. Small wonder that the plastics materials manufacturer is constantly faced with opportunities and questions on diversification. Small wonder that manufacturers of finished goods having entered plastics fabrication for a particular reason almost invariably diversify further from that point.

It takes about three years to build a polymer plant; the units are large and the capital cost is high. Different types of plant or different plant arrangements are required for different grades of a given polymer to meet different application requirements. The big production polymers and the monomers from which they are made are now articles of international trade. The new polymers designed for particular outlets or for extremes of performance, certainly so far as a UK manufacturer is concerned, demand an international marketing operation if they are to be successfully exploited, and in some cases the first full-scale manufacture must be in a bigger market than that which can be provided by the United Kingdom. The need for long term planning on a company basis is self-evident. For this to be rewarding demands a lively and intelligent appreciation of the likely intentions and aspirations of one's competitors, both national and international.

It might well be asked whether our reorganization has resulted in improved profits. Certainly our profits have improved and indeed there is plenty of room and need for this.

There have been many factors at play—not least of which in the last two years has been a greater than forecast increase in the market demand. However, we are completely convinced that our reorganization has enabled us to take significantly greater advantage of opportunities offered than otherwise would have been the case.

26 | Evaluating and Controlling Marketing Projects—The Ford Capri

by ROY HORROCKS

THE Ford 'Capri' story is a practical example of a marketing decision which, because of its investment and timing implications, straddles the frontier between short-term marketing and long range corporate planning.

What was involved?

1. Four years of research, planning, testing, evaluation and development to produce a product with a market life of at least another four years.
2. A detailed matrix of product, feature, performance, engineering, cost and timing objectives.
3. An investment of £22 million.
4. The recognition that the achievement of every one of the myriad performance targets we had set ourselves was mandatory to the success of the total programme.

Such a project could never have been undertaken without the well understood system of operating discipline exemplified by the Ford procedure for product planning.

Product planning in the motor industry is a demanding discipline. The lead times involved in planning a new car are such that the point soon arrives in the four-year cycle when decisions can no longer be changed. In fact, changes are only feasible up to two years before Job 1, but even then carry with them heavy cost and

ROY HORROCKS is Merchandizing Manager, Car Sales, Ford Motor Company Ltd. This paper was first presented to the National Conference on *Long Range Planning for Marketing and Diversification*, held at The University of Bradford Management Centre and sponsored by The British Institute of Management, June 1969.

timing penalities. After that the course is set and so a new model programme has to be right the first time. It can be no guessing game. It can only be a series of carefully taken decisions after having weighed all the facts and considered all the recommendations. To this must be added that entrepreneurial touch which turns a middle of the road selling 200 000 units during its lifetime into a world beater of one million plus.

How did it all begin?

Back in the early sixties we had begun to consider the future of motoring in Europe with particular regard to the coming decade— the seventies. We had seen the introduction of the 'Mini' in August 1959, our own Anglia one month later in September 1959 and more recently the Imp in 1963. During the second half of the fifties the level of disposable income had increased by 50 per cent and was still rising strongly. In fact by the mid-sixties it was to reach a level twice that of ten years before. Not only was this an increase of money spent on motoring in absolute terms, but when we examined the allocation pattern of disposable income we saw that between 1957 and 1965 there was a 12 per cent increase in expenditure, on food, drink and tobacco, but the increase on cars mounted to no less than 197 per cent.

Looking at another set of figures, in 1950, for example, £185 million was spent on shoes and the slightly higher figure of £214 million was spent on cars. In 1960 the amount spent on shoes had increased to £289 million, but expenditure on cars had increased nearly four times to £847 million. Clearly many more people prefer to ride than to walk. During this same period the car market had broken the 500 000 unit sales barrier, reached 750 000 unit sales by the start of the sixties and was running close to the, at one time thought to be impossible, one million unit sales level.

The Mini and the Anglia it seemed, in their own different ways, had brought personal motoring to the masses. Literally millions of motorists in the early sixties had been rendered able to throw off the shackles of their dependence on public transport. Ford had foreseen this overwhelming demand for economical and reliable family motoring, and the Cortina was added to our range. The Cortina matched this trend offering, as it did, big car, family size space at a low price. As we said at the time—with the Cortina you get a lot for your money.

It was at this point that the Capri concept started. We, in Marketing, concluded that having crossed the threshold of car ownership many would be anxious to graduate beyond the convenience that owning a family size car afforded. We felt a new formula was required for the European car in the seventies—a formula which would give the emancipated motorist a symbol of affluence and independence in contrast to the unexciting experience of owning a functional or somewhat starkly appointed motor car.

In 1962, using the Mark I Cortina bodyshell as a base, we produced a prototype of a two seater car—the Saxon—which attempted to match the anticipated trend. The attempt was not, however, considered strong enough and the car was never developed beyond the prototype stage. Our stylists continued work on what was purely an unofficial design exercise. However, a 'theme' began to emerge, a 'theme' which was in fact to enthuse management into the positive consideration of adding a fifth car line to our four car range. The stylists moved ahead to produce in 1964 a full size model or 'clay' which was their interpretation of the theme and the fifth car line moved a step nearer reality.

During this time a number of models had been introduced into the car market, offering a higher level of performance, trim and appointment within a standard bodyshell. Early examples were the Mini Coopers, Wolseley 16/60, and the Singer Gazelle and Vogue. In 1963 cars of this type accounted for just over 3 per cent of the UK car market; in 1964 this had grown to 3.4 per cent and when in 1965 we began to probe this area with the Executive version of the Mark III Zodiac, it had grown to 4.6 per cent.

This trend was to continue. In 1968 with GT versions of the Escort and Cortina, Executive versions of the Cortina, Corsair and Mark IV Zodiac, the Mini-Cooper and the MG, Wolseley and Riley versions of the BMC 1300 range, the Triumph 1300, the Imp sports and Chamois, the Gazelle and Vogue and the Viva SL90, the share held by 'developed' cars had grown to over 12 per cent of the market. And in terms of FORD—GT, a name which had at first earned derisory comment, accounted for no less than 15 per cent of Escort and Cortina sales. But that was to come.

Our job in Marketing was to decide if trend there was, what direction it would take and at what point of time, and in which sector of the market it would generate sufficient volume to enable us to participate with a reasonable pay-off. It was becoming clear in 1965 that the motoring public wanted, and would be prepared to pay for, added distinction and performance. This desire to be different was manifesting itself in other directions. The phrase 'You can have any colour you like, providing it's black', has associations with Ford as strong as the Model T and mass production. And yet by

1950 we were offering eight body colours, and by 1965 that had increased again to fourteen.

The same multiplication had been applied to the cars themselves, with the major UK manufacturers playing increasing variations on a common theme or reapplying the marques, once proudly displayed by the smaller manufacturers they had ingested, to their standard bodyshells. The realization was growing that the car owner of the future was likely to become much more demanding and much more extrovert about his most expensive purchase after his house.

The dreary terraces of the early twentieth century had been supplanted by the anonymous semi-detached of the thirties. With material and labour costs rising, the mass builders were able to make little improvement post-war but the owners themselves with the availability of a vast range of choice, ensured that however much alike their homes might appear externally, there were not two houses in the country which had the same furnishings, the same colour schemes and the same equipment. We in Marketing believed that the car owner would begin to think of reflecting his taste and his personality in his car, just as he was in his house. He would want to exercise his right to choose.

And then on 17th April 1964 the Mustang burst on to the American scene. During the remaining eight months of that year sales were nearly 300 000, and in 1965 in a market nearly ten times the size of the UK it achieved a share of 5.6 per cent. In addition, one out of every two Mustangs sold represented conquest business.

While the Mustang was introduced at the lower end of the price scale in the American market, and thus its concept was not strictly relatable to the trends appearing in the UK, it demonstrated that marketing opportunities were there for the taking in an industry where product development had been described as evolutionary not revolutionary. At the end of 1964 we sat down, weighed the trends, measured the opportunities and decided which one to seize.

A car exciting to own and rewarding to drive

One of our first conclusions was to question strongly the appropriateness of producing yet another box on wheels, and emphatically our decision was underlined by the brief Marketing gave to the product planners—'What we have to do is put the fun back into motoring with a personal car which will be exciting to own and rewarding to drive'. Armed with this brief, the planners, engineers and designers set out to define what constituted excitement and fun in motoring.

In recent years manufacturers had tried to satisfy the demand existing for such a vehicle in two distinct and different ways. Grand Touring Cars and out-and-out Sports Cars—but most of these failed on at least one of several counts. Either they were too expensive or they were impractical, they didn't have more than two seats or they had rudimentary luggage accommodation. These compromises were discarded at the outset. We were sure that with the technical resources of the company we could provide a far better solution at a realistic family budget price.

In the end the planners came up with the following definition of what was wanted in the seventies.

A personal car which was:

extremely good-looking
roomy enough for four or five people with their luggage
having a wide choice of performance and equipment to meet individual needs
offering exceptional ride, handling and control with very low noise level
available at family budget prices.

The targets were accepted, the project was code named COLT and the programme began.

The first requirement was to give the designers details of the interior dimensions for power unit, luggage and people. The wide choice of performance predicted alternate engines, but it was the passenger compartment or interior package which would have most influence on the critical factor—the shape. Normally the interior package size results from an intricate technical routine of life-size drawings which identify the package dimensions available from a series of design concepts. In the case of Capri we sat four men on four car seats and measured the space around them. So instead of producing a design and forcing four people into it, we had an interior designed around four people in the first place.

During the next three months various design concepts were eliminated; some failed to stand up to wind tunnel aerodynamic tests made with quarter-scale glass-fibre models, and others were discarded on appearance grounds. Finally, the choice was reduced to two—the Flowline and the GBX. All this, three months after the basic requirements were first accepted.

Having narrowed the field of choice, we then did the obvious— we asked the customers of tomorrow what they thought about the two prototypes. Space was booked in the Martini Centre in Brussels, in Earls Court in London, in Hamburg and in Geneva, and the early prototypes were taken to these locations. Members of the public were invited to talk about the car over a cup of coffee. They were not told the price or the name of the manufacturer; they were merely asked to comment on the car, which they did with great interest, some of the discussions going on late into the night.

These styling clinics amply confirmed our concept that we were getting close to 'the car you always promised yourself'. While this marketing research was going on, engineers were developing mechanical components in disguised 'slave' cars. It had been decided that the existing range of power units would be able to provide the variety of engines available. Thus the engineers were faced with a minimum of engine development and were free to concentrate on transmission, drive line and back axle research. The slave cars used were Corsairs with dummy badges, a foreshortened boot and tracked out to simulate Capri.

Product Planning had already prepared a document which re-stated the targets to which the Product Committee had agreed, requesting the Directors of Engineering, Manufacture and Finance to prepare outline submissions. This executive paper was the basic trigger which caused the various operational areas of the company to develop facilities planning and cost estimation. Meanwhile Product Planning had posed the following questions, and was researching the answers in concert with the operating areas.

What is the new model's sales potential?
What will be the effect on our model lines?
How much incremental sales potential does it possess?
What is the export sales potential?
How much will the programme cost?
What investment is required?

Project Colt

On April 18th 1966 the Engineering and Product Planning Committee reviewed our forward model passenger car product strategy with emphasis on 1969 and 1970 model years. They selected the design concept known as GBX and instructed Product Planning to produce a programme for Executive sign-off.

This programme paper was in effect a prospectus of the COLT project designed to 'sell' the concept to the committee. Firstly it outlined the product, relating it to the other models planned to be in our line-up during the 1969 model year. Next it dealt with the product objectives providing a product description which spelt out in operating terms the conceptual description signed off by the Product Committee months before. It covered shape, tyres, trim and ornamentation, seats, wheelbase and track, steering and levels of ride and handling. Following this came performance, safety features, pricing and sales volume. The package dimensions were detailed next, covering both exterior and interior, also luggage capacity and curb weight. These were related to competition. Then performance objectives were spelled out giving levels for acceleration, top speed and customer fuel consumption for the base and additional power units—again compared with competition. A features list was detailed identifying common and unique features by derivative providing information, for example on brakes, instrumentation and appointment detail, even proposing which models should be fitted with a vanity mirror.

The financial aspect

Financial considerations were dealt with next. Although the Capri programme was expected to produce incremental sales volumes, the financial feasibility of the programme, however, was evaluated at constant volume. In other words, the previously approved long range sales volumes for the total model line-up were redistributed across a new model line-up, including COLT, on the assumption that we would make no conquest sales whatsoever. Domestic and Export sales volumes were estimated for the first three years of the model's life.

This led naturally to the next section which covered capacity planning volumes—calculating the adjustments to assembly facilities and relating the resultant required capacity to the current corporate facilities programme. In essence, incremental investment was identified for additional storage, building and material handling equipment, together with some additional operating costs. Next came variable costs. Piece costs were identified by major product area such as bodyshell, wheels and tyres, driveline, suspension, brakes and steering, and related to Cortina with the variances analysed. Then fixed expenditure was detailed under five headings—namely, special tools, machinery and equipment, related manufacturing expense, engineering and styling and the costs of launching. Early on we had decided we required a remote gearshift (this part of the programme paper told us we had to invest over half a million pounds to get it). The paper ended by stating the total expenditure and deducting from this anticipated government investment incentive grants thus producing a net amount on which the programme profitability was based.

Target prices were then calculated—ex-works for Domestic and base prices for export—again a comparison with competition was made. With this information a profit forecast was arrived at and return on assets employed after tax was calculated together with the effect on overall company profit. Finally, before the recommendation for approval the date of the first Capri to be built was projected—for October 1968.

Two years and three months before that date—on 14th July 1966 —the Product Committee bought the Capri programme. This acceptance had the effect of introducing the Capri project into the official company timing programme. Immediately Product Timing and Product Planning fell into step.

Using the targets agreed by the Product Committee in the programme paper, Product Timing set up an interlocking timing programme designed to time their achievement. They established using Critical Path Network techniques the key actions required in the programme on the part of Engineering, Manufacturing, Purchase, Finance and Sales, and reported progress to Senior Management on a fortnightly basis. The programme had become part of the operational web of the company. The controls began to operate. Finance staff, using Engineering assumptions as their base, calculated piece and investment costs part by part. They described each part in detail relating it to an existing comparable part where possible, and laying down target costs.

The Red Book

This information is collated into a document termed the Red Book which details all parts, even those costing less than a penny. Every responsible executive in Product Development, Manufacturing and Purchase signs the book, thus signifying personal commitment to meet the objectives in individual areas. Achievement against objective is reported on a regular basis. Facilities costs were detailed and capital expenditure budgets established against which Purchase and Manufacturing could operate. Styling continued with the approved shape being translated into a mass of dimensions so that the engineers could release drawings to provide temporary tooling to permit the testing and evaluation programme to start. Full-size models of interiors were constructed to develop seating, fascia and instrumentation layouts and to ensure the feasibility of packaging the gearbox and driveline. Prototypes became more and more representative, clay gave way to fibreglass. Then metal skinned models were produced from temporary tools, and finally fully engineered prototypes were built.

Later in 1966 test and development was well under way. The first prototoypes were tested not only by engineers but also by men and women—representative of the general car driving population, chosen from within the company. A secretary who broke one of her long fingernails when opening a car from the inside caused a revision of interior door handle design and a scratch on her high-heeled shoes from the brake-pedal as she got out also brought that particular component under review. During the following months and into 1967 hot and cold weather testing was carried out, at the same time the opportunity to check the adequacies of the target service intervals was taken.

The European concept

At the meeting of the Product Committee which gave the go-ahead for COLT it was decided that the car would be manufactured in both Britain and Germany so that it would be available for the largest possible market. Furthermore this provided an opportunity for an interchange of design and engineering expertise, thus promoting a truly European approach. British and German engineers worked side by side on developing the early prototypes, and this now entailed a complex Pan-European timing programme. The first ten prototypes produced were subjected to punishing tests to reveal areas where design improvements were necessary.

Engineering work continued with a mounting tide of releases detailing specification, dimensions and use of each part, everyone of which would be subjected to an appearance and cost check before procurement was authorized. These costs were fed to Finance Staff, who compared them with the Red Book objectives already established, feeding the results into the reporting system for piece cost and investment control. Tools were being made and facilities installed, and all this activity was reported by Product Timing as achievement or delinquency against programme. And in parallel Product Planning through the Product Committee continued to co-ordinate the direction of these activities.

Marketing staffs, as had already been said, had been involved from the inception of the Capri programme. Apart from the development of the original concept, their commentary on all the product proposals prepared by Product Planning was used as input to the Product Committee and they had responsibility to research in depth certain aspects of the programme. Implicit in the acceptance of the Capri programme by their member of that committee was the commitment by Marketing to the sales, market shares and price objectives on which the financial viability of the programme had been based.

Towards the middle of 1967 at one of these programme reviews, it was revealed that people who had ridden in the rear seats of the prototype had reported difficulty in seeing out and a feeling of claustrophobia. The stylists were set to work to re-design the rear quarter window.

By mid-1967 we had arrived at a point in the programme where major marketing decisions were required. We knew the sales potential existed. The trends Marketing had forecasted in the early 60s had been borne out. Already the emergence of the 'fastback' as a shape, midway between saloons and sportscars, had been seen in the American and Continental markets. Everybody who had contact with the car during the programme, even the most self-critical—and this is a state of mind we encourage—was enthusiastic about the shape. The signs and portents were good.

But what to call the car? Colt with its happy connotations of Mustang was not open to us. A Japanese tractor company had already recognized its appeal and held the world copyright. What posture should the new model adopt in the market place—a sporty car with room for the family or a family size car with sporting appeal? Unless we were precise with our point of aim, the whole weight of our initial merchandizing effort would be expended in the wrong direction. Only a fraction of the sales potential would be realized. The programme would be unprofitable and we would be worse off by £20 million.

Final marketing survey

So in October 1967 we held our final marketing survey in London. We set out to establish which of the two marketing approaches was most credible. The sports car with space for the family or a family size car with sporting appeal. In order to plan component procurement, manufacturing build-up and calculate profitability, we asked for an assessment of the likely buying pattern between 1600 cc and 1300 cc engines. And finally we sought to obtain a reaction to the exterior and interior styling and interior roominess of the car. Five hundred people were exposed to a white glass-fibre model, an interior trim full-scale model or buck, a seating buck and a luggage compartment buck. The people were divided into three matched samples. One was shown the car 'cold'; the second saw a three minute television commercial and visual material highlighting the sporty approach and the third followed the same routeing but adopting the family approach.

The conclusions were that the 'sporty' approach was superior to the 'family' approach; and showed greater buying interest and significantly less resistance. It was also clear from the data that the re-design of the rear quarter window was more than justified. The data also revealed other things—that this was a car for the young in heart, the bachelor, the young marrieds, the more mature driver with older children. The car was regarded as a unique combination of value for money and sports car styling: that the great majority of motorists would at heart like to drive a sports car but domestic and social responsibilties restrain them, thus they have to consider the welfare, needs and comfort of family and friends. A dangerous thing this last fact because the psychologists had begun to mutter darkly that a guilt complex might deter some prospects. And finally one major item: the car was something which excited people emotionally.

In Marketing we summarized the findings in this way: a shape at a price and, rather more lightheartedly, everyman's dream car at a price everyman can afford . . . even though he's up to his neck in mortgages and kids. This last research clinic served to confirm the decisions made to restyle the rear quarter window. Marketing came out strongly with a product platform introducing the car as a new concept in motoring—a unique totality. Management agreed—we were finally and irrevocably committed. We knew where we were going—our aim was to put the fun back into motoring. And the name we chose with which to do it was—Capri. The date was November 1967.

Marketing the Capri

A detailed product platform was now prepared and the advertising agencies were briefed. The marketing men talked two prototypes out of the engineers and the agency teams left for Portugal and Sicily to shoot movie and still photography against a basic list of advertising and sales promotion requirements. In July 1968 a marketing guide to the Capri was prepared and circulated to all staffs concerned. It provided a background of facts, objectives and policies, against which all merchandizing plans, particularly the introduction plans, were prepared.

During June and July 1968 our plant at Halewood was reaching the end of a recruiting programme aimed at increasing manpower to handle the additional production, and, at the same time, running through the 'functional build programme', which is designed to ensure that the parts fit together and to prove-out the installed assembly facilities. The vehicles are assembled by supervision and management and form a training and familiarization programme at the same time. These models were used for more photography, for advertising and literature. During their short life they were to carry many badges, and the agency and company support teams were once again to thank the developers of that indispensable item for all mock-up men—double-sided adhesive tape. Other functional build units were assigned to Service Department as they, in turn, could dis-assemble them. This apparently circular exercise was to provide the basis for training courses for Ford Dealer mechanics and to provide material for the owners' handbook and the workshop manual.

On July 30th 1968 the Pilot Build programme was started at Halewood. This enabled the practical experience of supervision learned while assembling Capris in the functional build programme, to be passed on to Training Department. Gradually training skills were accelerated and more men were brought in from the training areas. This process continued through August and September until, on 14th October 1968, Job I was driven off the line twenty-seven months after our decision had been taken.

Someone once said that in industry there are three jobs worth doing—making 'em, selling 'em and ringing up the till. Marketing were now facing the selling 'em part of the trio.

Promotion

On August 2nd 1968 the agencies presented their campaign. They had chosen the phrase—Capri—'The Car You Always Promised Yourself'—as the introduction strap line. A little lacking in grammar for the purist, perhaps, but, coupled with a shot of the side elevation of the car, gave us a message certain to do the job we wanted. The media programme was then developed, the advertising themes and sequence decided. It was to be shape and concept followed by price, package, performance and choice. Sales literature was finally approved and the presses began to roll.

During this period the Sales training programme was set up. Designed to brief company management, sales staff, dealer management and salesmen, written, audio and visual material was produced describing the product attributes of the Capri and comparing them with competition. This programme reached an audience of over 5 000 company and dealer personnel before launch day.

o

Well before Job I the manufacturing area had been supplied with the model specifications giving the mix of engines, different trim and appointment combinations, optional extras and 'skin' colours so that the massive production build up we had planned would be in the assortment most likely to match demand. This selection was particularly critical since to satisfy the personal preferences we were sure were likely to be expressed towards the Capri by many prospects, we had decided to complement the wide range of engines by one equally wide range of option packs. With over 7 000 units to be built and shipped before public announcement it was vital that the stock should be what the customer wanted.

Plans were also developed to build greater flexibility into our delivery system. Although 'saleable' production started on 14th October, units were to be released to the dealers before January. If this build-up was allowed to flow into our distribution system in an uncontrolled fashion, it would swamp the regular deliveries of our existing models, thus lengthening delivery times and giving rise to customer dissatisfaction and dealer difficulties.

Meanwhile, my colleagues in the Public Relations Department were working hard on their presentation of the Capri to the press, a vital aspect of our car launch. A favourable and enthusiastic press gives a tremendous send-off to a new car and establishes right from the start the right aura of success. They gave their initial presentation to the motoring correspondents of all the leading national and provincial newspapers; broadcasting media; motoring, technical and glossy journals just before Christmas in London. This was, of course, a static presentation of the car and was designed to excite and enthuse the press but also to give them a long lead time on our announcement plans and the time they needed for special issues.

Presentation in Cyprus

The next major presentation of the car was in Cyprus, where all our enthusiasm and judgment was literally put to the test. Over 250 top motoring journalists from Britain and Europe drove the Capri in Cyprus, evaluating and considering the car. The result: universally acclaimed as a winner—and not even a word about the car had yet been written.

Why did we go to Cyprus? Our weather in January is too unpredictable to attempt a major introduction like this on British roads. Moreover, speed restrictions are not helpful when you are trying to achieve top speed figures and acceleration times. Also Cyprus offers, as many of you will know, an ideal setting for introducing a new car—the variety of road conditions enable you to drive on ice and snow in the Trudos Mountains and an hour or so later to bask in the sunshine on the coast. Another important aspect, too, was the opportunity for the press to talk to top management, who accompanied them to Cyprus, on any aspect of the car's design, engineering, production, sales or marketing.

Less glamorous perhaps was the really massive job put in at home in producing press material, special features, arranging interviews, technical reviews, and so on, to ensure that every motoring correspondent and editor had all the information at their fingertips for the press announcement.

For those of us who had lived with Capri from the beginning, enthusiasm and belief in the potential of the product had grown until enthusiasm and belief had combined into a conviction the product was right. The problem was how to convey this mental attitude to the front line of our sales and marketing effort—our dealer body. An exciting and glamorous product like Capri had to be revealed to them in exciting and glamorous surroundings. They had to see it in motion and, as we ourselves had learnt, they had to have the next reaction satisfied: they had to be able to drive it.

Malta marketing conference

This posed problems of facilities, climate, and security, and as Britain and October/December is a combination which does not equal ideal driving appraisal conditions—problems of currency, accommodation and transportation as well—we found the answer —Malta GC. And in the early days of December 1968 nearly 2 000 dealer personnel from the UK and Eire attended a marketing conference on the island.

They were given the product story, details of the sales potential of Capri, its relationship to our own and competitive models and predictably they clamoured to drive it. Once they had done so, they joined the ranks of the converted—their enthusiasm exceeded even our own.

Again we recognized a potential danger—life still had to go on and we and our dealers had to maintain a balanced operation. If we concentrated on the Capri to the exclusion of all else we would be neglecting 85 per cent of our volume. So in the midst of the final dramatic acts of the Capri introduction programme we designed an advertising and sales promotion campaign for the Cortina.

The sales promotion team had been developing point of sale material reflecting the marketing platform of the Capri since mid-1968 together with a wide variety of handout and courtesy items.

We had angled our approach to a predominantly male audience but had also catered for children with the provision of painting books and cut-out models.

During evaluation, testing and market research clinics, we had identified a marked feminine appeal in the Capri and so our product visibility programme reflected this. In addition to displays at railways stations, airports and hotels during the period of launch, we arranged co-operative promotions with dress designers, hosiery manufacturers, cosmetic manufacturers, Capri sun-glasses and even a Capri hair style.

The launch

On launch day itself we had nearly 500 showrooms throughout the country in which our dealers had excelled themselves in preparing compelling displays featuring the Capri. Our dealer support was tremendous. To a man they were with us with all their know how and expertise. Malta was paying off. Our final task remained in the launch cycle: we had to measure the effectiveness of our whole programme—how aware were our potential customers—how credible were our claims—what level of recall had been achieved?

With the Capri launch we had an ideal opportunity. Fourteen days before the planned public announcement date of 5th February 1969, the Brussels International Motor Show ended. This would have been an admirable platform for the European launch—the snag, however, was that dealers' stock would not reach the required level until two weeks later—5th February 1969. Needless to say, to launch a car without stock is a quick way to achieve massive customer frustration. In these particular circumstances, however, the Capri was an addition to our range and therefore there was no danger of loss of sales of a model being replaced. So we took the opportunity of two bites at the cherry.

We revealed the Capri at the Brussels Show on 24th January and announced it to the public across Europe on 5th February 1969. The press, television and radio did us proud. We received greater visibility and more editorial coverage than any other UK automotive launch before—and I may say since.

During the last week in January 1969, after press announcement and before public announcement, we checked public awareness of the Capri in Britain. We found 74 per cent of motorists were aware of Capri—57 per cent of whom mentioned the car unprompted. Of the total, 76 per cent had learned about Capri from newspapers, 15 per cent by word of mouth and 12 per cent from television.

Sixty-five per cent were favourably impressed by Capri, 68 per cent mentioning something as liked—styling being the main point (so our PR people had done a good job!).

After public announcement we asked again. The reading of 74 per cent had now become 98 per cent awareness, of whom those who mentioned the car unprompted had reached 89 per cent. Sources of awareness had changed dramatically, with newspapers moving from 76 per cent to 91 per cent, television from 12 per cent to 55 per cent, with magazines and posters at 36 per cent and 31 per cent respectively. Of the 67 per cent who had seen the car, 34 per cent had seen it on the road and 35 per cent in a showroom. A tribute to our dealer efforts. Favourable impressions had been left with 68 per cent, an increase of 3 per cent, and 69 per cent mentioned something as liked.

Sales took off like a rocket, with the Capri selling at twice the anticipated rate during the days immediately following launch. And then a labour dispute disrupted Halewood production, cutting off vital replacement supplies and thus reducing sales volumes. Nevertheless this we did know: a lot of motorists have made themselves a promise to buy a Capri, and though their keeping of it may be a little delayed this time, next year many thousands will be driving the car they always promised themselves—the Ford Capri.

27 | Strategies for Diversification— Cadbury

by JOHN HARVEY

THE concept of growth has always been a fundamental part of the Cadbury philosophy, as it must be for any successful business. Such a concept provides new opportunities for the company's employees and generates the high morale which is essential in motivating people in the right direction. A continuously expanding company can offer competitive rates of pay, nurture positive management skills, and realize expectations for higher profits which, in turn, attract an adequate flow of new capital to sustain the company's momentum of meaningful growth.

The founders of Cadbury's, an exceptionally talented family, believed that the cobbler should stick to his last. Until the end of the second world war there had been sufficient scope for growth within the cocoa and chocolate market. Certainly the company's record of expansion in these years was quite spectacular. The high level of chocolate consumption in the UK was to a large extent the result of skilful marketing by the Cadbury Group.

Selecting a strategy

Confectionery consumption was State controlled through war-time rationing until 1953. Immediately afterwards the industry enjoyed a sales bonanza. It soon became evident, however, that it was going to be difficult to increase the UK weekly level of confectionery consumption beyond $7\frac{1}{2}$ oz per head of the population. Although this was higher than anywhere else in the world, during the fifties, the confectionery market had reached a plateau.

JOHN HARVEY is Sales and Marketing Manager, Foods Division, Cadbury Brothers Ltd. This paper was first presented to the National Conference on *Long Range Planning for Marketing & Diversification* held at the University of Bradford Management Centre and sponsored by the British Institute of Management, June 1969.

There were many other commodities competing for the consumers' marginal purchasing power and it seemed clear that people
were not going to eat much more chocolate. Cadbury's had a substantial share of this market. To increase it in the face of growing
competition, was going to be difficult and expensive. Profit margins
looked like declining and the return on capital employed was going
to suffer.

Many companies find themselves in Cadbury's predicament—a
dominating share, built up after generations, in a market that has become static. The classic response is 'diversification'—but which way?

Buy it?

Firstly, it can be done by investing in a range of unrelated activities. A few of the rare successes of this method rank among the
big US 'conglomerates' of today. Little is known about the many
failures. Since the fifties, numerous fingers were burnt through
sticking them into enterprises of new and unrelated fields, such as
tobacco companies going into textiles and engineering. Diversification for its own sake is now viewed with suspicion, for it tends to
assume that cash and flair for financial management are all that are
needed to gain the best long-term returns on capital. It sometimes
works but any appreciation of really successful companies illustrates that this is not a satisfactory development of an organization
with deep roots in an industrial economy.

Take it over?

Secondly, diversification may come through the acquisition of
businesses in similar or related fields. For example, the Beechams
and Unilever approach or the more recent dramatic experience of
Mr Weinstock's GEC technique. It usually means that the bigger
company imposes its policies on the acquired partners. Such a company expresses it diversification strategy by grafting an organization
with, say, particular research and development skills; a branded
range of products; or useful distribution networks, on to itself. The
precise method of doing so varies in time and degree of emphasis
between financial and managerial control. It is often a painful and
difficult diversification technique but at present the most popular,
with many notable successes.

Do it yourself?

Thirdly, diversification many mean a fundamental re-orientation
of the whole organization from within. This can be extremely difficult but, if successful, certainly the most satisfying and rewarding

method. It has been particularly used by companies which have a keen awareness of their distinctive skills and individual marketing idiom. Such companies assume that their previous success has stemmed from more than effective financial management. Past success was based on a corporate identity whose character permeates the whole organization from the chairman down. Organizations such as Marks & Spencer, Sainsbury's and Tesco in consumer goods distribution, and odd bedfellows like Rolls-Royce, Heinz, and ourselves as manufacturers have this kind of identity.

It means that when responding to the need for diversification, one is searching for activities in which one's particular 'view' about the market can be extended. The product is less important than the attitude that permeates the organization.

The M & S attitude to quality/value meant that their diversification into 'own label' foods was a 'natural'. It can be predicted that Tesco's decision to move into durables will have the sort of cut price bargain approach which they operate with such flair in their food stores.

The Cadbury choice

Cadbury's have evolved on a philosophy which required mass market products to reach a distinct quality standard, rather than a price. The quality control aspects over the company's products have always been of primary importance. Over the years this attitude has become more significant than our chocolate/cocoa 'know-how'. It was therefore the reputation for quality which was considered our biggest asset in determining the most effective diversification strategy.

Our decision to diversify through products bearing the company name has meant that we have been less concerned than most expanding organizations with buying or taking over the brands or 'know-how' of smaller companies. As far as the 'Food and Drink' market was concerned, the Cadbury name provided the foundation for diversification.

Food and drink

It was against this background that the Board planned to overcome the limitations imposed by the confectionery market. The company decided that it was in the business of satisfying people's needs for food and drink. This offered scope in markets where expenditure was likely to grow as living standards throughout the world continued to improve. People were unlikely to eat more but they would eat better and more conveniently. They would want more variety and they would be prepared to pay more for good convenience foods.

When deciding to diversify from within, one cannot start completely fresh without a heritage of tradition and experience, particularly in a company which has been successfully engaged in an expanding business over a long period of time. When looking for profitable areas of diversification, one must define in some detail where one's existing strengths lie.

In the case of Cadbury's the main strength lay in:

Food technology: The manufacture of a wide variety of confectionery products. Many skills were acquired which had a wider application. Cadbury's, for example, are one of the largest users of milk in the UK. Confectionery has to have long shelf life and requires high standards of packaging.

Promotional 'know-how': The competitive conditions of the confectionery market (second largest advertisers in the UK) has led the company to develop skills in advertising, promotion and presentation.

Distribution techniques: A large proportion of chocolate is bought on impulse and needs, therefore, to be widely distributed. In achieving this distribution the organization had already grown familiar with the developments of the rapidly changing food trade.

Corporate identity: The enlightened social policies pursued by Cadbury's throughout this century, the reliable quality standards of their products and the sustained heavy advertising over a long period had established a distinct corporate identity. Our market researches indicated that the company image gave a positive advantage to any food products bearing the Cadbury name.

Once we had taken the decision to diversify through the food market, it was necessary to isolate specific areas which would yield the most rewarding returns from applying the company's strengths.

Hazards

The Food and Drink market in 1967, the latest year for which data is available, was worth approximately £5 700 million. It is composed of numerous specialized markets such as soups, breakfast cereals, coffee, provisions, etc. There are vastly different standards between them.

On the one hand, we have highly organized markets such as soup —£50 million, breakfast cereals—£48 million, coffee—£52 million, generated and sustained by leading brands through heavy advertising and promotional expenditure. On the other hand, we have commodity markets which are fragmented and where fluctuating prices are the most important influence.

Just to introduce new lines by no means guarantees success. They have got to be seen by the consumer to have demonstrable advantages. They have got to be an improvement on existing products. They require heavy advertising and promotional investment in the early stages. Too many new lines at any one time can have a depressing effect on a company's profitability in the short term. Alternatively, inadequate initial support can damage long-term profitability and open the door to pre-emption by competitors.

The risks are not only financial; what for example would be the repercussions of a monumental failure on the company's image in the eyes of the consumer and the distributor? What about the time and effort lost for developing something else? There are deeper hazards, too, such as having to face a redundant labour force and idle plant.

Although these negative possibilities haunt the imagination of management in the early stages of any diversification programme from within, fortunately they had never become a reality to us. By any standard, Cadbury's diversification strategy was a success, and these were our methods.

Implementing a strategy for diversification

We believed that one of the first essentials was to create an atmosphere receptive to new ideas, where everyone and any department feels free to put forward new ideas. I am certain that any commitment to new product development needs to be constantly inspired at all levels.

We do not believe that this is the exclusive sphere of the Research & Development Department. It is the current practice in the Foods Division of Cadbury's for a marketing specification to be drawn up before the work commences, outlining the essential features of the product and the kind of performance it will be expected to have. For example, if we were going to develop instant chips we would state that they should overcome the negative features of preparation, long cooking and cooking smells which are associated with home-made chips.

They would have to have the basic selling promise of 'perfect chips every time in seconds'.

At each stage of the development the product and the concept will, as far as practicable, be put to the consumer. Frequently a development will change direction as the work proceeds.

It is important to closely inter-relate all stages between research and development, market research, and marketing.

The diversification into food has been the responsibility of the marketing department of the food division. It is our view that it needs to be very closely allied to the marketing function if we are going to develop products with a real chance of success. Looking around the food market in general, one sometimes feels that some of the so-called new products have arrived there because their conception has been regarded as an end in itself.

Making decisions

In the early stages we allocated the work to product managers of going products. This gave them a firm base from which to work and had the added advantage that their proposals were at least likely to be practical. In recent years the amount of work and the number of new areas being investigated have grown rapidly. Some of the areas being explored are further removed from existing markets. This has made it necessary to appoint a new development manager to work within the sales and marketing department of the division. He has the responsibility of examining and sorting out the new ideas, making recommendations and, if these are accepted, to progress their development. If they survive continuous and rigorous tests in the market place, then he is responsible for seeing them through to the test market.

It is important that top management should be well informed on new development work and that their approval should be sought at each major step forward. Difficult investment decisions are often needed in determining whether or not to proceed with a particular development. These decisions are perhaps easier to make if top management have grown familiar with the issues during the development process. At the same time effort and resources can be saved if the development work is reviewed at regular intervals.

We deal with this by having a development group under the control of the divisional chairman, who receives reports on the progress of work in hand and regularly reviews the priorities. The detailed work is in the hands of a number of satellite working groups comprising research and development, marketing and cost control.

Market selection

Where do we look for new development? Fortunately we are living in an age of change, especially in social behaviour, and a number of influences, e.g. television, foreign travel, motor cars, eating out, are changing people's eating habits. There are opportunities for more convenient treatment of traditional products. One of the keys to success rests on being in tune with the consumer. Mistakes in the past have arisen very often from bad timing rather than poor products. Markets and consumers are changing continuously and the effect of new developments can be cumulative.

I believe that the sustained growth of the instant coffee market, for example, has produced a consumer attitude more likely to accept instant tea, whereas ten years ago this product would have been rejected. As consumer 'education' improves, there tends to be greater acceptance of 'new' processes such as AFD.

Currently there is a trend among marketers to develop research techniques designed to find new products by a systematic analysis of the market. It seems to me that the most useful part that market research can play is to provide a broad picture of the market under consideration. I still think that informed intuition and judgment must be used to identify the gaps.

Even sensitive attempts at precise measurement in the ideas stage with some of the more elaborate techniques for concept testing tend to inhibit and mislead. This does not mean that we should not try to think early about total concepts with all the trimmings of brand names, rough packs, advertising imagery, etc. In the Foods Division we try to move fairly early on to complete product ideas. We apply the results of research to modify and improve them, rather than systematically 'compose' new products piece by piece. At the same time we attempt to harmonize the inter-relation between company identity, the product packaging, and advertising claims.

There are certain fundamental consumer needs, some or all of which we expect a food product to meet—nutrition, consistency, taste satisfaction, convenience, variety.

So far, our interest has been in product groups with large markets where there has been lack of convenience or consistency in the traditional product—cakes (£250 million), milk (£350 million), potato (£180 million), tea (£? million).

There is a growing need for food in convenience form. I am not suggesting that manufacturers should 'instantize' everything. Convenience is also achieved through packaging, e.g. the ready-to-serve dinner, Vesta, Duo-Can etc.

What's my line?

In the food industry there is plenty of scope for new products. We, like others in the industry, have more ideas than resources to develop them. The difficult part of the exercise is to decide which are likely to succeed and prove most profitable. Usually there are plenty of good reasons for not going ahead with a particular proposition. In the case of instant milk, for example, all the indications were that fresh milk was a very convenient product anyhow. It was certainly instant and quite easily available. There also seemed to be a rooted prejudice against dried milk. Instant potato had a graveyard reputation and a number of manufacturers had tried and failed, probably because dehydration was not accepted as a process which made as good a potato as 'fresh' ones.

Any assessment of a new line has to be as objective as possible. It is here that we apply market research. We want information on the new line's acceptability—what benefits does it bring consumers? We use market research to help us assess the potential market, the life-cycle of the product, and what the reactions of competitors are likely to be.

Why should our new product be of use to the consumer? Where does the benefit lie? Is it a benefit which will be readily seen and understood? Does it save work? Offer a better standard of quality? Is there a noticeable improvement in flavour?

These propositions must be tested on the consumer. In tea, for example, preliminary investigations of the tea market revealed that there were several benefits from using instant rather than the traditional product.

One cup when alone—too much trouble to make a pot.
Strength difference—two or more people don't agree on strength.
Convenience—saves time, mess and trouble.
Early morning—quicker and easier.

Similarly with our instant milk line 'Marvel' and instant mashed potato product 'Smash', a variety of claims could be made—

Marvel	*Smash*
Mixes instantly with cold water.	Tastes as good as fresh potato.
Stirs into tea, coffee.	Perfect results every time.
Long life.	Cuts out chore of making mash.
Easily stored.	Milk already in the product.
Good flavour.	Makes a quick meal possible.
Cooking advantages.	Recipe opportunities.
High protein content.	Outdoor use—picnics, camping, etc.
Relatively cheap.	

The domestic market for potato is worth £160 million, and of this 40 per cent is used as mash. Consumer enquiries suggested that 'Smash' may offer a direct substitute for fresh potatoes and it is, therefore, not unreasonable to expect that at some future date at least 50 per cent of mashed potatoes will be made from instant mash.

A study of the potential market very often gives an indication of the possible life-cycle of the product—a concept about which it is relatively easy to speculate but where it is considerably more difficult to predict with any accuracy.

Finally, in making an assessment of a new line's performance, one must consider how well the new development blends with the company's resources, its public image, marketing 'know-how', distribution pattern and budgeting control.

Marketing strategy for new lines

To make an impact in a competitive market such as food, it is essential to have an integration between product, packaging, name, promotion, and display, and to do this we must at an early stage decide what the marketing strategy for each new line is going to be.

As regards cakes, research suggested that there was general dissatisfaction amongst consumers with the quality being offered and that many firms were marketing down to a price. It was therefore decided that our strategy was to use butter, to emphasize quality, and to guarantee freshness by sale or return—unique in this country.

For Instant Milk there were two alternative concepts—slimming and convenience. Thirteen per cent of people claimed to be definitely slimming to reduce weight at the time of the interview. A further 17 per cent said that they were trying to slim and keep their weight down, but not seriously. Twelve per cent claimed that they had slimmed recently.

From the convenience point of view, there were strong indications from our research that more than half the sample of housewives ran out of milk at some time or another.

It was difficult to determine the best strategy. In this case we developed advertising commercials for both approaches. In practice, we decided that slimming offered less scope for our product, so we went for the convenience angle.

In the case of 'Smash', there was a scepticism that processed potato could taste as good as the real thing and so it was decided to tackle this problem head on, and the object of our strategy was to persuade people that Cadbury's product is indistinguishable from the real thing.

An advertising agency, if properly used, can, I believe, make an important contribution to the success of a product.

Advertising budgets

Having established the marketing strategy for our product, the next stage is to develop the right marketing mix. Of all the ingredients, perhaps the one which gives rise to the greatest debate is the size of the advertising appropriation. Obviously, it is the most easily varied and possibly the most difficult to measure in terms of effectiveness. Because of this, it is perhaps tempting to reduce it, to launch the product with inadequate advertising support so as to reach the profit-making stage more quickly.

It seems to me that with advertising and promotional costs at their present level, you cannot make any meaningful impression with a major new product unless you are prepared to spend at a national rate of half a million pounds per annum. Launch advertising also needs to be sustained over a fair period of time, and one has to overcome the temptation of reducing it too early and letting competitors flood the new market.

Many of the companies rated as big league spenders are US based. Is it because the American accountant has a more positive appreciation of the importance of advertising in a diversification programme? Is he better conditioned to accept a long-term plan and has he more confidence in its success?

The impact of your investment

The need to invest large sums of this kind in establishing a new product obviously poses some very tough problems. You need to decide whether you can achieve sufficient volume at a price which will enable you to sustain this level of advertising investment. How long before you achieve sufficient volume at a margin which will enable you to justify these levels of advertising? How long are you prepared to wait for the new development to pay off? You also have to estimate the commitment of your competitors and 'guestimate' their expenditure plans.

At this point your sales estimate acquires prophetic significance —the old story about the world beating a path to the door of the man with the best mousetrap is very comforting but it certainly didn't allow for the problems of marketing with mass communication media. You have got to tell people about your new product idea, persuade them it is really worth trying. The results we achieve

—sales—depend on how well this is done; in other words the penetration, frequency and creditability of our advertising.

The potential of the market may be enormous. How much of the potential we achieve will depend on how well we communicate our idea to the consumer and how successful we are in persuading him or her to sample our new product. A new product's sales estimate is perhaps the most difficult of all, especially as we require this over a fairly long period if we are going to compute a pay-off plan.

Our guessing will probably be done more intelligently if we have tested our new line at every stage. Prolonged test market experience certainly improves the accuracy of our guess.

Test marketing

The theoretical case for test marketing is generally appreciated. Its purpose is to replicate, in miniature, the national marketing situation, to observe what happens, and then project the results to national proportions. The scale of the test can be varied to suit the particular product.

The strongest argument against test marketing is the fact that notice is given to the competition. If it is important to 'get in first', time may be lost by the need to extend before we have adequate performance data.

In practice, test marketing does not always work out as smoothly as the theory. We are supposed to find out what we expect the new product to achieve not only in terms of sales, but also consumer awareness, distribution, shop purchases, repeat purchases, etc., so that we can detect where the weaknesses exist.

A growing problem of effective test marketing in the food trade arises out of resistance from distributors. The very people who are likely to gain most from the new product are reluctant to participate in test marketing because they find it interferes with their central control. The new line is not easily accommodated by the computer. It upsets rationalization of stock control. American distributors have a very much more positive approach to new product introduction. This is illustrated by the following figures from the 36th Annual Report of the American Grocery Industry produced by the *Progressive Grocer*:

New Items in the 1967 Supermarket

Account for 55 per cent of items now handled.
Contribute 52 per cent of unit sales.
Represent 52 per cent of dollar sales.
Earn 57 per cent of dollar margin.

Own labels—A new line's hazard

Since Cadbury's decided to diversify into other food markets, the record shows four major successes and one failure. It may still be early to reach a final conclusion.

In the case of Cakes and Instant Milk, the markets have been transformed, sleeping giants have been awakened.

The competition to Marvel is divided into two camps, the own labels and manufacturers' brands. Here, the place of the private label in new product development is an interesting one. I have not so far seen evidence that the distributors who are so keen to take advantage of a growth market, once established, are prepared to participate in the expensive business of developing the market or to make any contribution to the costs of research and development. On the contrary, it seems that in some cases their main objective is to arrest the development of the new market by forcing prices down to a level which does not allow adequate money to be spent on promoting the new product to consumers.

It is interesting to speculate on how much scope for new developments the food market could offer if the promotional resources passed from the manufacturer to the distributor.

On the other hand, the retailers' pressure has positive side-effects. It provides continual stimulus to the manufacturer who can only survive under these conditions by continued technical advance and development. To do so, he has to ensure that adequate resources are directed to this end.

It takes time

These stages in our development work on Marvel give some indication of the time scale involved in developing a new major line in the food industry—

1960-61		Product Search—analysis of USA and Continental products.
1961		Usage and attitude research into milk and milk products.
		Agreement with European supplier.
1962	June	Consumer product test.
	August	Container research.
	Sept.	Name research.
	Sept.	Label design research.
	Autumn	Decision to test market.
1962-63		TV and Press advertising tests.
1963	March	Store siting test.

P

1963	April	Consumer Panel extended use product test.
	June	Test market—Tyne Tees and Southern measured by market research.
	Dec.	Decision to extend.
1964	April	UK production of product.
	May	Extension Westward.
	May	Research on value for money and price expectancies.
	Oct.	Extension to London, Anglia, Midlands and TWW.
1965	May	Usage of Marvel.
	August	National Marketing.

Diversification—The after effects

The effect of successful new development is cumulative. I think that in the early days of our diversification programme most consumers suspected that Cadbury's really only knew how to make chocolate cakes and that perhaps Marvel had a chocolate flavour. Within the company there was some concern as to the effect the development of instant milk might have on the Company's established products in the confectionery market, e.g. what would happen to the reputation of the glass and a half of full cream milk if heavy advertising support were given to Marvel? It was because of this that the Cadbury name was played down in the initial stages, but in practice this proved a groundless fear.

The success of these ventures appeared to establish a changing corporate identity for Cadbury's. They were beginning to be considered as pretty good at new products. When Smash was introduced there seemed to be some feeling that in view of the success of Marvel this too might be worth a try. I think that we finally made our mark when we introduced our instant tea—Fine Brew.

At the beginning I suggested that diversification could be expensive and needed to proceed slowly. Because of the demands for more rapid growth, we are just entering a new strategy for diversification where two very large companies like ourselves and Schweppes are joining together as equal partners. We share a mass of common points of view and are both determined on growth in the food and drink market. Clearly we still retain the positive identity of our two companies in creating a new image and character. Nevertheless, this development offers a good example of the way progressive top management has to think to devise new strategies for diversification.

28 | Growth Planning—Geigy

by CARL EUGSTER

IT is now almost a truism to state that the modern business corporation has become one of the dominant institutions of the free world. Energies, goods and services are being produced, marketed and consumed in such quantities and in such multiple varieties that people call our socio-economic structure an economy of abundance or still more paradoxically, an economy of waste. This is, of course, a contradiction in terms. We would not economize freely available goods. Relative scarcity is still at the heart of economic matters.

On the other hand, the enormous overall productivity of our present economic system (which is basically a free enterprise system coupled with mass consumption in democratic societies) is so manifestly demonstrated by its material results, that we tend to overlook its essentially human nature and human build. An industrial corporation is a social institution. It is man-made to a far larger degree than we may realize on first reflection. It is in fact a cluster of organized human behaviour, with its preconceptions and with its wonderful power for adaptation and renewal.

My main theme is to explain the human character of Geigy as a business enterprise. What makes it a vital enterprise? How can it be a leading multi-national firm in fine chemicals and pharmaceuticals?

The keyword is co-operation

The answer is simple: We believe that organized and well-planned co-operation is the key-word for continued corporate success.

DR. CARL EUGSTER is Head of Corporate Development, J. R. Geigy, S.A., Basle, Switzerland. This paper was first presented to The National Conference on *Long Range Planning for Marketing and Diversification* held at The University of Bradford Management Centre and sponsored by The British Institute of Management, June 1969.

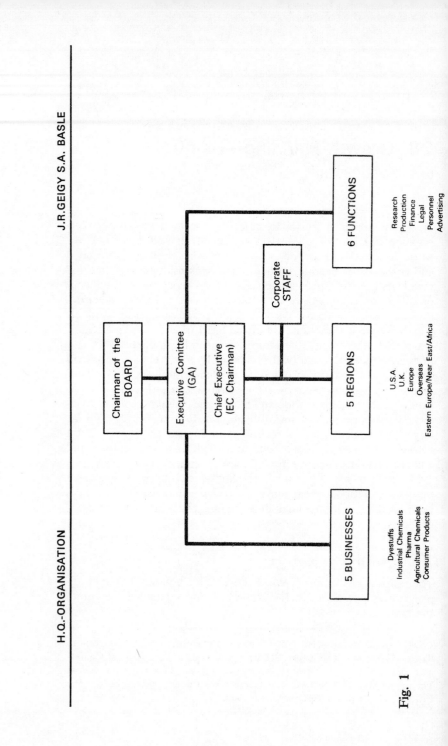

H.Q.-ORGANISATION

J.R. GEIGY S.A. BASLE

Chairman of the BOARD

Executive Comittee (GA)

Chief Executive (EC Chairman)

Corporate STAFF

5 BUSINESSES

Dyestuffs
Industrial Chemicals
Pharma
Agricultural Chemicals
Consumer Products

5 REGIONS

U.S.A.
U.K.
Europe
Overseas
Eastern Europe/Near East/Africa

6 FUNCTIONS

Research
Production
Finance
Legal
Personnel
Advertising

Fig. 1

You will recall that Geigy is a multi-national corporation with a consolidated turnover of some £300 million. We are active in some 145 countries: the bulk of our sales derives from thirty-two subsidiaries operating in twenty-two different countries, as well as from a number of independent agents. The total corporation owns and comprises sixteen chemical plants, seventeen compounding plants and twenty-eight selling companies. Furthermore, it maintains an important participation in seven joint-ventures. We have a relatively simple organization-structure at Geigy which is largely man-made. We have really rebuilt it recently from within and with the help of professional consultants over a period of decisive learning and adaptation (see Fig. 1).

The emphasis in our organization is now clearly on individual accountability within certain well-defined spheres of activity or tasks. We have corporate legislation to insure that each position carries with it the authority to get things done: the results achieved are measured and periodically compared with plan. Since operating plans are firm personal commitments, the control of current performance largely takes on the form of self-control.

The emphasis is also on personal responsibility. This term has a larger connotation. It always points to a common ground, a comprehensive set of underlying values. The 'way we do things around here'[1] implies that we actively evolve a working philosophy for co-operation which reflects social change. Executive development, in fact, is an endeavour to prepare people for such responsibility. Therefore, accountability and responsibility are twin concepts. They govern our work and teamwork in vital areas of business enterprise. It follows from this conception that the principle of delegation is consistently applied throughout the entire company.

Decision preparing and decision-making is, in fact, pushed down to the last unit which sufficiently masters a concrete problem-situation. Decisions are thus action oriented and are made most of the time by those who also in fact implement them.

International character of Geigy

In Geigy, executives at all levels have to participate actively in the world-wide management process because we have practically no home market. In fact, only $2\frac{1}{4}$ per cent of our group sales to third parties are effected in the Swiss market. The rest is business with the world at large. We were for many years and still are handicapped by our geographical location and basic market condition, particularly if we compare our potential and our resources with those of our large competitors who have a firm and established position in their home market and conduct their internal divisions with the backing strengths of fully integrated and well-diversified home operations.

We had to turn a problem into an opportunity. We had to overcome the niggardliness of Nature, as Adam Smith used to say, and seek our wealth as a corporation jointly with other nations. We had to develop the proper attitudes to do business internationally, to co-operate intensively and consistently with friends in all parts of the world and gradually to evolve the structure and create the management processes of a truly multi-national corporation. (And all the time, our lawyers keep reminding us that legally speaking the animal does not exist, and rightly so! Our concern is made up of a number of independently incorporated units which are entities in themselves.)

If you consider that Geigy has been growing from within over the last fifteen years at the rate of 15 per cent p.a. compound you can imagine that we must have experienced something of the 'perpetual open frontier' which is so characteristic of our modern industrial life. We tend to attribute most of this growth and historical change to scientific innovation, to our speciality products and the quality of our services. This is doubtless an important ingredient.

On the other hand, it was absolutely imperative for us to develop Geigy citizens throughout the world who jointly carried the load. During these last fifteen years we have reached a total size eightfold as big as our 1953 base, relying exclusively on internal development. This was possible only because there was also *inner growth*. People underwent an enormous process of learning and adaptation, of self-development and common, largely informal, education. This is clearly more than the joint pursuit of profits which you maximize from accounting period to accounting period. This is rather a matter of fundamental motivation. In a free enterprise system you have to give people the chance and the challenge to do meaningful work in a reasonable way.

I do not pretend that we in Geigy have mastered all issues of decentralization and of co-ordinated control, but we have a working conception derived from common experience, and we have the living understanding that we can do a lot together. In abstract, our scheme of regional management and multi-national decision-making is shown in Fig. 2.

The essential feature seems to me to be this: the authority of direct order, of outright command, has long lost its power in a dispassionate world of science and industrial performance. Leadership

MULTINATIONAL MANAGEMENT
SPECTRUM OF AUTHORITY LEVELS

Decision		Country Management	H.Q.-Management (R., F., B.H., G.A.)
LOCAL	I	Decision	—
LOCAL	CI	Decision	Advice
LOCAL	APD	Decision	Approval
CENTRAL	CC	Advice	Decision
CENTRAL	WCC	—	Decision

I   Complete independent authority

CI   Coordinated authority
(Decision made after obtaining advice from higher management but country chief executive is not bound by such advice)

APD   Approval prior to decision

CC   Basle decision with country chief's consultation

WCC   Basle decision without country chief's consultation

Fig. 2

is now more subtle: it draws on the art of persuasion and integrated planning. The personal dialogue insures resilience and is essentially relevant to striking realistic goals.

Obviously, our systems people take all this into their account. Their procedures are said to be flexible, embracing the factual inputs as well as the considered points of view of our subsidiaries. The manuals have only been enacted after careful international hearing, critical examination and suggestion processes have been duly completed. They could not be put successfully to work had their global acceptance not been meticulously prepared in this joint process of development of the concepts and forms—which procedure, by the way, resembles the legislative process in free countries to a striking degree.

As a planner of corporate growth, I have the firm conviction that this is all very necessary and helpful indeed, but that it is fundamentally not sufficient. Current profitability and good procedures are a basic requirement to further success, but they are not satisfactory in themselves. The continued prosperity of a corporation surely stems from its ability to 'generate vitality under all the circumstances that confront it, not only in times of crisis but just as much under conditions of success that may have persisted through many years'.[2] It is the profound task and inspiring mission of growth planning to prepare the ground for the new seed. Evidently, business is a practical affair.

Action thinking and reflective thinking

Most of our activities in operational planning, implementation and control do take place within the existing structures of the enterprise system. We would not optimize current operations if we did not accept certain given objectives, strategies and action programmes and carry them out within the existing framework of available resources and technologies. All these activities are governed by a prevailing pattern of *action-thinking,* which is immanent in the entire management process. The vitality of the enterprise system would soon be impaired without its having deep roots in another type of endeavour, which may be termed *'reflective thinking'.*

To rise above everyday worries and concerns in order to strike a new horizon is the task of every leader. Corporate staff people are, of course, reflective thinkers *par excellence.* They professionally extend the performance and the potency of top leadership. There is the searching activity of minds which critically review the adequacy of current operations. More significantly still, we have those who systematically probe into the undisclosed future. Possibilities for growth must gradually be converted into selected opportunities.

This thought-process thus helps to generate vitality in times of relative stagnation and to regenerate it particularly in times of prosperity and easy confidence. I mentioned earlier that modern corporations are institutions. As such they are subject to historical change: by this term I mean something more than quantitative variation. A corporation can grow or decline and even decay. It has a history, a more or less intensive present, and it may have a future. Put another way: institutions are clusters of organized human behaviour, and fundamentally a pattern of prevalent thoughts.[3]

Therefore, and because it is fundamentally human, an institution can also be changed and improved. A vital business corporation has the capacity to rejuvenate itself: it has, so to speak, the capacity to effect a renaissance of its structure and its style.

Growth planning, as we conceive it in Geigy, is this preparation for the future enterprise structure. It is a speculation in futures. Planning generally is not an aim in itself: it is a preparation for policy. In growth planning particularly, the element of being forerunners, leaders, plays an important role. As I have tried to explain, this is necessary for *internal* use, above all. Since sustained growth is essentially dependent on learning and assimilation, an important function of the early supporters of the 'Grand Design' is to make its components explicit. They must be able to campaign for the acceptance and appropriation of the new ideas and projects. This is the most difficult but also the most rewarding phase of corporate development planning.

Guide-lines into principal

Let us now look at the conceptual framework used in Geigy. Up to now, we unfortunately do not possess a formal corporate policy in Geigy. When we started our staff work we therefore had to interpret the underlying currents of thought and aspiration. We formulated working hypotheses which we used as guide-lines for our study. By now, they are pretty well accepted as principles.

Our heuristical assumptions appear on Fig. 3.

We then explained the place of *growth planning* within our planning system as shown in Fig. 4.

Further, we described the most important *categories* of growth planning as in Fig. 5.

We also used a familiar matrix in order to typify in a simple graphic way the different possible *growth directions,* as in Fig. 6.

Fig. 7 shows how we described to our mangament the *environment* in which we operate and our *competitive position* in the chemical industry.

I pass over the detailed description of the why and how of

growth and give you as a last feature our attempt to underline the eminent importance of the psychological climate for growth, in Fig. 8.

Thus we return to our point of departure, i.e. the *human* element in all growth planning. In Geigy we are convinced that this is not an exercise for animated slide-rules. We have to serve vital interests and values.

In Geigy, we are also convinced that in order to secure continued corporate success we must strike a balance between corporate objectives and educational aspirations. Corporate growth essentially flows from *inner growth*.

Remember the proverb:

> 'Should you plan for a year,
> then plant grain,
> should you plan for ten years,
> then plant a tree,
> should you plan for a whole life,
> then train people.'

To sum up, in Geigy we have had to consider and solve the problems connected with decentralization in a specific way. Our very condition forced us to evolve a pattern consistent with the multi-national framework in which we operate. Individual accountability and personal responsibility are key concepts. Over the years we have built up a Republic of Geigy citizens, with an *esprit de corps* and a *modus operandi* based on mutual respect, frank response and incontestable reliability. This climate of opinion can subsist only if top management takes a vital interest in people, in their learning and adaptation—in their inner growth.

Growth planning with its two dimensions of *corporate development* and of *executive development* is thus an essential function of top management. It flows from reflective thinking on the continued success of the corporation as a human institution. It challenges our ability to develop people and thus to give a vital sense to our professional tasks. I sincerely hope that some of you will take up this challenge, and please remember the classical words of Hamlet: 'The readiness is all'.

REFERENCES

1 Bower, Marvin. (1966) *The will to manage. Corporate success through programmed management* (New York).
2 Kappel, Frederick R. (1960) *Vitality in a business enterprise* (New York).
3 Eugster, Carl. (1952) Thesis, B. Veblen (Zurich).

Growth-Planning at Geigy

Key-Assumptions

(1) A *healthy* enterprise *grows*

(2) In growing, it *changes*

(3) A corporation which *does not grow,* loses its *vitality*

(4) Our industrial *environment* is rapidly *expanding* and is also continually *changing* with the increasing multiplicity of needs, products and services

(5) Geigy *must* and indeed *wants* to grow in order to continue being a leading multinational enterprise

(6) *Geigy* also wants further to *participate significantly* in the *scientific* and *industrial changes* of our time

Fig. 3

Industrial Growth-Planning

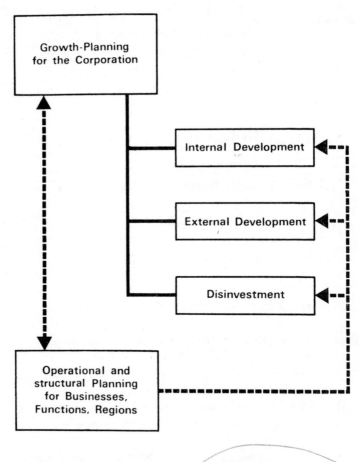

Growth = Expansion + Diversification

Fig. 4

Categories of Growth-Planning

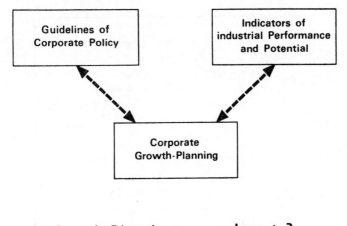

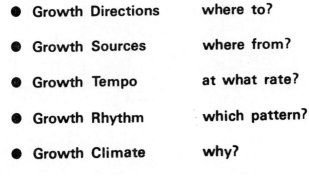

- **Growth Directions**   where to?

- **Growth Sources**   where from?

- **Growth Tempo**   at what rate?

- **Growth Rhythm**   which pattern?

- **Growth Climate**   why?

Fig. 5

Directions of Industrial Growth

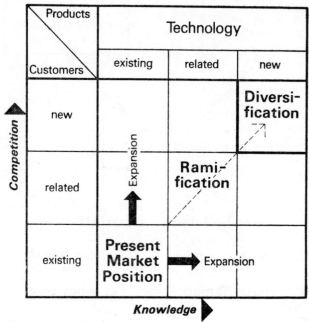

Fig. 6

The Chemical Industry

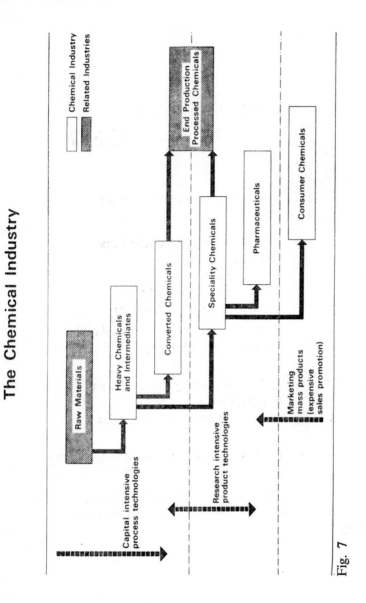

Fig. 7

Industrial Growth:
Why?

The Climate for Growth

● Adaptive movements *forward* are
achieved
> more easily
> more effectively
> more enthusiastically

than efforts at *contractive* adjustments
(Principle of positive steps)

● *Progress* essentially flows from an
individual and group process
> of *learning* and *adaption*

● Leaders *grow* with increased responsibility

● An executive sets a *living example*
when he tackles new projects creatively

Fig. 8

Appendix

LIST OF PARTICIPANTS AT THE NATIONAL CONFERENCE ON LONG RANGE PLANNING FOR MARKETING AND DIVERSIFICATION, HELD IN JUNE 1969 AT THE UNIVERSITY OF BRADFORD MANAGEMENT CENTRE

ABEL, JOHN P., Group Sales Director, Leyland Paints Ltd, Preston.

ADAMSON, EDWARD, Sales Manager, Granville Chemical Co., Keighley.

AKEROYD, M. H., Managing Director, Dictaphone Company Ltd, London.

ARNOLD, E. M., Managing Director, E. J. Arnold & Son Ltd, Leeds.

AXELRAD, J. P., Sales Director, Qualitex Yarns (Leicester) Ltd, Leicester.

BAGNELL, M., Manager Industrial Electronics Group, The M.E.L. Equipment Company Ltd, Crawley.

BARNARD, J. P., Staff Manager, Norwich Union Insurance Societies, Norwich.

BECKETT, ROY, Planning & Special Projects Director, Malga Products Ltd, Southall.

BEEDHAM, P. J., Financial Director, Pearson & Foster (Bradford) Ltd, Bradford.

BELL, H., Manager, Industrial Products Marketing, Rolls-Royce Ltd, Crewe.

BELOK, F. C., Director, Corsets Silhouette Ltd, London.

BIRMINGHAM, R., Manager i/c Planning, Legal and General Assurance Society Ltd, London.

BENNETT, RICHARD W., Marketing Services Executive, British Thornton Ltd, Manchester.

BICKEL, J. N., Director, Fairview Estates (Enfield) Ltd, Enfield.

BITTLESTON, J. R., Group Chief Planning Executive, Rank Hovis McDougall Ltd, London.

BLUMSON, JOHN D., Planning Manager, Electrolux Ltd, Luton.

BODEN, J. C., Sales Manager, Rowan & Bowden Ltd, Paisley.

BOWEN, J. D. M., Marketing Director, Avana Group Ltd, Cardiff.

BRADLEY, MRS. D., Production Development, Analysis & Data, Raleigh Industries Limited, Nottingham.

BRIGGS, P. R. A., Director and General Manager, Davy and United Instruments Ltd, Sheffield.

BROMLEY, A. K., Assistant General Manager, Martins Bank Ltd, Liverpool.

BROOMER, P., Commercial Manager, Aircraft-Marine Products (Great Britain) Ltd, Stanmore.

BROWN, WALLACE J., Corporate Planning Engineer, Tayforth Ltd, Camelon.

BUTEUX, L. H., Managing Director, Carrington Printers Ltd, Belfast.

CANTLEY, M. F., Lecturer & Consultant, Lancaster University Operational Research Dept., Lancaster.

CHITTY, V. C., Marketing Plans Manager, Ford Tractor Operations, Europe, Ford Motor Company Ltd, Basildon.

CHRISTOPHERSEN, G. R., Sales Director, J. John Masters & Co. Ltd, London.

CHURCH, G. R., Technical Director's Staff, Fibreglass Ltd, St. Helens.

CLARIDGE, J. E. A., General Marketing Manager, Bernard Wardle (Everflex) Ltd, Caernarvon.

CLARK, D. A., Economic Adviser, Imperial Tobacco Group, London.

CLARKE, E., Divisional Planning Staff, Smiths Industries Ltd, London.

CLEMENT, JOHN, Marketing Director, Milk Division, Unigate Ltd, London.

CLEVERLEY, G. A. W., Director Manpower Development Department, IPC (Group Management) Ltd, London.

COLES, M. A., Manager: Supplies and Systems Services, CAV Ltd, London.

COPE, D. J., Director, Fairview Estates (Enfield) Ltd, Enfield.

CROME, D. V., Group Budget Controller, Boulton & Paul (Joinery) Ltd, Norwich.

CROSSLEY, SIR CHRISTOPHER, Manager, Wm. Brandt's Sons & Co. Ltd, London.

DAVIES, H. M., Sales Director, The British Vacuum Flask Company Ltd, Huyton.

DAVIES, H. Q., Region Director, South, Milk Division, Unigate Ltd, London.

DAVIS, S., Director, Norbury Printers Ltd, London.

DAVIS, T. A. G., Marketing Strategies Manager, Rootes Motors Ltd, (Parts Division), Birmingham.

DENTON, J. S., Deputy Chairman, E. W. Nickerson & Sons, Grimsby.

DESHAYES, J. H., Planning & Corporate Director, Golden Ltd, L'Oreal of Paris, London.

DUGDALE, DR. IAN, Planning Manager, Ancillary Businesses, British Railways Board, London.

DYER, R. H. H., General Manager, William Kenyon & Sons (Power Transmission) Ltd, Hyde.

ESLING, A. G., General Sales Manager, Silent Channel Products Ltd, Huntingdon.

ELLIOTT, A. H., Director, John Haddon & Co. Ltd, London.

ELLIS, J. B. B., Sales Director, Barfords of Belton Ltd, Nr. Grantham.

FEHLER, S. J., Sales Director, Wood Brothers Glass Company Ltd, Barnsley.

FISHER, A. P., Field Research Officer, Rubery, Owen & Co. Ltd, Darlaston.

FITZGERALD, G., Group Economist, The SGB Group of Companies, Mitcham.

FOX, JOHN F., Sales Director, Ethicon Ltd, Edinburgh.

FOX, M., Marketing Officer, Gyroscope Division, Sperry Rand Ltd, Bracknell.

FREEDMAN, MICHAEL, Consultant, Leasco Systems & Research Co. Ltd, London.

GARNER, B. R., Financial Controller, Aircraft-Marine Products (Great Britain) Ltd, Stanmore.

GILES, G., Sales Manager, Ames Div., Miles Laboratories Ltd, Stoke Poges.

GILROY, DESMOND, Head of Research and Development, Palgrave Murphy Ltd, Dublin.

GOLDING, H., Organization and Methods Manager, Aero Zipp Fasteners Ltd, Glamorgan.

GOODENOUGH, I. M. H., Marketing Manager, The Borden Chemical Company (UK) Ltd, Southampton.

GORMAN, M. J., Commercial Controller, Newcastle Chronicle & Journal Ltd, Newcastle-upon-Tyne.

GORROD, K. M., Financial Planning Dept., Glaxo Group Ltd, London.

GOULDEN, D. A., General Manager, Yorkshire Post Newspapers Ltd, Leeds.

GRAY, A., Production Manager, Aircraft-Marine Products (Great Britain) Ltd, Stanmore.

GREEN, C. F., Head of Long Range Planning, National Westminster Bank Ltd., London.

GRIMWOOD, G. L., Marketing Director, Thomas Broadbent & Sons Ltd, Huddersfield.

HARRIS, E. S., Smiths Industries Ltd, Rugby.

HARRISON, P. R., Head of Group Corporate Planning, Firth Cleveland Group Ltd, London.

HARTLEY, JAMES W. H., Managing Director, Shaw Carpet Co. Ltd, Barnsley.

HAYHURST, C. E., Marketing Manager, Dictaphone Company Ltd, London.

HEATH, R., Plessey Telecommunications Ltd, Liverpool.

HERON, M. G., Marketing Manager, BOCM Ltd, Reading.

HEWITT, P. A., Finance Controller, Grocery Division, Rowntree & Co. Ltd, York.

HIRST, W. A. E., Product Manager Sales Marketing, Cadbury Brothers Ltd, Birmingham.

HOBBS, F. A., Sales Manager, Universal-Matthey Products Ltd, Enfield.

HOLDING, J., Plessey Telecommunications Ltd, Liverpool.

HUMPHREY, D., Plessey Telecommunications Ltd, Liverpool.

HUTT, S. E., Smiths Industries Ltd, Rugby.

INMAN, G. E., Managing Director, Joshua Tetley & Son Ltd, Leeds.

JEWSON, S., Asst. Managing Director, E. Green & Son Ltd, Wakefield.

JOHNSON, R. B., Marketing Manager, Geo W. King Ltd, Stevenage.

JONES, BRYAN, Deputy Group Managing Director, Leyland Paints Ltd, Preston.

JONES, B., South Region Manager, Alkaline Batteries Ltd, Stratford-upon-Avon.

JONES, J., Technical Planning Officer, Fibreglass Ltd, St. Helens.

JOUGHIN, D. A., General Manager, Carding Specialists Co. Ltd, Halifax.

JUKES, W., Business Training Manager, Volvo Concessionaires Ltd, Ipswich.

KEOUGH, J., Head of Product Planning and Market Research Departments, Smith Kline & French Laboratories Ltd, Welwyn Garden City.

KING, T. C. H., General Brand Manager, John Player & Sons, Nottingham.

LEDERER, P., Director, Richard Costain Ltd, London.

LEE, J. H., Marketing Manager, Ford Tractor Operations—Europe, Ford Motor Company Ltd, Basildon.

LEISER, G., Administration Director, J. E. Lesser Group of Companies, Hounslow.

LEPERE, J. M., Marketing Director, P. J. Carroll & Co. Ltd, Dublin.

LISTER, D. W., Managing Director, Smith & Nephew (Manchester) Ltd, Oldham.

LONG, P. A., Consultant, I.C.I. Ltd, Central Management Services Department, Wilmslow.

LUCAS, K. S., General Managers' Assistant, Lloyds Bank Ltd, London.

LYTH, T., Managing Director, J. John Masters & Co. Ltd, London.

MACKIE, R. L. M., Director of Marketing, Cerebos Ltd, London.

MACLEOD, N. J., Deputy Director Marketing, Williams & Glyns Bank Ltd, London.

MANN, R. T., General Manager, Knitwear Group, Remploy Ltd, London.

MARSH, A. M., Grocery Brand Manager, Rowntree & Co. Ltd, York.

MCCLURE, JOHN, Sales Director/General Manager, The Doagh Spinning Company Ltd, Belfast.

MCCUNN, P. A., Traffic Manager, Cable & Wireless Ltd, London.

MCDONALD, N. F., National Sales Director, Fishburn Printing Ink Company Ltd, Watford.

MCHATTIE, DR. G. V., Development Executive, Imperial Chemical Industries Ltd, Pharmaceuticals Division, Macclesfield.

MCMULLEN, V. G., Consultant, Peat, Marwick, Mitchell & Co., London.

MIGHALL, B. M., Marketing Controller, C.W.S. Ltd, Drapery and Fashions Group, Manchester.

MILLS, MISS DIANA, Head, Market Research, Vickers Ltd, London.

MOORE, J., Operations Manager, Standard Telephones & Cables Ltd, London.

MOORE, K. D., Deputy Chief Executive, The British Oxygen Company Ltd., London.

MORGAN, J. C., Technical Sales Manager, General Descaling Company Ltd, Worksop.

MORRIS, A., Managing Director, Boulton & Paul (Joinery) Ltd, Norwich.

MORTIMER, G. F., Economic Adviser, Smiths Industries Ltd, London.

MOULSON, R. L., General Manager (North), The A.F.A. Group, Leeds.

MULLER, DR. E., Marketing Director, Engineering, Chemical & Marine Press Ltd, London.

MULLIS, B. R., Marketing Director, British Thornton Ltd, Manchester.

MUNRO, G. H. J., Managing Director, Aircraft-Marine Products (Great Britain) Ltd, Stanmore.

NELLIGAN, J., Merchandise General Manager, Freemans (London SW9) Ltd, London.

NORMAN, R., Managing Director, Cecil M. Yuill Ltd, Hartlepool.

OFFORD, A. J., Group Marketing Executive, Electrical & Industrial Securities Ltd, London.

O'NEILL, K. E., Managing Director, Edge & Sons Ltd, Shifnal.

PARES, MICHAEL, Business Planning Officer, Food Services, The British Oxygen Company Ltd, Brentford.

PEARCE, D. A., Commercial Sales Manager, Willment Ready Mix Concrete Ltd, Twickenham.

PICKTHALL, D., Marketing Department, Fibreglass Ltd, St. Helens.

PLUMB, F. A., Works Manager & Local Director, Vickers All Wheel Drive, Swindon.

PORTER, DR. M. R., Development Manager, Lankro Chemicals Ltd, Manchester.

PRICE, A., Director and General Manager, Volvo Concessionaires Ltd, Ipswich.

QUEVATRE, L. A., Commercial Manager, Lightning Fasteners Ltd., Imperial Metal Industries Ltd, Birmingham.

REA, R., Director, Warwicks and Richardsons Ltd, Newark.

RICHARDS, B. A., Industrial Market Research, Albright & Wilson Ltd, London.

RICHLEY, R., Sales Manager, Cecil M. Yuill Ltd, Hartlepool.

RINGROSE, R., Product Manager, Abbott Laboratories Ltd, Queenborough.

ROBB, FENTON F., Publicity & Marketing Projects Manager, The Gas Council, London.

ROULLIER, J. H., Managing Director, S.B.D. Construction Products Ltd, Rickmansworth.

ROWE, J. D., Marketing Manager (UK), Vickers European Group Sperry Rand Ltd., Kingston.

SANDERSON, C. J., Planning Officer, Northern Gas Board, Newcastle-upon-Tyne.

SAYER, F., Chairman & Managing Director, Sayers (Confectioners) Ltd, Liverpool.

SAYER, T., Director, Sayers (Confectioners) Ltd, Liverpool.

SCOLLAY, I. J., Manager, Market Development, Morganite Crucible Ltd., Norton.

SELLARS, W., Sales and Development Manager, Doncasters Blaenavon Ltd, Blaenavon.

SHANNON, R. S., Marketing Officer, West Cumberland Farmers Ltd, Whitehaven.

SHAW-TAYLOR, W. E., Partner, Binder, Hamlyn, Fry & Co., London.

SHORT, P. L., British-American Tobacco Company Ltd, London.

SMAIL, R., Group Economist, Turner & Newall Ltd, Manchester.

SMITH, A., Director, Boehringer Ingelheim Limited, Isleworth.

SMITH, D. N., Sales Marketing Director, Redland Pipes Ltd, Reigate.

SMOUT, J. K., Director and General Manager, Lightning Fasteners Ltd, Imperial Metal Industries Ltd, Birmingham.

SOCHOR, P. Z., Marketing Director, Carrington Printers Ltd, Belfast.

SPELMAN, M. J., Manager, Marketing Services, British Leyland Motor Corporation Ltd, London.

SPENCER, A. C., Group Brand Manager, John Player & Sons, Nottingham.

STACK, E. G., Senior Marketing Executive—Consumer, The Wellcome Foundation Ltd, London.

STEELE, D. F., Director, Smith and Nephew (Manchester) Ltd, Oldham.

STEVENS, G. R., Sales Director, J. E. Lesser Group of Companies, Hounslow.

STROUD, RICHARD M., P. A. to the Managing Director, Stroud, Riley Group of Companies, Bradford.

SUTTON, M., Head of Statistics Section, Morganite Carbon Ltd, London.

TAVERNER, P., Marketing Director, Times Newspapers Ltd, London.

TAYLOR, D., Group Promotion Officer, Northern Region, Economic Forestry (Management Services) Ltd, Berkhamsted.

TAYLOR, DAVID, Planner, Morganite Research and Development Ltd, London.

TAYLOR, K. R., Marketing Director, Belfast Ropework Co. Ltd, Belfast.

THOMSON, A. W., Secretary/Accountant, Brooke Reid & Company Ltd, Leeds.

TOLL, RAYMOND, Head, Industrial Development and Marketing Division, Metra Consulting Group Ltd, London.

TROTMAN, P., Marketing Director, Aircraft-Marine Products (Great Britain) Ltd, Stanmore.

TUCK, M. W., Economist, Imperial Chemical Industries Ltd, Agricultural Division.

TUNNICLIFFE, G. E., Managing Director, Marfleet Refining Company Ltd, Hull.

TURNER, STANLEY W., Administrative Director, Leyland Paints Ltd, Preston.

VACCA, J. A., Marketing Manager European Group, Vickers European Group Sperry Rand Ltd, Kingston.

WAKEFIELD, M. A., Deputy Manager, Marketing Strategy Department, International Computers Ltd, London.

WALKER, A. B., Assistant General Manager, Nairn-Williamson Ltd, Lancaster.

WALKER, T. C., Marketing & Sales Manager, Westool Ltd, Bishop Auckland.

WALLEY, B. H., Management Consultant, Turner & Newall Ltd, Manchester.

WALTERS, S. R., Group Planning Officer, Pillar Ltd, London.

WARD, A., Plessey Telecommunications Ltd, Liverpool.

WARD, JOHN, Director of GLH Marketing Limited, Young & Rubican Ltd, London.

WHEELER, T. M., General Manager, Rank Audio Visual Ltd, Brentford.

WHITE, J. C., Market Research Manager, Lessona Ltd, Heywood.

WILLIAMS, J. F., Tarmac Derby Ltd, Wolverhampton.

WILLIAMSON, J., Marketing Manager, Royal Insurance Group, Liverpool.

WILTSHIRE, R. G., General Manager, Willment Ready Mix Concrete Ltd, Twickenham.

WITTMAEKERS, ROBERT F., Sales Director, Crabtree-Mann Ltd, Leeds.

WOODTHORPE, A. W., Commercial Director, Crabtree-Vickers Ltd, Leeds.

WYLIE, A. L., Marketing Director, Rexel Ltd, Aylesbury.

YATES, I. H. N., Director & General Manager, Bradford & District Newspapers Ltd, Bradford.

ACADEMIC TUTORS

TAYLOR, BERNARD, Director of Post-experience Programmes, University of Bradford Management Centre.

WILLS, GORDON, Professor of Marketing, University of Bradford Management Centre.

Index

AC Nielson Co., 110
Accountancy system, planning and organization, 403
Action thinking, at Geigy, 440
Adler, L., 110
Advertising budgets, in diversification, 431
Agricultural tractors, market survey, 389
Airbus, potential market, 357-8
Aircraft manufacturers, market share, 356
Aircraft type, for the RB211, 358
Air transport, growth of, 352-6
Alfred, A. M., 274, 281
American Management Association, 191, 195
American Motors, 37
Amperex, 368
Andrews, Kenneth R., 225, 230
Ansoff, *Prof* H. I., 52, 62, 193, 195, 385
Archimedes, 396
Arla Chemical Company, 287, 296
Assortments and product ranges, 139, 144-5, 149
Avon Beauty products, 32

Becker, S. W., 263, 281
Beechams, 423
Beer, S., *and* Wills, G. S. C., 292, 297
Bell Telephone Laboratories, 366-7, 377
Benn, Anthony Wedgewood, 292
Berg, T., *and* Shuchman, A., 261, 280
Bioriented films, 399
Board of Trade, recommendation for octane rating, 346
Booz, Allen *and* Hamilton, 110

Bower, Marvin, 437, 448
Bowes, Henry, 383
Brands, analysis of, 95, 139-40
appeal of, 98
developing new, 100
multiple, 149
place of, 298
research for, 146
Brands manager, 300, 304
Bread-board model, 266-7, 270
British Industry Week, 1968, 293, 297
British Market Research Bureau, 278
Buck, G. H., 269, 281
Burns, Tom, *and* Stalker, G., 263, 281, 283, 296
Business mix, 28
criteria, 44
developing, 43
Business, how defined, 29
strategy, 28
Business planning, at I.T.T., 326-7
Buying decision, basis of, 73

Cadbury Brothers Ltd, strategies for diversification, 422-34
Carroll, Lewis, 172, 194
Catherwood, Frederick, 292, 297
Chief executive, and corporate strategy, 50
Chrysler, 37
Civil turbine engines, world demand (graph), 355
Classification of new products, 16
Clayton Act, 367
Cleveland Petroleum Co. Ltd, 340
Combine harvesters, market survey, 389
Companies, specific action programmes for, 82
technology based, 254

Company strengths and weaknesses, 12
economic analysis of, 71
Company objectives, 85
Competitive tactics, 31
concentration on, 32
innovation, 31
strength and weakness of, 33, 80
timing, 32
Components industry, electronics, 368, 378
Computers, 373, 375, 379
Conglomerate, the, 69
Consumer attitudes, 105
Consumer industry, revolution in, 351
Control Data, entry into computer market, 32, 376
Convergent marketing, 204
Corey, E. Raymond, 125
Corporate planning, 9, 64, 69, 329
long range, 406
objectives of, 28
process of, 325
strengths and weaknesses in, 60
Corporate strategy, 10
business portfolio, 42
developing a statement of, 47
and the marketing concept, 51
objectives of, 53-4
Cost and investment, relative significance of, 74-5
Cousins, Frank, 293
Critical path network, the Capri programme, 413
Customer
analysis, 73
location, 29
relationships, 335
service to, 334
size, 30

Davies, J., 281
Day, R., 277, 281
de Bono, E., 110
Decision-taking, 269, 427
Delphi technique, 293
Deployment, of companies, 38, 39
Design, August 1964, 266, 281
Detergent materials, 26-7
Development department, 403-4
Diesel engines, market survey, 389
Directors, responsibilities of, 58

Diversification, 68, 385, 397, 422-3, 426
advertising budgets for, 431
approach to, 154
check list, 163, 168
criteria, 163, 189
failures in, 206
forms of, 153
meaning of, 152, 161
objectives of, 155, 182, 187
planning, 163
procedure, 157
strategies for, 151, 172, 385
see also Product diversification
Drucker, Peter, 28, 273, 281, 305, 307
Du Mont, 374-5
Dynamic technology, effect of, 36

Earth moving machinery, 391-4
Eitel-McCullough, 368
Electronics Industry, 363
history of, 364-8, 370
growth in, 379
Emerson Radio and Phonograph Corp., 369
Equities, investment in, 54-7
Esso (Standard Oil), 301
Eugster, Carl, 441, 448
European Economic Community, 292
Extrapolation, 45

Family expenditure, 348
Farm machinery, market for, 387
Farnsworth, 368
Federal Bureau of Commerce, USA, 278
Ferguson, Harry, 387
Financial feasibility, the Ford Capri, 412
Food and drink (Cadbury's), 424-5
in convenience form, 428
Forecasting, non-technical, 109
Ford Motor Co. Ltd, 37, 406
Fortune, 383, 384
Foster, F. G., 275, 281
'Frontier of knowledge', approach to the, 255-6
Funds requirements, 46

Galbraith, J. K., 282, 296
Gap analysis, 107

Geigy, S.A., Switzerland, 435
General Dynamics, 33
General Electric, 371
General Motors, 384
Gift choice technique, 143
Goodwill, as an asset, 55
Gordon, W. J. J., 110, 263, 281
Government agencies, influence of, 259
Green Shield Stamps, in service stations, 344
Growth market prediction, 91-3
Growth, the plastics industry, 397
Growth planning—Geigy, 435, 441-8
Growth vectors, 62-8
Gruber, W. H., *and* Marquis, D. G., 295, 297
Guardian, 'Think Tanks', 293, 297

Hall, P. D., 293, 297
Harris, Alanson, 386
Harvard Business Review, 'Marketing Myopia', 59, 70
Harvey, John, 67
Hayhurst, R., *et al*, 285, 296
Hetrick, J. C., 296, 297
Heyworth Committee on Research in the Social Sciences, 263, 281
Houston, John, 67
Hughes, Ifan, 265, 281

Industrial equipment, Light, 390
Industrial Marketing, 205, 206, 216
Industrial Training Act, 1963, 260
Industry
  profitability of, 78
  significant trends, 78, 79
  structure of, 77
  supply and demand, 72
Industry dynamics, 28, 35, 39, 41
  definition, 39
  strategy, 34, 39
Innovation
  definitions of, 258
  examples of, 372
  favourable conditions for, 258
  financing of, 321
  in distribution, 32
see also Competitive tactics
          Radical innovation
          Technological innovation
Integration
  industrial, 38, 67

I.T.T. Europe Inc., Brussels, 325
  planning principles, 326
International commerce, 37
Investment
  appraisal, 272
  capital programmes, 135
  discounted cash flow, 274
  in new products, 431
  timing, 40
  see also Cost and Investment

Jantsch, E., 110
Johnson, S. C., *and* Jones, I. C., 280, 281
Joyce, T., *and* Channon, C., 143, 150

Kaplan, A. D. H., 172, 178, 180, 181, 194
Kappel, Frederick R., 440, 448
Kearney & Trecker, Mult-au-matic machine tool, 32
Kelly, G. A., 110
Keynesian theory, 285
King, Robert I., 65, 70
King, S., 110

Launching a new product, 420
Leach, G., 264, 281
Learned, E. P., *and* Aguilar, F. J., 287, 296
Levitt, Theodore, 28, 60, 90, 110, 125, 283, 296
Light industrial equipment, 390
Linear programming, 133, 135, 136, 137
Lockheed Aircraft Company, 362
Lorsch, J., *and* Lawrence, P., 266, 281

McCarthy, E. J., 280, 281
McCormick, E. J., 268, 281
Mace, Myles I., *and* Montgomery, G. C., 244
Maclaurin, W. R., 312, 318, 324
Macro context, 258
Malcolm, P., *et al*, 204, 216
Management control, 241
Management spectrum, 439
Management Today, 69
Market
  development, 385
  distribution techniques, 387
  opportunities, 83, 340, 386-7
  information, 251

penetration, 65
research, 338, 352
selection, 427
share of, 390
Marketing
characteristics, 72-4
concept, the, 65, 88
creative, 298-307
functions, 340
future opportunities, 341-3
imbalance, 89
penetration, 332
Marketing man, creative role of, 306
'Marketing Myopia', (Theodore Levitt), 59, 70
Marketing strategy, 25-50
for new lines, 430-2
influence of long range planning, 330-1
long term, 299-301
objectives, 42
opportunities, 84
policies, 46
reason for, 26-8
Markets
development of, 95-8
new strategies and attitudes, 351
presenting the product, 276-9
'Marvel', Cadbury's, 429
Massey, Daniel, 386
Massey-Ferguson, development of, 385-8
Mergers
objectives of, 231
types of, 233
concentric, 234, 236-8
conglomerate, 235, 236-8
horizontal, 234
Merrett, A., *and* Sykes A., 273, 281
Micro wave, 368, 380
Miller, Rogers *et al*, 367, 369, 384
Miller, T. T., 125
Monopolies Commission, 346
Monopoly, element in profitability, 97
Motor Car manufacturers, 349, 407
Motor oil sales, 343
Motorola, 372, 381
Multi-dimensional specification, 14

National Defence Research Committee, 370

National Economic Development Council, 273-4, 281
National market, 279
National Research and Development Corporation, 259, 291, 322

Octane numbers, 345
Owen, Geoffrey, 303, 307
Oxenfeldt, Arthur R., 149, 150

Passenger traffic, airline, 354
Peters, L., 291, 296
Petrol sales growth, 342
Planning
contingency, 41
long range, 298, 330
problems in, 305
see also Strategic planning
Plastics industry, 397
consumption of sectors of, 399
diversification, 405
Playboy magazine, 31
Polymers, 398
Pricing, of consumer products, 74
for increased penetration, 337
Product development, 270-1, 385
Product diversification, 196
advantages of, 218
definition of objectives, 203
planned approach, 222
product criteria, 209
reason for, 198
resource audit, 207
selection for, 210
situation analysis, 206
Product innovation, 260
Product market strategy, I.T.T. Europe, Inc., 325
Product planning, the Ford Capri, 413
Product range, 13, 77, 126, 139
choice of, 139-50
definition of, 29, 143, 148
improvements in, 336
life cycle, 247, 252, 299
mature products, 383
new product developments, 83, 87, 91, 93, 113-25
optimal product mix, 131, 134-5
planning, 126-38
product grouping, 127
profit contribution, 128
research in, 140-1

strategic view, 30
timing, 413
use of, 73
Profits, 75, 76, 131, 136, 302, 388, 405
Production schedules, 275
Public Relations Department, 418

Quinn, J. B., 111

R.B.211, Rolls-Royce, 352-62
Radar, devolpment of, 368, 370, 379, 380
Radical innovations, 316
Radio, early years of, 365
companies, 367, 371, 380
Railroads, reasons for decline in USA, 59
Rank Xerox, market penetration, 332-9
Rawle, L. J., 276, 281
Red book, at Ford's, 413
Resale Price Maintenance, abolition of, 1965, 344, 346
Research departments
applied research, 263
in plastics, 402
Research and development, 245
mix, 248
investment ratio, 254
Research departments, 258-9
Research Services Ltd, 272, 281
Resource audit, 207
Retail outlets, 347
motor accessories, 350
service stations, 343
Return on capital employed, as an objective, 52
Reverse profitability analysis, 301
'Revised sequence' (Galbraith), 283-9
Reynolds, W. B., 282, 296
Risk level, 44
Robinson, C., 111
Rolls-Royce Ltd, planning for the R.B.211, 352-62
staff allocation, 359
sales techniques, 360
Ross Federal Corporation, survey by, 197, 216
Rothman, J., 278, 281

Schon, D. A., 283, 296

Schwartz, C. R., 191, 195
Shoes, annual sales of, 407
Servan-Schreiber, J. J., 291, 297
Servomation, the example of, 32
Sloan, Alfred P., 384
'Smash', Cadbury's, 429
Smith, Adam, 438
Stacey *and* Wilson, 125
Strategic alternatives, 76
Stravinsky, Igor, 290, 296
Sunday Mail, 68
Synergism, 45, 156
'Synergistic myopia', (Galbraith), 283

Take-overs, implications of, 57-8, 136
Tate, B., *and* Rothman, J., 278, 281
Tate, B., *and* Totham, L. J., 146, 150
Taylor, C. W. *and* Barron, 262, 281
Technological concept, demonstration of a new, 320
Technological forecasting and social planning, 291-3
Technological innovation: its environment and management (1967). Report to Department of Commerce, Washington, 322, 324
Technological innovation research, 311-24
Technological obsolescence, 377
'Technological profile', 246, 250
Technology
some implications of, 76
social planning of, 291
transfer and balance, 293-6
Television, history and development of, 368, 373, 374, 380, 381
Test marketing, theory and practice, 279, 432
'Think Tanks', *The Guardian*, 293, 297
Thixotropic paints, development of, 265
Thomson, D. C. & Co., printing capacity, 68
Thomson Organization, packaged tours, 60
Top management, and new products, 87
responsibilities of, 93

Totham, L. J., 146, 150
Trading Stamps, 344, 346
Transistors, development of, 377-9
Tyres, batteries and accessories, market development, 349

Unilever, 423

Varian Associates, 368
Vectors, growth, 62-8
Vehicle population growth, 342
Vertical integration, earth-moving machinery, 393

Warren, E. Kirby, 303, 307
Weinberg, Robert A., 32
Westinghouse, 371

Wilkinson razor blade, 31
Williams, B. R., 274, 281
Williams, Gertrude, 259, 280
Wills, G. S. C., 111, 291, 296, 297
Wilson, Aubrey, 266, 281
Wilson, Harold, 260, 280, 292
Woodgate, H., 275, 281
Wooster, Clive, 259, 280
World production, growth in (graph), 353

Xerox copier, development of, 265-6

Zenith, entry into FM, 373
Zinkin, M., 111
Zworykin, 368